Carl Rogers Counsels a Black Client:

Race and culture in person-centred counselling

Edited by
Roy Moodley, Colin Lago
and Anissa Talahite

PCCS BOOKS
Ross-on-Wye

First published in 2004

PCCS BOOKS Ltd
Llangarron
Ross-on-Wye
Herefordshire
HR9 6PT
UK
Tel +44 (0)1989 77 07 07
www.pccs-books.co.uk

This collection: © Roy Moodley, Colin Lago & Anissa Talahite 2004.

Chapter 2 © Guilford Press; Chapter 4a © Guilford press; Chapter 8 © Carfax Publishing, Taylor and Francis Group; Chapter 24 © Howarth Press.

Chapter 1 © C. Clarke & M. Goldman, 2004; Chapter 3 © R. Moodley, 2004; Chapter 4b © B. Brodley, 2004; Chapter 5 © G. Lietaer, 2004; Chapter 6 © C.S. Rhys, W.R.S. Black & S. Savage, 2004; Chapter 7 © S. Mier & M. Witty, 2004; Chapter 9 © K. Chantler, 2004; Chapter 10 © C. Clarke, 2004; Chapter 11 © S. Dhingra & R. Saxton, 2004; Chapter 12 © C. Lago & J. Clark, 2004; Chapter 13 © M. Charleton & M. Lockett, 2004; Chapter 14 © J. McLeod, 2004; Chapter 15 © W. West, 2004; Chapter 16 © S. James & G. Foster, 2004; Chapter 17 © A. Talahite & R. Moodley, 2004; Chapter 18 © C. Lee, 2004; Chapter 19 © W.A. Hall, 2004; Chapter 20 © J, Pankhania, 2004; Chapter 21 © S. Whitehead, 2004; Chapter 22 © G. Richards, 2004; Chapter 23 © W. Stillwell, 2004; Chapter 25 © C. Lago, 2004.

All rights reserved.
No part of this publication may be reproduced, stored in a retrieval system, transmitted or utilised in any form by any means, electronic, mechanical, photocopying or recording or otherwise without permission in writing from the publishers.
The authors have asserted their rights to be identified as the authors of this work in accordance with the Copyright, Designs and Patents Act 1988.

Carl Rogers Counsels a Black Client: Race and culture in person-centred counselling

A CIP catalogue record for this book is available from the British Library

ISBN 1 898059 44 6

Cover design by Old Dog Graphics
Printed by Bath Press, Bath, UK

CONTENTS

Acknowledgements
An Armor-Plated Man
Foreword — *Clemmont E. Vontress* — i
Introduction — *Roy Moodley, Colin Lago and Anissa Talahite* — vi

PART 1   REVIEW OF 'THE RIGHT TO BE DESPERATE' AND
'ON ANGER AND HURT'

1   Summary of 'The Right to be Desperate'   1
    Christine Clarke and Michael Goldman
2   Summary of 'On Anger and Hurt'   9
    Debora C. Brink and Debra Rosenzweig
3   Looking Back 'On Anger and Hurt'   17
    Roy Moodley

PART 2   ANALYSIS AND CLINICAL REFLECTIONS OF THE THERAPY

4a   Uncharacteristic Directiveness: Rogers and the 'On Anger and Hurt' Client   36
    Barbara Temaner Brodley
4b   2004 Postscript to 'Uncharacteristic Directiveness'   47
    Barbara Temaner Brodley
5   Carl Rogers' Verbal Responses in 'On Anger and Hurt':
Content Analysis and Clinical Reflections   52
    Germain Lietaer
6   Rogerian Empathic Listening: Applying Conversation Analysis
to 'The Right to be Desperate' Session   71
    Catrin S. Rhys, W. R. Selwyn Black and Shauna Savage

PART 3   RACE AND CULTURE IN PERSON-CENTRED COUNSELLING

7   Considerations of Race and Culture in the Practice of
Non-Directive Client-Centered Therapy   85
    Sharon Mier and Marge Witty
8   'The Right to be Desperate' and 'On Anger and Hurt' in
the Presence of Carl Rogers   105
    Roy Moodley, Geraldine Shipton and Graham Falken
9   Double-Edged Sword: Power and Person-Centred Counselling   116
    Khatidja Chantler
10   The Person-Centred Challenge: Cultural Difference and
the Core Conditions   130
    Christine Clarke
11   Cross-Racial/Cultural Matching: Three Approaches to Working
Transculturally   139
    Shukla Dhingra and Richard Saxton

12	Growing Race Awareness in the Therapist *Colin Lago and Jean Clark*	148
13	Using the Videotapes of the Sessions to Examine Ways of Helping Counsellors to Work with the Person-Centred Approach in a Transcultural Setting *Mary Charleton and Melanie Lockett*	160

PART 4   VIEWS FROM OTHER PERSPECTIVES

14	'On Anger and Hurt' Sessions: A Narrative Social Constructionist Perspective *John McLeod*	175
15	Points of Departure: A Humanistic-Spiritual View *William West*	190
16	Horizons of Alienation: Culture and Hermeneutics *Susan James and Gary Foster*	200
17	Therapist's Faces, Client's Masks: Racial Enactments through Pain, Anger and Hurt *Anissa Talahite and Roy Moodley*	213

PART 5   PERSONAL REFLECTIONS AND INTERPRETATIONS

18	Twenty-First Century Reflections on 'The Right to be Desperate' and 'On Anger and Hurt' *Courtland Lee*	228
19	A Credit to One's Self, One's Race and One's Community *William A. Hall*	231
20	The 'Armour-Plated Man' in Cross-Racial Counselling *Josna Pankhania*	235
21	The Man He Has Become *Stephen Whitehead*	239
22	'Tripping' in 'The Right to be Desperate' and 'On Anger and Hurt' *Gella Richards*	244
23	Multiple Interpretations: Stories, Lies and Videotapes *Will Stillwell*	247

PART 6   HISTORICAL DOCUMENTS

24	Interview with Carl Rogers on the Use of Self in Therapy *Michele Baldwin*	253
25	Carl Rogers on Multicultural Counselling: Excerpts from letters from Carl Rogers to Jean Clark, 1979–1983 *Colin Lago*	261

Contributors' Biographies	266
Index	290

ACKNOWLEDGEMENTS

We would like to acknowledge the support and help from the following people:

First, a depth of gratitude to Geraldine Shipton and Graham Falken for introducing the idea of writing about the videotaped sessions in the early 1990s, and the subsequent presentation at the Centre for Psychotherapeutic Studies, University of Sheffield, UK.

We would like to acknowledge the painstaking efforts of Christine Clarke, a counselling practitioner from Northumberland, England who spent many weekends transcribing the videotapes and produced the working document from which many of the contributors in this book began their analysis.

To colleagues at Support Service for Looked After Children, Sheffield NSPCC, particularly Deb Moore, Michael Savage and Emily Weir; thank you for the many hours of creative discussion on the 'On Anger and Hurt' Sessions.

A special demonstration of appreciation goes to Michael Goldman, PhD candidate in Counselling Psychology at the Ontario Institute for Studies in Education at the University of Toronto who methodically double checked the excerpts in each of the chapters for authenticity and accuracy.

There were many of our close colleagues and friends in the UK, USA and Canada who have in many different ways offered their help and support in making this project possible. A thank you to: Barbara Brodley, Bruce Meador, Christine Davidson, Clemmont Vontress, Danny Kavanagh, David Russell, Errol Reid, Mahdi and Sharon Asgari, Sharon Mier, Shukla Dhingra, Stephen Palmer, Stephen Whitehead, William Hall, Will Stillwell and William West.

To Natalie Rogers representing the Carl Rogers estate for your help and support.

To the Ontario Institute for Studies in Education at the University of Toronto for the Connaught Start-up grant which Roy received, part of which supported this project.

To Pete Sanders and Maggie Taylor-Sanders at PCCS Books, thank you for your patience and encouragement and belief that we could one day deliver this manuscript, after having missed many deadlines.

And finally, a very special thanks to the people in our lives who were patient, understanding and supportive during our absences from them whilst we edited this book: Roisin, Maya, Tara, Zina, James, Daniel, Rebecca and Gill.

THE EDITORS AND PUBLISHER WOULD LIKE TO THANK THE
FOLLOWING INDIVIDUALS AND ORGANIZATIONS FOR
REPRODUCING PREVIOUSLY PUBLISHED WORK

For permission to summarise and reproduce excerpts from the transcripts of the films: Carl Rogers Counsels an Individual: 'The Right to be Desperate' and 'On Anger and Hurt' (produced and directed by John M. Whiteley; American Personnel and Guidance Association, Washington DC, 1997).

For permission to republish the summary of 'The Case of Anger and Hurt' by Debora Brink and Debra Rosenzweig; and, 'Uncharacteristic Directiveness: Rogers and the "Anger and Hurt" Client' by Barbara Brodley, previously published in Barry A. Farber, Debora C. Brink and Patricia M. Raskin (eds) (1996) *The Psychotherapy of Carl Rogers*. New York: Guilford Press. © Guilford Press.

For permission to republish '"The Right to be Desperate" and "Hurt and Anger" in the presence of Carl Rogers', by Roy Moodley, Geraldine Shipton and Graham Falken published in *Counselling Psychology Quarterly* (2000), Volume 13(4): 353–64, edited by Waseem Alladin. © Carfax Publishing, Taylor and Francis Group: <http://www.tandf.co.uk>.

For permission to republish 'Interview with Carl Rogers on the Use of Self in Therapy', by Michele Baldwin, originally published in Baldwin, M. and Satir, V. (eds) (1987) *The Use of Self in Therapy,* pp. 45–52. New York: The Haworth Press and subsequently in Baldwin, M. (ed) (2000) *The Use of Self in Therapy* (2nd edn). New York: Haworth Press. © Howarth Press.

IMPORTANT NOTE ON SPELLING CONVENTIONS

It is always possible to standardise spelling according to British English or American English. However, in keeping with the multicultural sentiments of this project we have retained the spelling of each contributor's country of origin, or current residence or allowed them to choose. The voices of Rogers and his client are written in American English. This demands more effort from the reader, as does engagement with any multicultural work.

AVAILABILITY OF TRANSCRIPTS

Throughout the book most excerpts have transcript numbers for further reference. Full transcripts of each film are available for research purposes as follows:
On Anger and Hurt available on request, subject to conditions, from Germain Lietaer, email <germain.lietaer@psy.kuleuven.ac.be>.
The Right to be Desperate available on request, subject to conditions, from Roy Moodley, email <roymoodley@oise.utoronto.ca>.

An Armor-Plated Man
(adapted from Carl Rogers' final comments in 'On Anger and Hurt')

an armor-plated man
sufficiently hurt
hides his real feeling
very deeply
    in this relationship
    the armor begins to crack
    just begins to crack
the first time
ever talked to anybody
haven't really been in control
in this understanding climate
    creep closer to the experiencing of his feelings
    walking all around his own private slew of despond
    the upper layer is anger
    further down in the slime are the unspeakable hurts
    the feelings of being tramped on, defeated, humiliated
gets so close to experiencing
that his expressions
become eloquent
nonverbal communication Ooooh!—Whew! ! Whew oh, phew! Got to stop
    at that moment
    he put his foot into this dreaded pit
    then he has to draw back
    the wisdom of the client—introjected self, cultured self, 'credit to his race'
    give him full permission
to be as angry
stops him completely
not his anger that he's afraid of, but the hurting, the vulnerable part
the mourning which accompanies unexpressed love
the love for his father-in-law which he was never able to communicate
gained from communicating it to me
    Finally,
    frightening aspects of his life
    the prospect of death
    a message for all of us
    present in the relationship
    an understanding companion on this trip

This piece was set in poetry style by the editors using some of Rogers' final comments at the end of the second and last session counselling an African-American client from the film: 'Carl Rogers Counsels an Individual on Anger and Hurt'. The editors used a form that is used by John McLeod in Chapter 14 of this volume.

Foreword

CLEMMONT E. VONTRESS

In many ways, culture is like people: it continues to grow and change. That is to say that culture is an embodiment of time as it constantly re-invents itself to respond to new ideas, technologies, environmental conditions, and politics, among other things. Even so, change in any society is apt to be uneven. Some areas of human existence change more rapidly than others. This may be because people live in a network of interdependent systems. One system impacts on the others. Some need to change quickly. There may be no motivation for others to change at all. For example, in the United States in the 19th Century, some enlightened citizens recognized that slavery was morally wrong. However, plantation owners in the cotton belt strongly supported it. Their views about the institution were based on economic consideration, not morality. The American political system is in a constant state of tension in which people with different opinions about almost everything take sides.

The general culture of a nation affects how people think, feel, and behave in that country. Theories of social behavior and personality are usually culture-specific, because theorists see events in terms of their own life experiences and times. Their personality is usually the product of a single culture. Their perception of the world around them is influenced by their native culture, which may act as blinders. They are unable to see or understand cultural differences outside their immediate view. The recognition of this problem contributed to the emergence of cross-cultural counseling in the last quarter of the 20th Century. Since the beginning of the Civil Rights Movement in the United States, much attention has been given to considering the usefulness of available psychotherapeutic theories for counseling minority-group clients, especially African-Americans.

In recent years, there has developed a body of literature that recommends for Black American clients counseling approaches based on the folklore of sub-Saharan Africa. Many of the writers espousing such a race-specific view of counseling appear to equate race with culture. In terms of the conception of culture presented here, it appears that in counseling blacks, they would focus, first, on the racial and ethnic culture and, secondly, on the other layers of culture. There is also the suggestion that the culture often designated 'African-American culture' is necessarily linked to Africa, the 'Mother Land'. Perhaps one reason the Black psychology and Afrocentric movement has gained a foothold in the United States and elsewhere is because there is little research or analysis of mainstream counseling theories to show how they can be used effectively with African-American clients. That is why this book, *Carl Rogers Counsels a Black Client*, is so valuable to the counseling profession.

Carl Rogers set the tone and direction for a blooming counseling profession in the middle of the 20th Century. Decades after the emergence of counseling as a recognized psychotherapeutic enterprise, counselors and therapists throughout the United States and other parts of the world espouse, reject, or borrow from Rogerian counseling principles. I first met Dr Rogers in the 1960s when I was a doctoral student in counseling at Indiana University, in Bloomington, Indiana. He was the keynote speaker at a statewide conference on counseling. I was among four graduate students to occupy the stage with him, in order to ask him questions after his presentation. I talked with him briefly before his speech and was struck by his presence. He was a man in his fifties, who had a way of looking at his interlocutors, as if to suggest that each was the complete focus of his attention. He made them feel comfortable and completely at ease.

In his speech he told us about his formative years. He was born into a middle-class family on January 8, 1902, in Oak Park, Illinois, a suburban community in the metropolitan area of Chicago. When he was 12, his parents bought a large farm 30 miles west of Chicago. He also indicated that his parents were very religious. As a child, he was an introspective loner and an avid reader. On the farm, he spent leisurely moments lying on his back on the ground in an open field, looking at the sky and thinking about his place in the world. I was astonished by his authenticity. He revealed a personal history that seemed out of place. I had been socialized in a family and sub-culture in which people psychologically concealed themselves from others.

Dr Rogers talked about his attending the University of Wisconsin, where both his parents and three of his siblings had also attended. At first, he majored in scientific agriculture. However, on campus, he became interested and involved in religious activities. During his junior year, he went to the World Student Christian Federation Conference in Peking, China, for more than six months. This experience was a turning point in his life. When he returned to the United States, he became interested in religion as a professional pursuit. After graduating from the University of Wisconsin, he attended the Union Theological Seminary, near Columbia University, where he began taking courses in psychology. He began to see the relationship between religion and psychology. Of course, his stay in China had exposed him to worldviews that he had not known before. Asian philosophies fascinated him. We, the graduate students in the audience, were spellbound by ideas that we had never heard before. Moreover, Dr Rogers talked about them as if they were commonplace. To me, what he said was not ordinary. It was a totally new way of looking at reality. The Asian way of life was entirely new to me. I had grown up in an environment where blacks had to be on guard. When my siblings and I left for school every morning, my parents admonished us to be careful. We lived in a hostile environment. Whites could assault blacks physically and psychologically with impunity any time anywhere. Every now and then, White teenagers or young adults raped Black schoolgirls, sometimes as young as 11 or 12, on their way home from school. Usually, their parents were afraid to report the incidents. The victims might be accused of and punished for seducing the rapists.

The decade of the 1960s was the peak of the Civil Rights Movement in the United States. Congress passed the Civil Rights Act of 1964 and the Voting Rights Act of 1965, guaranteeing basic civil rights to all Americans, regardless of race. However, it took several years of protests and marching, ranging from the 1955–56 Montgomery bus boycott to the student sit-ins of the 1960s, and the huge march on Washington in 1963, to achieve these measures of relief. Most Americans had a television set in their home. Therefore, they were unable to escape the nightly televised images of brutality and injustice inflicted on African-Americans. Black and White Americans alike were affected by the nation-changing events.

Our professors had encouraged us to prepare for Rogers' campus visit. I came to understand that the Rogerian counselor is an alter ego for the client. The counselor creates a therapeutic environment conducive to the client becoming congruent. The atmosphere consists of empathy, unconditional positive regard, and counselor congruence. Client change is initiated by attitudes of the counselor—not knowledge, theories, or techniques. Clients solve their individual problems by drawing upon personal inner resources activated by the counselor. The psychotherapeutic procedure depends on the counselor and client working together. When White schools started integrating in the 1950s and 1960s, many Black parents doubted that White counselors would be able to empathize with their children. They felt that race would be an insurmountable psychotherapeutic impediment for most of the counselors. I, too, wondered how whites, no matter how well meaning they were, could recognize and identify the feelings, emotions, passions, sufferings, and torments that blacks and their forebears had experienced in the United States for over three hundred years.

I was therefore prepared to ask Dr Rogers a question that I had rehearsed mentally all night before he arrived on campus. I asked him about the relevancy of his theory for counseling African-Americans who might feel hostile toward whites for historical reasons. In clarifying my question, I wanted to know how empathy, counselor congruence, and positive regard about which he talked would affect the White counselor-Black client dyad. He responded that these therapeutic ingredients would still apply, if the Black client perceived them in the White counselor. His reply suggested transference, which was not a part of the parlance of graduate students in counseling back then. He said nothing about how White counselors perceived Black clients, a topic that would have suggested countertransference, a concept that was also unknown to many of us at that time.

I was not completely satisfied with Dr Rogers' response. Although I was a true 'Rogerian', in my counseling interviews with Black clients, the person-centered approach was not working. I tried to apply the techniques that my professors had taught me. However, they did not seem to solicit the expected response from my clients. I remember one client in particular. I continued to ask him about his feelings. He seemed unable to talk about them. I continued with the Rogerian techniques. Finally, the client exploded with 'What's all this talk about feelings? I feel like you feel when something like that happens to you!' On that occasion, I learned a great deal about the theory of counseling that I was using and the clients I wanted to help. I realized that some people are not socialized to talk about their feelings. Many Black Americans, especially males, resist personal self-disclosure.

I was also frustrated in my attempt to diagnose many of the problems presented by clients. In graduate school, we were exposed to essentially two approaches to counseling, the Rogerian, on the one hand, and the Williamsonian on the other. EG Williamson, dean of students at the University of Minnesota, had little faith in the ability of clients to define and find solutions to their problems. Why else would they consult a counselor? Trained as a clinical psychologist, he advocated a directive approach in counseling. The counselor used test data and other information to define the client's problem. Once a problem is defined, the counselor could take active measures to solve it for the client. It is clear how his approach to counseling differed from Rogers'. Graduate students often used as a conversation starter the enquiry, 'Are you Rogerian or Williamsonian?'

Today, it appears that many African-Americans are reconsidering not only the use of the Rogerian counseling approach with Black clients, but Western-based theories in general. Three factors contribute to the reconsideration. First, there is an increasing advocacy of Afrocentric counseling among African-American counselors, psychologists, and counselor educators. Secondly, membership in Black psychology associations is growing, especially among Black graduate students. Thirdly, the first two factors have contributed to a large literature devoted to counseling by race and ethnicity. That is, it takes one to know one. In other words, it takes an African-American to understand an African-

American. Over the last twenty years, a great deal of research has been conducted to ascertain counseling style preferences of culturally and racially different clients. However, little or no research indicates why preference styles exist.

In terms of the relevancy of person-centered counseling for helping African-Americans, I wonder if the concern may not be stated differently. Perhaps person-centered counseling as used by others is quite different from that demonstrated by Dr Rogers. Moreover, it is doubtful that a theorist can be aware of all of the therapeutic ingredients of his theory. After all, theory is a product of his culture and personality, the internalized facsimile of that culture. Culture is largely unconscious, invisible, and emotionally laden. It is difficult for cultural bearers to recognize and explain their beliefs, prejudices, and actions. If Rogers failed to discuss race and racially related issues to the satisfaction of blacks in his audiences during his lifetime, he was simply reflecting the attitudes and behavior of the White American culture in which he had been socialized. From listening to his presentations during his later years, I got the impression that he had a greater understanding of the imperfections of the world at large than he did his native country. To me, he seemed more comfortable talking about peace in the world than he did talking about peace between the blacks and whites in the United States. That is, he appeared to focus more on the universal culture than he did on the national or racio-ethnic cultures.

Carl Rogers had a major influence on the growth and development of the counseling profession in the United States and other countries. During his professional career, many people of my generation perceived him to be its progenitor. I believe that this book, *Carl Rogers Counsels a Black Client*, contributes significantly to understanding the life and contributions of one of the most important contributors to the counseling profession. Since he lived through the Civil Rights Movement in the United States, it is most appropriate to understand how the movement and its controversy affected his approach to counseling. People are affected by the culture in which they are socialized. The chapters in this book should contribute importantly to the already large literature on Carl Rogers. The contributors to the effort present a wide range of theoretical and empirical accounts of the Rogerian approach to counseling. These analyses of Rogerian counseling are powerful. They constitute a unique and close-up view of client-centered counseling. Moreover, the conversational analyses demonstrate a unique research method that ought to excite the interest of other researchers in our profession. This closer look at a way of counseling that has affected several generations of counselors should benefit worldwide the entire psychotherapeutic profession.

Clemmont E. Vontress, PhD
Professor Emeritus of Counseling, George Washington University

INTRODUCTION

ROY MOODLEY, COLIN LAGO AND ANISSA TALAHITE

> *There is only one way in which a person-centred approach can avoid becoming narrow, dogmatic, and restrictive. That is through studies ... which open new vistas, bring new insights, challenge our hypotheses, enrich our theory, expand our knowledge, and involve us more deeply in an understanding of the phenomena of human change* (Rogers, 1986/2002:12).

We have chosen these words of Rogers' to begin the book, as it suggests that Carl Rogers was very open to a developmental approach in psychotherapy, counselling and education. It also suggest that he may have, towards the end of his life, 'intuitively' felt that the person-centred approach may be tending to become 'narrow, dogmatic, and restrictive'. Since the death of Carl Rogers[1] there has been much development, change and controversy in the person-centred movement; many of these accounts have been examined and discussed by some of the significant contributors in this field, perhaps in some way to 'avoid becoming narrow, dogmatic, and restrictive' (see Lietaer, Rombauts and Van Balen, 1990; Mearns and Thorne, 2000; Patterson, 2000; Cain, 2002; Wilkins, 2003). Yet, in all these developments there seems to have been very little in the way of examining issues of race, culture and ethnicity in person-centred therapy (see Chapter 3 for discussion).

The various chapters in this book have attempted in a small way to redress this imbalance, many of them are written by person-centred practitioners who are concerned about, and seek the inclusion of, issues of race, culture and ethnicity

---

[1.] Carl Rogers was born on 8 January 1902 in Chicago, and died suddenly on 4 February 1987, after surgery for a broken hip. He was very active at the Center for the Study of the Person, in La Jolla. Rogers is world renowned for originating and developing the now prevailing humanistic trend in counseling, psychotherapy, pioneering research in this field and influenced all fields related to psychology (Gendlin, 1988: 127).

in Client-Centred Therapy. Through the investigation and exploration of these issues in 'a single case study' of one of Rogers' own demonstration films, this book in a sense hopes to generate multiple understandings of how person-centred therapy can be more inclusive of black and ethnic minority clients. Rogers himself had suggested the need for a, 'meticulous analysis of the single case ... as a source of emerging knowledge and generative hypotheses' (Rogers, 1986/2002: 12). This 'emerging knowledge' Rogers refers to could in some way be the inclusion of issues of race, culture and ethnicity. Although Rogers makes no overt mention of cross-cultural and transcultural issues here, he was nevertheless greatly involved with cross-cultural work around this time of his life, viz., cross-cultural encounter groups in South Africa, Mexico, Russia and the USA (see Sanford, 1999). In this sense, we feel that this book is connecting with current debates concerned with race, culture and ethnicity in counselling and psychotherapy but with a specific focus on the person-centred approach. We undertake this exploration, guided by Rogers' own thinking and ways of working—'meticulous analysis of the single case ... as a source of emerging knowledge'—to interrupt and disrupt the theory and practice of person-centred therapy in relation to race, culture and ethnicity. The analysis of the videotaped sessions also provides a critical point of departure from the often separate worlds of client-centred therapy and multicultural counselling (see Chapter 3, for discussion).

The sessions explored in this study were originally filmed in 1977; shows a young black man in a state of remission from leukaemia in therapy with Carl Rogers at the Centre for Studies of the Person, La Jolla, California.[2]

In the sessions which took place on two consecutive days, and which were

---

[2.] The year 1977 was also an important year for Rogers, for many reasons. Gay (Swenson) Barfield writes, that at UC Berkeley, 3,000 people gathered at the Association for Humanistic Psychology's Annual Meeting honouring Rogers on his 75th birthday. Barfield records that at this meeting Dr Richard Farson had this to say about Rogers:

'... through his advocacy, battled at every juncture so that, in turn, psychologists, social workers, marriage and family therapists, school counsellors, pastoral counsellors, lay and peer counsellors and facilitators of self help groups such as AA, women's groups, etc., could eventually "counsel" individuals. In that regard, Rogers paved the way for most of these groups to emerge, develop, become recognised for their unique services to society, and for many to forge powerful professional associations which would ultimately come to certify, licence and monitor their own' (Barfield, 2000:12).

Barfield argues that without Rogers' efforts there might not be in existence today organisations or orientations outside of the physicians' medical model enabling people to do private counselling and psychotherapy. This view is shared by Robert Sollod when he says that Rogers, 'was instrumental in the political fight for psychologists and social workers to practice psychotherapy alongside their medical colleagues' (Monte and Sollod, 2003: 484).

filmed as *'Carl Rogers Counsels an Individual: 'Right to be Desperate'* and *'On Anger and Hurt'* (Whiteley, 1977) [3] the client, whom Rogers described as 'an armor plated man', tells of the difficulty of being black in a white-dominated society and of the trauma of being 'a credit to his race'.[4]

This latter statement becomes a critical 'declaration of identity' which is repeated many times throughout the session. The issue of race appears to be the axis which creates the emotional movement. The client feels that he is the 'victim' of the race conflict in society which, to him, is worse than the leukaemia. He is quite emphatic that the leukaemia has been brought on by the socio-political process although he takes responsibility for his illness. He also speaks of loss, separation and hurt in his life: loss of his marriage, loss of his (white) wife and loss of children (he was separated from his wife and children during the period of the illness), loss of property and the loss of his father-in law who had died recently. The client indicates a number of times that he is desperate, angry and hurt; and hopes the therapist can 'give him the answers'. He also talks about his anxiety at not being in control and reflects on death and dying. The conversation interweaves between these themes with the issues of race and racism taking centre stage for the client.

The videotaped sessions offer a rare opportunity to see one of the 'founding

---

[3.] These titles appear to have arisen from the sessions themselves. For example, in the first session: 'The Right to be Desperate, Part 1', the client says: *C11: ... I didn't find anybody that allowed me to be desperate that could understand some of the things that I did and wanted to do ...*

Rogers' voiceover commentary after this exchange: *V3: I can let him feel desperate. Friends and family cannot allow this. It is important that someone can really permit it ...*

Rogers senses that the client can feel desperate with him, or senses after the events that he (Rogers) has allowed the client to feel the right to be desperate: 'The Right to be Desperate'. *V3: ... I also go back to his earlier feelings of hurt. I want to get a more complete feeling for his inner world but he as you will see doesn't pick up on this particular portion.*

This of course happened in the second video session, which is aptly titled: 'On Anger and Hurt'.

[4.] In the 'Carl Rogers Counsels an Individual' films, the client is named as 'an Individual' in the title; the client is not named in the actual session. But this is not the case with the therapist—Rogers is named by the client. For example, early on in the beginning of therapy, seen in 'The Right to be Desperate' session, the client tells Rogers: *C52: ... just sitting here talking with you, you know, whether you are Carl Rogers or Jesus Christ or whatever you know like. T53: Or, Jo Docs ...C53: Whom ever, you know, it's a (pause 2 seconds) still it's a very difficult thing for me to ... (T: yeah, yeah), you know. And I don't know ...*

To be acknowledged by name in the session even once is critical; naming or being named offers a particular status of the 'self' in the intersubjectively relating in therapy. Rogers could be seen as 'a man' with a big name. The client of course is 'a man' with no name (in therapy); but with many names in this book. For example, he is called an 'Individual', 'Dione', 'Hurt', 'Karl' (a spelling difference to Carl, as in Rogers' first name).

fathers or mothers' of counselling and psychotherapy working with a black client. There are of course no similar records of other pioneers of psychotherapy, such as Freud, Jung, Klein or Lacan working with their patients, let alone a black patients. Rogers, on the other hand, was filmed with as many clients as possible to demonstrate the person-centred approach. These session were made precisely so that a 'meticulous analysis of a single case' would offer 'a source of emerging knowledge' to support creative ways of working in the clinical room. Many of these films have already been given a 'meticulous analysis' by prominent scholars working in this field; some of which can be found in *The Psychotherapy of Carl Rogers* (Farber, Brink and Raskin, 1996). Clearly, it was 'brave' of Rogers to have allowed himself to be filmed in this way; knowing fully well that not only would the client-centred approach be under scrutiny, but also his own strengths and weaknesses as a therapist be exposed.[5] As Maria Villas-Boas Bowen writes in the foreword to *The Psychotherapy of Carl Rogers*:

> Carl Rogers was a courageous man. At a time when what happened in psychotherapy sessions was only known through the account of the therapist, he broke the taboo of secrecy by allowing himself to be recorded ... by doing so, he not only introduced one of the most valuable methods for teaching psychotherapy but also put himself under the microscope for scrutiny by his friends and foes (Bowen, Villas-Boas, 1996).

An analysis of the video sessions will, we hope, begin a process that will highlight some of the challenges and transformations which appear to be taking place within the field of counselling and psychotherapy, especially in relation to race, culture and ethnicity. In this respect, this book is very much focused on counselling and psychotherapy in the context of today's multicultural, multiracial and multiethnic society. Almost three decades after these demonstration sessions were filmed, we find that they are still widely used in psychotherapy and counselling training programmes to illustrate how the core conditions are employed in therapy, and sometimes to demonstrate therapy with black clients. This issue is further compounded by the lack of literature relating to these filmed sessions, and to the paucity of research on issues of race and culture in client-centred counselling and psychotherapy. A study by Brodley (1996) and

---

[5.] Rogers was extensively filmed throughout his career, in a variety of settings: working with individual clients; in small and large groups; and, in conversations with other therapists about counselling, particularly about the client-centred approach. In addition to his writings, these films, videos and transcripts have been critical in transmitting Rogers' humanistic approach to psychology and psychotherapy and his theories of non-directive client-centred approach to generations of therapists worldwide. All are now part of the Rogers collection at the Centre for Studies of the Person, University of California, Santa Barbara, and also in the United States Library of Congress, Washington, DC.

one by Menahem (1996) appear to be the only recorded studies of the 'On Anger and Hurt' sessions at the time of writing this book. They provide us with an insight into the way in which Rogers attempted to counsel this particular client (Brodley's study is included in this book, see Chapters 4a and b). Another study by Moodley, Shipton and Falken (2000; reproduced as Chapter 8 in this volume) focuses on issues of race and culture in the interaction between Rogers and his black client. It is this article which acted as an impetus for the development of this book as an attempt to understand further the ways in which person-centred practice can be applied to issues of race, culture and ethnicity.

This book was therefore written to fill in a gap by presenting a range of theoretical and empirical accounts of the issues facing students in training, professional counsellors, psychotherapists, social workers and others who use counselling and psychotherapy as part of their professional engagement. The aim was to understand better the nature of current shifts in professional and clinical practice, for example, transcultural matching, race in the clinical room, power relations in person-centred therapy, and many others. Therefore, the ideas presented in this volume tend to form a critical interrogation of the dominant discursive regimes of conventional psychotherapeutic and counselling theories and its applications in terms of difference and diversity. Although it focuses entirely on the question of race and culture in relations to the 'Carl Rogers Counsels a Black Client' sessions, it nevertheless has very important lessons for the 'other' equity and social justice issues of gender, class, disability and sexual orientation.

The book begins (in Part One) with summaries of the two sessions. In the first, *The Right to be Desperate* summary by Christine Clarke and Michael Goldman, the client tells of his childhood, the sense of alienation he experienced at an early age, the tensions that resulted from his marriage with a white woman (and his divorce), and finally the leukaemia which created a crisis and a need for him to reconsider his life. In the summary of the second session 'On Anger and Hurt' by Debora C Brink and Debra Rosenzweig, the client explores the difficulty he has in expressing his feelings of anger and hurt and talks about other painful experiences such as the way his 'white family' rejected him after his divorce. Part One also includes a chapter by Roy Moodley contextualising the therapy sessions against the background of multicultural counselling and person-centred therapy. Part Two (*Analysis and Clinical Reflections of the Therapy*) follows with a textual analysis of the sessions. It begins with Barbara Brodley's demonstration of Rogers' 'uncharacteristic directiveness' in *On Anger and Hurt* as a departure from his usual practice. Using extracts from the session, Brodley reveals how Rogers is in fact using therapeutic strategies that seem to go against his own theory of non-directiveness. Many contributors in this book have referred to this seminal study of Rogers' unusual practice, first published in 1996 and reproduced in this volume. Rogers' verbal responses are also the focus of Germain Lietaer's chapter which examines the wide range of 'techniques' used by Rogers in *On Anger and Hurt*, providing numerical data analysis involving the frequencies of the various types of responses which Rogers uses with his client. This quantitative analysis is followed by a qualitative study of Rogers' responses which focuses on the therapist's capacity for empathy, his 'presence' and his profound engagement with the client. Catrin S. Rhys, W. R. Selwyn Black and Shauna Savage offer a more specific analysis of Rogers' use of language through a detailed examination of his use of 'minimal encouragers', particularly his use of 'mm hmm'. Using Conversation Analysis as a theoretical tool, they offer a breakdown of the interactive practices in the sessions and discuss empathic listening in relation to the issue of race.

The descriptive analysis of Rogers' verbal responses offered in Part Two forms the basis for the more contextual investigation presented in Part Three: *Race and Culture in Person-Centred Counselling*, which critically examines the white therapist-black client relationship. This part begins with Sharon Mier's and Marge Witty's reconsideration of Rogers' responses to the client's references to race in the sessions. Mier and Witty review the sessions in detail, identifying the points at which they, as therapists, could have responded to the 'racial content' present in the client's communications differently. The alternative hypothetical responses which they suggest, provide a more explicit and specific exploration of the client's references to race in the context of multiculturalism and diversity. In a similar manner, Roy Moodley, Geraldine Shipton and Graham Falken focus on the racial dimension in the client's narrative, arguing that it is possible (and perhaps, essential, if effective therapy is to take place) to work with racial identity psychologically. Their chapter examines the client's and the therapist's 'separate journeys' during the sessions and the difficulties for a white therapist and a black client to form a relationship. The status differential between Rogers and his client as well as the ways in which Western psychotherapy and counselling have developed represent the background against which the authors examine the therapeutic process.

The idea of the therapeutic relationship as the product of structural positionings resulting from race, gender, disability, class and sexual orientation seems to be a central concern for many contributors. Khatidja Chantler, for example, argues that therapeutic healing can only take place when such positionings are acknowledged and negotiated as part of the counselling process. This view often leads to the argument that person-centred counselling has historically de-contextualised the 'person' by excluding factors involving the group to which he/she belongs. However, contributions in this book at the same time suggest that the Rogerian practice is also (paradoxically) conducive in terms of acknowledging the 'other' in therapy. Christine Clarke, for example, uses specific examples from the sessions to demonstrate that, through empathy and congruence, Rogers is able to engage with his client's reality. Her analysis is followed by the case study of one of her clients, a young woman of Pakistani parentage experiencing marital problems, a case that offers an insight into some of the complexities faced by clients seen as 'racial others'.

Another key focus in our analysis of race and culture as reflected in the sessions is the relationship between the white therapist and the black client. By addressing the question of racial and cultural matching between therapist and client, Shukla Dhingra and Richard Saxton, for example, argue that being able to choose one's counsellor—on the basis of race and gender affinities—is an essential aspect of the therapeutic process. While the previous chapters have at times offered a strong critique on the absence of race as a discourse on the part of Rogers with this client, Colin Lago and Jean Clark make a strong case of Rogers' growing awareness and sensitivity to issues of race and culture through the analysis of another video session showing Rogers with another African-American client in the mid-1980s, called *Carl Rogers Meets With a Black Client, 1985*. This interview is an interesting demonstration since it shows Rogers using a completely opposite approach to the way in which he 'worked with' the client in 'The Right to be Desperate' and the 'On Anger and Hurt' sessions. This time, Rogers addresses the race issue more directly, thus posing an interesting contrast with the earlier sessions.

In addition to presenting a theoretical analysis of race and Person-Centred Therapy, the book also intends to offer practical suggestions about how to conduct therapy with culturally diverse clients. Many contributors have selected specific parts of the sessions and offered alternative suggestions about responding to the client's references to race. Furthermore, since demonstration videotapes (of the films) are used widely in counselling and psychotherapy training, it seems critical that the book also addresses these videotapes as tools for teaching and training. Mary Charleton and Melanie Lockett, for example, suggest possible ways in which the training of therapists could respond to issues of race within therapy. By providing a set of 'questions to students' which are interspaced with the authors' discussion of the videotaped sessions, their chapter offers a practical perspective on the ways in which the person-centred counselling model can be used effectively in a transcultural context.

Another key aspect of the book is that, in exploring different interpretations of a single event, it tends to adopt what could be described as a hermeneutic approach. This is clearly reflected in Part Four: *Views from Other Perspectives* which offers different theoretical perspectives leading to multiple ways of understanding the client's distress. John McLeod examines the sessions using a social constructionist perspective to focus on the way in which the client provides 'vivid personal stories' that constitute his personal narrative. The analysis he offers reveals the scarcity of such personal narratives in the sessions, an aspect of the therapy which is seen as a critical factor in the inability for the client to fully express his psychological distress. William West's chapter follows with a Humanistic-Spiritual view of the client's distress which leads him to examine the points of departure between Person-Centred Therapy and humanistic spiritual therapy. Using a culturalist perspective, Susan James and Gary Foster reflect on the ever-changing context which constitutes a person's life experiences in order to examine Rogers' interaction with his client. Their aim is to understand the role of the therapist as supporting the client's understanding of the social, religious and cultural circumstances that constitute his sense of self. A further exploration of the white therapist/black client dyad is offered by Anissa Talahite and Roy Moodley through the lenses of the theories on race and alienation developed by Frantz Fanon. By exploring the socio-historical dimension of the client's distress, their argument is that unresolved tensions regarding race identity can lead to aggression, guilt and mistrust.

Adding to the multiplicity of views on a single event is the inclusion of brief and immediate, and at times intuitive, observations gathered in Part Five: *Personal Reflections and Interpretations*. The authors in this section were invited to write brief spontaneous responses on the sessions from their respective perspectives and personal experiences. Many contributors have examined the sessions taking into account the history of African-Americans as a key factor in the interaction between Rogers and his client. For example, Courtland Lee examines the way in which the social history of the United States informs the therapeutic exchanges in the sessions before considering some of the limitations of Rogers' non-directive approach when working with African-American clients. He looks at the client's difficulty in experiencing his blackness and at the silence surrounding issues of race during the sessions. Lee suggests methods which could have allowed the client to engage with his blackness in a creative and positive way through the use of black art forms. These ideas, he suggests are made with the benefit of almost thirty years of knowledge and practice related to cross-cultural counselling, which of course was not available at the time Rogers was conducting the sessions. From a similar perspective and with a personal identification with the client, William A. Hall turns 'a credit to your race' (which is one of the client's key repetitive statements) on its head, as it were, by giving it positive interpretations. He also contextualises some of the client's experiences which are embedded in the history and the psychology of African-Americans by focusing specifically on the question of trust. For him, trust not only involves counselling dyads but also organizations and institutions of counselling and psychotherapy at large.

Following a similar socio-historical perspective, Josna Pankhania offers a personal view of what she describes as 'troubling' moments in the therapy sessions.

She suggests that some of the problems originate from the history of racial domination, colonialism and cultural imperialism which inform the white therapist/black client relationship. She reflects on the 'armour-plated' Western European therapeutic institutions and practices which can hinder black clients' therapeutic process. It is the relationship between dominant ideologies and the construction of identity which seems to lie at the core of many of the analyses made in this book. For example, Stephen Whitehead examines the discourses of race and masculinity in the client's narrative to demonstrate how both race and masculinity are meanings that have been imposed on the client. He discusses the ways in which the constructions of race and masculinity overlap as factors that contribute to the client's identity. Gella Richards explores an further aspect of dominant discourses through her experience as a black female psychologist. Her chapter examines the notion of 'tripping' in the client's narrative. She argues that 'tripping' is used by the client as a term which comes to encompass his experiences of racism and rejection but also resistance and survival.

Part Five ends with Will Stillwell's contribution which also goes beyond the clinical room and reflects on many different stories and narratives that were circulating around the making of these films. Using some of the rumours in Rogers' circle at the time when the filmed sessions were being previewed, Will Stillwell offers a reflection on the meaning of 'truth' in therapy and comments on Rogers' ability to go beyond the literal meaning of the client's narrative to explore deeper levels of truth. These ideas are supported by excerpts from Sanchez Boda's observations on the use of 'reflection', 're-perception' and 're-visioning' as key therapeutic activities in Rogers' sessions with the client. Finally, in order to offer a complete context(ualisation) of *Carl Rogers Counsels a Black Client*, which could be used as a reference for further research in the field of Person-Centred Therapy and multicultural counselling, we have included historical documents in Part Six. This part comprises an interview with Carl Rogers conducted by Michele Baldwin on the use of self in therapy; and extracts from letters, edited by Colin Lago, which Rogers wrote to Jean Clark, one of his colleagues, about multicultural counselling in the UK.

Finally, it is important to acknowledge that the task undertaken in this book is not without certain limitations. An analysis of an event which lasted two hours, took place over two days and, for all intents and purposes, was a staged demonstration, presents numerous problems. Also, such an analysis is fraught with many difficulties, some of which are absent in real therapeutic encounters. For example, we can only rely on the view that the camera chooses to show, thus missing aspects of non-verbal communication and finer emotional exchanges between Rogers and his client. When we then turn to the written text and the transcripts for a deeper analysis of the therapy, we may need to keep in mind the words of Maria Villas-Boas Bowen (1996: viii):

That as valuable as verbatim transcripts of interviews are as a means to study psychotherapy, key aspects of the therapist's work are lacking. In Carl Rogers' case, transcripts fail to convey the incredible quality of his presence, which he expressed through his eyes, posture, and tone of voice; this presence was certainly a central element of his therapy. Often, it was not so much what he said or did that made the difference, but how he said it and his way of being with the client.

Furthermore, it is difficult to ascertain what the therapy would have been if a different method was used, since what we have in front of us is a session unravelling as a result of Rogers' interventions, some of them directive as observed by Brodley (see Chapter 4a, this volume). The client's narrative might have been totally different if a Freudian or Jungian approach had been used. Another limitation lies in the fact that we are reflecting on the video sessions many years later and in the words of William West (see Chapter 15, this volume): 'from the safety of our armchairs'.

As viewers, we remain outsiders to the process in the sense that we have no sense of immediate involvement with the client's material. Ours is mainly an intellectual reflection 'after the event' without taking any risks. The fact that we are analysing an event which took place in the 1970s from the vantage point of the twenty-first century is yet another parameter which has to be taken into consideration. Many of the contributors in this book have commented on these limitations inherent in the process of analysing videotapes of the filmed sessions. However, this does not make their analysis less valid. What this book intends to achieve is not so much a rendering of the 'truth' but an exploration of the multiplicity and diversity of ways in which the 'meticulous analysis of the single case [can be] a source of emerging knowledge' (Rogers, 1986/2002: 12), to support the emerging dialogue between person-centred therapy and multicultural counselling.

REFERENCES

Barfield, G (2000) 'Letter of Nomination of Carl Rogers to Time Magazine "Person of the Century"'. *Renaissance, Quarterly Newsletter of the Association for the Development of the Person-Centered Approach, 17*(2): 1–3; 13–14.

Bowen, M, Villas-Boas (1996) 'Foreword', in BA Farber, DC Brink and PM Raskin (eds) *The Psychotherapy of Carl Rogers*. New York: Guilford Press.

Brodley, BT (1996) 'Uncharacteristic Directiveness: Rogers and the "Anger and Hurt" client', in BA Farber, DC Brink and PM Raskin (eds) *The Psychotherapy of Carl Rogers*. New York: Guilford Press. Reproduced as Chapter 4a in this volume.

Cain, DJ (ed) (2002) *Classics in the Person-Centered Approach*. Ross-on-Wye: PCCS Books.

Farber, BA, Brink, DC and Raskin, PM (eds) (1996) *The Psychotherapy of Carl Rogers*. New York: Guilford Press.

Gendlin, ET (1988) 'Carl Rogers (1902–1987).' *American Psychologist, 43*(2): 127–8.

Lietaer, G, Rombauts, J and Van Balen, R (eds) (1990) *Client-Centered and Experiential Psychotherapy in the Nineties*. Leuven: Leuven University Press.

Mearns, D and Thorne, B (2000) *Person-Centred Therapy Today: New Frontiers in Theory and Practice*. London: Sage.

Menahem, S (1996) 'The Case of "Anger and Hurt": Rogers and the Development of a Spiritual Psychotherapy', in BA Farber, DC Brink and PM Raskin (eds) *The Psychotherapy of Carl Rogers*. New York: Guilford Press.

Moodley, R, Shipton, G and Falken, G (2000) '"The Right to be Desperate" and "On Hurt and Anger" in the Presence of Carl Rogers: a racial/psychological identity approach.' *Counselling Psychology Quarterly, 13*(4): 353–64. Reproduced as Chapter 8 this volume.

Monte, CF and Sollod, RN (2003) *Beneath the Mask: An Introduction to Theories of Personality (7th edn)* Hoboken, NJ: John Wiley.

Patterson, CH (2000) *Understanding Psychotherapy: Fifty years of Client-Centred Theory and Practice*. Ross-on-Wye: PCCS Books.

Rogers, CR (1986/2002) 'Carl Rogers on the Development of the Person-Centered Approach', in D Cain (ed) *Classics in the Person-Centered Approach*. Ross-on-Wye: PCCS Books.

Sanford, R (1999) 'Experiencing Diversity', in C Lago and M MacMillan (eds) *Experiences in Relatedness: Groupwork and the Person-Centred Approach*. Ross-on-Wye: PCCS Books.

Wilkins, P (2003) *Person-Centred Therapy in Focus*. London: Sage.

Whiteley, J (1977) Carl Rogers Counsels an Individual: 'Right to be Desperate' and 'On Anger and Hurt' Sessions (film producer and director).

Chapter 1
SUMMARY OF
'THE RIGHT TO BE DESPERATE'

CHRISTINE CLARKE AND MICHAEL GOLDMAN

The Right to be Desperate is the first of two sessions titled *Carl Rogers Counsels an Individual* which shows Carl Rogers in conversation with an African-American client. In this interview, the client reflects on his childhood, his anger and hurt, and his present state of health. He also reflects on death and dying. He is reconsidering his life and is struggling to get back to a childhood sense of self. At the beginning of the session, Rogers welcomes the client and acknowledges that he has limited details about him except for an awareness of his state of remission from leukaemia. The client is then invited to begin the session and responds with a reflection of his childhood recalling the time when he was a seven-year-old and had sought refuge in his basement as a way of 'closing the outside world ... concentrating on what I wanted to do and wanted to be'. Rogers tentatively reflects that his client is in a similar 'space' to where he was at age seven, trying to discover and come to terms with his self. At this point in the videotape, Rogers provides a voiceover of his own reflection about the client's narrative and states that 'he has rehearsed the first portion' and views this type of prepared material as a common form of initial engagements in therapy, which should be carefully understood and respected.

The client describes the impact of leukaemia as a critical time in his life, which allowed him to put his life in order; believing that he had only a year to live. The client focuses on the fact of having a year to live and states that it was a 'trip'. In response Rogers says, 'It was a trip into a fairly dark place I suppose.' The client talks about the way he accepts death but also explains that there has been a lot of hurt in his life:

Client: Because, you know, in being a credit to your race in being an outstanding

> *student and an outstanding (T: Hm mm) scholar an outstanding (T: Hm mm) football player, whatever, er, leaves you little room to, to be.*

Rogers reflects to the client that he has been meeting other people's expectations. Up until this time in the session, the client appears to be reporting his experiences, but the expression in his voice changes, reflecting inner feelings. The client describes his feelings of hurt, as well as the emotional conditioning and preparation to die. He then returns to the dichotomy of accepting death and yet fighting it. Rogers responds by saying, 'If it's going to be death, okay, you'll take it but you are not going to take it unnecessarily.'

In a voiceover, Rogers comments on the need for the client to be understood 'in the darkest portions of his experience'. He also notes the way he is being a companion to the client in trying to discover just how the prospect of death seems to him.

The client switches thoughts and talks about the way he had always put others first over the course of his life as well as during the time he was ill. He is experiencing a new feeling of not having control as a result of leukaemia; he is not able to work, and, with the prospect of having four weeks to live, no one allowed him to be desperate. He states: 'I didn't find anybody that allowed me to be desperate that could understand some of the things that I did and wanted to do. And er that brought on another guilt trip.'

In his voiceover, Rogers comments on the importance of allowing his client to feel desperate and of acknowledging the hurt he has experienced to obtain a more complete picture of his inner world. The client does not take the path of hurt after Rogers' reflection and, instead, talks about the impact of his father-in-law's death. His father-in-law had difficulty accepting his daughter's marriage to a black man; however, after a period of time, the client explains that he and his father-in-law had 'fought it out tooth and nail', before an eventual reconciliation. The relationship between them developed into a strong bond. After his father-in-law passed away, the client felt that he had become 'just another nigger' to his wife's family:

> Client: *… a loss I could never talk to my wife or anybody else about … I gave a lot to that family, you know, for five, I don't know, seven years I guess and when I went back there were just some things that happened that showed me there wasn't very much of a connection, there wasn't very much of a connection between all of that love and whatever that I put in and then all of a sudden I became just another nigger …*

Rogers reflects the resentment in his voice and empathically responds 'So, it hurt not to get that love back.' Rogers' voiceover comments on the importance of attending to the vague feelings of hurt and resentment, which his client has not yet voiced clearly.

The client's body becomes more active with an increase in hand movements. The quality of his voice is increasingly more emotional as he discusses his hurt and survival, as well as the burden of not being able to tell anyone he was dying. The client explains his need to keep his illness to himself when he states, 'You see, because I had to take care of myself, and I had to be better than anybody else because I was always told that.' Rogers reflects to the client, 'And in striving for that one reason you really weren't heard, was that you didn't dare express the person you were, the sick person you were at that time.' The client agrees and talks about his desperation which influenced the decisions he made at that time, such as giving up his job and moving to California where he felt that he had to spend money to keep himself alive. The client expresses his feelings about relying on other people to obtain money:

> Client: *I was scared to death to say that you know. (T: Hm mm Hm mm). You know, I needed some money because of er I think I must have invented about ten stories ... because I developed a professional attitude about myself ... because you know because you know you have to be perfect (laughs).*

Rogers replies, 'Yeh, so it's not acceptable even to you to, to do some of the things that you did. I gather to live behind that, erm, façade of falsehood for quite a while, I mean not telling anybody what the score was.' The client concedes and Rogers explains in a voiceover that the 'hurt and fear of revealing himself as ill is almost worse than the illness'. The client engages with Rogers' statement and explains, 'that was very difficult that was the most difficult part of I think of (T: Hm mm) I think that was the most difficult part of my illness.' In his voiceover, Rogers describes the importance of recognising and accepting his client's experiences, without reacting to his feelings of death and dying. The client continues to vacillate in his thoughts between helping others rather than himself; misleading people about his illness and being human, yet having the power to live.

The client returns to his feelings about having to lie to obtain money, which was worse than having leukaemia and asks Rogers if that made any sense. Rogers agrees and the client says, 'I said it,' indicating that he had just admitted and voiced something he had previously only dared to think. Rogers reflects that being false was more burdensome than his leukaemia. Again, the client agrees. Rogers' voiceover explains that this is a significant point in any first session, where his client voices previously unrecognized feelings.

The client then digresses into a discussion about his changed expectations for his children as he did not want them to grow up as he did and 'take the world on their back and change things ... I don't want to raise my children like that'. Rogers responds by saying, 'You don't want them to carry the kind of burden [client: 'no'] the image [client: 'no'] that you carried.' The client agrees and describes how bad he had felt being a 'credit to his race.' He becomes silent, then comments, 'So (sighing), that's a start' and they both begin to laugh.

Rogers comments in a voiceover that he is comfortable with the silence and is eagerly waiting for his client to choose where he goes next as Rogers believes his client has 'come to the end of his rehearsed part and now he is in new territory'.

The client begins talking about the time he had discovered being in remission from leukaemia; there is a pause of four seconds, he describes taking a motorcycle ride, which was his first emotional reprieve from his illness, after which, he changes course and discusses the hurt and bitterness he had felt from his divorce.

> Client: ... on top of having the leukemia I was fighting a divorce and having my property ripped away ... married into a family ... that was of a different race ... I learned later as my wife told me that she didn't know that a whole community wanted to divorce (Rogers laughs) ... And I was hurt by that too. How very good Christian upstanding people can make some pretty serious judgments without knowing, you know, the whole story.
>
> Rogers: And I catch an amount of bitterness there, feeling that they really make judgments without, without knowing the picture.
>
> Client: For sure, for sure, but the, but the thing that was incredible that I didn't (pause for 3 seconds) forget about I guess is that (pause for 5 seconds) to understand that I forget for, for maybe a couple of years that I am going to oversimplify this next thing but, but I forgot that I was black ...

He struggles to describe how he wants to rid himself of bitterness as he understands that he has a right to feel desperate. Rogers, in his voiceover, explains that this is a step towards his client accepting himself as a desperate person.

The client shifts between different experiences and talks about leukaemia and the impact of having to lie to get money and the need to pay off his debts before he passed away. Rogers comments on his client's sense of duty to maintain his standards that he and other people set for himself. The client acknowledges this and notes a change in his outlook, which, perhaps, gave him enough strength to live as he talks about being tired of internalising other people's standards.

The client returns to the physical and psychological impact of having cancer and the loss of control he felt at that time. Rogers states 'Yeah, the way you describe sounds like a lot of, err, real hatred for yourself for your body doing such things to you.' The client agrees and comments on his desperation and the sense of responsibility for his children: '... I was so desperate to er I had a young wife who had two young children and those children were of mixed er parentage living in a, in a (pause) isolated community, what would happen to those children you know ...' Rogers reflects his client's hatred of his body and his 'heavy burden'. The client affirms this sentiment and pauses, while Rogers' voiceover comments on how this feels like his client is catching up with himself and his feelings.

The second part of the session starts off at a much slower and considered pace with more pauses and frequent silences as the client is experiencing and attending to his internal self, rather than talking about or reporting on his experience. The client initiates a discussion about some positive changes he had experienced after moving to California such as the leukaemia taking him away from Michigan, which led to the dissolution of his marriage. Also, he acknowledges that his move from Michigan helped to relieve stress as he had not felt accepted there.

Rogers states in a voiceover, 'Previously, the divorce was a hurt. Here it sounds more like a blessing. I wish to follow and be with each feeling as it arises, no matter how ephemeral it may be.' The client's voice slows down and he acknowledges how the move to California was a 'rough scratchy road ... and it is extremely difficult for me to talk about it now'. Rogers highlights in a voiceover the way in which the client's speech has slowed down and he says, 'it shows he is working on himself. A client's whole speech pattern changes when he is exploring difficult new terrain.'

The client discusses the need to 'come to grips' with being so far away from his family as well as the difficulty of understanding the way others perceive him:

> Client: She [wife] called and everything was really great and she began to talk about a lot of other people and what their attitudes and what their opinions was and that night I got very little sleep and was ready to go back to the hospital and was ready to have leukemia too.

Rogers responds by tentatively reflecting his client's sense of being ready to become ill, or accepting what is said to him so that he is ready to be ill. The client responds, 'It seems like you know, I didn't believe that. I didn't believe that statement that you just made, (T: mhmm) sometime ago (T: mhm mm) but I believe it (T: mhmm) now. I believe it.' Rogers' voiceover comments: 'A fascinating awareness of the psychological source of his symptoms.'

The client recalls another time when he had felt a sense of control over his illness, 'It's incredible, it really seems like somehow, somehow I have got control of that in some way but I am not really sure but I am convinced that I have some control but I am not sure how ...' Rogers responds and notes how, previously, his client thought he deteriorated because of outside influences but now is beginning to feel some internal control. The client tentatively agrees.

Rogers' voiceover explains, 'This raises the whole question of what is illness? In what sense is it psychological, in what sense physical? I can only go with the psychological reality as he presents it to me.'

The client continues to discuss the way in which he is able to have control over the leukaemia, such as having a positive frame of mind as well as being involved in activities that he enjoys. This also helped him realise that he could rely on his internal sense and take back control from the doctors:

> Client: *I remember one doctor saying to me ... I don't really know who's got you into playing tennis ... but you need to come in here and get err have a transfusion. And I said, 'Really? For what? I'm doing okay.' You know? (T: Mhmm mm hm mm) that's well I'll not say what that is (Rogers laughs) but you know like to some extent though that confirms some things to me about not trusting doctors to take care of myself.*

In affirming that he has control over the leukaemia, he returns to having lost the ability to be himself:

> Client: *... I think it that I have, that I do have that control and like, since I was seven to some extent why went down that basement turned that light off or whatever and I shut the outside world off or whatever, somehow I lost that. Because somehow in the process of becoming educated, and socialized and whatever, I let other people control what I wanted, what I wanted to do.*

Rogers takes time to summarise the significance of this, reflecting the client's return to the self he discovered at age seven. The client continues to talk about his experiences as a seven-year-old and the way in which he was trying to trust himself. Rogers addresses this sentiment and reflects an earlier phrase the client used in their session, 'credit to your race'. The client reflects on the significance of that phrase for him.

> Client: *Oh yeh, 'You are extraordinary. You are a credit to your race.' ... Because in a way by accepting that kind of praise and their kind of buying into their kind of their system ... like I gave up something that I knew already at seven years old.*
>
> Rogers: *And that something is, I get it is, your giving up something of yourself.*

There is a substantial silence of 13 seconds as his client agrees with the statement. At this point, it appears that the client and Rogers are struggling together to put a difficult and painful realisation into words. In his voiceover, Rogers describes his client's experience of loss of self as 'the very heart of therapy', where his client engages his feelings rather than simply describing them.

The client discusses the way in which he had felt connected to the universe as a child and contrasted that with the feeling of a loss of himself as he grew older. In Rogers' voiceover, he explains the importance of helping his client 'get back to the realness he had as a child', as the client had depicted the 'picture of the wholeness of a child and its disruption by society'. The client continues to discuss the sense he had as a child, '... I was really the best person that I could be ... I was just taught, conditioned or something that to not trust that any more ...' Rogers says, 'But then that's just childish, that's just (C: Right, right) you know (C: Yeh) don't, don't trust that stuff (C: Hm mm) telling you what's right (pause for 4 seconds).' The client, laughing, describes being in touch with a lot of suppressed anger.

In the voiceover, Rogers explains using his intuition in therapy when he reflected society's voice to his client, 'that's just childishness we're telling you what's right'. This was a way of following and trusting his own felt sense in therapy and it appeared to facilitate his client's release of anger in the session. Rogers also notes that he has learned to trust his instincts in therapy.

The client continues discussing his sense of being black as a child and the need to be '200 percent better than everybody else to achieve.' Rogers slowly and tentatively reflects how those standards dominated his client's life. The client considers this and slowly remarks that the standards feel as foreign as the leukaemia. Rogers responds, '... Damn it, that seven-year-old was more right than all that's gone on in between.' The client responds tentatively to this and states that he would have probably handled the leukaemia better as a seven-year-old. This statement is followed by a 14 second pause and the client takes a drink of water; he then says, 'Yeah, that's, err (pause 3 seconds), feels some kind of release, I don't know.'

Rogers' voiceover comments on the way his client expresses himself, '... his voice has slowed, become more thoughtful and calm,' which reveals that, 'He's getting closer to himself by revealing some of himself and it feels good.'

The client turns his awareness to the issue of trust in his interchange with Carl Rogers and states, '... I'm really wondering about trusting too right now, (M: mhmm) you know? 'cos I have trust a lot of other people too.' Rogers reflects the client's concern about trusting him with all the intimate details he has shared. Rogers' voiceover examines the issue of feeling vulnerable in therapy as, 'Clients often have such doubts and I respond in a way which helps him to realize that I recognize and accept that question.' The client states that he has learned about himself through the therapeutic encounter with Carl Rogers. He continues reflecting about his relationship to trust and acknowledges it has been difficult for him.

> Client: ... I don't know if I haven't just allowed myself to be open you know and to be needy or whatever but you know it's that junk you know that credit to, you know, that really makes me mad ... Credit to my race,

credit to my race. You know, I remember that teacher so well, big boobs, and she'd put my head right in them and she'd say I was a credit to my race and, err, you know, how it burned my, err, that burned me up.

Rogers reflects his feelings and states, 'Damn it I am really angry at her for doing that to me.' The client agrees and talks about his children and how he does not want them to be a 'credit to their race', he then says, 'I know that now (pause for five seconds and the client smiles) getting militant (Rogers laughs and another pause for 10 seconds) it's incredible.' Rogers states in a voiceover the way the client finds it difficult to experience his anger and also mentions that they are 'really in the relationship'.

Rogers lets his client know that they are coming to the end of the session. The client says that he would like to say something to feel positive about himself. He says, '… I think I really want to say that I want to be comfortable in saying you know, I got, I got raked over the coals and I resent it, I am mad and I am angry and I need to get that to be angry'. Rogers reflects his anger and comments, 'Okay. I was really, I was really screwed by a lot of people and I have reason to be angry …' The client then says he needs to say this but hasn't yet, and he states, '… that's just part of being civilized maybe'. Rogers acknowledges this and tells his client he is talking in a very civilised manner. The client says he would like to '… go back and kick some butts', pauses for 3 seconds, and says he has been militant enough. Rogers brings the session to an end and arranges to see him the next day.

In his commentary, Rogers describes the way his client has moved between a presentation of himself to an exploration and from talking politely to honestly, which was facilitated by his ability to attend to every feeling that was presented to him. Rogers comments on the session and explains that it provides evidence that 'the child is open to all experiencing'. The child has an internal locus of evaluation and the client is open to all his experiences, but exchanges love for living up to others' expectations. Rogers states that therapy 'means slowly discarding those introjections and gradually recapturing the person as he was in childhood'.

REFERENCE

Whiteley, JM (Producer) (1977) *Carl Rogers Counsels an Individual —The Right to be Desperate* [Film]. American Personnel and Guidance Association.

Chapter 2
SUMMARY OF
'ON ANGER AND HURT'[1]

DEBORA C. BRINK AND DEBRA ROSENZWEIG

Before this 1977 interview began, Carl Rogers explained to the audience that it was the second session with a man who had leukemia, but he was in a state of remission. He described that, in the first interview, one of the client's important realizations was that at the age of seven he valued himself but that he had lost that valuing of self as a result of conforming to social expectations. During the first interview, the client had begun to feel angry about the loss, but he had not yet expressed his anger.

The reader should be aware that this summary cannot convey the full emotional impact of this often moving and sometimes frustrating session. The client (who is nameless throughout this session) speaks for the most part in a groping manner (see example below), as if in a thick fog; Rogers often changes the tone and intensity of his voice in what seem to be attempts to be either empathic or encouraging of the client's struggles to express his feelings.

Rogers asks the client where he wants to start, and the client replies that he has thought a great deal about their earlier talk of anger:

>Client: I'm not sure that, uh, I really don't want to be angry, you know, and I'm not sure if anger, being angry now, is a part of the process and I've got to do that, but I'd like to. I guess my mind, uh, academically or something, you know, and something, that emotion or whatever, would like to tell that, uh, I'd like to, uh, not be angry and skip over that part, if that's part of the process, you know? But I'm not sure I can do

---

[1.] First published in 1996, *The Psychotherapy of Carl Rogers*, Barry A Farber, Debora C Brink and Patricia M Raskin (eds). New York: Guilford Press. Reprinted with permission.

> *that (small laugh), you know.*
> *Therapist: Your mind says sort of, 'Oh, cool it, don't get into, uh, some strong emotion.'*

The client agrees with Rogers, then says it seems to him that he feels pulled into such traps by whatever environment he is in. Rogers responds that his mind is now speaking for the system, telling him to 'do the proper thing', while another part of him is saying, 'Yeah, but there's some anger there.'

The client affirms Rogers' statement and then says that in this country there seem to be only two positions possible with regard to race—being racist or anti-racist. He no longer wants to be the latter, nor does he want to be a reflection of the larger society. Rogers responds that he (the client) seems to want to connect with his own inner reality. Agreeing, the client acknowledges that he can more easily trust his own experiences than external circumstances. He realizes, he adds, that the things they discussed in the first session were, strangely, worse than the leukemia—that the suffering caused him by people was worse than that of the disease. For, if he had died, he would have had no awareness of past or present, but now he is too well aware of what is currently happening in his life. The bodily deterioration due to the disease, he says, 'is the same thing that happened to my mind.' Rogers suggests that society has given him 'a cancer of the mind'. The client agrees with Rogers' restatement of his words and adds that he really does want to say those words, but that a part of him, his culture, says that he should not be angry because militancy is disapproved of. He adds that, traditionally, blacks became militant when angry.

He cannot find anyone who can be blamed for starting what is happening in the culture; it would be better, he thinks, if he could blame someone and try to 'do that person in'. Rogers understands this to mean that he thinks identifying that one person might justify his rage, and the client then wonders how one can blame another who is sick—for those who are responsible for racism are really sick. At the same time, he questions whether he is being forgiving or trying to accept their sickness; he also states that he has not had the opportunity of anyone accepting his own sickness. Rogers hypothesizes that the client has so many reasons for not venting his anger that he would like to discuss them all.

The client says, with a small laugh, that some day he just might be angry and feel better for it, adding that when he is smiling 'there's a lot of anger there … but it's not in my nature to be angry.' Groping, he arrives at not knowing 'how you'd be angry in a productive way'. He says that before, when people gave him double messages, he tried to avoid giving offense, but now he says, 'Hey, that's a bunch of crap.' He now rejects negative nonverbal messages that contradict positive ones. Rogers interjects, 'I get what you're saying, and I also feel quite strongly that I want to say it's OK with me if you're angry here.' After a pause, the client replies that he is not sure how to be angry, that it is hard for him. Rogers reassures him that anger is not demanded of him, it's simply OK for him to be angry if he feels angry.

Client: You really believe that?
Therapist: Damn right.

After a 27-second pause and a sigh, the client says that he does not know how to respond because part of the anger is the hurt. Maybe if he really vented his anger he would be face to face with his hurt. That realization comes as a revelation to him, and he doubts that he wants to risk getting angry. For him, his anger means an open admission that he is hurt, and that is more frightening than facing death and its symptoms. 'And for God's sake … having to show somebody … that I'm hurt … how can I trust that to somebody?' He wishes he could justify his fear ('I'd like just to say it's my conditioning'), but he finds this unacceptable. He explains by putting his hand on his chest, stating that he can express the hurt with words but that he always 'keeps something down here'.

The client then talks about not knowing how to fully express his feelings and that he does not want to have the kind of emotional experience that would represent, implying that he does not drink alcohol because of his fear of losing control and experiencing too much. He realizes that during his last session with Rogers he would have liked to have been able to say, 'Yeah. I was screwed over and I got hurt and everything else like that, or whatever, but it's almost an admission, in a way, on another level, of saying that they got the best of me … they beat the hell out of me.' He has no regrets about caring, or loving, but in a way too he is 'a kid' who also wants to be loved. So he is going to start expecting some in return. He agrees strongly with Rogers' statement: 'You want love to be mutual' and adds that he does not want his present situation—fear of letting anyone see his hurt—ever to recur. The client says that his dread has to do with being a man, with 'the race thing'. with a relationship that failed, and with being an absentee father. It adds up to his feeling like a victim, and unable to let it out.

After a pause of 18 seconds, he says he does not know at all how to get those feelings up and then laughs. Every time he comes close to it, he says, he takes a drink of water (he laughs as he says this) and wonders if that serves to keep things down. Maybe 'exorcism' can free him, he says, because it feels 'like there's something there', sometimes a big lump in his throat. Not believing in cookbook answers, he nevertheless wishes someone could tell him what to do to get rid of the hurt and be left in peace. He wonders if Rogers is holding something back from him, then realizes that he is holding out on himself.

Rogers suggests that if the client could let out his hurt, it would be 'the voice of the victim'. In response, the client wonders whether he has 'any control' over the victim inside him. He relates that one time he saw the effects of culture in another's intellectualizing, and he 'really wanted to just ... deck him', a reaction not in his 'nature'. A friend who was present at the time cautioned him that one day he might really 'lose it'. The client explains that he wants to free himself of what was done to him, or at least find the skills to cope with it constructively. When he sees the things done to him now being done to others it makes him angry, and he has started to strike out on their behalf. Yet, he is not sure what he has ever done to protect himself. If only he could cry and have things be all right—but crying is a 'trip'. Maybe, suggests the client, if he went to a tear-jerker movie he would have an excuse to cry. However, he doubts that crying for himself can be 'constructive'. Rogers then offers what seems to be an interpretation: 'Hmm. You say you're not sure whether crying for yourself is constructive. I feel also you're afraid of crying for yourself.' Agreeing, the client says he was conditioned from the time he was a little boy to believe that men should not cry; he remembers crying but doing so alone. Laughing, he adds that a mere two or three people in the world have ever seen him cry. He describes his ex-wife's frequent crying as most likely 'healthier' than his own way, which is to work hard and not think about it. Rogers says that the client tried to be too busy to have these sad thoughts, but that the sorrow was still there.

Asked by Rogers what he would cry for if he did cry, the client describes the very long hours away from his family. He says that all of his time working, missing seeing his children grow, even his leukemia, might have been worthwhile if at least someone had benefited from it. He also wants to cry for his father-in-law who was killed six months before the onset of the client's leukemia, and to tell him that he loved him very much. Despite their sharp differences, including the fact that they were of different races, they really loved each other, went fishing together. His father-in-law encouraged him to free himself from 'that stuff' and to do what he really wants. A week after he had agreed to help the client finance his own restaurant, he died in a hunting accident.

The client considers his father-in-law to have been 'straighter' with him than many people. With his father-in-law's death about eight months earlier, all communication ceased with his ex-wife's family. He says that even they, his own family, had begun to 'take on the attitudes of the culture'. Recently he has come to see his relationship with them as lacking: 'It wasn't real ... I wasn't getting any nourishment back ... smiles and polite kisses ... That is part of the hurt.' He would have preferred blunt honesty to false niceness. He wishes he could have been outspoken about how he was hurt. Still, he believes that saying they were racist or terrible does not really express his feelings. And they would not understand his hurt because they see black people as not being human. In response to Rogers' statement that he (the client) would get some satisfaction out of expressing to his family how hurt he had been, even if they failed to get the message, the client remarks that he cannot trust them enough to state his true feelings because then he would get 'squashed'.

Rogers' remark that the client has opened up to him elicits agreement. The client says, 'You know that I'm a person, and I don't really want that denied to me ... ever again.' The client adds that he does not want to love anyone again the way he had loved his father-in-law. That love was nourishing and then taken away. No more in-laws for him, of whatever colour: 'It's crazy to love. It's just like loving a pet rock or something.' He doubts that telling his in-laws he was hurt would make a difference; he does not think they can understand. It had taken six or seven months from the time he left her for his wife (of seven years) to understand that he had felt hurt and desperate. He might as well try to get understanding from Dick Nixon. Nixon could not relate to his situation; he is as remote from the client's reality as 'that family' was. It seems 'insane'; in one way he feels all right for having loved them but not all right about any further sharing with them.

The client then describes his belief that his body must have gone through changes that have made it impossible for him to let out his locked-up feelings. Despite knowing all the reasons for letting them out, he cannot work up the strength to get them out. Still, he says, talking to Rogers really helps: 'It's incredible ... This is the first time that I've talked to anybody ... that I haven't been in control ... I've given up a lot of control to you.' Agreeing with Rogers that letting feelings loose is a new experience for him, the client says he wants to work to be able to feel and not fear crying. He says that, if he could, he would have doctors cut him open and 'get that out'. Rogers laughs while saying, 'Hmm. Probably it'd be simpler to have an operation.' The client agrees and sighs. He says he really does want to tell Rogers how hurt he is, but that he cannot. Rogers replies, 'I understand that ... It visualizes in my mind you're walking all around the edge of that pit, but you're not really letting yourself go down into it, so you're letting me know all about it, but not it.' The client agrees with Rogers' vision of his experience and adds, '[I] don't know how to do that.'

Rogers says that what he hears the client saying is that he really does want to get to it, but it has to be at his own pace. The client agrees. He feels that it is a sick part of him: 'That's really the cancer, you know ... If I could eliminate it, I could eliminate all the cancer from my body.' He goes on to blame his illness on his lifestyle, on stress, and on racism. He wants to give, but not like before.

The client then mentions that, on his way to the session, he thought of yelling but now he has doubts about it. Encouraged by Rogers to give it a try, he laughs, saying it would not be 'cultured'. If he were to express his anger it might come out in obscenity, calling someone a bad name. He does not know what effect it would have, but he would really like to do that:

Therapist: You'd like to just tell off the bastard.

Client: Yeah, right, right, right. For sure. (Laughs.) Oh my goodness! (Laughs.)
Therapist: You can't even do that.
Client: (Sighs) Oh, it's incredible. I don't know. Phew! I'm getting warm!

The client then talks about how he used to use words like 'bastard' and 'goddamit' with his wife but not with his teachers, his family, or his colleagues. He indicates that he does not think he wants to speak that way to them: 'I was raised properly.' Still, he knows that, for himself, he needs to get those feelings out in the open. He feels rotten, really screwed. Rogers reflects this sentiment: 'The bastards really screwed me.' The client concurs and tries to describe what had been done to him: 'To describe that hell to somebody is just the hardest thing ... It's like somebody knocking you down ... stomping on you and spitting on you ... and feeling like garbage.' And although his friends would say that he has everything, he feels that this is not true. He states, 'I didn't have everything, certainly didn't have that respect as a person.'

The client then says he will not allow himself to be treated with scorn again, because he is weary of fighting. He does not know what will happen in terms of his getting out his feelings; he does not want to say he is 'hurt' because that does not sufficiently describe his experience. Rogers restates these thoughts: 'Yeah, to say a word like that or several of the words you've used just isn't at all the same as feeling those feelings inside and really feeling them fully.' The client agrees, then likens his inner feelings to the green slime that the girl spewed up in the movie *The Exorcist*. The feelings are now part of him and his body wants to get rid of them, but he fears looking 'horrible' if he were to express that kind of hurt and anger. However, at the moment his overriding concern is not with expressing his feelings but with maintaining control for fear of getting sick again. Laughing, he says he knows his fear to be illogical. Then he sighs.

After a 20-second pause the client says he feels beaten 'right now,' not knowing why. He has things to say and thinks he will feel better—but maybe he will not. He says he is talking in circles. Rogers suggests that if 'only something could come out, you wouldn't feel beaten.' After another pause the client says that what he has been through has almost turned him into something inhuman. 'It damn near made an animal out of you,' Rogers replies. The client follows this up with another emphatic statement: he never again wants a repetition of what has happened to him. No one, he says, has the right to do that to anyone, neither teacher nor spouse, 'Just like somebody took a big goddamned tree and just rammed it u-, ooh, so you know? (Sighs.) Hard to describe, you know?' Rogers then asks, 'Took a great big stick and rammed it up your ass—is that what you're saying?' The client responds, laughingly, that he never said that. Rogers, though, asks him if that was what he meant to say. The client admits that it was, and Rogers responds, 'OK. That's what I want to know, whether I was catching your meaning correctly.'

The client states that such a thing would probably be very painful but that he still does not know how to tell Rogers how badly he has been hurt. Rogers says, 'Goes beyond words'; then, a moment later, clearly being empathic, he adds, 'You're feeling some of that hurt now.' The client agrees and tells Rogers about how he was thinking of a wino on the street who continues to drink and does not have anywhere to go, but he thinks that 'there may be some reasons'. He says that he himself has become more sensitive to such people because of what he has been through. Rogers tells the client that it seems to him that he (the client) knows what it is like to feel desperation and that he knows to what depths it can bring someone. The client agrees and says that his heart goes out to people like that. He says that he used to have a lot of money, but it is all gone and he is happier now. He is uncertain about where to go next, except for not wanting his old kind of life again. He wants to give, to help, to talk to people, but first he wants to get his own thing together, part of which may be the admission of being hurt and expressing it, to 'reaffirm the fact that I'm a person'. After the client speaks a bit more about how he needs to keep his hurt inside and how he manages to convince himself that nothing hurts and that he is fine, Rogers, somewhat uncharacteristically, but in an apparent attempt to be empathic, says, 'That's a lot of bullshit. Yeah, that's right, hmm. And just for a moment there, I felt you really were experiencing that too, really feeling that stick shoved up your ass.' The client, after appearing a bit flustered, declares that his natural reaction when he has 'felt stuff like that' has been to put it out of his mind by bringing it down to a 'safe level'.

When the client asks whether it is all right to blame one's problems on others, he and Rogers both laugh. Rogers then suggests that the client feels others are to blame but that his mind holds on to the sense that he probably has a share in it too. The client then says he let himself be hurt by giving too much most times, by sharing and loving in a total way.

> Client: But ... I've never really been this beaten ... and if I show you how much I've been beaten ... I'd probably become nothing in this chair. (20-second pause) Really too much for me.

Rogers and the client agree that he has gone about as far as he can. Rogers summarizes:

> You've walked around that pit of hurt and pain and beaten-ness, and you've felt some of it, and perhaps that's as far as you can go right at this moment ... Even though you know there's more there, you know that you're keeping some of it down, and to know those things may be helpful too.

The client begins to explain how he can talk about the leukemia, but Rogers interrupts him, pointing out that it is easier for him to discuss his cancer than to talk about all the hurt he has suffered. The client, sighing, says: 'Whew, oh, I really ... I have to stop. OK?' Rogers reaffirms that he has gone as far as he can go, and that they should 'call it quits'.

In his post-session commentary, Rogers reviewed the session:

> *Here is an armor-plated man. He's been sufficiently hurt but he hides his real feelings very deeply. But in this relationship, the armor begins to crack—just begins to crack ... We find the upper layer is anger, but further down in the slime are the unspeakable hurts.*

Rogers went on to say that he did not regret that the client held back. He regarded it as a demonstration of the wisdom of the client. It is the client who knows where his most tender places are, what he is capable of, and what pace to go at.

Rogers noted that he was fascinated by certain intellectual and theoretical aspects of the interview, for example, the extent to which the client's introjected self was his 'cultured' self. In addition, Rogers spoke about the client's fantasy that if he let his feelings out, it would make him sick again. He noted, too, that when he repeated the client's own words, the client realized how ridiculous this assumption was. Another theoretical aspect of the interview Rogers discussed was the client's reaction to being given permission to be as angry as he wished. Rogers explained that this permission stopped him from feeling angry and helped him realize that it was not the anger but the hurting and vulnerable part of him that he feared most. Finally, he described how the client gained from speaking about his love for his father-in-law, as he had never before been able to express those loving, mournful feelings.

Rogers ended his commentary by providing his own feelings about the client, the interview, and what others could gain from it. He stated: 'Finally, he (the client) makes it very clear that for him, there are many more frightening aspects of his life than the prospect of death. Somehow this seems to contain a message for all of us. As for me, I felt very present in the relationship, an understanding companion on this trip of exploration which seems so potentially dangerous to him. I think it's a good example of how I work with an articulate client.'

REFERENCE

Whiteley, JM (Producer) (1977) *Carl Rogers Counsels an Individual on Anger and Hurt* [Film]. American Personnel and Guidance Association.

Chapter 3
LOOKING BACK 'ON ANGER AND HURT'

ROY MOODLEY

When the 'Carl Rogers Counsels an Individual: The Right to be Desperate' and 'On Anger and Hurt' sessions (referred to as the 'On Anger and Hurt' sessions in this chapter) were filmed in the 1970s, a majority of studies on counselling and race concluded that minorities responded more favourably to counsellors of the same culture, engaged in greater self-exploration and felt they were better understood by minority counsellors than by white counsellors (see Carkhuff and Pierce, 1967).[1] The reasons for this are complex but, as some more recent authors suggest, historical mistreatment of minorities contributed towards the perception that whites were potentially racist and not to be trusted (Priest, 1991; Fong and Lease, 1997; Moodley et al., 2000). In the 'On Anger and Hurt' sessions, the Black client appeared to relate favourably, engage in greater self-exploration, and

---

[1] Throughout the late 1970s and 1980s research demonstrates a greater acceptance of cross-racial matching in therapy. This may be seen as a development in cross-cultural therapy or as, less happily, a period in which the climate of 'race neutralising', as noted by Bell (1992) and Hacker (1992), called for an increase in multiculturalism rather than the confrontation of racial and ethnic barriers to therapeutic development. In the 1980s and 1990s, however, research contradicted the notion that the minority counsellor/minority client dyad was the most effective way of resolving conflict in black clients. For example, Heppner and Dixon (1981) reported that the effects of the counsellor's race in the interpersonal process did not consistently support the notion that racial similarity is sufficiently powerful to influence client perception. In a study by Pomales et al. (1985), the client/counsellor composition was found to be less important than a culture sensitive process. Wade and Bernstein (1991) in a study of the effects of black female client perception of counsellors and counselling found that culturally sensitive counsellors and counselling affected the process more than the race of the counsellor (see Moodley et al., 2000).

at various times indicated that he was being understood by a white therapist. Although he brings up the issue of trust a few times, he seemed to have no difficulty in sharing personal issues, such as the pain he felt about his marriage breaking up and the subsequent loss of his children, and particularly his anxiety about death and dying. Clearly, it seems that this client appears not to fit into the research profile of the time regarding minority clients in counselling. Rogers too, on the other hand, appeared to have been uncharacteristic in his approach with this client by being unusually directive and engaging himself much more in therapy. Barbara Brodley, in her analysis of the 'On Anger and Hurt' sessions, observes that Rogers was 'uncharacteristically directive'. She argues that:

> Not only does Rogers' session with the 'Anger and Hurt' client have a higher frequency of responses from the therapist's own frame of reference ... but many of these responses seem to reveal that Rogers had specific goals for the client ... [an] uncharacteristic behavior in which Rogers manifests a directive attitude in the pursuit of an objective he has for the client (Brodley, 1996: 312; also Chapter 4 this volume).[2]

Therefore, it seems that an analysis of this 'uncharacteristic engagement' by both the Black client and Rogers may yield valuable insights in the way that counselling and psychotherapy, particularly Person-Centred Therapy may be conducted cross-culturally. By looking back on—rather than in—anger (as in John Osborne's 1957, *Look back in Anger*), we can attempt to understand some of the critical issues facing multicultural counselling and its relationship to the person-centred approach, and vice versa. Such an analysis must be seen in relation to the wider context within which these approaches or movements are themselves embedded—in their own history and culture, their evolution and development, and the challenges they face in relation to theory and practice by their critics.[3] I have written elsewhere (Moodley, 1998, 1999a, b) about the problematics of

---

[2.] Ivey et al. (2002: 245) exploring a different case and client with Rogers suggest that: 'Rogers is more directive than he thinks. By focusing on the individual and selecting certain key words (e.g., blame and anger) Rogers actually does shape the interview.' Could it be that Rogers was just doing what most therapists in counselling and psychotherapy were doing at the time? According to Patterson (1978), therapy in the 1970s was directive and controlling where the problem was defined by the counsellor, and there was a subtle imposition of the solutions from within the therapist's culture. Or was Rogers just following the strategy that many multicultural therapists were advocating at the time?

[3.] 'Rogers' work has been so controversial, maligned, and misunderstood as well as accepted and embraced' (Kirschenbaum and Henderson, 1990: xv). Rogers too was also profoundly aware of the negative view of the Person-Centred Approach by many, as he says, 'we are underrepresented, badly misunderstood, mistakenly seen as superficial' (Rogers 1986/ 2002:11), and according to Cain, 'the caricatured view of Client-Centered Therapy as the mindless parroting of the client's words' still persists (Cain 1990/2002: 381).

multicultural counselling and psychotherapy, so I will not go into any detail here, but suffice it to say, that multicultural counselling, with its compendium of hyphenated descriptors and diversity of nomenclatures, appears to be constrained by its preoccupation for 'cultural competency templates' and 'racial identity theories' as the critical clinical component in cross-cultural intervention.[4] The intensity of their own internal focus (and survival) has led multicultural counselling and Person-Centred Therapy to concentrate research and collaborative energy away from each other, thus giving the impression of occupying two separate worlds, particularly in the USA and Canada, which of course was not the case in the past. In the 1970s and early 1980s, there appeared to be a greater collaborative engagement. Ivey et al. (2002) records this involvement and collaboration by referring to Clemmont Vontress' work in the pioneering days of multicultural counselling. They say,

> Clemmont Vontress has long been a proponent of multicultural counseling and therapy (Vontress, 1979, 1986, 1995a, b). He was drawn to the concepts of empathy and positive regard of his colleague Carl Rogers but expanded on his approach by focusing in even more depth on the therapeutic relationship as an expression of intimacy, openness, and real human exchange (Ivey, D'Andrea, Ivey and Simek-Morgan, 2002: 253).

In the 1990s, in the US and Canada, with the exception of a very few, the client-centred theorists and the multiculturalists very rarely 'talk' to each other, appearing in fact to entrench their views on wanting to live in their two separate worlds. The very few papers that eventually see 'the light of day' are themselves a 'harsh' critique of each others' position. Some of these can be seen in recent pronouncements, for example, Pittu Laungani (1999: 146), in *Client-Centred or Culture-Centred Counselling?*, offers a very critical view of Person-Centred Therapy arguing that 'client-centred therapy/counselling runs into serious

---

[4.] The various names by which multicultural counselling and psychotherapy are known: cross-cultural (Pedersen, 1985), transcultural (d'Ardenne and Mahtani, 1989), culturally different (Sue and Sue, 1990), intercultural (Kareem and Littlewood, 1992) and multicultural (Pedersen, 1991; Pope-Davis and Coleman, 1997). *Ethnopsychotherapie* (Nathan, 1985), *ethnopsychiatrie* (Devereux, 1983), new cross-cultural psychiatry (Littlewood, 1990), and transcultural psychiatry (see Cox, 1986) have focused on culture and ethnicity as key variables in therapy, while antiracist (Moodley, 1991), Afrocentric (Hall, 1995), black feminist (Pankhania, 1996) and race and culture (Lago and Thompson, 1996) focus on race as a major construct. Other practitioners, e.g., Atkinson, Morten and Sue (1993), Cross (1971, 1978), Cross, Parham and Helms (1991), Helms (1990), Ponterotto (1988) and Sabnani et al. (1991), have constructed race and racial identity models as a way of making therapy more relevant to minority patients, while Vontress (1979, 1985) has developed the idea of existentialism as a cross-cultural therapeutic modality. In essence all these approaches are deconstructing the racial, cultural and ethnic identities of clients from minority communities (McLeod, 1993).

problems not only among the indigenous members of Western society but more importantly among the members of ethnic minorities'. While, on the other hand, there appears to be plenty of anecdotal evidence to suggest that many person-centred practitioners are not in favour of any engagement with multicultural and diversity 'politics'. There are of course many other person-centred practitioners who are working at 'building bridges' or finding ways in which the 'gap' could be closed, such as Holdstock (1993) and Patterson (2000) to name but a few.

Some multiculturalists, on the other hand, while commending the work of Rogers appear to still have doubts and are less charitable in their views of the Person-Centred Approach (see Ivey, D'Andrea, Ivey and Simek-Morgan, 2002; Helms and Cook, 1999). For example, Ivey et al. say,

> The positive philosophy of Rogers is applauded by many of a multicultural orientation, but the nature of Rogerian methods—slow reflection and a lack of action and immediate problem solving—seems inappropriate for multicultural clients. The tendency for existential-humanistic counseling to ignore person-environment transactions in daily practices also can be a major limitation. The intense preoccupation with the individual and free choice is at times incompatible with a more environmentally oriented and contextually aware approach ... the existential-humanistic philosophic tradition does not speak to multicultural concerns (Ivey, D'Andrea, Ivey and Simek-Morgan, 2002: 258).

In supporting these views Arciniega and Newlon argue that,

> This [person-centred] theory emphasizes self and real self, which can be counterproductive because it obscures relational and broader environmental issues that may be a priority with these [Latinos, Native American, African-Americans, and Asian-Americans] minority groups ... the focus on individual development can be at odds with cultural values that stress the common good and cohesion of a person's group (Arciniega and Newlon, 2002: 437).

The greatest criticism, however, comes from one of Carl Rogers' closest friends; a colleague and professional ally, Maureen O'Hara. She says, 'there are aspects of it [Person-Centred Therapy] that, whether consciously or unconsciously, serve to preserve, maintain, and protect the interests of the Eurocentric, patriarchal, Judeo-Christian world' (O'Hara, 1996: 286).[5] Indeed, on this point, both O'Hara and

---

[5.] O'Hara is also critical of Rogers, when she says, 'There were times that not even the empathic genius of Carl Rogers could bridge the gap and reconcile the fundamental differences in "world view" ... "construction of reality" ... "ways of knowing" ... between Rogers—a famous, powerful, successful, upper-middle-class, white American male—and myself—a young unknown immigrant, working-class, white English female' (O'Hara, 1996: 185).

the multiculturalists seem to be in agreement. This is the same argument offered by the multiculturalist who argues that traditional counselling and psychotherapy is Eurocentric and at times racist (see Moodley, 1998, 1999a, b). [6]

The situation in the UK, on the other hand, appears to be somewhat different, i.e., many Black and ethnic minority counsellors train as person-centred counsellors (the majority of university courses appear to be humanistic and person-centred), and probably work as person-centred therapists. With the exception of Pittu Laungani's critique (mentioned above) there appears to be very little (published) criticism of Rogers' work in multicultural counselling in the UK. This may be due to the fact, as mentioned above, that many Black and ethnic minority counsellors are person-centred practitioners themselves, and view the process positively. However, there still appears to be very little or no research and publications in terms of how race and cultural diversity issues can be part of the Person-Centred Approach. In general, however, there appears to be no scholarship connecting the theory of the client-centred approach with the issues of race and cultural diversity. This absence of scholarship and literature and the lack of any substantive cross-cultural person-centred research is one which is slowly being recognised by some practitioners. For example, Wilkins (2003: 19) in *Person-Centred Therapy in Focus*, suggests that the 'whole area of working with people who are culturally different is under-explored in terms of person-centred theory and practice (indeed, that is the assertion made in Holdstock, 1990, 1993, among others)' but he stops short of suggesting how this challenge could be taken up.

So it seems that by *looking back* 'On Anger and Hurt' we may begin to 'bridge the gap' that now seems to exist between the person-centred world of therapy, and the multicultural counselling movement. It seems that the best place to begin looking is at the source of the theory itself, that is with Rogers and, perhaps, his (in)famous words—'that which is universal is most personal' (Cain, 2002).

[6.] The multicultural counselling movement argues that counselling and particularly psychotherapy's close relationship to psychiatry, and the lack of a culturally inclusive approach could be seen as essentially Eurocentric, ethnocentric, individualistic, patriarchal and social-class oriented (see, for example, Bhugra and Bhui, 1998: 312; d'Ardenne and Mahtani, 1989: 86; Feltham, 1997: 123; Kareem and Littlewood, 1992: xii; Littlewood and Lipsedge, 1982/1997: 305). Even some of the early writings of psychoanalysis and psychotherapy have been criticised for expressing 'racist' views, particularly some of the writings of Jung. Even Freud has been critiqued on this issue. Some of these ideas were taken into more contemporary practice. For example, practitioners, such as Kennedy (1952) and Waite (1968), have emphasised racial differences and stereotypes as causes for black and ethnic minority patients' psychopathology. Kennedy, after treating two black women, observed that the cause of their neurosis was the result of conflicts arising from a hostile white ego ideal (cited by Carter, 1995: 38).

'THAT WHICH IS UNIVERSAL IS MOST PERSONAL'

Many classical person-centred theorists would argue that if the client-centred approach is practised in its 'purest' form, it would take into account the whole person and his or her social and cultural constructions, so issues of race, gender, class, culture, ethnicity, disability and sexual orientations would be an integral part of the process. If this is the case then surely it is multicultural in both its philosophical and practical applications. In other words, race and cultural issues would be an integrated aspect of the client's self, but appear as 'actors' which need interacting with, but only if the client wants it to be this way. The client's conversation may suggest this in obvious ways, but it may not necessarily be observed in the therapist's responses. This seems to be the case in the 'On Anger and Hurt' sessions: the client focus is on race issues, while the therapist responses can be seen as avoiding the race issues. This seems to be the overwhelming criticism of Rogers by the multiculturalists.

However, this criticism of the 'disavowal of race' cannot be made of Rogers when we observe him at work with another African-American client. Recorded in 1984, and recently made available as: *'Carl Rogers meets a Black client, 1985'*, it shows the client, Dadisi, unlike the client in the 'On Anger and Hurt' sessions, talking freely and openly about race issues. In this case, Rogers acknowledges the client's concerns around race issues and freely engages with these issues. Rogers' responses appear to be unlike his reactions to the 'On Anger and Hurt' client whose repeated articulations and concerns around race and racial tensions went unvocalised. For example, the client's mentioning of his earlier upbringing as being a 'potential credit to my race' becomes a critical utterance for the client, also repeated many times in an almost obsessive way shows that there are many complex unconscious projections and introjections to deal with in therapy. Perhaps 'credit' should be offered to Rogers for not 'jumping onto the "race band wagon"' by seeking clarification and reification of race matters. However, as time went on in the therapy, Rogers' focus on the 'anger and hurt' feelings and his 'uncharacteristic directiveness' (Brodley, 1996) in wanting the client to express these feelings, could easily be perceived as a 'disavowal of race', although this may not have been Rogers' intention. The client, on the other hand, also uses a much more complex and confounding textualisation of race, interweaving it throughout 'his story', while at the same time offering narratives of anxiety and fear of death and dying. In this intricate and elaborate composition of thoughts, the issues of race appears to be the axis which creates the emotional movement; he feels that he has been the 'victim' of the race conflict in society which he feels is worse than the leukaemia. The conversation interweaves between these three themes—race, anger and hurt—with the experience of race being a central focus for the client, and 'anger and hurt' being a central focus for the therapist. It is this issue of the 'disavowal of race', understood in this way almost three decades after the event, that seems to generate the complexity and controversy in the study of the 'On Anger and Hurt' sessions.

In another example, perhaps regarded as the third demonstration film, of Rogers with a Black client, we see another way in which Rogers' words—'that which is universal is most personal'—can be understood in therapy. This therapy session was filmed in London in October 1983, on one of Rogers' many trips to the UK. It shows Rogers in conversation with a Black British woman, called Ms G. In her conversation with Rogers, Ms G makes no reference either directly or indirectly to race and cultural issues, but shares very personal details of her life; and just as critical to the process is the fact that Rogers too does not introduce race matters. As Tony Merry says of this interview,

> Rogers tried to stay as close as he could to Ms G's feelings and thoughts without attempting to interpret them or diagnose her in any way. Carl Rogers was fond of saying, 'If it's personal, it's universal'. At first, this appears to be a rather paradoxical statement. While it seems the more personally we speak about ourselves, the more unique and separate we become, at a different level, the opposite is true. Although Ms G describes circumstances and feelings that are hers, the general human concern she touches on are very much part of all our lives (Merry, 1995: 35–6; also see Merry, 1995 for a detailed analysis and the transcript of the Ms G/Rogers interview).

As indicated by Merry above, this philosophy highlights the contradiction and the paradox inherent in the client-centred approach. Cain highlights this contradiction when he says,

> A paradox of the client-centred approach is that it acknowledges and values the uniqueness of persons, yet does not specify how the differences in clients might affect therapeutic practice. Rogers and most other client-centred scholars and practitioners offer little in terms of how therapists might modify their response styles to meet specific client needs and preferences (Cain 1990/2002: 380).

Perhaps, in the final analysis, it is Rogers himself that can offer Cain a response to his critical statement:

> I am trying to determine whether my understanding of the client's inner world is correct—whether I am seeing it as he or she is experiencing it at the moment. Each response of mine contains the unspoken question, 'Is this the way it is in you? Am I catching just the color and texture and flavor of the personal meaning you are experiencing right now? If not, I wish to bring my perception in line with yours.' … this means laying aside our own judgments and values in order to grasp, with delicate accuracy, the

exact meaning the client is experiencing (Rogers, 1986/2002:13–14).

Around the time of writing these ideas Rogers was also engaging in activities that appeared to overturn the notion 'that which is universal is most personal'. In the last few years before his death, he and his colleagues conducted a series of workshops in which it seems that 'the personal' could only be actualised in the 'universal' (see Lago and MacMillan, 1999). In Rogers' encounter groups 'people caught up in religious, racial, political, and ideological conflicts … with supposedly irreconcilable differences, ancient prejudices, anger, suspicion, hostility, and despair apparently learnt to communicate with each other … and find ways to peaceful resolution of interpersonal and intergroup relationships' (Combs, 1988/2002: 132). But these developments are not to be seen as merely just 'performances abroad', there was a genuine need to engage local minority communities in personal change, as Ruth Sanford writes in her chapter titled, '*Experiencing Diversity*':

> The idea of departing from the usual or traditional pattern of person-centred workshops evolved rather slowly … for most part the participants in person-centred workshops were white, middle-class professionals … need for going beyond elitism … need for more outreach to various minority groups … both within and outside the New York City area … The deepest experiencing of celebrating differences occurred … when several African-American participants shared in depth the pain and disappointment they suffered in finding their place in the life and culture of the US (Sanford, 1999: 78–81).

REFLECTION ON THE THEMES OF PAIN, ANGER AND HURT

Another reason to look back 'On Anger and Hurt' and the relationship between Rogers and the Black client, would be to understand the pain, anger and hurt that the client experienced, so that we can share in the 'deepest experiencing of celebrating differences'. The repetitive and circular conversations on the themes of pain, anger and hurt between Rogers and his client seem to suggest that the racial tensions of society can only be 'acted-out' and 'exorcised' in the clinical room, where it is 'safe' and under the core conditions of empathy, unconditional positive regard and non-judgemental acceptance of the client's experience. This of course is relevant for all the other social justice themes, viz. gender, class, disability and sexual orientations. Sometimes these notions of identity are 'played-out' through an individual paradigm or sometimes in multiple cultural ways. For example, in the 'On Anger and Hurt' sessions, the theme of pain, anger and hurt appear to intersect also with gender and masculinities, in a way that may be saying something about the invisible and often confounding issues of masculinity and masculinist discourses which appear to still remain hidden and undisclosed in therapy. In the case of the 'On Anger and Hurt' sessions, we gaze upon two men attempting to understand their respective, whether literal and figurative, Black and white positions through the bodily dysfunction of leukaemia. Very little is constructed in their therapy about the various masculine positions that they take. Yet, in watching the videos one cannot help but notice that so much is being conveyed between the two men in terms of body language, erotic transference and masculinities. As Patricia Raskin says,

> Because the sessions occurred in 1977, when Black consciousness and issues of race were both influencial and controversial, the client's reluctance to express the extent of his anger within the session may have reflected a sense on his part of the importance of the relationship between race and power in our society ... he (Rogers) may not have been aware of the extent to which black culture, particularly at that time, proscribed the display of strong emotion in the presence of white people (Raskin, 1996: 140).

Furthermore, she argues that Rogers 'would have needed a more culturally expanded self-awareness' (p. 140) to attend to, reflect upon and inquire about 'the client's thoughts and feelings about the "system"' (p. 140), but,

> Rogers was a product of his time— a white, middle class male who assumed a place of privilege in a white, male-valuing society ... his capacity for empathizing with women, by definition, was limited. So, too, was his capacity for empathizing with black people. Indeed, if one views the case from a cross-cultural counseling perspective, one cannot help but note these limitations (Raskin, 1996: 139).

In the interview with Dadisi, the conversation also appears to suggest notions of hurt and anger (see also Chapter 12 for a detailed discussion on Dadisi). A small excerpt from their conversation for example, seems to allude to this:

> C: ... *I realize that one thing that I would, I need to do is to go back to get the credentials to do that but, I have a lot of resistance to doing that.*
> T: *Mhm, mhm ... So intellectually you know the thing to do is to go back to school and get the degree. But inwardly you feel, 'the hell with that'.*
> C: *Right (pause 5 seconds). And at times it makes me angry that I have to do that.*
> T: *Mhm, mhm ... 'Why should they be demanding that' of you?*
> C: *Right.*
> T: *It does make you mad.*
> C: *Mhm, mhm ... (pause 15 seconds). It's making me mad thinking about it.*
> T: *Mhm, mhm ... Just thinking about it makes you really feel, 'damn it ... it's frustrating, it's unfair', or something like that ...*

> *T: ... but partly because of your anger and frustration you do more things out in the world uh ...*

It is also interesting to note that this theme seems to recur with Rogers' Black British client, Ms G as well. In the therapy with Ms G it is Rogers who once again appears to put words into the client's mouth, so to speak (see Merry, 1995). In his 'reflecting back' and 'interpreting' of the client's story and feelings Carl Rogers appears to introduce vocabularies that suggest hurt, anger and pain. For example:

> *Ms G: I ... er... For a long time I've felt like there, there is this thing in me and I don't know what it is ... and ... sometimes when I hear other people talking I ... and it's not so much the words that they are using but the feelings are touching the same kind of feelings in me.*
>
> *Carl Rogers: They're touching that secret part of you that you don't quite know what it is.*
>
> *Ms G: Mm a lot of the time that is hurt or pain and sometimes it's anger as well.*
>
> *Carl Rogers: But you feel that whatever this is sort of frightening within, is of negative feelings of pain and hurt and possibly anger (see Merry, 1995: transcript of Ms G.).*

It is difficult to tell if the black client came into therapy with these feelings of 'Hurt and Anger', or if in the 'presence' of Rogers these feeling arose in the client. One also wonders if the evocation of these feelings is a result of the expedited use of the core conditions. As Rogers says in voiceover 4 (see Figure 1): 'I always try to sense the feelings just below his words and he welcomes that. I try to catch the resentment and the hurt which he hasn't yet voiced very clearly.'

Whatever the case maybe, it seems that with this particular group of three individuals these feelings are talked about, felt and attempted to be examined, no doubt enhancing the therapeutic benefit for the client (and possibly the therapist also). Of course, it is not enough to draw conclusions by looking at selected excerpts of these interviews, neither would a detailed analysis of all three black clients' sessions offer reliability or validity of our hypothesis. We would merely be speculating and generalising on a critical aspect of Rogers' projective feelings regarding hurt and anger amongst black clients. However, it raises interesting possibilities of 'transference' issues as well as 'countertransference' reactions, especially since Rogers' use of a particular set of words happens to be directing these clients towards the themes of anger and hurt. This is not only seen in the conversations with the client but also in Rogers' voiceovers (see Figure 1: V3, V4, V22). Clearly the voiceovers say much more than this as I will demonstrate next.

ROGERS' VOICEOVERS: MULTIPLE CONFIGURATIONS OF CULTURE, THEORY AND PRACTICE

One of the interesting features about Rogers' demonstration tapes are the voiceovers which appear to be added on after Rogers himself has had a chance to see the films, and reflect on the conversation between himself and his client. This process it seems offers Rogers an opportunity to provide us with another insight—a conscious secondary reflection—in hindsight, as it were, to possibly elaborate appropriately and accurately on the dynamic intersubjective and psychic relationship of the therapy. In the 'On Anger and Hurt' sessions, the voiceovers when brought together (Figure 1) seem to appear as a critical document that illustrates this multifaceted, multitheoretical and possibly multicultural configurations that intersect within Rogers' thinking, feeling and practice of Client-Centred Therapy. For example, in the first voiceover (V1) Rogers shows his willingness to accommodate the client's narrative irrespective of its 'reality', when he says: 'Clearly he has rehearsed this first portion ... Whether it is superficial or deep ... true or false, real or imaginary, this kind of presenting material is very common in first sessions and is to be expected and it is to be respected.' Rogers' response is in relation to the client's opening story about being in the basement with a book by Jung.

> Client: ... when I was about ... seven or eight years old and I remember reading a book ... by Jung, I think it ... I used to go down in the basement of my home and uhm turn off the lights. And in a way that was kind of closing the outside world (T: Mmm ... mhm) ... and today I am in the same position ...
>
> Therapist: ... shutting out the world or shutting yourself into a space where you are trying to figure out ... What it is that ... you want or who you are.

It seems that the client is inviting Rogers into the basement of his mind (unconscious), perhaps also saying that Jung has been with him even at that early age. But now the 'little seven-year-old' wants to get out of the basement and Rogers' help is asked for, but in a way that is pitted against another 'big name', another 'founding father' of psychotherapy. Indeed, it is not just Rogers that appears to be confronted by the client's (perhaps unconscious) performance of 'show and tell' of cultural artefacts of childhood but the viewer (counsellor and/or researcher), too, is presented with this material and the possibilities of constructing a comparative analysis between Rogers and Jung, and between analytic psychology and Person-Centred Therapy.

In the second voiceover (V2) (see Figure 1), Rogers' comments appear to be theoretically expanding the possibilities of the Person-Centred Approach to explain the black client's experience. For example, he says, '... a client needs most to be understood in the darkest portions of his experience ...' One could speculate that there appears to be a continuation of the Jungian theme in the notion of the 'darkest portions', the 'shadow part' of the client. Understood in this way one could hypothesise that the initial or opening statements and remarks by the client could easily set the pattern of thinking and feeling in a therapist, even if it means, as with this particular case, a therapist adopting ways of reflecting and interpreting that are non-person-centred, i.e., psychoanalytic and psychodynamic. Expanding on this theme it would not be difficult to see how in voiceover (V18) (see Figure 1) Rogers appears to further move into psychoanalytic territory, for example: '... of the wholeness of the child and its disruptions by society. I'm trying, as in all my therapy, to help him get back to the kind of realness he has had as a *child*', and also in V23 (see Figure 1) he says, 'On a more intellectual level this session provides dramatic evidence of the theory that the *child* is open to all experiencing'. When Rogers talks about the *child* in this way one wonders whether his previous training in psychotherapy and its psychoanalytic ideas continue to stay with him, even if unconsciously expressing itself in these voiceovers. If this is the case then clearly some aspect of the Person-Centred Approach connects with the traditions of psychoanalysis to accommodate the black client. Clearly this is an important area for further research.

However, it is the key ideas of person-centred theory—'self' and 'feelings'—that Rogers' voiceovers place the greater emphasis (see Figure 1). For example, in V6 Rogers says, '... I feel it is highly important to be right with him, to recognise and accept his feelings' and in V7: '... he voices a feeling ...', in V13: '... I wish to follow and be with each feeling as it arises ...', V17: '... the client can experience his buried feelings ...', and in V23: '... I have followed every feeling I could ... I have tried to stay with and respond to the most central of his feelings.' When Rogers talks about the client's feelings or his own in this way it seems that Rogers does more than just reflect on feelings. He wants to acknowledge and 'celebrate' the client as a feeling and thinking being. In fact Rogers argues that he objects to the notion of 'reflections of feelings'. As Rogers says,

> I know that many of my responses in an interview—as is evident from published examples—would seem to be 'reflections of feelings'. Inwardly I object. I am definitely *not* trying to 'reflect feelings' ... I know that from the client's point of view we are holding up a mirror of his or her current experiencing. The feelings and personal meanings seem sharper when seen through the eyes of another, when they are reflected. So I suggest that these therapists' responses be labeled not 'Reflections of Feeling', but 'Testing Understandings', or 'Checking Perceptions'. Such terms would, I believe, be more accurate. They would be helpful in the training of therapists (Rogers, 1986/2002: 13; italics in original quote).

It is not just feelings that are commented upon in the voiceovers, Rogers also comments on the physiological responses of the client, for example, he observes the changes taking place in the client's speech and voice in V14 and V20 (see Figure 1), thus informing us that in therapy the whole person must be attended to, a view that is consistent with multicultural counselling.

Even the idea that 'culture and society' is a variable in therapy is alluded to in the voiceovers. For example, in the use of particular phrases, such as V18 (see Figure 1): '... disruption by society' and in V19 (see Figure 1): '... reflecting society's voice ...', we see Rogers positioning 'culture and society' as a critical part of the person's self; this is especially evident in V23 (see Figure 1) when he says: '... the family, the educational system and the culture pound home the lesson don't believe in your experience, but learn to live by others' expectations then you'll be rewarded by love.' Rogers continues to add, 'Therapy means slowly discarding those introjections and gradually recapturing the person as he was in childhood' arguing earlier in voiceover V17 (see Figure 1): 'He's experiencing his loss of self. This is the very heart of therapy.' In any analysis of the 'On Anger and Hurt' sessions, these critical, perhaps profound, thoughts of Rogers will define how practitioners and researchers come to understand the conversation between Rogers and his black client. It will also highlight the theorising that went on in Rogers' mind through the voiceovers of their conversation, a process which is obviously intended for us as viewers (practitioners); perhaps, to grasp some ways of working with a black client in Person-Centred Therapy.

Figure 1: **Carl Rogers' voiceovers in** *The Right to be Desperate*

Rogers' voiceover V1: Clearly he has rehearsed this first portion and yet the material is of interest. Whether it is superficial or deep I want to understand the exact meaning his experience has for him. Whether it's true or false, real or imaginary, this kind of presenting material is very common in first sessions and is to be expected and it is to be respected.

V2: I like the way I'm being a companion to him trying to discover just how the prospect of death seems to him. I find that important because a client needs most to be understood in the darkest portions of his experience.

V3: I can let him feel desperate. Friends and family cannot allow this. It's important that someone can really permit it. I also go back to his earlier feeling of hurt. I wanted to get a more complete feeling for his inner world but he as you will see doesn't pick up on this particular portion.

V4: I always try to sense the feelings just below his words and he welcomes that. I try to catch the resentment and the hurt which he hasn't yet voiced very clearly.

V5: The hurt and fear of revealing himself as ill is almost worse than the illness.

V6: One of the hardest things for a dying person is the reaction that others have to him, so when he is talking of death and dying I feel it is highly important to be right with him, to recognize and accept his feelings.

V7: I think this is the first time he voices a feeling he has not realised before. That's a significant point in any first interview.

V8: He has come to the end of his rehearsed part and now he is new territory. I am comfortable with the silence and I am eager to see where he goes next. It's his choice.

V9: This is a real step into self-acceptance. The acceptance of himself as a desperate person.

V10: It is so good to feel understood, it's releasing. It shows the value of really getting inside the client's world and understanding it and communicating that understanding to the client.

V11: Little by little he is experiencing his bitterness and his real desperation.

V12: This is the first comfortable pause. I feel he is kind of catching up with himself and with the feelings that he has voiced.

V13: Previously the divorce was a hurt. Here it sounds more like a blessing. I wish to follow and be with each feeling as it arises, no matter how ephemeral it may be.

V14: Notice how his speech has slowed down. It shows he's working on himself. A client's whole speech pattern changes when he's exploring difficult new terrain.

V15: A fascinating awareness of the psychological source of his symptoms.

V16: This raises the whole question, what is illness? In what sense is it psychological, in what sense physical? I can only go with the psychological reality as he presents it to me.

V17: This really touches him. He is letting it sink in. He's experiencing his loss of self. This is the very heart of therapy. When I can provide a climate in which the client can experience his buried feelings rather than describe them or be told about them, it has a much more powerful and enduring effect.

V18: This has been a marvelous picture of the wholeness of a child and its disruption by society. I'm trying, as in all my therapy, to help him get back to the kind of realness he had as a child.

V19: I was reflecting society's voice when I said 'that's just childishness we're telling you what's right.' It was simply intuitive on my part but it released his anger. I like to follow my intuition and I've learnt to trust it.

V20: Notice how his voice has slowed, become more thoughtful and calm. He's getting closer to himself by revealing some of himself and it feels good.

V21: Is it safe to trust me with this more vulnerable part of himself? Clients often have such doubts and I respond in a way which helps him to realize that I recognize and accept that question.

V22: He finds it very hard to experience his anger, he only talks about it rather coolly. The sigh though, is one of real letting down, of relaxing, of trusting. We really are in relationship.

V23: He has revealed more of himself than he expected to. He's gone from a presentation of himself to exploring himself from talking politely to talking honestly about anger. I believe this has happened because I have followed every feeling I could; even when he seems to be scattered, to be talking about several different things, I've tried to stay with and respond to the most central of his feelings. I feel like we've made a start. On a more intellectual level this session provides dramatic evidence of the theory that the child is open to all experiencing. That he or she feels the locus of evaluation is in the self, then the family, the educational system and the culture pound home the lesson don't believe in your own experience, but learn to live by others' expectations then you'll be rewarded by love. Therapy means slowly discarding those introjections and gradually recapturing the person as he was in childhood.

CONCLUSION

While this chapter attempted to seek a rationale for the engagement and analysis of 'The Right to be Desperate' and the 'On Anger and Hurt' sessions by arguing for more collaboration between the person-centred therapists and the multicultural counsellors, it also sought to highlight the potential for a way of working with issues of race in the palimpsest of Rogers' voiceovers.

It is through the process of 'looking back *On Anger and Hurt*' rather than looking back *in* anger ... that some of the critical issues in race, culture and person-centred counselling and psychotherapy can be explained towards a developmental framework of collaboration. Rogers himself towards the end of his life was not excited by 'looking back'. But for multicultural counsellors and person-centred therapists there may be a need to consider their past and present relations before they can 'push forward to new horizons', which Rogers felt he rather do than look back. This view he shared with Arthur Combs at the American Psychological Association Convention, held to honour his work and its influence in psychology and social sciences, on his seventy-fifth birthday. Rogers in a quiet chat said: 'I really can't get excited about *looking back*. I'd much rather *push forward to new horizons*' (Combs, 1988/2002; italics present author). In many ways, Carl Rogers' life and work appeared to embrace the spirit of this philosophy. His attention and focus moved from the inner world of 'conflict' of individuals in clinical rooms to the outer world of conflict of the social and the political, viz. Russia, South Africa and Northern Ireland. Clearly towards the end of his life Carl Rogers rose above the collective conflict of individual psyches and attempted to engage the collective unconscious and the global complexity of the universal aspects of humanity. But has person-centred therapy also made this journey with Rogers? Maureen O'Hara (1996: 298) reminds us that, 'If Client-Centred Therapy is to survive and thrive in this new postmodern pluralistic world, it will need to incorporate ... multiple "other ways of knowing"'. One way to achieve this is for person-centred therapists and multicultural counsellors to start 'talking empathically', 'working unconditionally' and 'developing positively' 'other ways of knowing', so that the 'push forward to new horizons' can be done together.

REFERENCES

Atkinson, DR, Morten, G and Sue, DW (eds) (1993) *Counseling American minorities: A cross-cultural perspective* (4th edn.). Dubuque, IA: Brown & Benchmark.

Arciniega, GM and Newlon, BJ (2002) 'Counseling and Psychotherapy: Multicultural Considerations', in D. Capuzzi and D. R. Gross (eds) *Counseling and Psychotherapy: Theories and Intervention* (3rd edn.). Columbus, Ohio: Merrill Prentice Hall.

Bell, DA (1992) *Faces at the bottom of the well: the permanence of racism.* New York: Basic Books.

Bhugra, D and Bhui, K (1998) 'Psychotherapy for Ethnic Minorities: Issues, Context and Practice.' *British Journal of Psychotherapy, 14*(3): 310–26.

Brennan, T (1992) *The Interpretation of the Flesh: Freud and Femininity.* London: Routledge.

Brodley, BT (1996) 'Uncharacteristic Directiveness: Rogers and the "Anger and Hurt" Client', in BA Farber, DC Brink and PM Raskin (eds) *The Psychotherapy of Carl Rogers.* New York: Guilford Press. (Reproduced as Chapter 4 in this volume.)

Cain, DJ (1990/2002) 'Further Thoughts about Nondirectiveness and Client-Centered Therapy', in DJ Cain (ed) *Classics in the Person-Centered Approach.* Ross-on-Wye: PCCS Books.

Carkhuff, RR and Pierce, R (1967) Differential Effects of Therapists Race and Social Class on Patient Depth of Self-Exploration in the Initial Clinical Interview. *Journal of Counseling Psychology* 31: 632–4.

Carothers, JC (1953) *The African Mind in Health and Disease—A Study in Ethnopsychiatry. WHO Monograph Series.* Geneva: WHO.

Carstairs, M and Kapur, RL (1976) *The Great Universe of Koto: Stress, Change and Mental Disorder in an Indian Village.* London: Hogarth.

Carter, RT (1995) *The Influence of RACE and Racial Identity in Psychotherapy.* New York: John Wiley and Sons.

Combs, AW (1988/2002) 'Some Current Issues for Person-Centered therapy', in DJ Cain (ed.) *Classics in the Person-Centered Approach.* Ross-on-Wye: PCCS Books.

Cox, JL (ed) (1986) *Transcultural Psychiatry.* London: Croom Helm.

Cross, WE Jr (1971) 'The Negro-to-Black conversion experience: Towards a psychology of Black Liberation.' *Black World 20*: 13–27.

Cross, WE Jr (1978) 'The Thomas and Cross models of psychological Nigrescence: A review.' *Journal of Black Psychology, 5*(1): 13–31.

Cross, WE Jr, Parham, TA and Helms, JE (1991) 'The stages of Black identity development: Nigrescence models', in RC Jones (ed) *Black Psychology.* Berkeley: University of California Press.

d'Ardenne, P and Mahtani, A (1989) *Transcultural Counselling in Action*. London: Sage.
Devereux, G (1983) *Essais D'Ethnopsychiatrie Generale*. Paris: Gallimard.
Feltham, C (1997) 'Challenging the Core Theoretical Model.' *Counselling*, 8(2): 121–5.
Fong, ML and Lease, SH (1997) 'Cross-cultural Supervision: Issues for the White Supervisor', in DB Pope-Davis and HLK Coleman (eds) *Multicultural Counseling Competencies*. Thousand Oaks, Cal.: Sage.
Freud, S (1910) *The Future Prospect of Psycho-Analytic Therapy, SE 11*, trans. J. Strachey. London: Hogarth Press.
Hacker, A (1992) *Two Nations: Black and White, Separate, Hostile, Unequal*. New York: Ballantine Books.
Hall, WA (1995) 'Counselling Black Students', in R. Moodley (ed) *Education for Transformation*. Leeds: Thomas Danby Publications.
Harrison, DK (1975) 'Race as a counselor-client variable in counseling and psychotherapy: A review of the research.' *The Counseling Psychologist*, 5: 124–33.
Helms, JE (1990) *Black and White racial identity: Theory, research and practice*. Westport, CT: Greenwood.
Helms, JE and Cook, DA (1999) *Using Race and Culture in Counseling and Psychotherapy: Theory and Process*. Boston: Allyn and Bacon.
Heppner, PP and Dixon, DN (1981) 'A review of the interpersonal influence process in counseling.' *Personnel and Guidance Journal*, 59: 542–50.
Holdstock, L (1990) 'Can we afford not to revision the person-centred concept of self?', in D Brazier (ed) *Beyond Carl Rogers*. London: Constable.
Holdstock, L (1993) 'Can client-centered therapy transcend its monocultural roots?', in G Lietaer, J Rombauts and R van Balden (eds) *Client-Centered Experiential Psychotherapy in the Nineties*. Leuven: Leuven University Press.
Ivey, AE, Ivey, MB and Simek-Morgan, L (1993) *Counselling and Psychotherapy: a Multicultural Perspective* (3rd edn.). Boston: Allyn & Bacon.
Ivey, AE, D'Andrea, M, Ivey, MB and Simek-Morgan, L (2002) *Theories of Counseling and Psychotherapy: A Multicultural Perspective* (5th edn.). Boston: Allyn and Bacon.
Kareem, J and Littlewood, R (1992) *Intercultural Therapy—Themes, Interpretations and Practices*. Oxford: Blackwell Scientific.
Kennedy, J (1952) 'Problems Posed in the Analysis of Black Patients.' *Psychiatry*, 15: 313–27.
Kirschenbaum, H and Henderson, VL (1990) *The Carl Rogers Reader*. London: Constable.
Lago, C and MacMillan, M (eds) (1999) *Experiences in Relatedness: Groupwork and the Person-Centred Approach*. Ross-on-Wye: PCCS Books.
Lago, C and Thompson, J (1996) *Race, Culture and Counselling*. Buckingham: Open University Press.
Laungani, P (1999) 'Client Centred or Culture Centred Counselling', in S Palmer and P Laungani (eds) *Counselling in a Multicultural Society*. London: Sage.
Littlewood, R and Lipsedge, M (1982/1997) *Aliens and Alienists: ethnic minorities and psychiatry* (3rd edn). London: Routledge.
Littlewood, R (1990) 'From Categories to Contexts: A Decade of the "New Cross-

Cultural Psychiatry"'. *British Journal of Psychiatry,* 156: 308–27.
McLeod, J (1993) *An Introduction to Counselling.* Buckingham: Open University Press.
Merry, T (1995) *Invitation to Person-centred Psychology.* London: Whurr Publications.
Moodley, R (1991) 'Interpreting the "I" in Counselling and Guidance: Beyond an Anti-Racist Approach.' Keynote speech, *Derbyshire FE Counselling and Guidance Conference,* February.
Moodley, R (1998) 'I say what I like': frank talk(ing) in counselling and psychotherapy. *British Journal of Guidance and Counselling 26*(4): 495–508.
Moodley, R (1999a) 'Psychotherapy with Ethnic Minorities: A Critical Review.' *Changes, International Journal of psychology and Psychotherapy,* 17: 109–25.
Moodley, R (1999b) Challenges and transformations: Counselling in a multicultural context. *International Journal for the Advancement of Counselling* 21: 139–52.
Moodley, R, Shipton, G and Falken, G (2000) 'The Right to be Desperate and Hurt and Anger in the presence of Carl Rogers: a racial/psychological identity approach.' *Counselling Psychology Quarterly 13*(4): 353–64.
Nathan, T (1985) *Sexualite Ideologique et Nevrose: Essai Clinique Ethnopsychanalytique.* Paris: La Pensee Sauvage.
Nickerson, KJ, Helms, JE and Terrell, F (1994) 'Cultural Mistrust, Opinions About Mental Illness, and Black Students' Attitudes Towards Seeking Psychological Help From White Counsellors.' *Journal of Counseling Psychology,* 41(3): 378–85.
O'Hara, M (1996) 'Rogers and Sylvia', in BA Farber, DC Brink and PM Raskin (eds) *The Psychotherapy of Carl Rogers.* New York: Guilford Press.
Osborne, J (1957) *Look back in Anger,* a play in three acts. New York: Criterion Books.
Pankhania, J (1996) 'Black Feminist Counselling', in M Jacobs (ed) *Jitendra: Lost Connections: In search of a Therapist.* Buckingham: Open University Press.
Patterson, CH (1978) 'Cross-Cultural or International Counseling or Psychotherapy.' *International Journal for the Advancement of Counseling,* 1:31–47.
Patterson, CH (2000) 'Multicultural counseling: From diversity to universality', in CH 'Pat' Patterson, *Understanding Psychotherapy: Fifty years of client-centred theory and practice.* Ross-on-Wye: PCCS Books.
Pedersen, P (1985) *Handbook of Cross-Cultural Counseling and Therapy.* New York: Praeger.
Pedersen, P (ed) (1991) 'Multiculturalism as a fourth force in counseling' (Special issue). *Journal of Counseling and Development,* 70: 4–250.
Pomales, J, Claiborn, CD and LaFromboise, TD (1985) 'Effects of Black students' racial identity on perceptions of white counselors varying in cultural sensitivity.' *Journal of Counseling Psychology,* 33: 58–62.
Ponterotto, JG (1988) 'Racial consciousness development among White counselors' trainees: A stage model.' *Journal of Multicultural Counseling and Development,* 16: 146–56.
Pope-Davis, DB and Coleman, HLK (ed) (1997) *Multicultural Counseling Competencies. Assessment, Education and Training and Supervision.* Thousands Oaks, California: Sage.
Priest, R (1991) 'Racism and Prejudice as Negative Impacts on African American Clients in Therapy.' *Journal of Counseling and Development,* 70: 213–15.

Raskin, PM (1996) 'Rogers' Therapy Cases: Views from Within and Without', in B A Farber, DC Brink and PM Raskin (eds) *The Psychotherapy of Carl Rogers*. New York: Guilford Press.

Rogers, CR (1986/2002) 'Reflection of Feelings', in DJ Cain (ed) *Classics in the Person-Centered Approach*. Ross-on-Wye: PCCS Books.

Sabnani, HB, Ponterotto, JG and Borodovsky, LG (1991) 'White Racial Identity Development and Cross-Cultural Counselor Training: A Stage Model.' *The Counseling Psychologist, 19*: 76–102.

Sanford, R (1999) 'Experiencing Diversity', in C Lago and M MacMillan (eds) *Experiences in Relatedness: Groupwork and the Person-Centred Approach*. Ross-on-Wye: PCCS Books.

Sue, DW and Sue, D (1990) *Counseling the Culturally Different: Theory and Practice* (2nd edn.). New York: John Wiley & Sons.

Sue, DW, Arrendondo, P and McDavis, RJ (1992) 'Multicultural counseling competencies and standards: A call to the profession.' *Journal of Counseling and Development, 70*: 477–86.

Vontress, CE (1979) 'Cross-cultural counselling: An existential approach.' *Personnel and Guidance Journal, 58*: 117–22.

Vontress, CE (1985) 'Existentialism as a Cross-Cultural Counseling Modality', in P Pedersen (ed) *Handbook of Cross-Cultural Counseling and Therapy*. New York: Praeger.

Vontress, CE (1986) 'Social and Cultural foundations', in M Lewis, R Hayes and J Lewis (eds) *An Introduction to the Counselling and Profession*. Itasca, IL; Peacock.

Vontress, CE (1995) 'The breakdown of authority: Implications for counselling African-American males', in J Ponterroto, J Casas, L Suzuki and C Alexander (eds) *Handbook of Multicultural Counseling (Vol. 1)*. Thousands Oaks, CA: Sage.

Wade, P and Bernstein, BL (1991) 'Culture Sensitivity Training and Counselor's Race: Effects on Black female Clients' Perceptions and Attrition.' *Journal of Counseling Psychology, 38*: 9–15.

Waite, RR (1968) 'The Negro Patient and Clinical Theory.' *Journal of Consulting and Clinical Psychology, 32*: 427–33.

Wilkins, P (2003) *Person-Centred Therapy in Focus*. London: Sage.

Chapter 4a
Uncharacteristic Directiveness: Rogers and the 'Anger and Hurt' Client[1]

BARBARA TEMANER BRODLEY

In 1977 Carl Rogers conducted two one-hour therapy sessions on consecutive days with a volunteer client. The sessions had been arranged in order to produce films demonstrating his way of working within the client-centered framework.[2] There was no audience for these demonstrations other than the film crew, and the resulting films reproduce the complete sessions. The film of the first session was titled *The Right to be Desperate* (Whiteley, 1977a). The film of the second session, the more famous of the two, was titled *Carl Rogers Counsels an Individual on Anger and Hurt* (Whiteley, 1977b).

Rogers never gave the client a pseudonym, and he has come to be known simply as 'the client from the film of *Anger and Hurt*'. Rogers had not met the client until the start of the first session. At their first meeting Rogers said to the client that he had been told only 'a few things' about him, 'all good things' and 'that you have leukemia but that you're in a stage of remission.' The client, a young black man who appeared to be in his late twenties, was attractive, articulate, and expressive. He exhibited a great range of emotions as he interacted with Rogers. This made him compelling to watch as his expressions changed from moment to moment. The entire session is rich and intense, full of the client's forays into his pain and Rogers' highly focused empathic responsiveness.

While Rogers' style of therapy evolved in some respects over the years, he never changed his basic assumption nor his basic theory as expressed in terms of

---

[1.] First published in 1996, *The Psychotherapy of Carl Rogers,* Barry A Farber, Debora C Brink and Patricia M Raskin (eds). New York: Guilford Press, pp. 310–21. Reproduced with permission.

[2.] Also referred to as the person-centered framework or approach.

the necessary and sufficient conditions for therapeutic change (Rogers, 1957, 1959, 1986a). Rogers' long-held basic assumption was expressed in 1986 as 'the person-centered approach is built on a basic trust in the person ... [It] depends on the actualizing tendency present in every living organism ... [It] trusts the constructive directional flow of the human being' (Rogers, 1986a: 198). Rogers' axiom, the actualizing tendency, and its corollaries of trust in and respect for individual persons, dictate the distinctive client-centered, nondirective attitude (Raskin, 1947) toward the client and the therapy process.

This nondirective attitude is implied throughout Rogers' presentation of therapeutic theory and practice, and it is expressed in his conception of the therapist's goals as 'limited to the process of therapy not the outcome' (Rogers, quoted in Baldwin, 1987: 47). He meant by this that the client-centered

Table 1 **Category system for Rogers' articulate verbal responses in therapy, with some examples from this case**

Category	Examples
Empathic following responses	'Your mind says sort of "oh cool it, don't get into such strong emotion."' 'Just like to have socked him!' 'You wonder about that—whether if you, let out all the—all the hell that you have experienced, it might, uh, it might bring back your illness.' 'It damn near made an animal out of you.'

Responses from the Therapist's frame of reference

Therapist comment/ observation	'I've thought a lot about what you had to say about that.'
Therapist interpretation/ explanation	'You say you're not sure crying for yourself is constructive. I feel also you're afraid of crying for yourself.'
Therapist agreement	'Yeah, maybe you haven't given it to them.'
Leading question	'If you cry, what would some of the themes of that crying be?'

Note. Vocal gestures such as 'M-hm' are not counted in this system although they contribute to the therapist's communication and to the client's perception that the therapist is attentive and following.

therapist's goals are exclusively to engender in him- or herself the therapeutic attitudes of congruence, unconditional positive regard, and empathic understanding in relation to the client.

According to Rogers, one way a therapist can help keep these goals for him- or herself appropriately limited and focused is by asking the question, 'Am I really with this person in the moment?' (Baldwin, 1987: 48). Thus, the client-centered therapist does not have specific objectives for the client and consequently does not direct the client. Instead, the therapist attempts to provide attitudinal conditions that support and facilitate the client's inherent actualizing tendency toward constructive change. The actualizing tendency is thought to be activated when the therapeutic attitudes are presented by the therapist and perceived by the client.

Accordingly, in Rogers' session with the 'Anger and Hurt' client, we would expect to observe him behaving in ways that are consistently implementing his therapeutic attitudes, exhibiting trust and respect for the client with a nondirectiveness that allows the client his own pace, direction, sense of importance of things, and perceived reality. We would also expect Rogers' therapeutic attitudes to pervade the form of his empathic responses, any references to himself, and his responses to explicit questions. We would expect him to be sensitive and adaptive to the issues and vulnerabilities that appear in the client. And, in fact, we do observe all of these expected elements in Rogers' session with this client; but we also find some unexpected elements.

Before sitting down to write this commentary, I had viewed the 'Anger and Hurt' film many times with my students. While I perceived the client-centered qualities and behaviors from Rogers I expected, it also appeared to me that he was, at times in the session, attempting to influence the client in a systematically directive way. Consequently, the session seems very different from other sessions of Rogers' that I have experienced.

In these other sessions, Rogers either behaved strictly empathically or he met Raskin's (1988) criteria of 'a freely functioning client/person-centered therapist'.[3] In this session, however, Rogers seemed to have specific objectives for the client, instead of the nondirective goals he espoused, of experiencing and implementing the therapeutic attitudes.

Because I felt Rogers was functioning differently in the 'Anger and Hurt' interview, I compared his behavior in this session with his behavior in relation

---

[3.] According to Raskin (1988: 2–3), the 'freely functioning client/person-centered therapist' is one 'who not only responds empathically but who may also offer reactions, make suggestions, ask questions, try to help the client experience feelings, etc. in a spontaneous and non-systematic way while maintaining a basic and continuing respect for the client as the architect of the process'.

to nine other clients he worked with at different points over a 40-year period. The research (Brodley and Brody, 1990; Brody, 1991), from which I drew the comparison, analyzed ten of Rogers' sessions, including this one. Brody and I classified the total number of Rogers' substantive verbal responses in the ten sessions into two categories: 'empathic following responses' and 'responses from the therapist's frame of reference' (see Table 1). The first consists of Rogers' responses that were intended to check[4] with the client whether or not Rogers accurately understood the client's immediate internal frame of reference. The second category consists of responses from Rogers' own frame of reference (in Table 1. 1, these are further subdivided into four subcategories).

The study shows that while 4.2% of the total number of Rogers' responses in the nine other sessions were from his own frame of reference, 22% of his responses in the 'Anger and Hurt' interview were from his own frame of reference. It is likely that such a high frequency of responses from the therapist's frame of reference is the result of attempts to implement specific objectives for the client. It is, however, not only the frequency of such responses that may reveal directiveness. The definitive test of directiveness is whether or not responses from the therapist's frame of reference systematically implement a directive intention or attitude in relation to the client. In short, does the therapist consistently express some specific objectives for the client in his responses? If so, that behavior is directive and inconsistent with client/person-centered principles.

Not only does Rogers' session with the 'Anger and Hurt' client have a higher frequency of responses from the therapist's own frame of reference compared with the other nine sessions in the sample, but many of these responses seem to reveal that Rogers had specific goals for the client at times during the session. Several sequences of interaction in the session reveal this uncharacteristic behavior in which Rogers manifests a directive attitude in the pursuit of an objective he has for the client. The first sequence that reveals systematic directiveness begins at the point of the client's 29th statement in the transcript.

> *Client: I don't know if I'm sounding confused or whatever, maybe, you know, but trying to accept their sickness, you know. (CR: M-hm.) And at the same time, I really haven't had the opportunity of letting anybody accept mine. (G.R.: M-hm.) Or maybe I haven't given it to them.*
> *CR: Yeah, maybe you haven't given it to them.*
> *Client: Right.*
> *CR: That's what I sense is going on now—that you feel, 'there's so many reasons why I really shouldn't express my anger. I'll, I'll talk about all those reasons.'*

[4.] Rogers (1986b) asserted that his empathic responses were not intended to reflect the client's feelings, but rather to check the accuracy of his own understandings.

> Client: Yeah (small laugh), for sure ... I don't know really, you know. Maybe I'll just be angry one day (small laugh) and maybe I'll really feel better or whatever, you know, and ... and I—when I, when I smile, I—I'm, uh, you know, I'm smiling but there's a lot of—and I'm sure you know that—there's a lot of anger there. (CR: M-hm.) You know, but it's not my nature to be angry. (CR: M.hm.) It's not my nature to be angry, but I feel angry.
>
> CR: Yeah, um, and, uh, so I hear you explaining and explaining that uh, uh, 'that's not my nature to be angry. It's just that I am angry right now.'
>
> Client: For sure (slight laugh), for sure.

In Rogers' first response above, he asserts the client's idea that he may not have let his needs be known to others. In his second response Rogers uses this to reinforce his *own* idea that the client is avoiding the expression of his angry feelings. This is an interpretation of Rogers' that implies that the client *should be* expressing his anger. It is also notable, and unusual for Rogers, that he states his interpretation in the assertive mode when he says, 'That's what I sense is going on now.'

The client appears to have been uncomfortable in reaction to Rogers' interpretation and eases himself away from the pressure in Rogers' statement saying, 'Maybe I'll just be angry one day.' Immediately following this statement, the client continues in a somewhat hesitant and ambiguous fashion: 'and maybe I'll really feel better or whatever, you know, and ... and I—when I, when I smile, I—I'm, uh, you know, I'm smiling but there's a lot of—and I'm sure you know that—there's a lot of anger there.' It is not clear whether the client was complying with Rogers' implicit direction to express anger when the client commented that his smile covered angry feelings, or if the client was revealing some anger toward Rogers in reaction to the interpretation.

In any case, Rogers does *not* give an empathic response that acknowledges that the client feels he has been provoked to feel angry and, consequently, has become angry. Instead, Rogers reiterates his interpretation that the client avoids anger by 'explaining and explaining', Ironically, it seems that Rogers has been so strongly goal directed in his attitude at this point that he bypasses the fact that the client has said that he is angry right at that moment.

Rogers' goal, for the client to be immediately angry, is explicit in Rogers' comment within the interaction following the one above.

> Client: I don't know how you'd be angry in a productive way, you know, in terms of ... It's like now when I, when I respond to people, if, if when you encounter people, whether it's in the street, whether it's in a professional situation or whatever, if people send out certain messages and, no matter what they're saying, there are certain kinds of messages

>   that I'm getting. They're saying, 'hey,' you know, 'that isn't for me' kind of thing. And that's before ... I'd like to work with that and ride it, like to try to communicate without alienating (CR: M-hm) people or whatever. But now I'm ending up saying, like, 'hey, that's a bunch of crap.' (CR: M-hm.) You know. Don't tell me about the way I should do it or give me all that nonverbal stuff about, um, saying that I'm OK, but by nonverbally saying 'hey,' you know, 'you're really not OK.' And I don't want to hear that kind of stuff anymore.
>
> CR: I get what you're saying and I also feel quite strongly that I want to say, 'It's OK with me if you're angry here.'
>
> Client: (Pause) But I don't, you know, it's hard to know how to be angry, you know, hard to—
>
> CR: Sure, sure, I'm not saying you have to be.
>
> Client: Sure.
>
> CR: I'm just saying it's OK with me. (Client: M-hm.) If you feel like being angry, you can be angry.
>
> Client: You really believe that?
>
> CR: Damn right!

The client's response to Rogers' statement of permission indicates that he interprets the permission as an encouragement. Although Rogers denies that he meant to imply that the client *should* get angry, the vehemence of Rogers' reassurance probably communicated the advocacy of anger to the client. In addition, Rogers sacrifices an opportunity for an empathic response and, in the process, again overlooks, and distracts the client from, the feelings he was immediately experiencing.

From here, Rogers responds nondirectively and empathically for many interactions. Then Rogers makes a comment that implies encouragement for another immediate feeling.

> Client: When I see other people doing it to other people, it grinds me, it makes me angry, you know? And I would think that in those situations, I've begun to kind of strike out, you know, or like, protecting somebody else or fighting for somebody else or whatever. (Pause) And, if I could cry and have it be all right—
>
> CR: That's what I was thinking.
>
> Client: That would be—
>
> CR: I was just thinking, if you could only cry.

Here, Rogers interrupts the client twice to state his own idea that it would be good for the client to cry. Even though Rogers supports the client's idea, he asserts it as his own thought. Again the encouraging response overlooks the client's ownership of the idea that immediate feeling and expression (crying) are desirable. After this, Rogers follows empathically for several interactions and then makes an interpretation.

> Client: I can cry, you know and have an excuse to cry. But crying for myself, I'm not sure that's going to be constructive, you know (laughs).
>
> CR: M-hm, you say you're not sure whether crying for yourself is constructive. I feel also you're afraid of crying for yourself.

This interpretation does not accept the client's doubt that crying for himself would be constructive. The interpretation carries the message that the client should cry, that he would be better off crying, and that the real experience the client is having is the latent one of crying. Rogers gives additional evidence of his directive attitude with respect to crying in his next response to the client when Rogers says, 'Probably your seven-year-old could cry.'

In this response, Rogers is referring to the client as a child, mentioned earlier in the session, who, lonely as he was, had an authentic self before he reacted to the falsifying pressures of culture. Rogers' statement implies that the client would be more authentic if he could cry for himself.

Rogers empathically follows during the next four interactions until he breaks the empathic process with a leading question.

> Client: I really don't know how to de—, and I really don't know how to deal with that. I really don't. I really don't (sighs). You know, just really giving so much of yourself, and it's just really crazy. Too much (sighs).
>
> CR: If you did cry, what would some of the themes of that crying be?

Here, again, Rogers overlooks and deflects an immediate feeling in his apparent effort to move the client toward immediacy and expression of feelings. The client is feeling his sadness. His words, sighs, and appearance indicate it very clearly. But Rogers' question redirects the client to draw out information and explanations, which distracts the client from the feelings he was experiencing before the question.

By the midpoint of the session, Rogers has already encouraged the client to feel angry and to cry in the session. Then he encourages the client to express another emotion, one of intense hurt or anguish.

> Client: I just don't want to get caught up into that anymore, and I want to continue to give, but I don't, I'm just not going to do it the way I did before. May— yelling, you know, one of those long, big long, you know. But I'm not sure I want to do that (smiles).
>
> CR: You could try it.

Rogers' encouragements and permission, his pressure on the client to express anger, to cry, and to yell out his pain, subvert in each instance, if only briefly, the client's actual immediate feelings. This type of deflection is characteristic of directive therapies (psychodynamic, Gestalt, family systems, etc.) but rare in client-centered work. Although a directive therapy may consider the immediate expression of feeling as desirable, the directive behavior often results in the therapist's overlooking and deflecting spontaneous feelings in the client. In contrast, the client-centered therapist's usual empathic attention and responsiveness leave the client free to experience a feeling or shift away from it according to his or her inner leanings. The deflections that appear in this session are unusual, possibly unique, in available examples of Rogers doing therapy. As if he were aware of this, each time Rogers' directiveness interferes with the client's immediacy, Rogers resumes empathic responding and, as a consequence, the client's feelings are re-established and a productive client-centered process is reinstated.

There is an additional way, other than through interpretations and encouragements, that Rogers conveys a directive attitude in relation to this client. In two instances in the session, Rogers conveys a directive attitude by expressly introducing a profanity into an otherwise empathic understanding response, as a means to press the client to express intense feelings. In the first instance, this stimulates embarrassment in the client.

> *CR: You'd like to just tell off the bastard.*
> *Client: Yeah, right, right, right. For sure. (Laughs) Oh, my goodness! (Laughs)*

The client's embarrassment about having profanity attributed to him (although he acknowledges that the sentiment is correct) may be caused by his awareness that the session is being filmed, or his beliefs about the correct manner of speech in therapy, or the fact that he is speaking to Rogers, an elder and a professional person. In any case, he is obviously uncomfortable with the attribution.

In the second instance of Rogers' modeling of profanity, the client had been talking about his resolve and determination that he would no longer allow other people to degrade or dehumanize him as had been done to him in the past. He speaks with strong emotion evident in his words and his manner.

> *Client: I don't think anybody has a right to do that to anybody. Nobody, teacher, wife, husband, whatever. Uh, uh, you know, and it, and it really wasn't my fault either, and I'm not the blameless, I mean, I'm not without any blame or whatever, but you know, you know, just like somebody took a big goddamned tree and just rammed it u-, ooh, so you know? (Sighs.) Hard to describe, you know, you know?*
> *CR: Took a great big stick and rammed it up your ass—is what you're saying?*
> *Client: (Laughs) I, I didn't say that.*

Rogers' response—one that refers to an emotionally charged situation and that focuses on a metaphor with a compelling emotional meaning—is a type that Rogers used often in his empathic responding. But in this instance he seems to have been pushing the explicit profanity that the client communicated quite well while avoiding the phrase 'up my ass'. And, as might be expected, given his previous embarrassed response to Rogers' use of the word 'bastard', the client reacts with nervous laughter and denies he used the phrase. The focus on stating the profanity deflects him from the strong emotion he appeared to be experiencing when he used his own metaphor but omitted the profanity. (An empathic response that Rogers could have made that would have respected the client's reserve in the session about profanity but also communicated the intensity of his feelings might be: 'Nobody has the right to violate you, or anybody, the way you've been violated, degraded and hurt.')

In these interactions and others, Rogers seemed to be working from an idea that the client would benefit from intensely and immediately vocalizing his feelings. It seems, paradoxically, that this idea led Rogers to responses that, at times, inhibited or undermined that very goal.

The client resumes contact with his strong feelings after several more interactions with Rogers. That such a recovery is possible seems to be the consequence of the activeness and intensity of the client's feelings and of Rogers' powerful nondirective empathy that, aside from moments of directiveness, predominates in the session. (Seventy-eight percent of Rogers' responses were empathic following responses.)

Near the middle of the session, the client makes an observation that expresses my perception that Rogers' oscillations between directiveness and his characteristic empathy, acceptant, nondirective attitude resulted in Rogers exerting control over the client in the session. The client says, 'It's incredible, you know. This is the first time I haven't really been in control. To some extent I've really given up a lot of control, uh, to you.' Clients of client-centered therapists often give up excessive controlling tendencies as a consequence of the relationship. But the client's muted words 'to you' express his sense that Rogers is in control—a different matter. The client's words speak to my perception that Rogers was trying to influence the client toward specific objectives—to immediately and intensely experience anger, sadness, and hurt feelings.

The question naturally arises as to why Rogers wavered in this session between an uncharacteristic, theoretically inconsistent directiveness and his usual, theoretically consistent nondirectiveness. I do not know and would rather not speculate. The purpose of my commentary has been to demonstrate Rogers' uncharacteristic directiveness in this session, not to explain it. For those who are inclined to speculate there are rumors which, if true, might support certain explanations.

One rumor has it that Rogers felt some reluctance to make the films, but that he responded to pressure from a colleague and went ahead with the project. Mixed feelings about the filming situation may have made him in some way impatient with the client's reserve, which may have caused him to lose his nondirective discipline with the client. Another rumor has it that the client misrepresented critical information about himself, for example that he suffered from leukemia; and although Rogers had no knowledge of this at the time the sessions took place, he may have sensed something in the client that threw him off of his usual congruent state in the relationship.

The peculiar, and disturbing, uncharacteristic quality of Rogers' work with this client was echoed in another way at the very end of the film. In the final minutes of the session, Rogers is purely empathic, expressing acceptant and accurate understanding of the client and, as a result, the client became very emotional. Tears came to his eyes and he requested that the interview be ended because he felt too emotional to continue. As the session closed, Rogers leaned toward the client and tenderly touched his knee in a gesture of support and care.

Then, immediately after this moving sequence of events, in his post-session comments (not in the client's presence), Rogers began his remarks by describing the client as an 'armor-plated man'. This metaphoric description is strangely and disturbingly at odds with the viewer's experience of the man who had been talking emotionally with Rogers during the hour. It was also an uncharacteristically harsh statement for Rogers to make about a client, and it seems contradictory to the caring attitude Rogers conveyed at the end of the session. This contrast supports other evidence that Rogers was not entirely himself in the session with this client.

Therapists often function in an imperfect manner with their clients, both in general, with respect to the ideal of their own theories, and more specifically for client-centered therapists, with respect to Rogers' conception of the necessary and sufficient conditions for therapeutic change. Nevertheless, clients feel and report progress and can be objectively assessed to show progress. Rogers' (1957) statement of his therapeutic theory makes it very clear that a therapist need not function with absolute consistency nor always provide the highest levels of the therapeutic attitudes in order to foster therapeutic change. Even so, during my examination of many sessions conducted by Rogers (Brodley, 1994), I have found that he often achieved an absolute level of therapeutic presence, but not with the *Anger and Hurt* client.

REFERENCES

Baldwin, M (1987) 'Interview with Carl Rogers on the use of the self in therapy', in M

Baldwin and V Satir (eds) *The use of the self in therapy* (pp. 45–52). New York: Haworth Press.

Brodley, BT (1994) 'Some observations of Carl Rogers' behavior in therapy interviews.' *Person-Centered Journal 1*(2): 37–48.

Brodley, BT, and Brody, AF (1990, August) Understanding client-centered therapy through the study of ten interviews conducted by Carl Rogers. Paper presented at the Annual Conference of the American Psychological Association, Boston, MA.

Brody, AF (1991) Understanding client-centered therapy through interviews conducted by Carl Rogers. Clinical Research Paper submitted in partial fulfillment of requirements for Doctor of Psychology in Clinical Psychology, Illinois School of Professional Psychology.

Raskin, NJ (1947) The nondirective attitude. Unpublished manuscript.

Raskin, NJ (1988) 'Responses to person-centered vs. client-centered?' *Renaissance, 5* (3 and 4): 2–3.

Rogers, CR (1957) 'The necessary and sufficient conditions of therapeutic personality change.' *Journal of Consulting Psychology,* 21: 95–103.

Rogers, CR (1959) 'A theory of therapy, personality and interpersonal relation- ships, as developed in the client-centered framework', in S Koch (ed) *Psychology: A study of a science: Vol. III. Formulations of the person and the social context* (pp. 184–256). New York: McGraw-Hill.

Rogers, CR (1986a) 'Client-centered therapy', in IL Kutash and A Wolf (eds) *Psychotherapist's casebook* (pp. 197–208). San Francisco: Jossey-Bass.

Rogers, CR (1986b) 'Reflection of feelings.' *Person-Centered Review, 1*(4): 357–77.

Whiteley, JM (Producer) (1977a) *The Right to be Desperate* [Film]. American Personnel and Guidance Association.

Whiteley, JM (Producer) (1977b) *Carl Rogers counsels an individual on anger and hurt* [Film]. American Personnel and Guidance Association.

Chapter 4b
2004 Postscripts to 'Uncharacteristic Directiveness'

BARBARA TEMANER BRODLEY

I doubt that there would be a field of 'multicultural counseling' if every therapist working over the past 50 years had been a client-centered (CC) therapist. The reason there has been a need for a distinct multicultural discipline in counseling is because all therapeutic approaches, other than nondirective CC, utilize diagnostic and culture-specific psychological concepts, and make assumptions about clients' mental health that directly affect the therapists' relationships with their clients. Once the baggage of these concepts and assumptions is introduced into the therapy relationship, it should come as no surprise that some of it might be racially or culturally insensitive. Directive therapists whose theories require them to have conceptions of what is best for the client and what the client's problem really is inevitably inject biases based on their own culture's values or characteristics into their therapy relationships.

In contrast to the directive therapies, CC Therapy is inherently multicultural in the best sense. While no therapist reaches his or her ideal of therapy, nevertheless CC Therapy, when practiced by an experienced therapist, is simply free of the defect of generalizing about individuals on the basis of their race or culture. It brings no such generalization because, unlike other therapies, CC theory does not assume that therapists should know what is good for their clients nor that therapists should direct and influence their clients toward these preconceived goals.

Client-centered theory emphasizes a whole and genuine acceptance of clients—including their cultural particulars—and requires a nondirective empathic understanding of the client from the client's internal frame of reference (Rogers, 1957; Brodley, 1996; Merry and Brodley, 2002). Its intrinsic values of respect for the individual, of acceptance toward the individual, and of dedication to the internal frame of reference of the individual client (Bozarth, 1998) tend to preclude the risks of stereotyping (Patterson, 2000) and cultural insensitivity.

Client-centered therapists learn what their clients need them to know about their cultures. This happens through their openness to individual differences and by deeply listening to their clients. The client-centered therapist is committed to respect for the client's culture insofar as it is a part of the client, and learns what is relevant to the client about his or her culture as the result of non-judgmental empathic understanding, and by checking these understandings with the client (Rogers, 1986).

ROGERS' SESSIONS WITH AFRICAN-AMERICAN CLIENTS

Among the films, tapes, and transcripts of Rogers' own therapy sessions, there are examples of his work with clients from various cultures: Dutch, German, British, Japanese, and South African clients. And there are three sessions with African-American clients—the two with Dione (pseudonym) in the films *The Right to be Desperate* and *Carl Rogers Counsels An Individual on Anger and Hurt* (Whiteley, 1977) and one with an African-American man, David (pseudonym), who volunteered to be Rogers' client in a demonstration (Rogers, 1984) for a workshop approximately seven years after the Dione sessions.

Both of Rogers' African-American clients speak to him about race and racism. As early as Dione's fourth statement to Rogers in their first session, he mentions how racial attitudes affected him as a child. But he does not develop his feelings about racism as such in either session. The session with David, the workshop client, is different in this regard from the two with Dione because about half-way into the interview, David specifically *focuses on* his feelings about race and racism and on his racial difference from Rogers. (Although race becomes part of his focus, this client hesitates before venturing into the topic, taking it on after Rogers encourages him 'to take a chance'.) More specifically, David alludes to or explicitly mentions race or racism in 19 out of a total of 55 statements—approximately 35%. Dione, in his first session, refers to race or racism in 21 out of 71 statements—approximately 30%. In his second session, Dione refers to race or racism in 25 out of a total of 135 statements—approximately 18% of his statements.

Rogers himself explicitly refers to race or racism 15 times to the 19 of David's statements that include race. (That is, Rogers includes words about race or racism in 78% of his empathic responses to that client when David's statements have included the topic of race or racism.) In contrast, Rogers explicitly includes racism in only one response to the 21 statements that include something about race or racism by Dione in their first session. Similarly, in the second session with Dione, Rogers explicitly mentions race in only one response to the 25 statements by Dione that include a comment about race or racism.

What accounts for this difference in frequency between Rogers' explicit references to race or racism in the 1984 workshop session with David (78%) and the one-each explicit references in the two 1977 Dione sessions? Was Rogers, as some have suggested, personally more open to, or more comfortable with, issues of race seven years later? Do Rogers' much more frequent explicit mentions of race or racism in his empathic responses to David exhibit, as one might infer from a multicultural counseling perspective, that he was more empathically attuned to the race of this client?

What did the clients think? In all three sessions, the clients indicate a high percentage of explicit agreement (e.g., 'right,' 'exactly,' 'yeah,' 'for sure,' 'Uhm hm') with Rogers' empathic understanding *checking* responses and comments. David expresses explicit agreements, indicating that Rogers has been accurately, empathically understanding him, in approximately 70% of his statements. In their first session, Dione expresses explicit agreements with Rogers in 62% of his responses; and in the second, he explicitly agrees that Rogers understands him in 72% of his responses. While other responses to Rogers by both clients do not contain explicit vocal confirmations to Rogers' empathic responses, the clients appear to confirm Rogers' accuracy by their nods or by the way they develop their narration about themselves (expressing only a few disagreements or qualifications in the three sessions). In short, the evidence in the interviews indicates that Rogers was perceived by both clients as being highly accurate in his empathic following of their meanings and feelings.

But what about the frequency of the clients' agreements with Rogers' responses to statements the clients make that allude to or explicitly refer to race or racism? If Rogers was less open to, or less comfortable with, Dione's references to race in those sessions, and if this was revealed by the fact that Rogers makes only two explicit references to race or racism, then we would expect that Dione would judge Rogers' responses to his statements referring to race or racism as inaccurate. We would then expect Dione to infrequently express an explicit agreement to those responses. Since Rogers frequently (78%) responds with mentions of race to David's remarks about race, we would expect that client to more frequently express agreements with Rogers' responses to David's statements that include something about race.

Actually, what occurs is contrary to these expectations. Dione expresses agreement with Rogers' responses to his statements including race or racism equally or more frequently than David. David explicitly agrees in 55% of his responses. Dione in session one agrees 57% and in session two agrees 72%. The greatest difference (17%) is between David (55%) and Dione in the 'Anger and

Hurt' session (72%). We find that Dione frequently explicitly indicated he felt understood by Rogers throughout the sessions, and specifically when Rogers made empathic responses to Dione's communications about race even when Rogers did not include explicit statements about race. (There is also considerable evidence in both sessions of therapeutic movement, another sign that Dione experienced Rogers' empathic responses as appropriate. Rogers summarized some therapeutic developments he observed in his remarks that were interspersed and voiced-over in the 'The Right to Be Desperate' session and in his remarks after the 'On Anger and Hurt' session.)

Thus the difference in Rogers' explicit reference-to-race responses is not evidence that Rogers under-responded to Dione about race, or was more sensitive to race or racist issues seven years later when relating to David. The difference in frequencies of Rogers' mention of race or racism is due to his differential responses to *different client presentations* about the issue. While David talks directly about the role of race and racism in his feelings and problems, Dione often incorporates mentions of race or racism in his responses only as part of his description of the situations underpinning his *feelings*, which are the focus of his responses, or he mentions race or racism within his statements but then shifts his focus to another aspect of his life or feelings before finishing his statement to Rogers.

All three interviews with the two clients are revealing about the nature of empathic responding in Client-Centered Therapy. Most of Rogers' responses reveal that he is attempting to empathically understand *what the client appears to intend*. He is not attempting to summarize each point that appears in the client's statements, or to emphasize an agenda of his own. (Granted there are instances of Rogers giving emphasis to feelings of anger and hurt in Dione's second session. These uncharacteristic directivities, however, occur after Dione has tentatively proposed them for himself.) When a CC therapist empathically responds, whatever is included in the empathic response should not be there because of the therapist's personal beliefs, psychological theories, or political agenda—whether they are against sexism, racism, ageism, or in favor of such humanitarian viewpoints as feminism or cultural awareness. Client-centered therapists should not be responding to clients in a manner that highlights features of clients' race or culture unless these appear to be the clients' intentions. Multicultural politics has no place in Client-Centered Therapy with cross-race or cross-cultural client/therapist pairings.

REFERENCES

Bozarth, J (1998) *Person-centered therapy: A revolutionary paradigm.* Ross-on-Wye: PCCS Books.

Brodley, BT (1996) 'The nondirective attitude in Client-Centered Therapy.' *The Person-Centered Journal.* 4(1): 18–30.
Merry, T and Brodley, BT (2002) 'The nondirective attitude in client-centered therapy.' *Journal of Humanistic Psychology,* 42(2): 66–77.
Patterson, CH (2000) 'Multicultural counseling: From diversity to universality', in CH 'Pat' Patterson, *Understanding psychotherapy: Fifty years of client-centered theory and practice.* Ross-on-Wye: PCCS Books, pp. 302–13.
Rogers, CR (1957) 'The necessary and sufficient conditions of therapeutic personality change.' *Journal of Consulting Psychology 21*: 95–103.
Rogers, CR (1984) *A client-centered demonstration interview during a workshop.* [Video] Center for the Study of the Person. La Jolla, CA.
Rogers, CR (1986) 'Reflections of feelings.' *Person-Centered Review,* 1(2): 125–40.
Whiteley, JM (Producer) (1977) *The Right to be Desperate* [Film] and *Carl Rogers Counsels an Individual on Anger and Hurt* [Film]. American Personnel and Guidance Association.

Chapter 5
CARL ROGERS' VERBAL RESPONSES IN 'ON ANGER AND HURT': CONTENT ANALYSIS AND CLINICAL REFLECTIONS

GERMAIN LIETAER

It has always been a trademark—and in that time a pioneering one—of Rogers that he recorded his therapeutic work and made it available for further research and commentary (Rogers, 1942). The many excerpts from therapy sessions one finds sprinkled throughout his work, along with the numerous audio, film and video recordings of therapeutic sessions he left behind, all testify to this (Lietaer and Brodley, 2003). In this chapter, I will discuss one of Rogers' sessions that appeared as a didactic film in 1977. It involves a second conversation with an African-American and was given the title *Carl Rogers Counsels an Individual— On Anger and Hurt*.

My first aim will be to make a detailed analysis of Rogers' responses in this session by asking the questions: what types of responses does he make and to what extent? And what strikes us as typical characteristics of his manner of working? But first, I will present in some detail the category system that will be used to objectively map out Rogers' responses. Thereafter, I will discuss the results of this objective analysis and provide some qualitative and clinical comments on it. In this way, I hope to present a nuanced and differentiated view of the manner in which the older Rogers facilitated the self-exploratory process of his client, and that this lively confrontation with 'the Master' might offer a resourceful and inspiring account both for person-centred therapists as well as for others.

A CATEGORY SYSTEM FOR THERAPIST RESPONSES

Over the years, several systems of categorizing a therapist's verbal behavior have been devised. However, comparative research has shown these to be largely overlapping and therefore lending themselves to grouping into a limited number of 'basic response intentions' (Elliott, Hill, Stiles, Friedlander, Mahrer and Margison, 1987; Greenberg, Rice and Elliott, 1993b). I based my own category system on Hill's (1986) but subdivided several of the categories and occasionally changed their meaning. This resulted in a system consisting of 18 content-verbal categories grouped into 11 main categories (see below the numbers 3 to 13 included). I believe this differentiated body of response modes provides a suitable framework in which to place therapist verbal behaviour in a clinically meaningful way.

The categories are mutually exclusive: each therapist response unit may be put into one category only. However, a total therapist response—by this I mean everything a therapist says between two client responses—may be split into several response segments, each with its own separate code. In counting frequencies and calculating percentages, identical codes coming from a single global response are calculated only once. I believe this to be the most clinically meaningful way of counting as these codes are largely made up of redundant statements of the same response intention.

A concrete description of the category system now follows. Each category is carefully defined and illustrated with a few examples (for an extended manual, see Lietaer, Leijssen, Vanaerschot and Gundrum, 1995).

1. Minimal encouragement

T (therapist) indicates that he is following C (client) and understands. Such responses encourage C to go on speaking without suggesting any particular direction and without approving or condemning. E.g.:
Hmm, Hmm ... ; I see.

2. Silence

Any silence lasting over 5 seconds, whether between or within T and C responses. They are graded according to duration, 2a being 5–10 seconds, 2b 11 to 20 seconds, 2c 21 to 60 seconds and 2d over 60 seconds.

3. Confirming, Reinforcing, Reassuring

In one way or another, T takes C's side. T supports, acknowledges or reinforces C's experience or behaviour *explicitly*; T tries to reassure C. E.g.:
I understand this very well; It will be all right; It's a good thing you dared doing that.

4. Information

4a. External information
T gives information unrelated to the content or progression of the therapeutic process. E.g.:
> *Tests showed your IQ to be slightly above average; I notice time is up; An orgasm is sometimes called 'little death'.*

4b. Information about the therapeutic process
T informs about the theoretical or technical aspects of the therapeutic process, about how the process of change occurs; he gives general information about his own working method. E.g.:
> *As I said before, focusing is paying inward attention to your feelings; Now that you see this so clearly for yourself, you have, no doubt, more freedom to choose; You may correct me if I'm wrong; I will always start off with a few relaxation exercises.*

5. Directive

5a. Process directive
T suggests or instructs C to do something specific or deal with his/her problem in a certain way here and now within the session. E.g.:
> *Place this critical voice on that chair for a while; Can we stop for today?; Take your time to feel your anger.*

5b. Advice/homework
T gives advice, suggestions or orders for C to use after the session. E.g.:
> *It may be important to do these relaxation exercises every day; Wouldn't it be better for you to go and live alone?; You should discuss that with your father.*

6. Closed Question

T asks a question requiring a short specific answer. Response units worded in a tentative or questioning manner but qualifying for another category are always put in this other category (and not in 6 or 7).

6a. Question about factual or situational matters
T wishes to obtain (more) information about a not yet mentioned aspect of the situation, event or reaction; or T wants to check the veracity of his own hunch about it. E.g.:
> *I gather you did go to see a general physician in the meantime?; Where were*

you when this happened?; Envy towards whom?; Did you talk about it with your partner?; You kept a diary?

6b. Diagnostic question about feelings
T *wants to know* whether or not C is having or has had a specific experience or feeling reaction; in doing this, T takes his own frame of reference as a starting point without connecting to C's current topic of conversation. E.g.:
> *Did you feel depressed at that time?; Are you shy once in a while?; Do you like your job?*

6c. Question intended to check feelings
An experiential content expressed by C or brought in by T is submitted to C for checking. This is most often done by means of a separate question. E.g.:
> *Do you also feel it now?; (Shyness:) Does that word feel totally right?; You say 'perhaps'?; (You seem very anxious today) Is that right?; (Rather disappointed, I would think.) Something like that?*

7. Open Exploratory Question

T explicitly invites C to explore his/her experience further or to describe a situation more concretely. This is done by means of an open question (not containing any content elements) or by means of a grammatically closed question obviously intended to facilitate further exploration (the content elements in it only being meant to stimulate or to illustrate possible responses). E.g.:
> *How does that feel to you?; How exactly did you prepare yourself for the exams?; Could you go a little deeper here?; Do you feel happy or sad or something else ... ?*

8. Reformulating Aspects of the Narrative

T reformulates sometimes more concisely, more clearly, more sharply, more concretely certain aspects of C's narrative: his/her behaviour (what C was doing), situational aspects, feelings and reactions of others. E.g.:
> *Not much was left of your car; Your father was very angry then; Thus, the whole family was present; You sometimes fantasize about therapy, you said?*

9. Reflection

9a. Reflection of expressed feelings
T restates sometimes more clearly or sharply C's explicitly stated experiences, inner processes or reactions: thoughts, feelings, emotions, wishes, intentions,

decisions, ways of handling experiences. E.g.:
- C: *This way, I feel much quieter already*
- T: *Now you feel more relaxed already;*
- C: *I don't show how hurt I feel*
- T: *You grin and bear it.*

9b. Reflection of underlying feelings

T *clearly adds something* to what C tells about himself/herself: T puts into words inner processes or reactions (whether of a feeling, a cognitive or a volitional nature) implicitly present in C's message but not yet named by C; T uses images or metaphors occurring to him/her when hearing C's discourse; T makes empathic guesses as to the deeper layers of experience. As opposed to interpretation, this is always an evocation or clear intensification (using words with a different content) of C's concrete experiencing itself, of an implicit aspect of his/her experience which T suspects to live in C *right now*. E.g.:
- C: *My best friend has been out with my sweetheart*
- T: *And this has hurt you?;*
- C: *I have nothing to say today*
- T: *Are you angry because I didn't answer your question?*

10. Intepretation

T brings clarification of a cognitive-insight type or proposes a new cognitive structure for C's behaviour or experience. This may mean: making a link between apparently isolated statements or events; naming underlying motives, defense mechanisms or resistances; interpreting transference reactions; exposing recurring patterns of experience or behaviour; linking present events with past ones; putting C's feelings and problems into a new framework. E.g.:
- C: *And you too abandon me!*
- T: *As your mother so often did;*
- T: *You have perhaps always been sensitive to criticism?*

11. Feedback

T formulates his observations about C from his/her own point of view: T's impressions about the way C is or was present in therapy, about the evolution T notices in C, about how T sees the mutual interaction. E.g.:
> *I notice you return to this quite often; I sense tension between us; I have never seen you so angry; I feel therapy comes along well; You kick with your foot.*

12. Confrontation

T indicates a discrepancy, not made explicit by C, between several of C's statements, between behaviour and words, between the real self and the ideal self, between fantasy and reality, between T's and C's perception.
T pushes C's nose against what C avoids or what C (repeatedly) runs away from. E.g.:
> *You say it's impossible (8) but would you like it?; You see yourself as incapable (9a) but you keep repeating the good points?*

Category 12 has precedence over all others except 13.

13. Self-Disclosure

13a. Task-related process disclosure by T
T communicates specific inner here-and-now reactions (feelings, thoughts, intentions) on his/her own task-oriented work or on C's process. This is a more personal and process-like kind of information than the rather general and static information in 4b. E.g.:
> *I feel a bit nervous with this video recording; A minute ago an image occurred to me ... ; I have difficulty following you; I'm guessing here and ... ; Let me see if I understand you ...*

13b. T's relational here-and-now feelings
T reveals something about his/her present position in his/her relationship with C or about C's interactional here-and-now impact on him/her (feelings which C evokes in T). E.g.:
> *I feel put under quite a bit of pressure from you; I really care about you ...*

13c. T's personal experiences and views
T reveals facts or experiences from his/her own life, how T feels or has felt in certain situations. He communicates something about his/her personal life philosophy and values, about his/her personal views on psychological or interpersonal functioning. E.g.:
> *I don't like violent movies; I have also been sad for a long time after my father died; I have lived in Antwerp in the past.*

14. Rest-Categories

14a. Social talk
Greeting at the beginning or the end of the session; chat about subjects unrelated

to C's problems. E.g.:
> See you next time; Great soccer yesterday, right?; It keeps on raining.

14b. Unclassifiable
Any unclear statements or any which after thorough consideration do not fit any of the categories; statements of 'not understanding' (e.g.: What did you say?); routine appointments.

QUANTITATIVE AND QUALITATIVE ANALYSIS

In the 'On Anger and Hurt' session, lasting 58 minutes, Rogers makes 114 content-verbal responses (categories 3 to 13). Approximately 25% of these contain various coded segments, in total comprising 144 codes. Table 1 (below) gives an overview of this. Although these quantitative findings do give us a picture of Rogers' style of verbal responding, they in themselves give little 'flesh' to that image. They tell us what Rogers does and how frequently he does it, but tell us very little regarding the quality of his responses. This raises several questions: To what extent is the content of his responses 'to the point'? How are they presented? How have these responses been timed? What is their significance and function in the context of the momentary process the client is going through? In light of these questions I will weave qualitative-clinical reflections into the quantitative material of the analysis and illustrate my commentaries with a selection of transcript excerpts (see T response numbers with asterix). Further I urge the reader to watch the video in order to acquire a more 'holistic' impression of Rogers' responses within the whole of the process.

Empathic reflections

It will undoubtedly cause no surprise that the categories 8 (Reformulating Aspects of the Narrative) and 9 (Reflection) occur very frequently in all responses, in this case representing 61%. After all, if Rogers is to go down in the history of psychotherapy for one particular reason, it would be in part for his emphasis on the 'reflection of feeling' as the royal way to following and deepening the self-exploratory process of the client. Here is a list of what appear to me to be the typical characteristics of this large group of responses:
- Rogers' reflections direct themselves largely to the internal experiential side of what the client lives through, and only sporadically to the reformulation of the situational aspects of the story (cat. 8). We note that not a single question is asked concerning situational data (cat. 6a). Perhaps Rogers underestimates the power of a 'on site reconstruction'. recalling

Table 1: Carl Rogers' verbal responses in *On Anger and Hurt*: frequency and percentage of response segments per category[1]

RESPONSE CATEGORIES		Freq.	%
3	Confirmation, reinforcement, support	3	2.1
4a	External information	–	–
4b	Information about the therapeutic process	4	2.8
5a	Process directive	3	2.1
5b	Advice/Homework	–	–
6a	Question on factual & situational aspects	–	–
6b	Diagnostic question about feelings	–	–
6c	Checking question	6	4.1
7	Open exploratory question	2	1.4
8	Restatement of narrative aspects	4	2.8
9a	Reflection of expressed feelings	76	52.8
9b	Reflection of underlying feelings	8	5.5
10	Interpretation	4	2.8
11	Feedback	11	7.6
12	Confrontation	6	4.2
13a	Task-related therapist comment	15	10.4
13b	Relational here-and-now feelings of T.	2	1.4
13c	Personal experiences or views of T.	–	–
TOTAL		144	100

to the mind a living and concrete scenario in which something important to the client happened. As Rice and Greenberg (1991) have written, mentally resituating oneself in a specific event and reliving it can bring the client closer into contact with the specific 'stimulus-characteristics' that elicited a particular feeling-reaction.

- Within the reflections of feelings (cat. 9a and 9b), one is struck by the fact that about 90% of the cases involve reflection of expressed feelings and only 10% reflection of underlying feelings. Rogers obviously sticks very closely to what the client himself has said. This does not mean that we are faced here, on the whole, with wooden or parrot-like reflections. Perhaps this really is the most striking aspect emerging from this analysis: the masterly talent with which Rogers takes up for himself the message

---

[1.] A transcript with numbered T responses and coded meaning units is available through the author upon request, see the second acknowledgements page at the front of the book.

of the client and gives it back to him. In fact, many of the reflections may actually be situated on the *borderline* between expressed and underlying feelings (T7*, T87, T90, T109, T148, for example). This point, among others, becomes clear in the reliability study; category 9b is shown there to be an unreliable category.

> C7: ... I don't really care to be an antiracist, if you know what I mean (T: Mmm) anymore. Uh, and I don't wanna be a reflection of any other ... of any other larger society at all. (T: Mmm.) I really don't want to ...
> T7: You'd like to get in touch with what's going on in you.
> C8: For sure.

- Clarity and liveliness appear to me to be two general characteristics of Rogers' reflections. It often strikes me how effective his responses are in achieving more clarity: the essence of what is expressed unclearly, mistily, laboriously or in piecemeal by the client is taken up by Rogers and usually precisely and concisely reflected back to the client (T39, T69, T93, T110, for example). The vibrancy of his responses have, in my opinion, a lot to do with the fact that he often speaks in the first person, taking the position of the client (as in T3*, T54, T74, T132, for example). His frequent use of image-filled language also contributes to this effect to a significant extent: sometimes Rogers himself initiates an image (T14, T61); yet more often he takes up the imagery suggested by the client as a sort of 'keyword' set in order to intensify the experience of the client and allow it to unfold further (T55, T114*, T117, T123, for example). In his post-session commentary Rogers emphasizes the 'power of metaphor in the deeper regions of psychotherapy'.

> T3: Your mind says sort of, 'Oh, cool it. Don't ... don't get into uh, such strong emotion'.

> T114: But there were a lot of people who, though they may or may not have beaten you physically, treated you in a way that just trampled on you and beat you up and spit on you and made you a nobody, a piece of garbage.

- When I now, on a microlevel, look into the precise manner in which Rogers carries further the experience of the client through his reflections, I am able to put together the following list of aspects: when the client tells what he does *not* want to be, Rogers expresses in positive terms what he *does* want to be (T7). Sometimes Rogers reflects the underlying attitude of the client towards himself, rather than the content of what the latter has been saying

(T96*). When the client describes the situation of drunkards who live on the street, Rogers shifts the attention from the story to its personal significance for the client (T131*). Rogers reflects the implicit meaning of nonverbal signals (T109). When the client questions his own behavior and asks the therapist for advice, Rogers sketches the poles of the conflict behind the question in a clear manner (T135*). Rogers, in my opinion, even smuggles in a suggestion under the guise of a reflection (T99): 'I hear you saying, "I really want to get to that, but it will have to be at my pace. I can't ... I can't force it"'; to my mind C98 and C99 rather suggest to us the client's sense of impatience and powerlessness. Although Rogers always gives back the feelings of his client in their full intensity, in some places his responses take the form of explicit modeling (T107, T112*, T125): he sets the example by daring to use aggressive or rough language. Within the context of the conflict the client experiences between social norms and his own experiencing, Rogers clearly takes the side of the 'experiencing self' (as in T5, T6, T55*, T81, for example). In the same line Rogers gives extra attention to everything that appears to be 'germinating' or growing: he emphasizes the client's positive intentions (T99, T124) as well as the changes he already notices (T95, T96); sometimes he even gives feedback that is more positive than the way in which the client himself experiences it (T83, T121).

> C96: ... and like I have been hurt and I really don't want to get involved anymore in terms of with people that can't return love and can't accept people. I just don't really want to get involved anymore. I'm sick and tired ... sick of it.
> T96: Sounds as though you're more accepting of yourself as a person who is vulnerable, who has been hurt, who is hurting, and who wants love ...

> C131: ... I was thinking a ... about a wino on a street that continues to drink, doesn't have a place to live. ... [C tells about his reactions to this scene.] ...
> T131: Mmm, mmm. It seems, it seems to me that you're uh feeling it ... you know what it's like to be in desperation and you know what it could drag you to, and so maybe that's what happened to some of them. Something like that.

> C135: ... is it all right to have everybody else to blame? (Laughs.) (T: laughs.) You know, for your, for your problem, instead of sharing some of that. But I shared, you know, I, I, I think I've really, I shared that, you know.

> T135: *I think ... I think what you're saying is, 'I feel as though, damnit, everybody else is to blame. My mind says, Oh, no, you have, you probably have a part in it too, but ... ' (C: Sure. Sure.) ... your feelings are ...*
>
> C112: *... Really rotten and I really feel ... you know, really screwed. I really feel ... (T: Mmm.) ... so badly.*
> T112: *'The bastards really screwed me.'*
>
> C55: *... and I've identified it. I think I've identified it, you know, because I know that there's some times when there is such a big lump in my throat, you know, and that I explain, I give myself a lot of reasons why I shouldn't be feeling like that, you know.*
> T55: *A big lump of hurt, though. (C: Mmmm.) (15-second pause.) And how to let that hurt come out in the open ...*

- A last aspect to which I would like to draw attention is the questioning-tentative character of his reflections. This comes unmistakably through in the checking questions (cat. 6c) and in a number of intervention segments from category 13a in which Rogers makes explicit his concern to accurately understand his client (T11, T61, T127, T139). This is also noticeable in the subjective-tentative manner in which he sometimes formulates his reflections ('Sounds as though ... '; 'And I guess ... ') or in the questioning tone in which he says these. Here Rogers is creating a climate of co-exploration where his checking intention is always clear and the experience of the client has the last word.

Interpretation, Feedback and Confrontation

Interpretation, feedback and confrontation often are described as content-directing responses that plainly emerge from the referential framework of the therapist. In this session this type of response comprises 14.6% of the total. And this is not a low figure for the founder of *client-centered* psychotherapy! But let us take a closer look at these responses. Are they really so different from the more following reflections of feelings? What are their typical characteristics?

- Four responses (T60*, T64, T68, T118) have been coded as interpretations because they were directed to cognitive structuring rather than to the unfolding of the concrete experience itself. In these four responses Rogers traces a link between the inability of the client to express his emotions and the social norms with which he was raised as a child: a genetic interpretation. It is nonetheless important to recognize that the client himself already mentioned these 'early influences'. Rogers rightly retains what he heard from the client; consequently it becomes a matter of highlighting, at the appropriate time, of a link of which the client himself is already aware. In T60 and T64, T65 it further appears that Rogers has the intention of not only sharpening the insight of his client, but equally to communicate his own understanding of the fact that the client has such difficulty in expressing his emotions. These two interpretive responses are 'filled in' further with an experiential reflection ('But …'), whereby the client is steered away from an 'explanatory' mode and brought back to feel his concrete experience of pain and sadness. In T68 Rogers uses an evocative image ('Probably your seven-year-old could cry … '), and also response T118 is formulated in an exceptionally concrete and vivacious way. This makes the line between interpretation and reflection of feeling in Rogers' responses an extremely thin one, and makes one think of Gendlin's rule of thumb regarding the experiential use of clinical knowledge: 'In using theories in practice, translate them into what one might feelingly find directly. Permit yourself any amount of complex reasoning privately, but make the intervention be a simple question, [say] whether the person feels something like … some way of feeling you can imagine he might find' (1974, p. 288).

C60: … it feels like I'm holding out on myself… (T: Mmm.) You know. Hell, you know. I don't know.

T60: I think it goes back to some of the things you mentioned. A man doesn't admit he's hurt … a black man especially doesn't admit that he's been hurt by anything. (C: Sure.) Uh, a father doesn't admit he's been hurt by being away from his children. Just too many things that say: no, no, no … don't let it out. (Pause.) But inside there's the hurt.

- The feedback responses form the third largest category. They demonstrate that Rogers not only 'participates' empathically but also 'observes' and explicitly brings in his observations. These observations, however, tie in so closely with the self-exploration process of the client that we certainly cannot speak of directing, 'track-shifting' responses. Two of these responses (T98, T121*) form an answer to an explicit question posed by the client. Six others (T102, T106, T133*, T134, T146, T147) are simply confirmation from within his own referential framework—in the sense of 'That's the way I see you too'—of what the client has just said about himself. Another two responses (T21, T74) simply lead up to or are in the service of a reflection of feeling. One last response (T145) is a reflection of a non-verbal behavior, with the connotation 'I see that that is enough for today'. Seen as a whole, it is clear that the responses closely follow the experiential path of the client, even if they arise within the referential framework of the therapist. Rogers' use of imagery is evident in this group of responses as well, with a clear 'preference' for the metaphor 'that pit of hurt and pain and beaten-ness' that he throws in at three different occasions.

> C121: ... God, I realize how I'm talking in circles. I seem to be talking in circles. Does it sound like uh?
>
> T121: No, not quite. It's more spirals, I think. (C: Laughs.) Getting, as you say, getting very close, you feel, you feel beaten right now as though, if only something could come out, you wouldn't feel beaten.
>
> C133: ... But at least I'm admitting to you that I'm hurt, you know.
>
> T133: Yeah, that's right, mmm. And just for a moment there, I felt you really were experiencing that too, really feeling that stick shoved up your ass.

- In the confrontational responses we are dealing with feedback and interpretations where Rogers takes his client by the collar, as it were, and makes him see something he was likely to have let slip by. Two of these responses might be seen as positive confrontations: in T83 he draws the client's attention that the latter can already show his feelings of pain in front of Rogers, even though he does not yet dare to do so in front of other people; in T71 he brings the client back to his sadness after having evoked his client's usual defensive behavior in T70. In T20* and T67 Rogers points out to his client his avoidance behavior with regard to his expression of anger and sadness. Finally, in T104 and T105 Rogers tries to make it clear to his client that the norms with which he has been raised have in fact become 'his own': this is no longer an interpersonal problem but an intrapsychic one. None of these can be said to be 'heavy-handed' confrontations, but they are moments where Rogers presses ahead in a steering manner.

> T20: That's what I sense is going on now ... that you feel 'there's so many reasons why I really shouldn't express my anger. I'll, I'll talk about all those reasons.'

Personal presence

When it comes to the question regarding the 'transparency' of Rogers in this therapeutic encounter, it is obvious that, in the first instance, we are looking at the subcategories under 'Self-disclosure.' We see here that Rogers does not bring personal experiences (13c) into the discussion and only two times (in the successive responses T22* and T23) gives expression to a relational here-and-now experience: it is for him totally acceptable if the client allows his anger to come out and we can see this as a communication of 'containment'. A much greater number of responses come under Task-related process disclosure, a category that should be understood to be somewhat relative. Under this rubric may be grouped nine response segments in which Rogers only mentions that something came to his mind, that he understood something, that he would like to understand or that he wants to check if he has indeed understood something. The remainder of the responses in category 13a might be grouped as follows: in one response (T2) he says that he himself did reflect further on what the client said about his feelings of anger in the first session; in three instances (T25, T58, T59) Rogers, in a personal and spontaneous manner, gives information on the therapeutic process and his own style of working; finally, in two more cases (T106, T148) he makes personal comments on the process the client is going through. All things considered, Rogers is quite sparing in his self-expression. Most of the time these responses comprise task-related 'mini-disclosures'. Yet I am of the opinion that this sort of response—however modest—itself gives a personal color to the working alliance: it reveals a therapist who uninhibitedly is himself and once in a while shares his personal reactions to the client's process.

> T22: *I get what you're saying and I also feel quite strongly that I want to say, 'it's OK with me if you're angry here'* ...

Still other categories, alongside 13a, b, c, contribute to Rogers' transparency as a therapist, particularly those responses involving feedback and confrontation, but also those of category 3 (T33, T63*, T146) where Rogers personally supports the experience of the client. In fact all of the categories mentioned point to forms of transparency in which Rogers, as a separate pole in the interaction, comes to the fore and therefore cannot be said simply to take the role of an 'alter ego'. This does not mean that the personal presence of Rogers—so evident in this session—only manifests itself in this sort of responses. His personal presence is just as much fostered through his remarkable 'power of listening': his full attention, his involvement with the 'whole of his being' in the experiential world of the client, his capacity to allow the client's message to resonate in himself and then reflect it in a personal manner.

> C63: ... *Annnd, if I could cry and have it be all right* ...
> T63: *That's what I was thinking.* (C: *That would be* ...) *I was just thinking, if you could only cry.*

Aim and Strategy

Alongside a detailed analysis of the sort of verbal responses Rogers employs, we might also look at his work in this session in a more 'molar' way. And here we come to the question: what is Rogers' objective and what 'strategies' does he use to achieve this? In order to facilitate a reflection on this point, let me refer to the theoretical framework advanced by Greenberg, Rice and Elliott (1993a). These authors state that an experiential therapist must allow him- or herself to be led by two groups of principles: the creation of a therapeutic relation and the facilitation of therapeutic work around specific tasks. I will not discuss the first group here; the authors refer largely to the Rogerian therapist conditions, and it is already evident from what has been said above that Rogers gave form to his 'own' principles in a brilliant manner. But what of the task-related principles? Here we can hardly speak of 'conscious' intentions on the part of Rogers, given that his work was never formulated in such terms and that he remained rather diffident towards all that whiffed of 'technique' and 'strategy'. Yet perhaps we are dealing here with 'tacit knowledge' (Polanyi, 1966), with an implicit clinical wisdom that Rogers unconsciously allows in. Greenberg et al. (1993a) put forward three task-related principles:

1. the encouragement of experiential (in place of purely conceptual) self-exploration;
2. the stimulation of growth and self-determination; and
3. a directedness to bringing therapeutic tasks to completion.

With regard to the first principle, they make a distinction between four types of explorative engagement that the therapist should seek to stimulate in a differential manner, that is, in function of what at a given moment is most needed for the client: directing one's attention to specific internal or external stimuli in order to enhance the contact with reality; exploring, differentiating and symbolizing one's own—sometimes vague and complex—idiosyncratic experience; intensively reliving and actively expressing one's feelings; and finally, focusing on what is happening here-and-now in the relation between client and therapist. Although none of these four forms of exploration are absent, it would seem evident to me that the majority of Rogers' responses are aimed at intensifying the feelings of the client and to help him actively express his anger and pain. Perhaps Rogers has missed an opportunity in not trying enough to make the experience of his client more concrete. Once he posed an open exploratory question (T72: 'If you did cry, what would some of the themes of that crying be?') that went in this direction, but he might perhaps have insisted on being more specific, on exploring one important event. This often offers the client greater possibilities of seeing how he is tied in to the situation and of looking more closely at his own role. In this case the exploration remained quite general. I say this, however, with some reserve: in the last analysis, we are dealing here only with a second session in which the client probably, and above all, has a need to talk in more general terms about what he has experienced in his life.

On the second principle, I have already—where I spoke of Rogers' empathic reflections—pointed to his 'selectivity' for everything that is budding, for the client's feelings in contrast to the normative grain, for his future-oriented intentions. Also the promotion of the client's autonomy, self-agency and freedom of choice come to the fore in this interview: the client himself determines what he will speak about (T1) and Rogers' concern for checking his perception is strongly evident throughout the exchange. This creates a work alliance with an egalitarian tint in which the client retains the role of captain with his experience as the main compass.

The third task-related principle requires a bit more comment. Does Rogers think in terms of tasks that must be completed? His theory (Rogers, 1957) says this is not the case: he sets no goals for his client yet sets for himself the objective of experiencing and communicating the therapeutic basic attitudes in the most profound way possible. Yet, I am of the opinion that, in this session, Rogers does set a goal for his client and quite systematically strives toward this aim. I am supported in this by Brodley who, in an analysis of the same session, came to the conclusion:

> Rogers seemed to be working from an idea that the client would benefit from intensely and immediately vocalizing his feelings ... that Rogers was trying to influence the client toward specific objectives—to immediately and intensely experience anger, sadness, and hurt feelings (Brodley, 1996: 318–19; see also Chapter 4 this volume).

To back her argument Brodley refers to the responses where Rogers, in a confronting and interpreting manner, points out to the client his defensive attitude (T19, T20, T21 and T67, T68), explicitly invites and encourages him to express his emotions (T22 to T25, T63, T72 and T101), and is himself an example in using rough language (T107 and T125). Brodley regrets this 'systematic-directive intention' on the part of Rogers. She sees it as a form of manipulation, one which happily is atypical of his work, and takes the view that because of this Rogers sometimes misses other feelings that are there (C125, T125, for example). She concludes that Rogers 'was not entirely himself in the session with this client' (Brodley, 1996: 319; also Chapter 4, this volume). I personally would take a more mild position regarding Rogers' directivity. True enough, the 'cathartic intention' is undoubtedly palpable in Rogers—also in a number of evocative reflections Brodley does not mention—but in my view it is never imposed. The client himself, at the beginning of the interview, makes it clear that he would like to talk about his feelings of anger; during the session he repeatedly expresses his desire to let himself go and show his emotions. Besides, Rogers always shows concern and understanding for the resistance in the client (T33, T56) and for his pace. As a result, Rogers' task-related focus on his client's reliving his anger and pain, is kept in balance with his relational focus on a work alliance in which the process itself remains in the hands of the client and is led by him.

CONCLUSION

In this Chapter I have attempted an 'objective' analysis of Rogers' responses in *On Anger and Hurt* with the aid of a carefully constructed system of categories. Use of the content analytic method required that I carefully 'weigh' each (sub)response in the aim of placing each in one of the categories in as valid a way as possible. This resulted in a quantitative overview (Table 1), with frequencies and percentages cited for the various categories. I should emphasize here that the percentages arrived at by this means need to be interpreted relatively: they are in fact the results of a number of coding and scoring methods behind which lie choices that other researchers might not have made. Thus, we did not include minimal encouragers (category 1) and moments of silence (category 2) in the research data; I have also counted response segments with the same code only once. In categories 6c (Question intended to check feelings) and 13a (Task-related process disclosure by T) one will find a number of intervention segments to which I have assigned a separate code, whereas other researchers might have judged them to be insignificant. The definitions I have given for the content of the various categories will also have had an influence on the frequencies. I was, for example, quite strict in the assignment of category 9b (Reflection of underlying feelings): for each entry it should have been clear that the therapist 'adds' something to what the client himself has said. In short, other choices would in some cases have led to other frequencies and percentages.

I pointed out that my category system is purely descriptive in nature and that each analysis could undoubtedly be improved with the addition of a qualitative and clinical evaluation of the responses in their respective contexts. This was indeed my approach in the study of this interview. Out of the mixture of quantitative and qualitative data, Rogers emerges in this session as a therapist who—with a high rate of responses—to a high degree deepens the process in a content-following manner. The clarity and freshness with which Rogers' empathic reflections are expressed are typical, as is the fact that they often lie precisely on the boundary between the expressed and the underlying experience. Further, it is striking that Rogers makes many responses that are usually described in the literature as directive and emerging from the frame of reference of the therapist: interpretation, confrontation, feedback and self-disclosure. This clearly shows that Rogers is not present in the therapeutic relationship simply as a 'twin'. On the other hand, this qualitative study demonstrates that, usually, this sort of response by Rogers closely connects with the client's experiential track, and that separating his responses into directive and following ones as a result becomes a far more complex task than would first appear. In conclusion, I would like to put forward several characteristics that Rogers communicates in a largely non-verbal and paralinguistic way: his profound engagement, his confirming attitude, his disciplined 'presence' which allows the client's process still to remain central, and his egalitarian stance as a companion in his client's journey of exploration.

When we look at this session from the standpoint of the client, I am of the opinion that we can, without hesitation, speak of an extremely fruitful session: the client begins to realize the fact that he is not, primarily, afraid of his feelings of anger but of the underlying feelings of pain and hurt; he is able to grieve over the loss of his father-in-law; it is the first time that he let go so much control; he can speak of all the pain that he has felt in his life, something that fills him with more anguish than the fact that he has leukaemia or the prospect of death. This appears to me to represent considerable progress for a second session. Rogers' contribution in this intense process is unmistakably great, but this does not exclude that other forms of intervention could have been equally facilitative. There are, after all, more approaches that lead to experiential process deepening. Other client-centered therapists might, for example, intervene less frequently, pose more open exploratory questions, bring in more experiential process instructions, or employ the empty-chair technique in order to work through emotions toward specific persons that have not as yet been dealt with. I personally have the impression that the interview is actually a little *too interpersonal*: the dialogue is a bit rushed with too few moments of silence and, as a result, the client is not sufficiently encouraged to delve into himself. As I said earlier, I also perceive the fact that the client tends to speak only in general terms about what has been done to him as a weakness in the exchange. A few mini-instructions to slow down the pace and direct the client's attention more within himself, a few questions regarding concrete circumstances and 'exactly how' specific events touched him, could have helped this.

This analysis demonstrates how Rogers, towards the end of his career, worked with what he, in his closing comments, called 'an articulate client'. The extent to which Rogers' reactions are determined by the type of client, and how he evolved as a therapist over the years, form the subject of a broader study designed to analyse 140 sessions and transcripts of his that have been preserved (Lietaer and Gundrum, study in progress). In anticipation of the findings of our own study, I might already refer to an analogous study by Brody that provides a comparison of this second session of *On Anger and Hurt* with nine other sessions (Brody, 1991). She comes to the conclusion that the number of therapeutic responses arising from the therapist's own referential framework make up a fully 22% of the total in this particular interview, while in the other nine interviews the average is only 4.2%. It would then appear that we are here dealing with a session in which Rogers markedly departs from his 'usual practice'.

REFERENCES

Brodley, BT (1996) 'Uncharacteristic directiveness: Rogers and the "Anger and Hurt" client', in BA Farber, DC Brink and PM Raskin (eds) *The Psychotherapy of Carl Rogers: Casebook and commentary.* New York: Guilford, pp. 310–21.

Brody, AF (1991) Understanding client-centered therapy through interviews conducted by Carl Rogers. Unpublished doctoral dissertation, Illinois School of Professional Psychology, Chicago.

Elliott, R, Hill, CA, Stiles, WB, Friedlander, ML, Mahrer, AR and Margison, FR (1987) 'Primary therapist response modes: Comparison of six rating systems.' *Journal of Consulting and Clinical Psychology, 55:* 218–23.

Gendlin, ET (1974) 'The role of knowledge in practice', in GF Farwell, NM Gamsky and FM Coughlan (eds) *The Counselor's Handbook.* New York: Intext, pp. 269–94.

Greenberg, LS, Rice, LN and Elliott, R (1993a) 'Treatment principles for a process-experiential approach', in LS Greenberg, LN Rice and R Elliott, *Facilitating emotional change. The moment-by-moment process.* New York: Guilford, pp. 101–17.

Greenberg, LS, Rice, LN and Elliott, R (1993b) 'What the therapist does: experiential response intentions and modes', in LS Greenberg, LN Rice and R Elliott, *Facilitating emotional change. The moment-by-moment process.* New York: Guilford, pp. 118–36.

Hill, CE (1986) 'An overview of the Counselor and Client Verbal Response Modes Category Systems', in LS Greenberg and WM Pinsof (eds) *The psychotherapeutic process: A research handbook.* New York: Guilford, pp. 131–60.

Lietaer, G and Brodley, BT (2003) 'Carl Rogers in the Therapy Room: A listing of session transcripts and a survey of publications referring to Rogers' sessions.' *Person-Centered and Experiential Psychotherapies, 2*(4): 274–291.

Lietaer, G and Gundrum, M (in progress) *Analyse van 140 sessie-transcripten van Carl Rogers.* Centrum voor client-centered therapie en counseling, K.U. Leuven.

Lietaer, G, Leijssen, M, Vanaerschot, G and Gundrum, M (1995) Handleiding bij een categorieënsysteem voor therapeutinterventies. Unpublished brochure, Centrum voor client-centered therapie en counseling, K.U. Leuven.

Polanyi, M (1966) *The tacit dimension.* Garden City, NY: Doubleday.

Rice, LN and Greenberg, LS (1991) 'Two affective change events in client-centered therapy', in JD Safran and LS Greenberg (eds) *Emotion, psychotherapy and change.* New York: Guilford, pp. 197–226.

Rogers, CR (1942) 'The use of electrically recorded interviews in improving psychotherapeutic techniques.' *American Journal of Orthopsychiatry, 12:* 429–34.

Rogers, CR (1957) 'The necessary and sufficient conditions of therapeutic personality change.' *Journal of Consulting Psychology, 21*(2): 95–103.

Chapter 6
Rogerian Empathic Listening: Applying Conversation Analysis to the 'The Right to be Desperate' session

CATRIN S. RHYS, W. R. SELWYN BLACK AND SHAUNA SAVAGE

In this chapter, we focus on the very salient but rarely examined minimal responses that Rogers makes in the course of a session, namely the 'uh huh's and the 'mm hmm's. The work on this paper began with the assumption that the counselling context is an institutional context and that institutional talk-in-interaction is regarded as a form of institutional *action* that is constitutive of both the institution and the institutional identities of the participants. In other words, participants in an institution 'talk the institution into being' (Heritage, 1984: 290) and, as a correlate of that, talk their institutional roles into being. So the question we began with was: how does Rogers do 'being a therapist'[1] in interaction with this client? Conversation Analysis involves an inductive methodology. It begins with what is described as 'unmotivated looking' (Psathas, 1995), that is, an examination of the data that is not driven by pre-specified analytic goals or theoretical constructs. Schegloff (1996: 172) observes that analysis may 'begin with the noticing of some feature of the talk and be pursued by asking what—if anything—such a practice of talking has as its outcome'. Faced with the question: what is most noticeable about Rogers' talk, our third author's response was: he doesn't really say very much, he just says 'mm hmm' most of the time. Our question then is, what is Rogers 'doing', when he says 'mm hmm'?[2] The

---

[1] This is an ethnomethodological turn of phrase that attempts to articulate a very bottom-up, participant-oriented perspective on social/institutional roles and practices.
[2] Minimal responses vary in form, the most typical being 'uh huh' and 'mm hmm' and the non-verbal equivalent, nodding. We argue below that the form of the minimal response is not consequential. Hence in this paper, 'mm hmm' is used to refer generically to the set of possible minimal responses.

ethnomethodological perspective of CA requires us to address this question by examining in detail not just when Rogers uses such minimal responses but also how the client responds when Rogers says 'mm hmm'. The focus on the client's reaction to these minimal responses allows us to apply our findings to reflect on whether the interactive function of these non-linguistic verbal responses is in keeping with some of the fundamental assumptions of Person-Centred Therapy, in particular the communication of empathy, as required by Rogers' (1957, 1959) sixth necessary and sufficient condition, and the question of non-directiveness.

This is a very different but probably complementary focus from so many other papers that also address Rogers' verbal responses, but focus on the much more infrequent responses with verbal content (for example, many of the chapters in Farber et al., 1996; Lietaer, this volume; Egan, 1998). These minimal responses are typically acknowledged but treated as a single, homogeneous and relatively uninteresting category of verbal response. For example, Brodley comments: 'Vocal gestures such as 'M-hm' are not counted in this system although they contribute to the therapist's communication and to the client's perception that the therapist is attentive and following' (1996: 313).

THE CONVERSATION ANALYTIC ACCOUNT OF 'MM HMM'

The use of 'mm hmm' needs to be examined in the light of our understanding of the basic system of turntaking in interaction as articulated by Sacks, Schegloff and Jefferson (1974). The most basic observation about ordinary interaction is that people take turns at talk, that these turns are not pre-allocated, but locally managed by the participants in the interaction. Furthermore, speaker change typically occurs without gap and without overlap. What this means is that participants do not generally wait for the current speaker to finish speaking to identify an opportunity to speak, since this would result in audible gaps between speakers. Furthermore, the opportunity to speak appears to be projectable, in the sense that a participant can tell where an opportunity will appear and start speaking at exactly that moment, hence the typical lack of overlap between speakers. In the Sacks, Schegloff and Jefferson (1974) model of turntaking in interaction, these observations are accounted for by a system in which turns are constructed out of Turn Construction Units (TCU), which can be anything from a word to a sentence. The endpoint of each TCU provides a possible speaker transition opportunity, and so is referred to as a Transitional Relevance Place (TRP). The model then provides a set of recursive 'rules' for speaker transition at the TRP which include the possibility that the current speaker continues to speak, resulting in an extended, multi-unit turn. In other words, whether or not speaker change actually occurs or not, the projectability of the

TRP for the participants in the interaction makes speaker change possible.

The interesting thing about this model for the analysis of 'mm hmm' is that there is thus internal pressure within the turntaking system towards short turns, since every TCU provides a possible speaker change point (Schegloff, 1982). We can demonstrate this by showing how speakers themselves often orientate to this minimisation of the turn by prefacing their longer contributions to the interaction with some kind of preliminary turn that not only says 'here comes a longer turn', but also often gives an indication of what the possible endpoint of that longer turn will be. Examples include story prefaces like: 'Did you hear about … ', or preliminaries like: 'Can I ask you a question?' or 'Can I ask a favour?' which often are followed by extended explanation or context setting (the long turn), before the question/favour (the projectable endpoint) is articulated.

Interaction, however, is a form of collaborative action and a longer turn is *jointly* accomplished by both the speaker and the hearer, in that the hearer, at each potential TRP at which he/she could become the speaker, does not initiate a new turn. Schegloff (*ibid.*) thus talks of the recipient of an extended turn 'enabling' the extended turn. Schegloff suggests that 'mm hmm' is used at a TRP to display an understanding that an extended stretch of talk is underway and not yet complete and hence to take the stance that the current speaker should continue that extended stretch of talk. In other words, it is a minimal way of passing the conversational floor back to the speaker. 'Mm hmm' does this precisely because when a speaker simply utters 'mm hmm' they are *explicitly, observably* passing up an opportunity to take a full turn at talk. Such uses of 'mm hmm' are termed *continuers* (*ibid.*).

It is important to note here that this analysis constitutes a claim that 'mm hmm' derives its interpretation from its sequential location in the interaction. That is to say, 'mm hmm' does not inherently mean something like 'go on', but gets this meaning by virtue of its lack of semantic content, combined with a sequential context in which its producer had the opportunity to produce a full turn with semantic content. An important corollary of this is that we cannot simply claim that 'mm hmm' means 'go on' or 'keep talking'. Rather the sequential context of any instance of 'mm hmm' makes relevant a particular interpretation of that instance of 'mm hmm'. Hence, in the analysis of Rogers' use of 'mm hmm', we argue that in contrast to existing accounts, such minimal utterances cannot simply be separated from their context of production and classed as a single homogeneous category of verbal response.

A further corollary of this contextualised account of 'mm hmm' is that the sequential context may make other more specific interpretations of 'mm hmm' relevant. An early finding of Conversation Analysis is that conversation is often structured by pairs of utterances, termed adjacency pairs, in which the first utterance, the *first pair part*, makes relevant a particular type of second utterance, the *second pair part*. The most obvious adjacency pair is the question answer pair where after a question, an answer is relevant and expected (and therefore if absent, *noticeably* absent). For certain types of adjacency pairs, 'mm hmm' appears to be interpretable as the unmarked second part of the pair. These include yes-no questions, invitations, and assessments. The sequential environment provided by the first part of each of these pair types makes a more specific interpretation of 'mm hmm' relevant: namely, yes, acceptance, and agreement respectively. Another very relevant sequential environment in which 'mm hmm' may acquire a more specific interpretation is following an utterance that might be deemed problematic in some way for either speaker or hearer. Schegloff et al. (1977) show that if the recipient of a problematic utterance is going to address ('repair') the trouble source in that utterance (for example, by disagreeing, or requesting clarification), they typically do so in the immediately following utterance. Given this, if a hearer simply utters 'mm hmm' after a potentially problematic utterance, the absence of repair might be interpreted as agreement with or understanding of the problematic utterance. This is illustrated below in the analysis of the 'The Right to be Desperate' session.

A further consequence of the claim that the interpretation of 'mm hmm' is contextually derived is that the form of the minimal response may not be consequential. Indeed, Schegloff suggests that by explicitly passing back the floor with a continuer, a hearer is demonstrating an understanding of the *state* of the interaction, which also displays their attention to the interaction. However, by simply passing back the floor the hearer is choosing not to make a more specific, contentful response. Hence, a series of tokens of the same continuer might be interpretable as incipient disinterest. Schegloff (1982: 86) thus suggests that speakers vary the form of the minimal response so as to 'mask the absence of other types of response token' and hence allay any impression of disinterest. As we might expect, Rogers does vary the form of the minimal response that he uses, mostly using 'mm hmm', 'uh huh' or a form somewhere in between (i.e., nasal but mouth open), although since we cannot usually see him, which form he has used is not always easily discernible.

Rogers' use of 'mm hmm'

As we have seen from the account of 'mm hmm' presented above, Rogers' use of 'mm hmm' cannot be analysed as a single category of verbal response unless we can show that he consistently uses 'mm hmm' in the same type of sequential environment. The use of 'mm hmm' as a continuer is consistent with the aim of the therapist to encourage the client to speak. It might also appear, at first blush, to be consonant with the client-centred aim to be non-directive since it passes the turn back to the speaker without comment. However, as we see below this turns out to be somewhat equivocal. Whether or not continuer use of 'mm hmm' is congruent with the aims of the therapist, we can only make claims about Rogers' use of 'mm hmm' by examining the sequential environment of each individual token of 'mm hmm'. In this process, the aim is not to quantify continuer and non-continuer uses of 'mm hmm'. Rather, we aim to examine the distribution of Rogers' minimal responses, the different types of sequential environment of the minimal responses and the subsequent effect of the distribution and type of minimal response on the client's talk. To do this, we firstly determine for each token of 'mm hmm' whether it is in the sequential environment of a continuer, namely at a TRP, where speaker change is relevant. If the token is at a TRP and no more specific interpretation is made relevant by the preceding turn, for example, by a particular first pair part of an adjacency pair, then it is interpretable as a continuer and we would expect to see the client simply continue their story in their subsequent turn as evidence of their interpretation of 'mm hmm' as a continuer.[3]

As we might expect, a large number of Rogers' uses of 'mm hmm' do look like continuers. The following example illustrates Rogers' use of 'mm hmm' as a continuer:[4]

Example 1

    C   and at seven years old I was I was into that (0.2) and to<u>day</u> (.) I'm in the same position (0.4) em (0.4) really you know, trying to find out what I want to do what I want to <u>be.</u> (0.6) and em I've learned a lot of things <I've learned a lot> of things since I've found out I had leukaemia=

⇒   R   = mm hmm

    C   which is about a year ago (.) eh this <u>June</u> (0.2) and eh (1.2) learned an ↓aw:ful lot of things

    R   I bet =

    C   =[heh heh

    R   [uh huh (0.2) and you're going through a stage, if I understand it correct, is a little bit like what it was at seven. sort of shutting out the world or shutting yourself into a space where you're trying to figure out (.) what it is that you want or who you ↓are.

[3.] Note, this reflects the ethnomethodological foundations of Conversation Analysis where the analyst aims to determine the meaning of behaviours for the participants themselves.
[4.] Examples are given using CA transcription conventions giving the level of detail required in this type of analysis. A legend for the transcription conventions is given at the end of the paper.

If we consider the token of 'mm hmm' marked by ⇒, we can observe a number of features. Firstly, it occurs at a TRP, a point at which the client might be interpreted as having finished his turn, and at which Rogers might therefore initiate a turn. It is latched onto the client's talk, which is to say that there is no perceptible gap between the client's talk and Roger's 'mm hmm'. The client then continues with his talk. Notice that the client even formulates his subsequent turn in such a way as to make it syntactically dependent on his preceding turn.[5] This is typical of continuer use of 'mm hmm' both in this data and more generally (Goodwin, 1986), and demonstrates an orientation on the parts of both Rogers and the client that the function of 'mm hmm' here is to *enable* the client to take an extended turn at talk.

This is an interesting example in that it clearly illustrates how in some sequential contexts 'mm hmm' does not have any of the more specific interpretations often suggested in the literature. We see this in this example because, in this instance, the lack of a more specific response is observably problematic to the client who repeats 'I've learned a lot of things' three times with a number of inter-turn pauses and then laughs rather than continue speaking, at which point Rogers gives a contentful response.

This analysis of 'mm hmm' as a continuer might suggest that 'mm hmm' as a minimal response offers a very useful, non-directive mode of interacting for the therapist. However, the following sequence presents a somewhat more equivocal view of the question of directiveness:

Example 2

```
         C    like the↑fun thing about it is is that I'm I'm finding out that some
              of the things that I think inside of me (0.2) are ok
⇒             (0.6) and like that is a (0.4) you know, I'm, I feel ↓ok
              and I'm in a process of <becoming ok but like I >
              haven't worked that out you know that ↓hurt is a hard thing to
              deal with and like em (0.4) conditioning yourself to ↓die
         R    mm hmm
         C    is another thing, you know.
              and em <you see> I didn't let my family in on that
         R    mm-
         C    until March of this year
              (0.6)
```

[5.] 'Which' at the beginning of the client's turn is a relative pronoun which marks the subsequent clause as dependent on and subordinate to his preceding clause, i.e., the clause preceding Rogers' 'mm hmm'.

R	mm hmm
C	.hh and so it was some months before hand eh
R	= carried that within
	(0.3)
C	Oh yeah, but I proceeded very meticulously to carry out a plan
R	°mm hmm°
C	where my children would ah (.) would live, in an area that
C	I [wanted them to live]
R	[mm hmm mm hmm]
C	eh (0.4) and that (0.4) I tried to c- I was trying to control something after I I I [died
R	[mm hmm mm hmm

This is a very useful sequence to examine in that unusually it affords us a simultaneous view of both Rogers and the client. The importance of this is that although so far we have focused on verbal continuers such as 'mm hmm', it is clear that there is a certain amount of blurring of the boundaries between verbal and non-verbal forms of communication.[6] When we examine interaction at a micro-level, it is apparent that meaning-making is a distributed process in which talk and gesture are co-occurring elements (Goodwin, 2000) within a single semiotic system (Rhys, forthcoming).[7] The interactive task of producing a continuer may be done non-verbally and indeed Rogers at places uses nodding to this effect.

Turning to the sequence above, we observe that the client produces an extended multi-unit sequence with a considerable number of TRPs. In other words, there are a considerable number of opportunities for Rogers to either take a turn at talk or produce a continuer. However, these are not all treated equally by Rogers. So, for example, at the ⇒, we have not only a TRP, but also a pause, yet Rogers neither responds verbally nor non-verbally. He sits still. In this extended turn, there is no response from Rogers while the client talks about being 'OK', but when the client turns to hurt and dying Rogers begins to produce responses, nodding at 'hurt is a hard thing to deal with' and finally producing a verbal continuer at 'conditioning yourself to die'. The subsequent sequence involves a verbal continuer at each TCU and concludes with a repeated token of 'mm hmm' at the point where the client not only describes but interprets his behaviour 'I was trying to control something after I, I, I died'.

[6.] Indeed, this blurring of the boundaries is discussed in other analyses to the extent that the 'mm-hmm' might be regarded as the pivotal connection between the verbal and the non-verbal (Natiello, 1996:124).

[7.] Note this is a claim about the functional relationship between the verbal and the non-verbal (and indeed the linguistic and the non-linguistic). It does not amount to a claim about the cognitive structures behind such a semiotic system.

There is a clear sense in which we might argue that Rogers is being directive here by being selective in the use of continuers. As discussed above, in uttering a continuer, its producer takes the stance that the speaker should extend their turn. However, by being selective in where the continuers are placed, Rogers implicitly directs the client to extend some parts of their talk and not others. According to Mearns and Thorne (2000: 191), the question that should be asked here is not 'is Rogers behaving directively?', but 'is the client being directed?' That is, do the client's responses to Rogers' use of continuers exemplify the client being directed by the absence/presence of 'mm hmm'? This fits well with the conversation analytic/ethnomethodological principle of looking to the behaviours of the participants themselves for evidence of any analytical claim. In the above example, we see that the client does not expand on the theme of 'becoming OK' but does expand on the theme of 'hurt' in response particularly to the presence of continuers where he talks of hurt. From this we conclude that the client *is* being directed.

In the following example, we also see the client clearly being directed, this time more by the *absence* of 'mm hmm', providing further illustration of the directiveness that is implicit in the placement of continuers:

Example 3

    C   and em, I remember in second grade I eh (0.2) I was a c- I would I was a potential credit to my race.
          (1.0)
    R   [°mm hmm°
    C   [that was one of the-
    R   °mm hmm°
    C   I used to always wonder why I couldn't be a credit to someone [else's race
    R   [he he he
⇒   C   also (0.4) but (.) em I think I ↑really conditioned (0.4) eh (.) to be something (0.8) eh to be some kind of a symbol [or whatever
    R   [mm hmm
          (0.2)
    R   mm hmm mm hmm
          (0.2)
    C   and eh
    R   mm hmm
    C   and not really being a person you know? I kinda missed out on my childhood
    R   °mm hmm°

In this sequence, we see how the client orientates to Rogers' withholding of any form of continuer. The client begins to talk about his childhood experience of racial issues, the pressure to 'be a credit to his race'. In the turn marked ⇒, we see that the client leaves pauses after two TCUs and completes a third on this theme, without any kind of response from Rogers. We then see the client dismiss this theme with 'or whatever' at which point Rogers begins to produce a continuer. Rogers then produces a number of continuers before the client resumes talking, and when he does, the issue of race has been subtly left out of the frame. The point here is that the continuers are *noticeably* and *relevantly absent*. We see this in the client's reaction to their absence in that he removes the racial dimension from his narrative about his childhood development. We thus clearly see the client being directed to shift perspective away from issues of race.

This is perhaps another example of the eurocentricism observed by O'Hara in Rogers' interaction with 'Sylvia' (1996: 291), which raises the question of empathic understanding or perhaps the failure of empathic understanding. In the sequence examined here, Rogers not only appears to fail to 'work within the frame of reference of the client' (Duncan and Moynihan, 1994: 295), his non-response appears to trigger a shift in the client's frame of reference. This draws us into a debate which goes beyond the confines of this chapter, namely the tension between the purported universality of the theory[8] and the issue of 'cultural awareness'. For example, Bimrose (2000, cited in Wilkins, 2003) argues that social contexts can be overlooked in counselling because of a preoccupation with the individual, while Wilkins contends that Person-Centred Therapy 'when properly conducted is "culture free"' (Wilkins, 2003: 59).

Non-continuer uses of 'mm hmm'
So far we have concentrated on continuer uses of 'mm hmm', which display an understanding of the *state* of the interaction, but do not directly display a response to the *content* of the interaction. However, the claim was that the sequential environment is what makes a particular interpretation of 'mm hmm' relevant. In particular, we saw that following a potentially problematic utterance, 'mm hmm' is interpretable as displaying the stance that the utterance is not actually problematic. This is best understood through illustration. If we return to Example 2, above, we see that the client at the end of the sequence shifts from describing his behaviour to suggesting an interpretation of his behaviour: 'I was trying to control something after I died'. At this point, Rogers' opinion becomes relevant in the sense that the client has produced an interpretation that Rogers might disagree with. (In contrast with the descriptions of his actions which do not

---

[8.] There is a consensus that Rogers appears to take the view that there are 'universal human qualities which override cultural differences' (Wilkins, 2003: 20).

present the same opportunity for disagreement.) In this context, 'mm hmm' becomes interpretable not simply as passing the opportunity to take a turn, but passing the opportunity to disagree with the interpretation and hence as agreement.

Another example of a more specific interpretation of 'mm hmm' follows the client's use of figurative language. By nature, the interpretation of figurative language is much more subjective and individual than the interpretation of literal language. Hence when a speaker uses figurative language, they run the risk of their hearer either arriving at a different interpretation from the one they intended or even simply not arriving at any intended interpretation. Thus, in the context of figurative language, the hearer's understanding of the intended meaning becomes relevant. If in this context, a hearer produces a minimal response such as 'mm hmm', they are passing up an opportunity to seek clarification in a context where their understanding is relevant. Hence, 'mm hmm' becomes interpretable as 'I understand'. We see this where the client says of his relatives: 'they all were throwing flowers on my grave' and Rogers' response is 'mm hmm', which is interpretable as communicating that he understands what the client intended by the figurative expression.

In both these last examples, the point is that it is the preceding utterance that gives 'mm hmm' the specific interpretation. We are not claiming that 'mm hmm' means 'I agree' or 'I understand' out of context. Note also that in both these examples, we cannot claim that Rogers is using 'mm hmm' to mean 'I agree' and 'I understand' respectively. Rather, since the simple continuer interpretation of 'mm hmm' is still available in both contexts, 'mm hmm' is ambiguous between the specific agree/understand interpretation and the continuer interpretation. We see the client orientate to this ambiguity in part of the session where Rogers identifies an aspect of the client's behaviour as being a 'martyr', and the client then seeks, not to reject the label, but to redefine 'being a martyr':

Example 4

> R   really ↓crucify yourself? is that what you are saying, be a martyr? You're not [quite sure-
> C   [oh I I I'm not really sure you know but I think the <u>activities</u> I was involved in, in terms of (.)trans-racial communication
> R   mm hmm =
> C   =<u>working</u> with groups
> R   mm hmm
> C   and helping people

	R	mm hmm
		(0.3)
	C	and eh that I would hope (0.2) very similar to what people like yourself do
	R	mm hmm
		(0.2)
	C	em (0.2) you know, always being available (0.2) for every̲body
	R	mm hmm
	C	[a̲ll the time]
	R	[mm hmm] mm hmm
⇒	C	and ah (0.4) I think that's that's being a (0.3) a martyr or [or something, °yeah°
	R	[°yeahm°

At the point marked ⇒ where the client concludes his redefinition 'I think that's being a martyr', Rogers' agreement or disagreement clearly becomes relevant. Rogers' minimal response then is ambiguous between agreement with the reinterpretation and the simple continuer interpretation.[9] The client displays his uncertainty as to Rogers' intention in his subsequent turn, where he downplays his claim: 'or something yeah'.

DISCUSSION

Most of Rogers' talk as a therapist is dominated by the use of 'mm hmm'. If the talk that constitutes that therapist in terms of his institutional role and practice is dominated by the use of 'mm hmm', then we would expect the tenets of the theory to be manifest in the use and effects of 'mm hmm'. In our examination of Rogers' use of 'mm hmm' we have been led to address the issues of directiveness, empathic understanding and the problematic issue of cultural awareness.

In the debate around non-directivity, Bozarth (1998) argues that a non-directive attitude remains fundamental to the Person-Centred Approach. While therapist non-directivity may be an aspiration in the person-centred therapeutic relationship, what this research demonstrates is that in practice an absolutist position is unachievable. Minimal responses are clearly a vital component of therapeutic interaction. However, if the therapist were to produce a continuer at every TRP, the interaction would become mechanical, and suggest

---

[9.] 'Yeah' is frequently used as a continuer when produced with the same intonation as other monosyllabic continuers such as 'hmm'. In fact, Rogers here uses a blend between 'yeah' and 'hmm' with continuer intonation.

inattentiveness on the part of the therapist. On the other hand, we have shown that by selectively using continuers, the therapist is inherently being directive. This evidence supports the shift in focus from non-directive therapy to the experiential orientation outlined by Lietaer (1998) citing Gendlin's work from the late 1960s on. However, while Lietaer suggests that the therapist becomes a 'process expert' in the marriage of the frames of reference of both client and therapist (*ibid.*: 66), what this research shows is that in relation to minimal responses the therapist may be unintentionally selective about when they opt in and out of the client's frame of reference. Opting out of the client's frame of reference leaves open the possibility of imposing that of the therapist rather than 'maximising the client's experiential process, using our own [sic] to do so' (Gendlin, 1970: 549).

Non-directivity is closely related to the question of empathic understanding which is also addressed in terms of how the therapist orientates to the client's frame of reference. In exploring empathy, the researcher does not have direct access to therapist empathy, but only to how empathy is manifested. In fact, Rogers (1975) observes that clients are better judges of the degree of empathy than therapists. Hence, the presence of therapist empathy should be evaluated from the client's responses. In addressing the question of empathic understanding in this session, it is not that we see Rogers' understanding or lack of understanding. Rather, we see the client subtly shift his frame of reference when Rogers does not acknowledge it. Viewing this as a failure of empathic understanding provides a clear counter argument to the reductionist view of empathy as a therapist behaviour or skill (Egan, 1998). In this, we are in agreement with Rogers that empathy is not a skill or a technique. Rather, we conclude that empathy is an interpersonal process (Bozarth, 1997; Duncan and Moynihan, 1994). Bozarth (1997) points out that Rogers, in his later writings, consistently referred to empathic responses as capturing the client's frame of reference and attempting to represent it in the immediate interaction. What we show here is that in the case of non-verbal responses and minimal responses, demonstration of empathic understanding may simply involve the *acknowledgement*, rather than the *representation* of the client's frame of reference. This is shown by the way the client responds to the failure to acknowledge the frame of reference as a failure of empathic understanding. The failure of empathic understanding that we identified in this research highlights the neglect in the Person-Centred Approach of problems posed by cultural difference (Wilkins, 2003). Our analysis of Rogers' minimal responses reveals this lack of engagement with questions of race and culture.

To conclude then, the application of Conversation Analysis to the 'The Right to be Desperate' film data in this chapter demonstrates the value of micro-level exploration of therapist/client interaction. The ethnomethodological principles of this approach require the researcher to provide evidence for any claim from the 'fine-grained' detail of the participants' behaviour rather than the analyst's subjective interpretation. In this case Rogers' directiveness, degree of empathic engagement and eurocentricism emerge without reference to any of his responses with linguistic content.

Transcription conventions

Punctuation marks are used to show intonation:

?	indicates the rising intonation that signifies a question
,	indicates a lower rise that typically indicates the endpoint of a phrase within a Turn Construction Unit
.	indicates falling intonation
↓	indicates higher pitch on the immediately following word or syllable
↑	indicates lower pitch on the immediately following word or syllable
°yeah°	indicates that the word or syllable is uttered very quietly
to<u>day</u>	underlining indicates that a word or part of a word is emphasised
(.)	Micro pause: a silence that is audible but too short to time
(0.4)	Silence given in tenths of a second.
[ ]	Used to demarcate overlapping talk. The brackets are placed round the talk of both speakers to show the overlap. Where the end of the overlap is not thought to be relevant it is often not transcribed with the].
=	Used to show that one speaker's talk is latched onto the previous speaker's
< >	Used to show that the talk between the angle brackets is delivered noticeably quickly
c-	the hyphen is used to show when a word is cut off

REFERENCES

Bimrose, J (2000) 'Theoretical perspectives on social context', in C. Feltham and I. Horton (eds) *Handbook of Counselling and Psychotherapy.* London: Sage.

Bozarth, JD (1997) 'Empathy from the framework of client-centered theory and the Rogerian hypothesis', in AC Bohart and LS Greenberg (eds) *Empathy Reconsidered.* Washington, DC: American Psychological Association.

Bozarth, JD (1998) *Person Centered Therapy: A Revolutionary Paradigm.* Ross-on-Wye: PCCS Books.

Brodley, BT (1996) 'Uncharacteristic Directiveness: Rogers and the "Anger and Hurt" Client', in BA Farber, DC Brink and PM Raskin (eds) *The Psychotherapy of Carl Rogers.* New York: Guilford Press. (Reproduced as Chapter 4 in this volume.)

Duncan, BL and Moynihan, DW (1994) 'Applying outcome research: intentional utilisation of the client's frame of reference.' *Psychotherapy, 31*(2): 294–301.

Egan, G (1998) *The Skilled Helper: A problem management approach to helping* (6th edn). Pacific Grove, CA: Brooks Cole.

Gendlin, ET (1970) 'A short summary and some long predictions', in JT Hart and TM Tomlinson (eds) *New Directions in Client-Centered Therapy*. Boston: Houghton Mifflin, pp. 544–62.

Goodwin, C (2000) 'Gesture, aphasia and interaction', in D McNeill (ed.) *Language and Gesture*. Cambridge: Cambridge University Press, pp. 84–98.

Goodwin, C (1986) 'Between and within: Alternative sequential treatments of continuers and assessments.' *Human Studies, 9*: 205–17.

Farber, BA, Brink, DC and Raskin, PM (eds) (1996) *The Psychotherapy of Carl Rogers*. New York: The Guilford Press.

Harrow, J (2003) *Active Listening*. http://www.draknet.com/proteus/listen.htm

Heritage, J (1984) *Garfinkel and Ethnomethodology*. Cambridge: Polity Press

Lietaer, G (1998) 'From non-directive to experiential: a paradigm unfolding', in B Thorne and E Lambers (eds) *Person Centred Therapy: A European Perspective*. London: Sage, pp. 62–73.

Mearns, D and Thorne, B (2000) *Person-Centred Therapy Today: New Frontiers in Theory and Practice*. London: Sage.

Natiello, P (1996) 'An argument for client self-determination', in BA Farber, DC Brink and PM Raskin (eds) *The Psychotherapy of Carl Rogers*. New York: The Guilford Press.

O'Hara, M (1996) 'Rogers and Sylvia', in BA Farber, DC Brink and PM Raskin (eds) *The Psychotherapy of Carl Rogers*. New York: The Guilford Press.

Psathas, G (1995) *Conversation Analysis: The study of talk-in-interaction*. Thousand Oaks, CA: Sage.

Rogers, CR (1957) 'The necessary and sufficient conditions of therapeutic personality change.' *Journal of Consulting Psychology, 21*(2): 95–103.

Rogers, CR (1959) 'A theory of therapy, personality and interpersonal relationships, as developed in the client-centered framework', in S Koch (ed) *Psychology: A Study of Science, Vol 3. Formulations of the Person and the Social Context*. New York: McGraw-Hill, 1959, pp. 184–256.

Rhys, CS (forthcoming) Gaze, aphasia and turn construction.

Sacks, H, Schegloff, EA and Jefferson, G (1974) 'A simplest systematics for the organisation of turn-taking for conversation.' *Language, 50*: 696–735.

Schegloff, EA (1982) 'Discourse as an interactional achievement: some uses of "uh huh" and other things that come between sentences', in D Tannen (ed) *Analysing discourse: Text and talk*. Washington DC: Georgetown University Press, pp. 71–93.

Schegloff, EA (1996) 'Confirming allusions: towards an empirical account of action.' *American Journal of Sociology, 104*: 161–216.

Schegloff, EA, Jefferson, G and Sacks, H (1977) 'The preference for self-correction in the organisation of repair in conversation.' *Language, 53*: 361–82.

Warner, MS (1998) 'Person-centered psychotherapy: one nation, many tribes', in C Wolter-Gustafson (ed) *A Person-Centered Reader: Personal Selection by our Members*. Boston: Association for the Development of the Person-Centered Approach.

Wilkins, P (2003) *Person-Centred Therapy in Focus*. London: Sage.

Chapter 7
CONSIDERATIONS OF RACE AND CULTURE IN THE PRACTICE OF NONDIRECTIVE CLIENT-CENTERED THERAPY

SHARON MIER AND MARGE WITTY

We are nondirective client-centered therapists who have trained at the Chicago Counseling and Psychotherapy Center, and have studied with Barbara Brodley (author of Chapter 4 in this volume), a colleague of Carl Rogers. We have questioned why Carl Rogers' empathic responses in the two films, *The Right to be Desperate* and *On Anger and Hurt* did not frequently include the client's references to racism. Our perspectives on counseling have been shaped by our experiences as White female nondirective client-centered therapists and our involvement in cross-cultural interactions both at a professional and personal level. We have provided training and therapy for a number of years in academic and community settings and have worked extensively with clients of different social classes, religions, racial and gender identities, ethnicities, and sexual/affectional orientations. Focusing on the delivery of mental health services to Black and ethnic minority communities, women, and other marginalized groups are experiences that have made us particularly aware of issues of marginality and difference. Our outlook has also been determined by our personal histories. I (Sharon Mier) have been profoundly affected by my experience as a White mother raising an African-American /Vietnamese daughter in the United States as well as having a Black Brazilian daughter-in-law and two Black Brazilian grandsons. I (Marge Witty) come to this discussion as a bisexual woman with a history of involvement in the Women's and Gay Liberation movements and the New Left.

In this chapter we explore questions of race and culture and begin with a note of agreement with Brodley (1996; also Chapter 4 in this volume), in which Brodley gives evidence of an uncharacteristic directivity in Rogers' therapeutic work in the film *On Anger and Hurt*. In this chapter, we will review the tenets of nondirective client-centered theory and address the attributes and perceptual processes of the nondirective client-centered therapist. In order to do so, we will review in detail the empathic understanding response process as evidenced in the 'The Right to be Desperate' and 'On Anger and Hurt' sessions, specifically in relation to the client's references to racism and Rogers' responses. Finally, we will discuss explicit responses to difference in relation to the practice of nondirective Client-Centered Therapy.

NONDIRECTIVE CLIENT-CENTERED THERAPY AND ISSUES OF DIFFERENCE

Nondirective Client-Centered Therapy is based on the belief in the uniqueness of the individual in the context of the universality of human nature. All individuals are seen to have the same basic tendency to actualize their nature as best they can under their prevailing circumstances. Consequently unique individuals perceive, process and experience their environments in unique ways.

Although client-centered theory is based on a personality theory and theories of development and includes an aetiology of disturbance, the therapy practice puts aside these systematic ideas in orienting to the specific individual. The characteristics of a person are seen as descriptive and not categorical. Translated into the therapeutic relationship, this means that the therapist's attitudes are sufficient to promote healing and development. The therapist enters the therapeutic relationship with a general knowledge of the universality of human nature and an openness to the myriad ways in which an individual may express that humanness. The therapist perceives the client before her/him in the present moment as unlike any client who will have come before this client, or any client who will come after. This means that the therapist working in a nondirective client-centered way would not make any assumptions about how the client's race and culture, for example, had impacted the client's experience and development. This is *not* to say the therapist is not *aware* of racial and cultural issues as impacting on the client's experience. Rather it is saying that the therapist is not preconceiving what the particular impact has been.

This would also mean that the therapist working in a nondirective client-centered way would not make assumptions, for instance, about the meaning of being a White therapist working with a Black, Asian, Latina or indigenous client, or being a Black, Asian, Latina or indigenous therapist working with a White client. It would mean that the therapist would not make assumptions about the meaning of the client's racial identity. It would also mean not making assumptions about the meaning to the client of being a therapist from the dominant racial, cultural or political majority working with a client from a racial, cultural or political minority.

The task of the therapist working in a nondirective client-centered way is to provide the core attitudes of empathic understanding, genuineness and unconditional positive regard and trust in the client's own self-actualizing process. Provision of these attitudes is considered to be the therapist's role in therapeutic change. There is also an assumption that each of the client's interactions with the environment will have less or more of an impact on the client's differentiating process. In therapy, it is up to the client to determine what aspect of this process will be spoken about to the therapist. And it is up to the therapist to try and grasp what the client is getting to. The effort to understand will play out through a process called the empathic understanding response process in which the client will speak, and the therapist will respond with the intention of checking with the client to see if she/he has correctly understood what the client has communicated. The client will then let the therapist know if she/he feels understood, by responding to the therapist's communication of understanding. In this process, the therapist will usually gain a more complete and accurate understanding.

It is important to note that nondirective Client-Centered Therapy is not attempting to solve particular problems. Rather, the therapy is promoting the autonomy of the person, and promoting the client's self-differentiation, while acknowledging the limitations of each person in that effort. The extent to which the therapist understands the client's communications will be determined by the skill of the therapist, as applied in any given therapeutic hour. What the therapist grasps will also undoubtedly be influenced by the therapist's various attributes and experiences and perceptual variations as well as by characteristics of the client, especially her or his openness to self-disclosure and capacities for self-awareness. What is most important is that the therapist is following the client at whatever level of awareness or self-disclosure the client presents.

In addition to differences among therapists in their levels of understanding of their clients, there will also be differences among therapists as to *what particular aspects* the therapist will grasp from the numerous ideas, feelings, or actions of personality expressed by the client. It is important to note here, however, that it is not necessary to grasp *all* of what the client is communicating in order for the therapy to be effective. If the client experiences the therapist as trying to grasp what she/he is saying, and if the core conditions of therapy can still be sufficiently provided, then therapy can still be relatively effective. In our analysis of the two therapy sessions with Carl Rogers, we believe that our individual experiences may have shaped our perceptions and influenced what we understand in the client's communications. We are not able to say why Rogers responded to the client as he did. We can, however, share some of our experience as a possible way of explaining our responses to the client.

ANALYSIS OF THE SESSIONS

There are some major limitations to the process of reviewing Rogers' sessions. Most importantly, in order to review these sessions properly from a nondirective client-centered perspective, we would need to include viewpoints from Rogers and the client. Unfortunately, we only have Rogers' brief voiceovers that were added to the films at the time of their production. We do know that the sessions were filmed in a film studio, and this may have created some pressure for him to demonstrate client progress within the session. The process may also have caused Rogers some distraction in the sessions. After the sessions were filmed, Rogers heard rumors that the client might have been misrepresenting his illness. Rogers later commented that misrepresentations of experiences by clients did not undermine the validity of the work, because a client-centered therapist works with the client's immediate intended communications and the feelings immediately expressed. In a longer therapeutic relationship some misrepresentations may be corrected when more trust is established, or simply the therapeutic effort will be made around them.

There are two other sessions where Rogers demonstrates his work with clients of color: 'Dadisi' and 'Grace'. From our perspective, both of these sessions provide good examples of Rogers' nondirective Client Centered Therapy. In the 'Grace' session, the client does not mention the issue of race. In the 'Dadisi' session, Rogers encourages the client, who is reticent, to speak about the issue (see Chapter 12 for a detailed discussion on Dadisi; also see Chapter 4b). Questions of Rogers' understanding of the race issue in the 'The Right to be Desperate' and 'On Anger and Hurt' sessions have come up because Rogers seems less responsive to the client's communications of racism than in the other existing taped sessions. Also, he seems less responsive to the race issue than some therapists believe they might have been if they had been the therapist working with this client.

In our review of the two sessions, we will be asking these questions:
- How does Rogers respond to issues of race mentioned by the client?
- Is Rogers communicating to the client his effort to understand him?
- Does the client express a sense at some level that he feels understood?

We will at times offer alternative responses to the client's comments that we believe address the client's experience of racism more explicitly. These responses are not intended as prescriptive but come from our own understandings of the client's expressed meanings. We will provide a discussion of responding explicitly to difference in the practice of nondirective Client-Centered Therapy later in the chapter.

We will focus our discussion more on the first of the two sessions, *The*

Right to be Desperate, as this tape provides a number of examples of client communications about the impact of racism on the client's experience. A review of the 'On Anger and Hurt' session is more complicated as there is another variable. In the latter session we believe Rogers' generally high level of empathic understanding is distorted by some uncharacteristic directivity (see Brodley, 1996; also Chapter 4a in this volume).

'THE RIGHT TO BE DESPERATE'

In the early part of *The Right to be Desperate*, after introductions, the client begins to speak about how he realized as a small child that he was being separated out, as being 'a credit to your race' and about his experience of having leukemia and thinking he was dying.

> *Client (C5): I think that I've listened for so long to other people about who I was (T: Mmhm) and uhm I remember in second grade I uhm I was a, I was a potential credit to my race (T: Mmhm) that was one of the (T: Mmhm) I used to always wonder why I couldn't be a credit to somebody else's race also ... uhm it was last June when I found out and, uhm I proceeded to get everything in order because I was told that I had, uhm, less than a year to live (T: Mmhm) and uhm that was a trip (T: I bet, mmhm) that was, that was a trip and uhh.*
>
> *Therapist (T6): It was a trip into a fairly dark place I suppose.*

Here Rogers' response picks up the client's communication relating to his experience about trying to make sense of his whole life, in the context of thinking he was dying. He is checking with the client to see if he is grasping his meaning. It is important to note in Rogers' checking response that he is not trying to summarize every detail of the client's statements. He is attempting to verify his understanding of the main issue.

> *Client (C6): Oh, yeah for sure, for sure (T: Mmhm) ... but there's some there's a lot of hurt too (T: Mmhm) there's an awful lot of hurt and I think I am just beginning to realize that uhm because you know, in being a credit to your race, in being outstanding student an outstanding (T: Mmhm) scholar an outstanding (T: Mmhm) football player whatever, eh leaves you little room to, to be.*

The client, in C6, validates Rogers' understanding of his previous comments by saying, 'Oh, yeah for sure' and then proceeds to elaborate on what he wants to communicate. In so doing, he returns to one of his earlier comments about being a 'a credit to your race'.

> *Therapist (T7): You've been meeting other people's expectations of you and that it seems that's what you should do, now I guess you are really questioning that very much.*

Rogers responds, in T7 above, by speaking to the client's conditioning to others' expectations, a response which provides a more general understanding of the client's comment on being, 'a credit to your race'. In the next response, the client begins with an acknowledgement that suggests he feels Rogers is following him:
> *Client (C7): Oh yeah, tremendously ...*

Rogers speaks in a voiceover:
> *(V2): I like the way I'm being a companion to him trying to discover just how the prospect of death seems to him. I find that important because a client needs most to be understood in the darkest portions of his experience.*

The voiceovers are helpful in our effort to understand what it was that Rogers heard in the client's comments. The voiceover here suggests that Rogers is trying hard to be with the client. And, in particular, he is hearing the client's expressed concern about dying. In our listening to the client's communication, we also hear the client speaking about racism and how it affected him from his recollection of an experience at the age of seven. If either of us had been the therapist, we might have checked on that aspect of the client's communication as well.

Further on in C12, the client speaks to the loss of his father-in-law and the effect on him:
> *Client (C12): Lost my father-in-law (T:Mmhm) which was uhm a terrible loss to me ... when I went back there were just some things that happened that uh uh showed me there wasn't, there wasn't very much of a connection, there wasn't very much of a connection between uh, between all of that love and whatever that I put in and then all of a sudden you know I became uh you know I, I became just another Black person I became just another nigger you know ...*
>
> *(T13): And I imagine. Perhaps I catch a little bit of resentment that you really poured a lot of love and caring into that family and you had gotten some back from him but after his death none of it paid off (C: right) for you in any way.*

Rogers' response picks up on the loss of connection with his wife's family, and the hurt of feeling rejected by them. Rogers does not check on the client's comment that he 'became just another Black person ... just another nigger'. We hear this last comment as an important one and are not sure why Rogers did not check his understanding of it. For us, the client's comment seems like a powerful expression of his feelings. The comment also seems descriptive of the racism he seems to have felt. As the therapist, either of us might have checked our understanding of the client's comment with a response such as: 'Losing your father-in-law was a terrible loss, and in its aftermath you began to realize that you had so little connection to others in the family. On top of that, you began to realize how without him in the family supporting you, you were just another Black man, just another nigger.'

The client's next response, however, seems to indicate that he felt Rogers did understand him to some degree and that he felt Rogers was grasping key elements of what the client was communicating. The client says:

> *Client (C13): For sure, yeah I think that you know what I wanted, what I wanted more than anything else was just you know I guess it was love (T: Mmhm) you know I guess it was that that uh (T: Mmhm) mutualness (T: Mmhm) you know what I felt for each of them ...*

In C16, the client returns to the issue of being '*a credit to your race*' when he says:

> *(C16): ... You see because I had to take care of myself and I had to be better than everybody else because I was always told that. You can uh in a majority society I had to, I had to be a hundred per-, two hundred percent better than my, than my white counterpart ... because that's what it took to survive (T: Mmhm).*
>
> *(T17): And, and in, in striving for that one reason you really weren't heard was that you didn't dare express the person you were, the, the sick person you were at that time.*

In this response, Rogers seems to grasp the client's dilemma that he could not speak to being a sick man, because he had been conditioned to be 'two hundred percent better' than his White counterpart, although Rogers again does not explicitly check his understanding of the racial component of the client's response. And still, the client expresses a sense of being understood in his next response:

> *Client (C17): Oh no, not that I really, I really had a fear of that you know (T: Mmhm) I really I guess maybe didn't trust some things that were happening ...*

The client's communications continue to speak to both his belief that he was dying, and his realization that he was not being true to himself, and Rogers' checking responses follow these threads:

> *Client (C26a): ... and things like that and always being controlled (T: Mmhm) and I never really mean to feel a part you see because I don't*

> if my second grade teachers thought they were doing me a favor by telling me that I was a credit to my race but uh (T: Mmhm, mmhm) they certainly did, and I didn't feel good about it then (T: Mmhm, mmhm) (pause 4 seconds) So (sighs). That's a start (joint laughter).

The client has returned to the earlier comment again, of his being told that he was a credit to his race. Rogers adds a voiceover here, and states that he senses in the client's pause that the client is beginning to get closer to expressing more of his feelings and his experience. Rogers does not comment on the client's return to being a 'credit to his race'. For us, as therapists, given that the client has now gone back again to speak about this experience one more time, we believe we would have checked our understanding of his comments here.

Rogers' next checking response comes after further comments by the client about the client's family's judgment about him:

> *Therapist (T27): And I catch an amount of bitterness there, feeling that they really make judgments without, without knowing the picture.*

The client's following response, implies that he feels Rogers understands him, and so he acknowledges that he feels understood and continues to say more:

> *Client (C27): For sure for sure ... I am going to oversimplify this next thing (T: Mmhm) but but I forgot that I was Black (T: Mmhm) in that family (T: Mmhm) in that community ...*
> *Therapist (T28): You were reminded all over again.*

In this response Rogers seems again to be right with him, and the client expresses this in his following response:

> *Client (C28): Oh for sure for sure and I think that also caused a lot of bitterness or whatever (T: Mmhm) and that kind of stuff I want to get out of me ...*

As the session unfolds, the client gets closer to his deeper feelings, and in C32, he speaks to them, saying:

> *Client (C32): ... and nobody really likes cancer patients I don't think I don't know, at least, you know maybe that's my attitude (T: Mmhm) but I didn't seem to be very liked when I had it but at the same time I didn't like myself (T: Mmhm) you know maybe I didn't like myself at all because I couldn't control it.*
> *Therapist (T33): Yeah the way you describe sounds like a lot of real hatred for yourself for your body doing such things to you.*

The client again expresses a sense that Rogers is understanding him, saying:

> *Client (C33a): For sure for sure it'd been much more uh easy better way to go getting shot in the head (T: Mmhm) you know or run over by a missile or something (T: Mmhm) like that much more dignified ...*

As we hear the client's words, we find ourselves considering these communications in relation to the client's expressed experience of racism. As the therapist, either of us might have commented more explicitly and said something to the effect of his experience as a Black man needing to be in control, of needing to be perfect. We are also aware, in our speculation of what we might have said, that we would not want to get ahead of the client and become directive by pushing him to make this connection that he may not have made yet.

In a response just a little further on, the client returns to his early childhood experience, saying:

> *(C39b): ... since I was seven to some extent when I went down that basement turned that light off or whatever and I shut the outside world off or whatever, somehow I lost that. Because somehow in the process of becoming educated, and socialized (T: Mmhm) and whatever, I let other people control what I wanted, what I wanted to do. And I really, I did and that was, Jesus, it was ... Yeah, well, what can you say?*

Rogers, in the following response, seems to get a bit closer in his understanding of the client and follows him in this communication, saying he wants to make sure he gets this, and slows down and checks in detail what the client has said:

> *Therapist (T40): That has a lot of meaning to me and I want to make sure that I'm getting it straight. Down in that basement as a seven-year-old, with the lights out, you are really finding yourself and I gather trusting yourself (C: Mmhm) and then life has said to you 'no no don't do that we have the standards for you to live up to our expectations. You got to be the image, you got to be just right and everything' and now you are gradually recapturing what you found as a seven-year-old.*

The client acknowledges that Rogers understands and begins his response with:
> *Client (C40): I, I, I believe that to be true.*
> He then continues to say more: ... *But I guess I did lose it, I did lose it but I still had it, but all this garbage about me being ...*
> Rogers responds: *(T41): is well buried ...*

And the client continues, with an acknowledgement that Rogers is getting what he means:

> *Client (C41): Yeah, yeah and then other people were shaping me up you know (T: Mmhm, mmhm) by saying well you know you are good if*

>   you do it this way or whatever (talked over)
> (T42): You're a credit to your race.

Rogers finally uses the client's language and speaks explicitly to the phrase the client has used several times in his effort to express his experience. The client lets Rogers know that he does feel understood, in his next response and then the client explores more deeply his feelings about this experience:

> Client (C42): Oh yeah 'You are extraordinary. You are a credit to your race', you know and I don't know, maybe, maybe they meant very well or whatever, (T: Mmhm) but it, it didn't do the job. It didn't do the job you know (T: Mmhm). Because in a way by accepting that kind of praise and their kind of buying into their kind of their system or whatever, like I gave up something that I knew already at seven years old.

After this exchange, the client begins to speak more deeply about being conditioned to not trusting himself and to not trusting what he knew as a child. Rogers seems to grasp an understanding of this and says:

> Therapist (T48): But then that's just childish that's just (C: right, right) you know (C: yeah) don't, don't trust that stuff (T: Mmhm) telling you what's right (pause 4 seconds).

The client responds with a comment that implies that he feels understood, and is able to speak much more about his feelings:

> Client (C48a): Yeah, you know, I really suppressed I guess a helluva lot of anger (client laughter) you know 'cause when you said that, you know, I felt, you know ... (pause 2 seconds) think of all kinds of words now.

The client seems to have been circling this material, going round and round it. Rogers seems to have been following him, carefully. He does not use the client's language that speaks more explicitly to race, and yet, the client is able to explore this material of race and racism, and in his circling of it, gets closer and closer to it, sharing more and more with Rogers as he goes. By the end of the tape, the client is able to describe in detail the critical incident that occurred when he was seven.

> Client (C53): ... it's that junk you know that credit to you know that really makes me mad. That really made me mad. I mean I keep in mind, I keep, as I'm talking it keeps coming back to me, you know. Credit to my race, to my race. You know I remember that teacher so well big boobs and she'd put my head right in them and she'd say I was a credit to my race and, err, you know that would, burned my oh, that burned me up.

The first session ends soon after this interchange, the client having got in touch with a core experience he had when he was seven, which he feels shaped his development as a Black man. We see in the session Rogers' effort to understand him, and we see the client's acknowledgement that he felt understood. Rogers is cautious in his use of language, relating to race. As therapists, we think our responses would have more often checked explicitly our understanding of the client's use of the language of race and racism. However, there is no way of knowing if our hypothetical responses would have been a correct understanding of what the client was trying to communicate. There is no way of knowing where different understandings from different therapists would have led. We are aware that our own vigilance on the issue of race with this client might have created its own directivity, that might have got in the way of the client's own process with either one of us as therapists.

We do see evidence, in the above empathic understanding response process, that Rogers is consistent in his efforts to understand the client, even without a more frequent explicit checking of his understanding of the client's language regarding racism. We also believe that, throughout the session, there is evidence of the client's experience of being understood.

'ON ANGER AND HURT'

In this session Rogers' uncharacteristically directive responses get in the way of his work, and he does not provide his unusually high level of core attitudinal conditions for the client (Brodley, 1996, also Chapter 4 in this volume). This creates another variable in trying to understand why Rogers' empathic responses did not include more explicit communications about the client's experience of racism.

The client begins the session by addressing his anger and putting it in a racial context by explaining:

Client (C7): Right ... you only have about two options, you know, when you deal with race ... you either have to be ... you're either a racist or you're an antiracist. (T: Mmm) ... I don't really care to be an antiracist, if you know what I mean (T: Mmm) anymore. Uh, and I don't wanna be a reflection of any other ... of any other larger society at all. (T: Mmm.) I really don't want to ...
(T7): You'd like to get in touch with what's going on in you.

Rogers responds to the client's initial reflections on his feelings of anger, but does not address the client's comment of 'being a racist or an antiracist', and the client returns to the topic to continue to clarify it:

Client (C15): ... It's, it's just traditionally, you know, when Blacks become

> angry they're, they're not angry ... they're militant. (T: Mmm.) You know what I mean (slight laughter)?
>
> Therapist (T15): I know. Another label.

If either of us were the therapist, we might have checked more closely on this comment by the client, to see if we understood correctly, by saying something like, 'when Black men become angry, they are seen as militant.'

Throughout the early part of this session the client continues to speak of his anger:

> Client (C21): ... there's a lot of anger there. (T: Mmm.) You know, but it's not my nature to be angry. (T: Mmm) It's not my nature to be angry, but I feel angry.
>
> Therapist (T22): I get what you're saying and I also feel quite strongly that I want to say, it's OK with me if you're angry here.
>
> Client (C23): (Pause) ... But I don't, you know ... it's hard to know how to be angry, you know ... hard to ...

We believe that at this point, Rogers is getting ahead of the client. The client seems to be expressing an awareness of the anger he has felt, which came to the fore in the last session, at the same time he is saying it is not something with which he is comfortable. Rogers jumps ahead of him by saying to the client that his anger would be acceptable. The client's response suggests he does not feel understood, although he does express a safety in being able to express this feeling, thus suggesting he believes Rogers is trying to understand: (T23): 'Sure, sure, I'm not saying you have to be.' (C: Sure.) 'I'm just saying it's OK with me.' Rogers' response suggests he is hearing the client's hesitancy, and yet still implies directivity, and the client's response reflects this: (C24): 'Mmm.' Rogers does not seem to let go of his directive comments, and he says: (T24): 'If you feel like being angry, you can be angry.' The client seems to be having trouble here, and says to Rogers: (C25): 'You really believe that?' Rogers responds with: (T25): 'Damn right.'

We believe that the next response by the client suggests he is feeling perplexed at this remark by Rogers, and tries to talk about it. He says:

> Client (C26): (12-second pause.) Well. (15-second pause.) (Sigh) I'm not sure how to respond to that at all, you know, because a part of that anger is, you know, the ... the hurt, and maybe if I ... maybe what's happening is that if I'm ... if I become angry and I really let it hang out, that I really will see how hurt I am.

After this exchange, Rogers seems to pick up that the client is not feeling understood, and he seems to try to refocus and hear more of the client's dilemma:

Therapist (T28): Perhaps at a deeper level you're afraid of the hurt that you may experience if you let yourself experience the anger.

As the session continues the client explores his feelings of hurt and of anger, more deeply:

(C44): You know, I really don't want anybody historically to get, have ... to have gotten the best of me ... but they did. They did. They beat the hell out of me.

(T44): You don't want to say, 'I really was defeated at times,' and yet that's the truth.

During this part of the session, Rogers' checking responses suggest he seems to understand the client and seems to grasp his deep feelings of hurt and of anger, although he still seems to be distracted from providing the core therapeutic conditions. We sense Rogers pressing the client to express his feelings, even to the point of overstating the client's expressed feelings, as in his response in T25: 'Damn right.'

As we hear Rogers' responses, we wonder if this uncharacteristic directivity confuses the client. We wonder if this directivity gets in the way of Rogers taking in what we hear the client saying. The client seems to be speaking to the experience he has had as a Black man in a White society, saying that getting in touch with his anger will force him to get in touch with his hurt. He says if he gets in touch with his hurt, he will be defenseless and vulnerable, and will then have to face the reality that he has been beaten down by the larger society:

Client (C45): Mmm. It is. (sighs) (pause) You know, being ... having it being all right to be defeated and be beaten and I don't know if there's any value in, you know ... maybe to myself ... admitting it to myself, or whatever, you know, but you know ... because I don't want to be beaten. (T: Mmm.) But I was, you know.

Client (C48): For sure, for sure. (T: Mmhm) And I don't want to have, uh get in the situation like I'm in now, you know, where I'm afraid to, to, to, show anybody that I'm hurt, you know (T: Mmhm, mmhm). Scared to death, terrified.

Rogers in this next response seems to express again a better understanding of the client:

Therapist (T48): Something really awful about showing ... letting anyone know that 'I'm hurt' (C: Yeah.) 'I'm hurting'.

In response to Rogers, the client again brings the material back to his experience of being a Black man:

> *Client (C49): Sure, sure. It's, you know ... it has something to do with being a man and it has something to do with with ... the race thing, you know.*

Rogers responds with 'Mmm' in T49, acknowledging he has heard the client.

We might have said more to check our understanding of this last statement by the client with something like: 'As a man, and particularly as a Black man, there is something awful about showing that you have been hurt.'

In the next set of responses, Rogers again gets more directive and seems to push the client to express his feelings, as in:

> *Therapist (T55): A big lump of hurt, though. (C: Mmmm.) (15-second pause.) And how to let that hurt come out in the open ... how to let it ... emerge and be out here instead of way down locked in here.*

The client continues to seem uncertain and confused by the directivity, to the extent that he says:

> *Client (C58): For sure. (Laughs) I have a suspicion that maybe you know some things that I don't know. (Laughs) (T58): (Laughs) No. (C59): Mmm.(T59): No, I'm not holding out on you.*

This response from Rogers seems to suggest that he is trying to stay with the client again, and he continues in the next response, saying: (T60): '... a Black man especially doesn't admit he's been hurt by anything.' The client responds with 'Sure'.

Later in the session, the client seems to get close to the core of his hurt when he says:

> *Client (C81): ... But they, but it, but it ... they wouldn't understand that, they wouldn't understand how a Black person could be hurt, you know, because if you don't accept a person as human, how can you, how can you think about, you know, like ... it's like thinking a dog could be hurt or whatever, you know, people that don't have dogs and don't understand them, you know?*
>
> *Therapist (T81): But you get some satisfaction out of saying, 'You people don't realize how much you hurt me'. They might not be able to hear that message, but you'd get some satisfaction out of ... out of expressing that, out of ... out of letting, letting yourself know, letting others know that, 'God, I've been hurt!'*

In this response, we find Rogers' directivity getting in the way of listening to the client. What we hear the client seeming to say is that he would like to tell people how much he has been hurt but doubts that they (White individuals in his family and environment) would understand, since he feels these same people have never considered Black people as human.

In spite of Rogers veering from his generally high level of empathic understanding, the client expresses some sense that Rogers understands and values him:

> *Client (C84): For sure. Mmm. I maybe think you can understand that a little bit (T: Mmm) in terms of about hurt and that, you know, that ... you know, that I, you know, that I'm a person (T: Mmm) and uh, (pause) you know, I'm a person. And I don't really want that denied to me (T: Mmm) you know, ever again.*

The client continues, exploring the issue of his anger and not being able to get it out:

> *(C85): You know. I could really get angry.*
> *Client (C91): ... so little chance for that group of people understanding me.*

In much of this next section, Rogers tries to stay with him:

> *(T93): It's still too much locked in.*
> *Client (C94): Yeah, for sure ... it's incredible, you know, this is the first time I've talked to anybody that, you know, that I haven't really been in control. To some extent I've really given up a lot of control uh ... to you.*

The client's communications speak again to racism, saying: (C101): '... And to some extent, I blame racism ...' In this response the client then speaks to feeling like he might like to yell, a big long yell, and says: 'But I'm not sure, I, that I want to do that' (smiles). Rogers again seems to get in front of the client when he says: (T101): 'You could try it.' This comment misses the client's expression that he might like to yell, and is not sure about it. A more empathic response might have been, 'I feel like yelling, but I am not sure I want to do it.'

Rogers' directivity is evidenced in a number of responses throughout the remainder of this session. His focus appears to be on getting the client to express more of his feelings as in:

> *Therapist (T121): ... Getting, as you say, getting very close, you feel, you feel beaten right now as though, if only something could come out, you wouldn't feel beaten.*

As we listen to the client, we pick up more of his hesitancy to express these feelings. He seems to have not resolved his dilemma that if he expresses these feelings he may well have to face an intense feeling of being exposed as a beaten man; for him, particularly as a Black man, this has powerful implications.

By the end of the tape, the client is beginning to express a feeling of being beaten:

> Client (C139): *But you know, I, I've really never been this beaten. I never ... you know, never have.*
>
> Client (C141): *Just beaten, you know, just really beaten, and I think that if I show you how much I've been beaten or whatever, you know, like I'd probably, you know, become nothing in this chair, you know, just ... (T: Mmm, mmm.) You know? (Laughs.)*
>
> Client (C143): *It's really too much for me.*

While the client is not here to clarify these comments, we wonder if he was feeling too pressed by Rogers to express feelings that he did not wish to expose.

In *The Right to be Desperate*, the client explicitly communicates about issues of race and racism on many occasions throughout the tape. Rogers' empathic understanding responses do not explicitly refer to racism until very late in the therapy session. Our empathic responses—and we suspect those of some other nondirective client-centered therapists—might have been more explicit in checking an understanding of these issues of racism throughout the therapy session. However, many of Rogers' checking responses *do* speak implicitly to the issue of racism. When the client speaks early on in the session to being told he was 'a credit to your race' as a child, Rogers' empathic understanding response refers to 'meeting other people's expectations of you'. Even if this is not a full understanding of the client's communication, it does imply an initial effort to simply follow and try to understand the client.

Often, in nondirective Client-Centered Therapy, if an important aspect of a client's communication is missed, if the client feels safe enough, then she/he will return to the topic, interacting with the therapist to make her/himself more understood. This seems to be what happened in this instance regarding this particular expression of the client's experience. The client seems to circle the experience of being told when he was seven that he was 'a credit to your race'. He returns to it a number of times, using the experience and his feeling about it to explore a particular aspect of the racism he felt and how it affected his awareness of himself as a person. Each time he brings it up, Rogers follows him if ever so cautiously. We believe that, each time, Rogers gets much of the implicit meaning of the client's communication. His response, 'credit to your race', appears quite dramatic and perhaps long overdue. At this point in the session, when Rogers does respond explicitly, the client readily delves into this material much further.

In *On Anger and Hurt*, the client is able to get more in touch with his feelings of anger and hurt. At the same time, he is speaking to some uncertainty about expressing these emotions. The dilemma, as he puts it, '... has something to do with being a man and it has something to do with, the race thing, you know'. In this session, Rogers is a little more explicit in his empathic understanding responses in addressing the client's communications about racism, as in: (T60): 'A Black man especially doesn't admit he's been hurt by anything.'

However, as in the first session, most of Rogers' empathic responses address the client's comments on racism implicitly. The difficulty in trying to assess Rogers' empathic understanding responses and the client's expressed feelings of being understood in this session are confounded by the variable of Rogers' uncharacteristic directivity within the session. There are numerous examples, as discussed earlier, of Rogers getting ahead of the client or pressing him to address his feelings as well as examples of the client expressing a sense of not being understood. Such interactions between Rogers and the client where Rogers seems to veer from providing the core client-centered conditions for therapy make assessing his empathic responses in relation to the client's expressed experience of racism problematic. These prevent this session from being a good example of Rogers' work in general.

Finally, we would like to note that, while our comments point to places in both sessions where we suggest alternate responses to the client, we in no way mean to suggest that we have clarity as to why Rogers responds as he does. Without Rogers or the client on hand to participate with us in this discussion, we can only present what we observe between Rogers and the client through our own perceptual lenses. Without the client present, we are not able to say how he would have experienced our alternative responses, nor can we say whether he would have felt any more understood.

OTHER RESPONSES TO RACE ISSUES

In formulating ways in which we would have responded more explicitly to the client's references to his experiences of racism and racial identity, we wish to clarify that this analysis is not an *instruction* that we give to ourselves or to our students of Client-Centered Therapy. We do not see this expressive behavior in our own therapy as representing any departure from the original practice of Client-Centered Therapy. To make an *a priori* decision to 'bring up race' whether the therapist is White (or of color) and the client is Black, Latino, Asian, or indigenous (or White) is a misguided strategy for attempting to address difference within the therapeutic relationship. Many students in American and British clinical psychology training programs are instructed to refer directly to racial difference in the first interview with a client. This instruction supposedly is to open up the subject and to convince the client that the therapist is sensitive and aware in dealing with racial issues, thus telegraphing the message that the client is safe and accepted in the counseling relationship. The problem with this instruction, in our view, is that too often the message is not true. The therapist may *not* be sensitive or aware while feeling that he or she ought to be. We believe this is a recipe for incongruence, self-doubt, and, thus, a distraction from being with the other person. Alternately, she or he may be open and accepting, but trying to function in accordance with the instruction of pointing directly at racial difference with a vulnerable client, something that one would not ordinarily do in client-centered work. This introduces ambiguity regarding the therapist's motives and possibly a sense of violating norms governing social interaction which in itself is confusing to the client.

This prescription to raise the issue of racial difference also neglects the consideration of the power of the therapist in posing a subject that may be a repository of great vulnerability, anger, and fearfulness as well as pride and meaning. The client may feel that the therapist is seeking reassurance that racial difference is not an issue, thus stimulating incongruence in the client as well. Therefore we want to emphasize that we are not prescribing this kind of 'problem-solving' approach to racial difference by pointing out differences in the ways we might have responded to the client compared to Rogers' responses in these two sessions. In the examples given above, in which we would have responded to the client's concerns with more explicit language, we are referring to something we have experienced spontaneously in our own work over time, not just with racial, ethnic, or other types of differences, but with any material about which the client may fear a judgmental response. When we express empathic understanding of what the client has communicated, we are conscious of speaking out of a fluid, constantly changing matrix of meanings and associations—a kind of local knowledge. Insofar as we are responding from within our own particular historical period, we may differ from Rogers who was working with the client in 1977; similarly, if Rogers were to be working with Black clients today, he would probably respond differently, too.

We are alert to the vulnerability and risk the client may experience in referring to wounding experiences he or she knows the therapist has not had, such as Rogers' client having been dismissed as 'just another nigger'. We are attuned to the fact that the explicit restatement of words like 'nigger' involves violating social norms. These are most often norms having to do with preserving each person's dignity, of not referring explicitly to anything which would rupture the functional, though false, assumption of our being 'just two human beings'. The social norm of tactful silence about the racial difference which is the implicit backdrop to the interaction may at times lead to the client's feeling that the difference is practically invisible, although he or she knows this is unlikely to be the case. Goffman has described these moments of encounter between persons of different master statuses as sociology's 'primal scene'. The White therapist thinks, 'I see that you are a Black person, and that you see me as White.' The Black person thinks, 'She is noticing my race and is trying to appear that she is not noticing anything. I am, however, keenly aware of this, and am trying to appear that I am not aware of it.' She thinks 'Oh dear! I hope he doesn't think that I am thinking about the difference between us!' (Goffman, 1963).

We believe that not all cross-racial dyads should succeed. If the therapist is unaware of his or her own discomfort with racial difference, and the client is affected negatively by this, it will not solve the difficulty by trying to inculcate a problem-solving approach with politically correct gambits. Better that the client should accurately perceive the problem and its true source in the limitations of the therapist and move on.

CONCLUSION

It is indisputable that the theory and practice of Client-Centered Therapy is not culture-free but is a product of a philosophical tradition that evolved from secular and democratic societies in the West. The theory is committed to a vision of a pluralistic society in which individuals can and will display a host of differences which should be appreciated and understood, and in which subcultures can exist independently within the context of a national policy. This is not to say that the practice of nondirective Client-Centered Therapy is not dynamic and evolving according to its various national, cultural, linguistic, ethnic and racial environments, as local practitioners find their own ways of being agents of change within their own contexts. If the therapist is functioning from a nondirective attitude, he/she has no goals for clients, but just the goal of experiencing the attitudes and expressing empathic understanding of the client's frame of reference. This stance precludes any systematic aims of promoting racial identity development in clients. It precludes educating women about sexism, and gays, lesbians, bisexuals, and transgendered persons about homophobia or transphobia. It also precludes giving working class and poor people a tutorial about multinational globalization and the concentration of capital.

Is any therapy—even the most empowering therapy—a necessary and sufficient practice to remedy oppression? We answer in the negative for a host of reasons, one of the most obvious being that, at least in societies without universal health services, like the USA, psychotherapy is a very scarce resource. The most seriously afflicted persons, the chronically mentally ill, are the most highly represented group among the homeless population. Therapy may be an emancipatory practice, but it cannot substitute for humane social policy, legal reform, and for massive organizing among the working poor and middle-class. Stereotyping, prejudice, discrimination and racial oppression have psychologically damaging effects which therapy cannot on its own rectify. Many Whites in the

USA still hold discriminatory attitudes and racial stereotypes (Kleg, 1993: 145). We also know that Whites tend to attribute blame for the suffering of racism to its victims instead of institutions (Ryan, 1971). The issue is whether therapists who are practicing from the client-centered or person-centered approach should try to promote social change within the therapeutic relationship in a direct way. This question is raised and addressed at much greater length by Holdstock (1990) in: 'Can Client-Centered Therapy transcend its monocultural roots?' We do not agree that the theory is deficient but believe that practitioners are deficient in terms of their ability to provide the core conditions. We also believe that the practice of Client-Centered Therapy tends to empower individuals over time, and that in an indirect way, this may have positive effects.

Devotion to the subjective realities of clients in authoritarian societies is undeniably subversive, although we argue that the practice of individual therapy is insufficient to alter power relations. Those aims are more effectively pursued in practices that Rogers evolved from individual therapy: peace and conflict resolution, large community encounters, and from traditions and practices which pursue human rights, among which the Person-Centered Approach rightfully belongs. Furthermore, we believe that Carl Rogers was consciously antiracist long before the two interviews he held with the 'On Anger and Hurt' client. Rogers' social conscience was expressed through his antiracist attitudes and conduct during the Second World War. He refused to meet in facilities that were not open to the African-American colleagues he worked with (Brodley, 2003). He does not need to be defended in terms of his own record of accomplishments. It is certainly true that his radical valuing of each person's internal experience as a trustworthy guide for living is still a radical position, opposing ideologies, religious or secular, which claim legitimacy over individual choice and individual freedom.

REFERENCES

Brodley, BT (1996) 'Uncharacteristic Directiveness: Rogers and the "Anger and Hurt" client', in BA Farber, DC Brink and PM Raskin (eds) *The Psychotherapy of Carl Rogers: Casebook and Commentary*. New York: Guilford, pp. 310–21.
Brodley, BT (2003) Personal Correspondence.
Goffman, E (1963) *Stigma: Notes on the management of spoiled identity*. Chicago: University of Chicago Press.
Holdstock, L (1990) 'Can Client-Centered Therapy overcome its monocultural roots?', in G Lietaer, J Rombauts and R Van Balen (eds) *Client-Centered and Experiential Therapy in the Nineties*. Leuven: University of Leuven Press.
Kleg, M (1993) *Hate, Prejudice and Racism*. Albany: State University of New York Press.
Ryan, W (1971) *Blaming the victim*. New York: Pantheon books.

Chapter 8
THE 'RIGHT TO BE DESPERATE' AND 'ON ANGER AND HURT' IN THE PRESENCE OF CARL ROGERS: A RACIAL/PSYCHOLOGICAL IDENTITY APPROACH[1]

ROY MOODLEY, GERALDINE SHIPTON AND GRAHAM FALKEN

In our viewing of the films we have chosen one key issue—*racial/psychological self-understanding*. The literature in multicultural psychotherapy and counselling as far as we are aware seems to be engaged with racial and psychological aspects but emphasises racial issues at the expense of the psychological (if these two can be separated at all). In this chapter, we are not attempting a purely psychological exploration but intending through the analysis of significant excerpts to explore how the client and psychotherapist/counsellor deal with racial identity psychologically and psychological identity racially. Carter (1995: 71) suggests 'although much has been written about the therapeutic needs of these [ethnic minority] groups, less is known about how race, as a psychological construct, influences the therapeutic process for members of various racial/ethnic groups and for White people'. And, Jones (1985) argues that psychotherapy and counselling in relation to race appears to be insubstantial compared to the detailed and sophisticated literature in therapy generally (see also Sashidharan, 1990; Sue and Sue, 1990). In attempting to understand the therapeutic content and context of the videos we consider it from outside any preconceived notions on the client-centred approach.

There are limitations of course to any methodology used in social science research particularly in psychotherapy and counselling research as we are constantly reminded in this particular audio-visual study. For example, paralinguistic effects and non-verbal behaviours such as nervous hand movements, staccato gestures and anxious laughs remain outside our analysis

---
[1.] A longer version of this paper was published in the journal: *Counselling Psychology Quarterly*, *13*(4), 2000: 353–64. Reproduced with permission.

for this chapter. We do not attempt a detailed critique of the sessions in the light of the main theories of the client-centred approach nor do we critique the therapist style and technique although it may offer interesting challenges to psychotherapy and counselling research: both of these aspects are beyond the more narrow focus of this chapter. Furthermore, concepts and terms such as race, culture, ethnicity, ethnic minority and black are not used in this chapter as essentialistic and fixed. These concepts are products of specific histories and geo-political experiences and so are problematised by their ambiguous usages (see Ahmad, 1996; Gates Jr., 1986; Grillo, 1998).

In examining the client's narrative, it seems important to have in mind the impact that specific historical and political movement and its mentors—the Civil Rights, Martin Luther King, the Black Consciousness, Malcolm X and others—had on the developments of multicultural counselling and psychotherapy. In analysing significant excerpts of the video sessions, we hope to show that racial/psychological self-understanding can be achieved irrespective of the particular approach a counsellor or psychotherapist uses with a black client/patient.

RACIAL/PSYCHOLOGICAL IDENTITY FORMATION

Theories about racial identity development and its influence in psychotherapy and counselling have been well documented (Atkinson et al., 1993; Carter, 1995; Cross, 1971, 1978, 1991; Cross et al., 1991; Helms, 1984, 1990; Ponterotto, 1988; Sabnani et al., 1991). For Carter racial identity theories describe psychological development from the perspective of racial, rather than ethnic identity. He cites Helms who says that:

> Black racial identity theories attempt to explain the various ways in which Blacks can identify (or not identity) with other Blacks and/or adopt or abandon identities resulting from racial victimization; White racial identity theories attempt to explain the various ways in which Whites can identify (or not identify) with other Whites and/or evolve a non-oppressive White identity (Helms, 1990: 5).

Cross (1971) suggests a five-stage theory for black identity development (in relation to living in a white dominated-society)—Pre-encounter, Encounter, Immersion-Emersion, Internalization and Commitment stages. Each stage is described in relation to the psychosocial process a person experiences and the psychological manifestation that result from such encounters. For example, in the Pre-encounter stage a black person 'consciously or unconsciously devalues their own blackness and concurrently value White values and ways. There is a strong desire to assimilate and acculturate into White society' (Sue and Sue,

1990: 94; Carter, 1995: 90). Cross et al. (1991: 322) suggest that 'at the core of Pre-encounter is an aggressive assimilation-integration agenda'. In the Encounter stage, a two-step process, the black person encounters a profound negative race experience causing him/her to reinterpret and challenge previously held ideas about the world and his/her relation to it. Feelings of guilt and anger are experienced for being 'brain washed' by White society (Sue and Sue, 1990). In the third stage, the Immersion-Emersion stage, the black person withdraws from white culture and immerses him/herself in black culture; the guilt and anger begins to dissipate; and, an increasing sense of pride develops. In the final stage, the Internalization and Commitment stage, the person experiences an inner security of his/her racial identity, and participates in society as a 'fully functioning person' (Cross, 1991).

Another five stages (pre-exposure/precontact, conflict, anti-racism, retreat into white culture, redefinition/integration) are offered for white identity development (see Sabnani et al., 1991). Sue and Sue (1990) whilst also offering black and white racial/cultural identity development models caution us on the limitations and essentialistic notions that prevail in the construction of these models. Many of these models tend to consider psychological development but do not develop the relationship between the two. For example, in Sue and Sue's Dissonance Stage for white identity development, the person experiences guilt, shame, anger, depression—but these are not explored fully in relation to any psychological theories of development. We are also reminded that these models are developed in relation to the experiences of the African-American and white American socio-political and cultural histories. Although the experiences of ethnic minorities in Europe are historically, culturally and socio-economically different with experiences of race and racism being understood in a variety of complex ways (see Solomos and Wrench, 1993), the basic principles of the racial identity theories still apply.

In Britain, Dupont-Joshua (1997) argues that if white counsellors are to work effectively across cultures then they must examine what it means to be white by working on their racial identity development and start owning their whiteness as part of their identity (see also Carter, 1995). Holmes (1992) indicates that there are several factors which limit therapeutic intervention when therapists do not fully interpret intrapsychic conflicts in relation to clients' racial explanations. These are: white therapist guilt, black therapist over-identification with the downtrodden (a particular form of countertransference problem), and warded-off aggression in clients and therapists. Tan (1993: 43) suggests that 'racial difference in the transference is an essential tool to be taken up and made use of in the resolution of the patient's emotional conflicts, a tool to be used via transference interpretations'.

In constructing racial identity models we may need to consider many factors other than racial history, such as the socio-economic and cultural histories that exist within and amongst minority groups. Constructing a single model to explain the diversity of experiences may be problematic for articulating the psychological complexities in psychotherapy and counselling. In establishing a racial/psychological model of identity we may also need to look beyond the post-colonial critique and place equal emphasis on the post-modern 'condition' of the individual 'subject' (see Foucault, 1980). We attempt to illustrate that within the therapeutic dyad each individual's psychological identity and racial identity are in constant movement in the shape of an elliptical figure. Whilst this is happening inside each person, a similar field of movement is played out between the dyads, so that in any given moment of psychotherapy and counselling there may be a convergence of their respective racial or psychological material. This dialectically opposite identity frame creates a tension which may be seen as a point (or a moment) of therapeutic resolution. However, the meeting of similar frames of references, i.e., psychological/psychological or racial/racial will engage the psychotherapist or counsellor in a negative model resulting in the disavowal or exclusion of the 'other' dimension.

In configuring racial/psychological identity we are positing racial and psychological identities as separate and manifested differently, but at the same time we are also suggesting that at the interface there are enormous possibilities for conflict, resolution and reformulations of self. For the purposes of this discussion we make such a distinction and separation in order to open up the area for exploration conceptually though we are aware that racial/psychological identity formation may be a singular process in the constitution of the 'subject'.

WORKING WITH THE RACE/PSYCHOLOGICAL 'SUBJECT'

In cross-cultural psychotherapy and counselling, the therapist needs to be aware of the impact of otherness in relation to the racial/psychological identity formation of the client. In *The Right to be Desperate* and *On Anger and Hurt*, the client emphasises time and time again the consequences of having his identity constructed for him:

> *Client (C5): I think that I've listened for so long to other people to who I was (T: Mm) and uhm I remember in second grade, I uhm, I was a, I would, I was a potential credit to my race (T: Mmhm) I used to always wonder why, why I could not be a credit to somebody else's race also. But uhm, I think I was really conditioned uhh to be something uhh, to be some kind of symbol or whatever (T: Mmhm) ... I kind of missed out on my childhood.*
> *(The Right to be Desperate)*

In the first minutes/moments of therapy the client introduces ('some kind of symbol or what ever') 'a potential credit to my race'. Although it takes the therapist 'thirty five minutes' to respond directly and acknowledge this in the client, it is consistent with the Person-Centred Approach.

The repression of the inner sense of 'self' as a result of the totality of the external environment may constitute for the 'subject', a 'gap' (see Parker, 1998) leading the client to understand that as a result: 'I kind of missed out on my childhood'. This may mean that the racial/psychological self may have been 'psychopathologised' during childhood (see Biko, 1978; Burke, 1986; Fanon, 1967). The client confirms the complexity of psychological/racial development, when he says:

> *Client (C48b): ... I'm minority you know and as a minority in terms of a minority you know my mother is, is old sage, you know she's part Indian, her family, that history (T: Mmhm) my father a descendant of black slaves (T: Mmhm) you know, because that's what it was you know certainly was you know 'cause I knew what was happening to other people in the class whether they were white or black or whatever, but it was you know, but I always you know, really understood, that I had to be two hundred per cent better than everybody else so I had to achieve (T: Mmhm) ...*

(The Right to be Desperate)

These 'invitations' by the client to deconstruct racial/psychological identity are not taken up by the therapist. Fanon (1967) develops related ideas which might be summed up in the title of his book, *Black Skin, White Masks*. Bhabha (1994: 62) believes that in the uncertain and ambivalent identification of the white-masked black man, that it is possible 'to redeem the pathos of cultural confusion into a strategy of political subversion.' In other words, the negative experiences of race and racism which contribute to the psychological and physiological dysfunctioning of the 'subject' can be redeemed through engaging in individual agency (positive self-concept, self-esteem) and group agency (community empowerment and cultural advancement). Biko's (1978) psychology of 'black consciousness' emphasises this process (see Moodley, 1998b).

Throughout the two sessions we find that whilst the therapist does not avoid the race issue directly, he does not actively engage the racial/psychological make-up of the client. The person-centred theory is 'a *passive* theory of the subject' (Millington, 1980: 109, italicised in original) and may therefore explain this particular approach by Rogers. Forming a relationship between Rogers, the white therapist and the black client in the 1970s was certainly not easy. Nor could it have been achieved by evading or neglecting the racial/psychological components of the client's utterances, as these sessions demonstrated. During this period race was an 'explosive' issue, as the client remarks and the therapist acknowledges:

> *Client (C15):* ... *I guess that part of me that's, that's my culture or is a part of the total, is saying that it's not all that good to be angry, you know, because militancy is frowned upon (T: Mmhm) or whatever (T: Mmhm), you know. And I guess I'm using mili-, militant in my sense because of it's, it's just traditionally, you know, because of white, blacks become angry. They're not angry, they are militant (T: Mmhm) you know what I mean (slight laughter).*
>
> *Therapist (T5): I know. Another label.*
>
> *(On Anger and Hurt)*

The therapist cannot possibly 'know'. He cannot say that he does 'know', as a white male American what an angry black militant might feel in America. 'Know', know-ing and know-ledge/able can be problematic in the therapeutic relationship with black people. An avoidance of race as a clinical variable may be the route the therapist undertakes in accordance with his/her theoretical orientation, but an active engagement of race, racial identity, racism may be the therapeutic moment. Carter (1995) suggests that white clinicians feel more comfortable examining cultural and ethnic issues than addressing racial issues. This is illustrated in the next excerpt:

> *Therapist (T11):* ... *You feel as though, um, what the culture and people and so on, have ... have done to you ... that's really caused you more suffering than the leukemia. Is that what you're really saying?*
>
> *Client (C12): I think so (T: Mmhm). I think so and to some extent that is mild. Like for instance, you know, either I don't know what happened if I died or if I will die, but I certainly know ... (T: Mhmm) ...*
>
> *Client (C14):* ... *or what's happened and to some extent that kind of leukemia, that deterioration of the body is the same kind of thing that happened to my mind ...*
>
> *Therapist (T14): Oh really, what the culture did to you is to give you cancer of the mind.*
>
> *(On Anger and Hurt)*

The therapist's avoidance of race (as in white, racism): 'what the culture and people and so on, have, have done' is a *mild* way of putting it, according to the client. The therapist assimilates the 'mild rebuke', rephrases the client's: 'deterioration of the body is the same kind of thing that happened to my mind, as the cancer of the mind' but still uses culture rather than race as a variable.

The client is in remission from leukaemia (white blood cells literally eat up the oxygen (life) carriers, red blood cells). The client appears to clearly suggest the association for the body/mind conflict here and at the same time offers a clear analysis of the socio-political variable of his 'problem'. Here we see clearly the therapist engaging in the race variable, although the language he uses differs from that of the client. However, at the intrapsychic level the therapist is not articulating anything new for the client who is left in a kind of 'no man's land'. Whilst Rogers' method may be consistent with the Person-Centred Approach it seems to have created tension in the client and reinforced some of the anger and hurt, as the excerpt below indicates:

> *Therapist (T6): There's some real anger there.*
> *Client (C7): Right. It's it's almost like in this country, and, and I've always felt like this, you only have about two options, you know, when you deal with race ... you either have to be, you're either a racist or you're an antiracist (T: Mmhm) and that doesn't seem really to be the kind of thing that I'm, you know, I really care to be an antiracist, if you know what I mean (T: Mmhm) anymore. Uh, and I don't want to be a reflection of any other, of any other larger society at all (T: Mmhm) I really don't want to ...*
> *Therapist (T7): You like to get in touch with something inside you.*
> *Client (C8): For sure.*
> *Therapist (T8): Not ... not with some label or other.*
> *Client (C9): For sure. I think I can probably trust that a lot better than, than than trusting what's happening or what has happened (T: Mmhm). And, um, and when I think about that, when I think about all of that, uh, the things we talked about, I, I, I think that, um, that's worst than the leukemia.*
> (On Anger and Hurt)

The 'subject' constitutes and is constituted by the 'larger society', so that 'getting in touch with something inside' may only be done through language ('with some label or other') in Western psychotherapy and counselling. However, there seems to be a tension point here. The client tends to agree with the therapist's analysis but at the same time raises questions about the process: 'I think I can probably trust that [something inside] a lot better than trust what is happening [something outside]', i.e., in the therapy.

The exploration of subjectivity is influenced by the degree and quality of the element of trust contracted into the therapist-client relationship. Vontress (1971) suggests that some black clients' mistrust of white therapists can prevent them from identifying with the white therapist's world-view. And if, which is often the case that the therapist is white, male, middle-class, able-bodied and heterosexual then, more often than not, a status differential exists between the black client and the white therapist which may lead to levels of mistrust that imbue therapy. In the above case study the status differential is not only emphasised by the historic period in which this event takes place (USA in the 1970s) but the personal circumstances in which the client finds himself emphasises this position, i.e., experiencing loss, death and dying. The question of trust, however, still remains in the frame of the relationship. For example, when the client says:

> Client (C50b): ... I'm really wondering about trusting too right now, you know (T: Mmhm) you know (T: Mmhm) 'cause I've trusted a lot of other people (T: Mmhm) too.
> Therapist (T51): And so you're wondering, Yeah but can I trust him?
> Client (C51): Mmm ... well ...
> Therapist (T52): Maybe part of that reason you feel, 'My god I've told him a lot, I've trusted him. Have I trusted him too much?'
> Client (C52a): For sure. Well I guess I've to deal with that in terms of I'm just going to have to trust myself to tell you (T: Mmhm, mmhm) you know. But I, I do have that, you know. I have that history ...
> (The Right to be Desperate)

The therapist in the above excerpt attempts to engage with this issue but stops at the edge, at the borderline of what confronts both of them in the session, i.e., race. Although Rogers does not himself feel this way since in his commentary (voiceover) at the end of the excerpt, he says: 'Is it safe to trust me with this more vulnerable part of himself? Clients often have such doubts and I respond in a way which helps him to realise that I recognise and accept that question.'

It must be remembered that the ambiguous status of trust is deeply ingrained in the socio-cultural and political histories of black communities, as the client points out. Slavery, indentureship and present-day racism can manifest themselves both consciously or unconsciously in psychotherapy. The acknowledgement of these knowledges/experiences may be indulged significantly in the therapeutic process, sometimes making un(re)presentable psychological narratives easily interpretable, or socio-political constructs of the client's self-concept empty and meaningless. Sue and Sue suggest that a therapist practising 'with a minority client is likely to experience severe tests of his/her expertness and trustworthiness before serious counseling can proceed' (1990: 91) and emphasise that 'the onus of responsibility for proving expertness and trustworthiness lies with the counsellor' (*ibid*.: 92).

CONCLUSION

Towards the end of the session in both *The Right to be Desperate* and *On Anger and Hurt,* Rogers and the client describe 'their talk' as 'circular' (client) and 'spiral' (therapist). This description or metaphor by the both of them is indicative of the separate paths/journeys/routes they were travelling towards transformation of the 'self'. The failure of a closer examination of the racial/psychological identity may have contributed towards the dialogue being experienced as 'circular' and 'spiral'. At various intervals in the therapy (in the recorded sessions), Rogers offers a voiceover commenting at times on the client, the existential moments, the clinical process and also about himself as a 'competent' clinician. These voiceover texts and the specific contexts in which they appear are themselves worthy of analysis and reflection.

In this chapter, however, we have suggested that it may be possible for psychotherapists and counsellors to 'work with' racial identity psychologically and psychological identity racially. In this way the internal representations of their racial/psychological identities will match more their external notations of self (i.e., verbal and non-verbal expressions and behaviours). In one way or another, psychotherapists and counsellors will be faced with the dilemma of how to engage the race and psychological material especially in black clients. This also applies to the other discursive practices of gender, class, caste, disability and sexual orientation.

To 'gaze' on Carl Rogers working with a black client in a socio-historical context 20 years ago may seem out of place in contemporary psychotherapy and counselling, and the new knowledge/s gained in social anthropology and political economy. As mentioned earlier, our investigation of the video presentation was not to offer a detailed line by line analysis of Carl Rogers at work, or an analysis of the client-centred approach with black clients, or critique the vignette in a way that focuses on the limitation of the principles of the approach. What seemed important was to refer to one of the 'founding fathers' in our exploration of racial/psychological identity when working with black clients irrespective of the kind of therapeutic approach a therapist uses.

REFERENCES

Ahmad, WIU (1996) 'The Trouble with Culture', in D Kelleher and S Hillier (eds) *Researching Cultural Differences in Health*. London: Routledge.

Atkinson, DR, Morten, G and Sue, DW (eds) (1993) *Counseling American Minorities: A Cross-Cultural Perspective* (4th edn). Dubuque, IA: Brown & Benchmark.

Bell, DA (1992) *Faces at the Bottom of the Well: The Permanence of Racism*. New York: Basic Books.

Bhabha, H (1994) *The Location of Culture*. London: Routledge.

Biko, S (1978) *I Write What I Like*. London: Heinemann.

Burke, AW (1986) 'Racism, Prejudice and Mental Health', in JL Cox (ed) *Transcultural Psychiatry*. London: Croom Hill.

Carkhuff, RR and Pierce, R (1967) 'Differential Effects of Therapist Race and Social Class upon Patient Depth of Self Exploration in the Initial Clinical Interview.' *Journal of Consulting Psychology, 31*: 632–4.

Carter, RT (1995) *The Influence of Race and Racial Identity in Psychotherapy*. New York: Wiley.

Cross, WE Jr (1971) 'The Negro-to-Black Conversion Experience: Towards a Psychology of Black Liberation.' *Black World, 20*: 13–27.

Cross, WE Jr (1978) 'The Thomas and Cross Models of Psychological Nigrescence: A Review.' *Journal of Black Psychology, 5*: 13–31.

Cross, WE Jr (1991) *Shades of Black*. Philadelphia: Temple University Press.

Cross, WE Jr, Parham, TA and Helms, JE (1991) 'The Stages of Black Identity Development: Nigrescence Models', in RC Jones (ed) *Black Psychology*. Berkeley: Cobb & Henry.

Dalal, F (1988) 'Jung: A Racist.' *British Journal of Psychotherapy, 4*: 263–29.

Deleuze, G (1994) *Difference and Repetition* (Trans. P Patton). New York: Columbia University Press.

Dupont-Joshua, A (1997) 'Working with Issues of Race in Counselling.' *Counselling, 8*: 282–4.

Fanon, F (1967) *Black Skin, White Masks* (Trans. CL Markmann). New York: Grove Press.

Fong, ML and Lease, SH (1997) 'Cross-Cultural Supervision: Issues for the White Supervisor', in DB Pope-Davis and HLK Coleman (eds) *Multicultural Counseling Competencies*. Thousand Oaks, Cal.: Sage.

Foucault, M (1980) *Power/Knowledge*. C Gordon (ed). New York: Pantheon Books.

Gates, HL Jr (ed) (1986) *'Race', Writing and Difference*. Chicago: University Of Chicago Press.

Grillo, RD (1998) *Pluralism and the Politics of Difference*. Oxford: Clarendon Press.

Hacker, A (1992) *Two Nations: Black and White, Separate, Hostile, Unequal*. New York: Ballantine Books.

Helms, JE (1984) 'Towards an Explanation of the Influence of Race in the Counseling Process: A Black-White Model.' *Counseling Psychologist, 12*: 153–65.

Helms, JE (1986) 'Expanding Racial Identity Theory to Cover Counseling Process.' *Journal of Counseling Psychology, 33*: 62–4.

Helms, JE (ed) (1990) *Black and White Racial Identity: Theory, Research, and Practice*. Westport, CT: Greenwood Press.

Helms, JE and Richardson, TQ (1997) 'How 'Multiculturalism' Obscures Race and Culture as Differential Aspects of Counseling Competency', in DB Pope-Davis and HLK Coleman (eds) *Multicultural Counseling Competencies*. Thousand Oaks, Cal.: Sage.

Heppner, PP and Dixon, DN (1981) 'A Review of the Interpersonal Influence Process in Counselling.' *Personnel and Guidance Journal, 59*: 542–50.

Holmes, DE (1992) 'Race and Transference in Psychoanalysis and Psychotherapy.' *International Journal of Psycho-Analysis, 73*: 1–11.

Jones, EE (1985) 'Psychotherapy and Counseling with Black Clients', in P Pedersen (ed) *Handbook of Cross Cultural Counseling and Therapy*. New York: Praeger.

Lago, C and Thompson, J (1996) *Race, Culture and Counselling*. Buckingham: Open University Press.

Maldiney, H (1967) *Le Moi* (Course Summary). Bulletin Faculte De Lyon.

Millington, M (1980) 'Client-Centred Counseling—An Interdisciplinary Examination.' *International Journal for the Advancement of Counseling, 3*: 107–18.

Moodley, R (1998a) 'Cultural Returns to the Subject: Traditional Healing in Counselling and Therapy.' *Changes, International Journal of Psychology and Psychotherapy, 6*: 45–56.

Moodley, R (1998b) '"I Say What I Like": Frank Talk(ing) in Counselling and Psychotherapy.' *British Journal of Guidance and Counselling, 26*: 495–508.

Parker, I (1998) 'Constructing and Deconstructing Psychotherapeutic Discourse.' *The European Journal of Psychotherapy, Counselling and Health, 1*: 65–78.

Pomales, J, Claiborn, CD and Lafromboise, TD (1985) 'Effects of Black Students' Racial Identity on Perceptions of White Counselors varying in Cultural Sensitivity.' *Journal of Counseling Psychology, 33*: 58–62.

Ponterotto, JG (1988) 'Racial Consciousness Development among White Counselors' Trainees: A Stage Model.' *Journal of Multicultural Counseling and Development, 16*: 146–56.

Priest, R (1991) 'Racism and Prejudice as Negative Impacts on African-American Clients in Therapy.' *Journal of Counseling and Development, 70*: 213–15.

Sabnani, HB, Ponterotto, JG and Borodovsky, LG (1991) 'White Racial Identity Development and Cross-Cultural Counselor Training: A Stage Model.' *Counseling Psychologist, 19*: 76–102.

Sashidharan, SP (1986) 'Ideology and Politics in Transcultural Psychiatry', in JL Cox (ed) *Transcultural Psychiatry*. London: Croom Helm.

Sashidharan, SP (1990) 'Race and Psychiatry.' *Medical World, 3*: 8–12.

Solomos, J and Wrench, J (eds) (1993) *Racism and Migration in Western Europe*. Oxford: Berg.

Sue, DW and Sue, D (1990) *Counseling the Culturally Different: Theory and Practice* (2nd edn). New York: Wiley.

Tan, R (1993) 'Racism and Similarity: Paranoid-Schizoid Structures.' *British Journal of Psychotherapy, 10*: 33–43.

Thomas, A and Sillen, S (1972) *Racism and Psychiatry*. USA: Citadel.

Thompson, CE and Jenal, ST (1994) 'Interracial and Intraracial Quasi-Counselling Interactions when Counsellors avoid Discussing Race.' *Journal of Counselling Psychology, 41*: 484–91.

Vontress, CE (1971) 'Racial Differences: Impediments to Rapport.' *Journal of Counseling Psychology, 18*: 7–13.

Wade, P and Bernstein, BL (1991) 'Culture Sensitivity Training and Counselor's Race: Effects on Black Female Clients' Perceptions and Attrition.' *Journal of Counseling Psychology, 8*: 9–15.

CHAPTER 9
DOUBLE-EDGED SWORD: POWER AND PERSON-CENTRED COUNSELLING

KHATIDJA CHANTLER

This chapter explores issues of power which are frequently hidden and implicit within person-centred theory and practice. There are many sites within which power operates that are relevant to counselling, for example, race, gender, class, disability, age and sexual orientation. In relation to power, I argue that personal power (one of the key aims of therapy) is very much mediated by our structural positionings, whereas for Rogers, the conceptualisation of power in therapy appears to operate in an intensely personal space. I further argue that not only do counsellors need knowledge and self-awareness about structural locations and their 'personal' and shifting places in it, but also about the ways in which they carry their conceptualisations of power (or lack of it) into the counselling relationship, and the consequences of this for cross-cultural counselling. As the film sessions *On Anger and Hurt* and *The Right to be Desperate* are between white, male therapist/black, male client dyads, issues of race, masculinity and power assume centrality in this chapter.

Carl Rogers was one of the first people in the counselling world who referred directly to the issue of power in counselling relationships. The power dynamic that Rogers makes explicit is that the counsellor by virtue of being a counsellor holds more power than the client (Rogers, 1951). Rogers' work stresses this theme by the importance given to being transparent and real—not hiding behind a professional, 'expert' mask (Rogers, 1959; Thorne, 1992). This attempt to redress the balance between counsellor and client and to strive for equality places person-centred counselling in a strong position to examine, interrogate and integrate issues of anti-discriminatory practice. Yet the evidence, both in the films and in contemporary counselling literature (e.g., Kearney, 1996; Lago and Thompson, 1996; McLeod, 1993), would suggest that person-centred counselling (as well as other Western therapeutic approaches) has overlooked the significance of power based on difference.

In discussing the films, it is important to contextualise them to get a sense of Rogers' work more broadly, highlighting themes both from person-centred theory and Rogers' work with groups that have particular relevance to these films and to cross-cultural work more generally. In terms of wider issues, the chapter begins by exploring the silences around power, issues around sameness and difference, the advantages and disadvantages of the notion of an individual as unique and the tensions between 'reality' and subjectivity. I then move on to elaborate on how these themes are present in the films. I highlight sections of the films that illustrate occasions when Rogers missed important cues from his black client or recognised and articulated aspects of his racialised and gendered 'self', the latter being when therapeutic movement appears to take place. It is argued that if the founder of person-centred theory and practice struggles to engage with this client, then it is incumbent on all of us to acknowledge the limitations of this approach. It is also crucial to build on what appears to work therapeutically in order to learn to work more effectively with black clients. The chapter also refers to the theory of person-centred counselling. It explores how conditions of worth, self-concept, locus of evaluation, the notion of fully functioning and the core conditions are strongly linked to our 'location' in society. More specifically, it introduces the notion of racialised, classed and gendered conditions of worth and argues for the centrality of these to be recognised and addressed in Person-Centred Therapy as a key mechanism for linking the external with the internal world.

SILENCES AND POWER

Key to the lack of engagement with issues of power based on difference is the unspoken and unstated assumption that the theory and practice of person-centred counselling is universal and equally applicable to all. Structural differences based, for example, on race, gender, and class which situate and locate people differently are hardly attended to; hence, the specific experiences of marginalised groups and individuals which contribute to the development of their self-concepts (in Rogerian terms) are rendered invisible. We should note here that such notions of universality are not restricted to person-centred counselling. In practice, structural omissions are a feature of a wide range of helping agencies and contribute to services and provision that cater largely for dominant groups (Chantler et al., 2001). In turn, such silences impact on minoritised people's access to services, including counselling services.

Neither does Rogers appear to fully grasp how his own privileged position as a white, middle-class, able-bodied, heterosexual male accords him (and others who enjoy such privileges) increased opportunities to both trust in his own 'locus of evaluation' and to maximise his own potential and move towards becoming 'fully functioning'. This is well illustrated in the following quote where Rogers writes about resolving intercultural tensions:

> Community tensions, racial and otherwise, can be eased by using the person-centred approach to empower the people on both sides of the conflict (Rogers in Kirschenbaum and Henderson, 1990: 438).

This statement is bewildering, for one wonders why both sides need to be empowered, when one side already has more power in relation to the other group? Empowering an already powerful group does nothing to redress the balance of power; all it does is shift the power dynamic along, complete with inequalities. Hence, an approach which fails to recognise such inequalities and differences in power between different (racial) groups is one of the main ways in which person-centred practice continues to struggle to work with issues such as racism, sexism, class and homophobia in therapy, or indeed in the training of counsellors (e.g., Kearney, 1996; Lago and Thompson, 1996; Waterhouse, 1993). The marginalisation of racism is also plainly evident in the films *On Anger and Hurt* and *The Right to be Desperate* as explored below.

SAMENESS AND DIFFERENCE

A key arena in which power operates is around issues of sameness and difference. The ways in which we see ourselves in relation to others and work with the power differentials between us whether based on race, gender, class and other factors provide us with rich material for exploring power dynamics between therapist and client and its impact on the therapeutic relationship.

In relation to the Person-Centred Approach, what is clear from Rogers' writings on racial situations is the importance that he attached to working with the similarities between different groups of people. The acknowledgement of points of commonalities or sameness between different groups of people (or individuals) is important. Firstly, it can be facilitative in that it *potentially* helps to break down barriers, reduces distance between groups or individuals and encourages emotional closeness. Secondly, working with sameness helps to overcome the view that 'others' are strange and alien. This is especially relevant where stereotypes of marginalised groups are prevalent in society and minoritised cultures often portrayed as deficient.

However, focusing on similarity can be interpreted as assimilative (i.e., conformity to dominant culture) and therefore as reproducing colonial-paternalistic relations. Hence, working purely with issues of similarities (as Rogers tended to do) and ignoring the issues of differences, both in terms of power and the qualitatively different experiences of marginalised groups compared to dominant groups, only serves to replay, collude with and further buttress systems of oppression based on inequalities. When Rogers writes, 'One of the most striking things about international groups is that they are so similar to every other encounter group. The national, racial and cultural differences come to seem unimportant as the *person* is discovered' (Rogers in Kirschenbaum and Henderson, 1990: 445; original emphasis); this implies that the racial or cultural difference *per se* is the barrier between people rather than the power and privilege which stem from being situated differently.

DOUBLE-EDGED SWORD

Following on, it is also argued that the insistence of the Person-Centred Approach of the uniqueness of the individual is a double-edged sword. On the positive side, particularly for oppressed or marginalised groups, the experience of being treated as a unique person, rather than being thoughtlessly grouped with others on the assumption of shared characteristics or traits, is to be welcomed. On the other hand, if this uniqueness and emphasis on the individual is dislocated and decontextualised from wider social processes (Squire, 1989), at best the core conditions will only be partially present and important cues from the client risk being missed. At worst, the therapeutic encounter will only serve to perpetuate existing systems of domination such as racism and sexism. Hence contemporary understandings of the conditions of worth need to be explicitly inclusive of inequalities based on race, gender, class and other factors. This is especially important given the discomfort, the silences and the 'scapegoating' that is far too frequently part of the experience of marginalised groups (and their allies) who attempt to raise and challenge issues of discrimination and oppression either individually or collectively. Therefore, an alertness to, and engagement with both the inner and the outer world of the client and how they interact with each other (without over or under-emphasising either) would seem crucial to effective therapy.

TENSIONS BETWEEN 'REALITY' AND SUBJECTIVITY

Elaborating on the emphasis of individual subjectivity a little further foregrounds one of my key criticisms of the Person-Centred Approach. As Carl Rogers sees it:

> I, and many others, have come to a new realization. It is this: the only

> reality I can possibly know is the world as I perceive and experience it at this moment. The only reality you can possibly know is the world as you perceive and experience it at this moment. And the only certainty is that those perceived realities are different. There are as many 'real worlds' as there are people! (Rogers in Kirschenbaum and Henderson, 1990: 424).

This belief points to a solipsism which makes it difficult to make connections between individuals, social and cultural structures and their material situation. It also leaves issues of responsibility, power and inequality purely in the personal domain. Are racism, sexism, homophobia and other inequalities purely individual perceptions? The danger of such individualisation combined with the central notion of personal responsibility in person-centred theory is that, first, abuse, violence and other effects linked to racism or sexism can be ignored, marginalised and made invisible. Second, the experiences of people from marginalised groups can be presented through therapy as somehow being their responsibility, hence it would be argued that people are only 'victims' if they choose to be. As Waterhouse writes,

> I have argued that counselling 'survivors' is not enhanced by reinforcing the burden of responsibility already felt by them. I think Rogers and, indeed, many person-centred counsellors fail to grasp that in the context of unequal power relationships, some people may have more responsibility than others for a particular life event (Waterhouse, 1993: 65).

Thus, for example, the popular refrain in domestic violence situations where the question 'why doesn't she leave?' is frequently posed to women in abusive relationships is indicative of where the responsibility for the abuse (and how to end it) is placed. Thus, it is the woman (rather than the perpetrator) who is expected to leave, to relocate, to uproot herself. This persists even in the face of evidence which illustrated that women who had recently *left* a violent partner were in a high-risk group for repeat assaults (BCS, 1996). Moreover, the notion of 'choice'—whether to stay or to leave—becomes decontextualised from issues such as the lack of appropriate housing, the lack of affordable child-care, poverty, racism, barriers to the job-market as well as the paucity of other practical, material and emotional support that is essential to women leaving violent relationships (Batsleer et al., 2002).

Furthermore, the message of personal responsibility clearly does not appear to recognise the dominance of systems of racism or sexism, for, however fully functioning people from marginalised groups may be or want to be, 'glass ceilings', poverty and closed-off life opportunities frequently severely curtail this. Also, it does not fully appreciate the many methods of resistance and challenge used by people from marginalised groups and how the 'therapeutic' process may indeed be used to re-enforce cultural, racial or gender stereotypes. For instance, Asian women may be viewed as being 'too passive' and not taking enough control of their lives, and African-Caribbean men seen as being 'too aggressive' and having 'a chip on their shoulder'. The contextual nature of the expression of feelings (i.e., the same emotion expressed by different groups) is given a different meaning depending on existing patterns of subordination and domination. This also needs to be recognised in cross-cultural counselling. Many of these themes are reflected in the filmed sessions 'The Right to be Desperate' and 'On Anger and Hurt'. In this chapter, three key factors are analysed from the films:

- The client's direct references to race and Rogers' responses to these.
- The centrality of racialised and gendered conditions of worth of the client.
- The therapeutic movement in relation to race and gender.

THE CLIENT'S DIRECT REFERENCES TO 'RACE'

From the transcripts of the films, a numerical count of the client's direct utterances on issues of race compared to Rogers' direct responses to race shows a wide gap in the articulation of what is clearly a central concern for the client. Whereas the client mentions race directly 23 times, Rogers only makes four direct responses to these. An example of this is given in the following extract from Part One of *The Right to be Desperate* where, amongst other central questions, the client brings relationship issues with his wife and her father who had recently died:

> *Client (C12):* ... I gave a lot to that family you know for five I don't know seven years I guess and erm when I went back there were just some things that happened that er showed me there wasn't much of a connection there wasn't much of a connection between all of that love and whatever that I put in and then all of a sudden I became, er, you know I became just another black person, just another nigger, you know, and I think it is important to understand that my wife is Ge-, er, is white ...
>
> *Therapist (T13):* And I imagine. Perhaps I catch a little bit of your resentment that you really poured love and caring into that family and you had gotten some back from him, but after his death none of it paid off (C: right) for you in any way.
> (*The Right to be Desperate*)

Clearly, Rogers is accurate in responding to the client's resentment, thus showing partial empathy. However, this empathy would be received at a much deeper level if Rogers had also been able to shadow his response more closely to the client and refer to his blackness. By not directly articulating the client's issues of race, Rogers is making them invisible and thus ignoring and masking the hurt and anger associated with the client's experiences of racism. Although there is nothing very subtle or nuanced in the way the client expresses his racialised identity in this interaction—the client's references to race are in fact straightforward and direct—Rogers fails to respond to them. Neither is this an isolated example; indeed, omissions of this kind are prevalent throughout the sessions. For example:

> *Client (C33): ... because I didn't at that time I didn't I, I just hadn't really decided that I could live (T: Mmhm) and I wanted to, you know, but I was so desperate to, uh, I had a young wife who had two children and those children were of mixed, uh, heritage (T: Mmhm) living in a, in a (pause) isolated community what would happen to those children (T: Mmhm) you know (T: Mmhm). My phone bills went up to ... my phone bill averaged about fifteen hundred dollars a month you know because I was so worried about (T: Mmhm) the children you know (T: Mmhm).*
> *Therapist (T34): So that was a big heavy burden too.*
> *(The Right to be Desperate)*

Here it is unclear which 'heavy burden(s)' Rogers means. Certainly, the financial aspect was a heavy burden. However, underlying the financial burden was the client's clear emotional burden about his 'mixed-race' children in an isolated (white?) community. It seems that what the client is trying to communicate is that, as the only black parent, he sees himself as carrying additional responsibilities to act as a positive role model to his children—something which he indicates cannot be entrusted to the children's mother or the community in which they live. Rogers' response is ambiguous and fails to engage with the client's 'race-speak'. Although the client goes on to agree that it was a heavy burden, I am left with a sense that the two of them may be in very different places within their understandings of what the heavy burden is constituted of. These extracts are only two of the many examples that could have been elaborated on in a similar way. In addition to the argument that the empathy being offered is partial, the consistent lack of engagement with and marginalisation of the client's racialised self is potentially damaging in therapeutic encounters and clearly does not show an acceptance or unconditionality of the client as he sees himself.

RACIALISED AND GENDERED CONDITIONS OF WORTH

Conditions of worth form a central plank in person-centred theory and practice. In summary, they refer to values, beliefs and behaviours which have become internalised. Many of these may be alien to the core self but have been absorbed into the self-concept to win approval from significant others. A key feature of

Person-Centred Therapy is to facilitate an exploration of the client's conditions of worth to enable him/her to dismantle those that are no longer valid, are stifling or in some way detrimental to the client's current situation or wellbeing. Within this framework, I am advocating the specific consideration of racialised and gendered conditions of worth which are elaborated in the following excerpts and analysis of the films. For instance, this is one of the many examples where the client makes direct reference to what can usefully be described as racialised and gendered conditions of worth:

> Client (C6): ... because you know, in being a credit to your race, in being outstanding student an outstanding (T: Mmhm) scholar, an outstanding (T: Mmhm) football player whatever, eh, leaves you little room to to be ...
> Therapist (T7): You've been meeting other people's expectations of you and that it seems that what you should do now I guess you are really questioning that very much.
> (The Right to be Desperate)

Rogers' response is clearly rooted in person-centred theory. In this sense the expectations that Rogers refers to are the client's conditions of worth. However, to make this more relevant to the client, there is a need to be more specific in responding, in order that the clearly verbalised racialised content of the client's frame of reference is not lost. Rogers' response is so generic that it could be applied to almost anyone without attending to the specific significance attached to the meanings of an individual client's conditions of worth. Hence, in this instance, the weight of being 'a credit to one's race' is overlooked. There is plenty of evidence throughout the sessions that the client's racialised conditions of worth have become internalised and that his experiences based both on race, gender and their intersections have given him little room to become fully functioning. A traditional Rogerian approach, assuming that the racialised dimension is acknowledged (and this is a big assumption to make), would then invite the client to reassess his conditions of worth and to shift from an external valuing process to an internal one. However, the brutality of the experiences of racism and the everyday nature of more or less dramatic incidents make it very difficult to ignore and totally re-evaluate racialised or gendered conditions of worth, as these are being re-enforced on a regular basis in a wide range of contexts.

Within these constraints, it is argued that it is not always feasible for people from minority groups to be completely reliant on an internal locus of evaluation. First, the external world and loci of evaluation make it very clear that there are barriers on the grounds of race and gender which deny people from minoritised groups the benefits, opportunities and privileges accorded to majoritised groups. Secondly, these processes continue to re-enforce messages about the inferiority of minoritised groups. As indicated by the client, the need to outperform white counterparts is a strategy for survival and could be viewed as a positive adaptation to a racist environment. It is also recognised that such a condition of worth, although necessary, can also be destructive, as the self-concept becomes more punitive and demanding than it would otherwise be. Moreover, if the therapeutic process ignores the wider political, social and economic contexts of clients (and counsellors) in the belief that an internal locus of evaluation is one of the desired outcomes of therapy, it is merely seeking a comfortable illusion, serving to delude both client and counsellor. Here it is important to recall that the client describes the impact of racism as worse than the leukaemia from which he is in remission. As the client talks about his illness and the struggles and strategies he used to manage it, there is the consistent theme of racism. However, it appears that Rogers is more comfortable with, or more alert to, listening to issues to do with the client's leukaemia than with the issues relating to racism, despite the connections that the client continually makes between the two. Plainly, it is not being advocated that the issue of racism takes priority, and that the leukaemia and the client's other issues are ignored; rather, all the issues brought need to be heard, connected and responded to.

One of the strategies that the client used to manage his illness was to keep this a secret from his family and his explanation for this was as follows:

> *Client (C16): ... in a way I used to feel like that I put myself in that position because no one knew (T: Mmhm) what was happening inside of me, you see because I had to take care of myself and I had to be better than everybody else because I was always told that. You can uh in a majority society I had to, I had to be a hundred per, two hundred percent better than my, than my white counterpart (T: Mmhm) or my brown counterpart (T: Mmhm) or what I had to do that because that's what it took to survive (T: Mmhm).*
>
> *(The Right to be Desperate)*

The client's drive for perfection based on his racialised and gendered conditions of worth as illustrated in the quote above meant that he was unable to ask for support as a black man, for to make such a request was totally incompatible with his self-concept based on his lived experiences. As the client goes on to say later, it was not the sort of information he could entrust to anybody else. More generally, this highlights another major concern for cross-cultural counselling. How is trust to be established and built on in cross-cultural encounters given historical and current patterns of subordination and domination? It seems crucial that effective cross-cultural therapy has a space where differences based on race, gender, class, sexuality and disability can be acknowledged and negotiated. This requires a major shift by counsellors and therapists to ensure that, firstly, they do not continue to deny powerful experiences that shape not only minority clients (and therapists) but majority therapists (and clients), and, secondly, to recognise that the dynamics based on difference will be present in the therapeutic relationship, whether articulated or not. If the therapeutic endeavour is about making previously invisible or unspoken-about experiences, thoughts or feelings visible, this would strongly indicate the need to engage with the dynamics of difference as manifested in particular therapeutic relationships. As d'Ardenne and Mahtani argue: 'Furthermore the therapeutic relationship cannot be effective if power differences are not acknowledged and tackled' (1989: 81).

THE EXPRESSION OF EMOTION, 'RACE' AND GENDER

Within these film sessions, the client acknowledges how hard it is for him to express either anger or hurt. When Rogers invites the client to express his anger, the client says he cannot as it would not be 'cultured'. Given the long-established stereotype of African-Caribbean men as aggressive, it is easy to understand why this client is reluctant to express his anger. Furthermore, whereas the expression of anger by a white man may seem acceptable or not even recognised as anger, a black man expressing the same emotion is frequently interpreted differently. As the client says, '... *traditionally, you know, when blacks become angry, they're, they're not angry ... they're militant.*'

Similar but different mechanisms are also in place in relation to women where the expression of anger is not well tolerated. In both situations, whether to do with women or with black men, the dominant view of who is 'allowed' to express anger (and the meanings attached to this) suggests that the expression of emotion is strongly influenced by a person's structural location (e.g., Waterhouse, 1993). The relative ease with which Rogers is able to use 'profanity' to express anger is in stark contrast to the client's discomfort with such language in public, especially perhaps under the gaze of a white man. Hence for the client, the intersections of being both black and male have a large bearing on the expression of anger.

It is equally difficult for the client to express his hurt and vulnerability and this, I suspect, is partly to do with the client's images of masculinity and in particular black masculinity. The outward expression of desperation or vulnerability for men is problematised and can be seen to have resonance in sayings such as 'Big boys don't cry' or 'Big girl's blouse'. The subtext in these is that, firstly, you cannot be a 'proper man' if you show sadness, and that, secondly, such a 'softness' is effeminate or womanly and therefore such a man must be gay. Thirdly, the sexist and homophobic sentiments present in these sayings also serve to privilege a particularly 'macho' type of masculinity. Such binaries or polarities are clearly unhelpful in the construction of masculinities. Moreover, the construction of black masculinities is further complicated by the histories of oppression and domination through slavery and colonisation as well as the strategies used to challenge and resist such processes. At a psychological level, it could be argued that in the face of both past and current brutality, one way of keeping hold of a sense of self is to hide the hurt and anger from one's oppressor. In this way, at least the oppressor does not gain the satisfaction of seeing the pain he inflicts. So, as well as the gendered messages about masculinity, the intersection with the racialised messages urge an even tougher image for black men in which the expression of hurt, especially to do with racism, is to be kept hidden. Additionally, it is a common experience of black people and other marginalised groups that when attempts are made at demonstrating hurt, vulnerability or anger in relation to oppression and injustice, these structural inequalities as well as the feelings generated by them are frequently denied and transferred onto the marginalised person with the familiar cry that it is they who have a 'chip on their shoulder'. Within these contexts, it is extremely difficult to begin to explore emotions whose expressions are so closely linked to structural positionings. However, the following section considers the therapeutic shifts that take place within the therapy sessions with particular reference to race and gender.

THERAPEUTIC MOVEMENT, 'RACE' AND GENDER

I want to emphasise that the following discussion looks at specific, yet consistent themes about the client's world, namely issues of race and gender. In focusing on these aspects, it is not being suggested that the only therapeutic movement that occurs or that should occur is to do with the client's racialised and gendered self. However, as the analysis above demonstrates, it is because these aspects are more often ignored rather than engaged with, that particular attention is being paid to them here. The aim is to recognise the omissions and what appears to work therapeutically in cross-cultural counselling. The first example discussed is from Part One of *On Anger and Hurt* when the client is talking about his experiences of both leukaemia and racism:

> Client (C9): ... and um, and when I think about that ... [racism] when I think about all of that you know, uh, the things that we talked about ... I, I, I think that, um that's worse than the leukemia.
>
> Therapist (T11): Let me see if I understand that ... you feel as though um what the culture and people and so on have ... have done to you ... have really caused you more suffering than the leukemia. Is that what you're saying?
>
> (On Anger and Hurt)

Despite the coyness of Rogers' terminology—culture rather than racism—there is a definite articulated understanding, acceptance of and engagement with the client's racialised self and his perceptions of his experiences. Rogers' direct reference to culture and the connection to leukaemia are relevant. His response is facilitative as space is given to a part of the client that he indicates is not normally well understood by others. Rogers' response encourages the client to explore further:

> *Client (C14): and to some extent that ... that kind of leukemia, that kind of deterioration of the body is the same kind of thing that happened to my mind (T: Mmhm). And um ... (T: Mmhm) you know, it's ...*
> *Therapist (T14): ... what the culture did to you was to give you a cancer of the mind.*
> (On Anger and Hurt)

This is a very powerful response from Rogers which accurately captures the deep sense of what the client is trying to communicate, and again there is a direct and unambiguous reference to, and linkage with, what Rogers terms as culture and the leukaemia. Later on in the session, in relation to the difficulties the client is experiencing in expressing his hurt, Rogers says, 'It goes back to some of the things you mentioned. A man doesn't admit he's hurt ... a black man especially doesn't admit that he's been hurt.' This summary of what the client has been saying similarly illustrates an acceptance and high level of understanding of the client and is facilitative in the ways outlined above. Unfortunately, this moment is then quickly lost, as Rogers takes the client away from this sense and focuses on his loss of being away from his children. Identifying points where therapeutic movement appears to have taken place in relation to race and gender is important in aiding our understanding of what effective cross-cultural counselling might look like. In the examples given above, Rogers' clear and direct references to the client's racialised and gendered self is therapeutic as these responses acknowledge the impact of the outer, external world and its connections to the client's inner world in a specific rather than generalised manner. These responses are in contrast to the many other instances in the sessions (explored above) where Rogers did not respond to these aspects of the client. Hence it is being argued that attending to, and verbalising, the racialised and gendered being of clients in an understanding, accepting and affirming way is a crucial component of therapy. The frequency with which Rogers did not respond to the client in this way when the latter was clearly articulating his racialised and gendered self is of concern. These omissions also highlight the ways in which a consistent invisibility of such issues by the therapist is potentially damaging in therapy.

CONCLUSION

This chapter concludes by suggesting the necessity to further develop and expand the Rogerian concept of power in a way that can bring person-centred counselling more in line with contemporary society. There needs to be a recognition that some of the key concepts of person-centred counselling such as the notion of being fully functioning, the internal locus of evaluation, and the sufficient and necessary conditions for therapy to be effective are largely based on a white, male majority perspective. Hence, the key to integrating other perspectives is to pay greater attention to structural inequalities and how they affect all of us—therefore a shift in perception from a purely individualistic approach to one which sees people as 'situated' is crucial. It is also argued that within these films, it is when Rogers was able to respond to his 'situated' client that a therapeutic movement took place in relation to the racialised and gendered aspects of the client. It is also argued that when Rogers was unable to respond in such a manner, opportunities for exploring what were critical concerns for the client were lost. Given the premium that is placed on counsellors' personal development, it is vital that this also includes an exploration of prejudice, power and privilege that may well be operating 'out of awareness'. I believe it is possible within the person-centred framework, to include wider social and political processes, yet these have tended to be marginalised and overlooked. Central to this marginalisation has been an overemphasis on points of sameness or commonalities between people without sufficient attention being paid to the differences. This needs to change if counselling is to be relevant and sensitive to the needs of minority groups. Therefore, an open and explicit engagement that acknowledges the differences in power in therapeutic encounters, together with specific consideration of what I have come to understand as racialised and gendered conditions of worth of both counsellors and clients, would offer new and much needed possibilities of working cross-culturally within the Person-Centred Approach.

ACKNOWLEDGEMENTS

In addition to the editors, I would also like to thank Liz Bondi, Erica Burman, Sue Hawkins and Anne Kearney for their helpful comments on an earlier draft of this chapter.

REFERENCES

d'Ardenne, P and Mahtani, A (1989) *Transcultural Counselling in Action*. London:

Sage.
Batsleer, J, Burman, E, Chantler, K, McIntosh, HS, Pantling, K, Smailes, S and Warner, S (2002) *Domestic Violence and Minoritisation: Supporting Women to Independence.* Women's Studies Research Centre: Manchester Metropolitan University.
British Crime Survey (1996) London: Home Office.
Chantler, K, Burman, E, Batsleer, J and Bashir, C (2001) *Attempted Suicide and Self-harm (South Asian Women).* Women's Studies Research Centre: Manchester Metropolitan University.
Kearney, A (1996) *Counselling, Class and Politics: Undeclared Influences in Therapy.* Manchester: PCCS Books.
Kirschenbaum, H and Henderson, VL (eds) (1990) *The Carl Rogers Reader.* London: Constable.
Lago, C and Thompson, J (1996) *Race, Culture and Counselling.* Buckingham: Open University Press.
McLeod, J (1993) *An Introduction to Counselling.* Buckingham: Open University Press.
Rogers, CR (1951) *Client-Centered Therapy.* Boston: Houghton Mifflin.
Rogers, CR (1959) 'A theory of therapy, personality and interpersonal relationships, as developed in the client-centred framework', in S Koch (ed) *Psychology: A Study of Science, Formulations of the Person and the Social Context (vol. 3).* New York: McGraw-Hill, pp.184–256.
Squire, C (1989) *Significant Differences—Feminism in Psychology.* London: Routledge.
Thorne, B (1992) *Carl Rogers.* London: Sage.
Waterhouse, RL (1993) 'Wild Women Don't Have the Blues: a Feminist Critique of "Person-Centred" Counselling and Therapy.' *Feminism and Psychology,* 3(1): 55–71.

Chapter 10
THE PERSON-CENTRED CHALLENGE: CULTURAL DIFFERENCE AND THE CORE CONDITIONS

CHRISTINE CLARKE

Under the shadow of the steel works, waking to the smell of the coke ovens, I witnessed inequality every day of my childhood. Men are gods, and women are there to serve. Children are wrapped in a cloak of invisibility. Power is abused, and 'might is right'. Cars and indoor toilets contrast with shoes with holes in and potties under the bed. Later, media images of free love, free expression, acceptance, equality, and women speaking out and being listened to gave me the power to change myself, and, later as a counsellor, other people's lives. Rogers and Kierkegaard 'spoke' to me (in Rogers, 1961: 181; also see Kierkegaard, 1941). The previous ideals of empathy, unconditional positive regard, and congruence became realities and not just ideals.

Initially, as a counsellor, I valued the self-defined autonomy of the fully functioning person and introjected the importance of the individual above all else (Rogers, 1959, in Kirschenbaum and Henderson, 1990: 236–57). I did not realise that White Male American cultural values were replacing my own (Clarke, 2000a). Listening to Holdstock, I realised I was denying a huge aspect of myself and my experience (Holdstock, 1996: 399). While connectedness and context had been underlying aspects of my practice, my emphasis had been on people becoming fully functional *individuals* rather than functioning fully within their families and their communities as well. Unexamined, Rogers' view that a person's 'valuing process would lead to emerging value directions which

---

I would like to dedicate this chapter to the memory of my close friend, colleague and teacher Hamish Garrett, who first showed me a videotape of the films: *The Right to be Desperate* and *On Anger and Hurt*.

would be constant across cultures and across time' led me to become culturally unaware for some considerable time (Rogers in Kirschenbaum and Henderson, 1990: 169). Therefore, this potentially led to my unacknowledged and unexamined cultural values being unknowingly transmitted to my unsuspecting clients.

As a woman, my sense of interconnectedness and identity through my relationship with others is as important as my separate and individual identity (Clarke, 2000a, b). I am part of a Western culture that defines 'self' as 'an independent autonomous closed entity that constitutes the unit of the social system' (Holdstock, 1996: 397). However, many cultures define 'self' through interrelationships and social contexts and can be only objectively viewed, rather than phenomenologically experienced. My developing cultural awareness increasingly enables me to understand people from different cultures more effectively, although it has serious limitations.

ROGERS AND HIS CLIENT

In transcribing the videotapes, several things really struck me, such as the client's continuous use of 'for sure' and 'you know', and Rogers' use of 'Mmhm'. While in speech what they say makes sense, writing down what they are saying can read as 'gobbledygook' at times. For example, the client says,

> Client (C88): ... I think that part of it, you know, more so than, than the risking loving somebody, just because their death ... death I know is inevitable. But it's that, that other collection of things around it, or whatever, but you know, it's crazy.
> (On Anger and Hurt)

For me, people's use of language often tells me more about them than the words alone. I am more likely to pick up inferred meanings from people with a linguistic background similar to mine through local dialect and regional accent. Both the client and Rogers speak American English with, what to me are, similar accents, but both are culturally different. Although he speaks the same language as the client, Rogers may not always be aware of the implications of his own and his client's very different upbringings and different ways of life. Consequently, he may miss the significance of some of the client's experiences, and the amount of distress that the latter contributed to the client's current state of being. For example, Rogers seems to ignore the frequent references to race and culture that the client makes. He seems to want to accurately understand the client's experience, focusing on conditions of worth, and feelings, whereas, to me, the client is struggling to understand his complex cultural experiences and his resulting contradictory feelings. The client talks about being 'a credit to his race' many times (e.g., C5, C6,) at the beginning of the first session, and yet Rogers does not respond. The client then changes his focus from not feeling good about this to being in remission (e.g., C7, C8). It is not unusual for clients to jump away from painful experiencing, particularly at the start of counselling. I have found that acknowledging the context as well as the feelings enables clients to stay with the current focus, even if they are talking about, rather than experiencing, their feelings at this point.

Towards the latter part of the first session, Rogers eventually paraphrases 'credit to your race', thus allowing the client to stay with his painful experiences of 'losing himself' at seven, and the effects of living between two cultures. Rogers notices his client's response and comments on the process as being at 'the very heart of therapy' (V17). According to Van Kalmthout, the therapist's task is to help the client to contact his inner source of experiencing, and to further the client's cognitive and emotional awareness of the role of past conditioning in present difficulties (1998b: 59). This may have happened earlier if Rogers had reflected on 'a credit to your race' nearer the beginning of the session.

Although the client is introduced as having leukaemia, one of his first statements ('I was a potential credit to my race', *The Right to be Desperate*, Part 1) suggests that these sessions are not just about his illness but about larger issues regarding his social and cultural identity. To me, this is typical, as I receive referrals that define the client's problem either through medical symptoms, or as a problem to be solved, while my clients, mostly, are really looking to function more fully as people (Van Kalmthout, 1998a:17). Rogers listens very carefully to the client's statement to identify just exactly what his client is bringing to therapy. Rather than elaborating on the leukaemia and what the client has learnt since being diagnosed, Rogers responds to his client's wish to find out about himself. This focus, which is the essence of the Person-Centred Approach, really sets the stage for the rest of the sessions. As Van Kalmthout says, '[Therapy is] a way of being that provides the climate for every individual to find for him- or herself what it means to live life to the full' (*ibid.*: 16). Having such a focus is tremendously freeing for both the client and the therapist as it gives both permission to wander through the client's world and his experience, trusting that the client is struggling to find the way forward for himself. Concentrating on the leukaemia would not have allowed him to do this, as the focus would have been restricted on external factors. By clarifying what the client really wants to talk about and by demonstrating an empathic understanding of him, Rogers is also showing that he values what the client is saying and expecting from the sessions (Rogers, 1961: 33).

Many elements suggest that Rogers engages with the client's reality at a deep level. For example, Rogers speaks to the client on an equal basis, not as an expert who has made a diagnosis. He rarely talks over the client, is respectful of his silences and uses his language. Rogers (1961) emphasises the importance of unconditional positive regard, which consists of a deep, warm valuing of the client, rather than the formal surface acceptance of his reality. When Rogers says, 'If you feel like being angry, you can be angry' (T2), the implications are potentially considerable. This is a turning point in the conversation as Rogers suggests that he will accept all of his client who, in turn, can trust this acceptance. If one takes into consideration the fact that, at this time, anger expressed by a black person was not acceptable and was seen as a threat to society by many white people, Rogers' statement 'your anger is acceptable to me' demonstrates the substantial depth of his acceptance. The client perceives the depth of the truth in this statement, strengthening the depth of their relationship. This allows the client to be much more open to his experiences from this moment, enabling him to explore really painful and difficult issues as openly as he can.

The person-centred challenge

Person-centred counselling can sometimes be perceived as not particularly challenging to the client. However, empathy, acceptance and congruence can be experienced as strong challenges. For example, Rogers' statement 'cancer of the mind' (T24) is the exact phrase which describes the client's experience and which, up until now, the client has been struggling to put into words. It is as if the client had been grasping for the words that exactly fit his experience at the edge of his awareness. By naming this experience so accurately, Rogers takes it from the edge to the centre of the client's awareness. The harsh reality of this empathic reflection causes the client to reflect on and accept this painful awareness with a new clarity.

Congruence offers a different type of challenge through allowing the person to be more his/her real self, rather than the false self he may be to others. At the start of the second session, Rogers sums up the client's incongruence when he says,

Rogers (T4): ... your mind is taking the place of the system in saying now uh, 'Play it right. Do the right ... the proper thing ... '
(T5) But some other part of you is saying, 'yeah, but there's some anger there'

Rogers challenges that incongruence a short while later when he says, 'If you feel like being angry, you can be angry' (*On Anger and Hurt*).

This permission to be congruent really strikes the client, as he says, 'You really believe that?'(C25) and Rogers responds, 'Damn right' (T25). Although the client does not respond through being angry, for the first time, he stays with the feelings he is experiencing for some length of time. To me, this is a turning point in the sessions. From this point on, the client is much more in touch with his feelings, and therefore more of his 'real self' than he was previously. By experiencing his feelings, rather than talking about them, he realises that he feels a much deeper hurt below his anger (Rogers, 1951).

Unconditional positive regard can also be challenging in its own right. The client has only felt accepted under certain conditions of worth and has denied his unacceptable feelings and experiences. When Rogers starts accepting the client's denied feelings and experiences, he challenges the client to risk experiencing them more deeply and acknowledging the depth of their significance, as shown in this interchange:

> *Client (C36): Yeah. It's uh ... I guess I would be ... and I'd really admit openly that I'm hurt. I, I said that I've been, I've been hurt. (T36: Mmhm.)*
>
> *Client (C37): And I think, you know, that I, I feel I've been hurt, but really ... to show that, you know ...*
>
> *Rogers (C37): To show it and ... I guess to let yourself sort of ... experience it, that ... that. I guess would be difficult.*
>
> *Client (C38): Yeah, I, I don't know. It ... it's, it, it's as scary, I think, as the possibility of ... that I had before ... more than before, about dying, you know.(T38: Mmhm, mmhm.)*
>
> *Client (C39): And maybe, you know ... guess I was really scared because of the symptoms, you know, of, of, you know ... not being able to walk and not being able to see, and things like that, you know. And having to depend on somebody, you know. And for God's sake, you know ... having to show somebody that I'm ... that I'm hurt (T: Mmhm). And how, you know, how can I trust that to somebody, you know. Mmhm ...*
>
> *Rogers (T39): Mmhm ... seems that's a horribly big risk.*
>
> *Client (C40): Yeah, it is (small laugh). Seems to be bigger and bigger as we talk!*
>
> *Rogers (T40): Mmhm, mmhm, mmhm. 'Suppose I expose to somebody the fact that I'm deeply, deeply hurt.' That in a sense would be comparable to having to be dependent on somebody when you can't walk or something like that.*
>
> (On Anger and Hurt)

I believe that in just these two sessions, where the conditions were met to cause personality change, the client was already experiencing change and discovering who he really was. I would argue that without Rogers' core conditions, the degree of change would have been less, and the client may never have risked being open to his deep, painful experiences (Rogers in Kirschenbaum and Henderson, 1990: 219–35). A person-centred approach may not be as overtly challenging, in the same way as some other approaches, yet it can challenge a client much more deeply and effectively because of its subtlety. The following case vignette demonstrates the ways in which a person-centred approach can be used in dealing with issues of race, culture and gender in a multicultural context.

CASE STUDY: SARA

Sara has given me permission to use this case study with some personal details changed to protect her identity. She is a Muslim woman in her late twenties, born in England, of Pakistan parentage. Sara has two young children, and at the start of counselling was living with her parents and her brothers and sisters, after leaving her husband from her arranged marriage. In the first session, we assessed the potential for counselling meeting her needs, the number of sessions needed and whether we could work productively together. As Sara told me why she had requested counselling, she sat demurely, spoke quietly and an occasional quiet tear trickled down her cheek. Quite often her eyes were downcast, and we had little eye contact. She told me of her fleeing her violent and adulterous marriage and disappearing with her children. Eventually her family had found her, and she reluctantly agreed to live in their home. They constantly reminded her of the shame she brought on them, the inappropriateness of her actions, and her ungratefulness. She felt that her only solution was to leave and cut herself off from them entirely. Sara sought counselling where someone would non-judgementally listen to her, while she explored the difficulties of balancing her own needs against the demands of her families. To decide whether I should offer counselling, I asked myself if I could provide the necessary and sufficient conditions of change (*ibid.*) and provide a climate in which Sara could take the risk of experiencing her reality in her own terms. I decided this was possible provided empathy was at the centre of the counselling process.

Sara was open and spoke freely with me. In turn, I recognised her internal conflict and how distressed she was. I understood her as someone who was trying to be true to both herself and her family and did not judge her. I attempted to explore with her aspects of her conflict and be open to her own experiencing, rather than have to censure it to fit with my values and beliefs. However, like Rogers with his black client, I also wanted to be perceived as being on her side and joining in her struggle for her to achieve the best possible outcome. We were in psychological contact, even though I was distracted by the fact that she was speaking English to me, and Punjabi to her children (present with her during the therapy sessions) in the same sentence. Another issue related to language is the fact that, while Sara was fluent in English, she found it difficult to express deep feelings about herself, her experiences and her family. The ways in which words are spoken, specific phrases and hidden meanings used in Punjabi cannot always be expressed in English. Therefore, I might not have been able to hear the right 'music behind the words' and, therefore, might not have been able to realise true empathy.

Sara's situation had deteriorated since I first saw her, and she was much more distressed. Both her parents and parents-in-law were angry with her because she had not dealt with her problems in the accepted way. Her own family found difficulty in celebrating Eid properly because of the shame she had brought on them, and her mother had had to cope with a lot of outside criticism. Sara had felt the burden of being the focus of her family's humiliation but also felt angry that they were not more supportive of her. They did not believe the reasons behind her leaving and thought she was being difficult in refusing to return to her husband. Throughout the sessions, I tried to understand what life was like for Sara. I offered no judgements and responded as empathically as I could in order to enable her to tell me some of the difficulties and traumas that she had encountered. As her trust in me grew, she was increasingly open to her experiences and was able to express some of her deeply felt emotions.

Struggling with cultural limitations

I tried to identify with Sara's struggle to find a voice for herself. As women, we struggle to voice our experience in a language which is predominantly male orientated and which does not have the vocabulary which accurately describes our experience. For Sara, the issue of language was even more complex. Even though she was fluent in English, she was trying to express her distress in terms of her own culture. As her family culture barely recognises her experience (leaving her husband is culturally unacceptable), her own language did not easily give her the vocabulary to voice it. This left it trapped inside her and potentially denied expression (see Hawtin and Moore, 1998).

Although Sara found it culturally and personally unacceptable to express her anger, she still experienced it. While she transmuted her anger into her eyes, voice and fists, she was able to acknowledge it. My interconnected sense of self helped me understand her shame at letting her family down and feeling weighed down by the burden of their humiliation. My individualistic sense of my self recognised the pain and hurt Sara felt as a result of no one believing her. Through her flashing eyes, slight change of voice and tightly clenched fists, I was also able to recognise her underlying feeling of anger, which she experienced but found difficult to acknowledge or express.

However, I am aware at the same time that, where Sara's experiences were culturally different from mine, I would not necessarily recognise them or recognise the ways in which she was communicating them to me. While she struggled to give voice to the edge of her awareness, I could not help her. Like Rogers', my empathy was grounded in my own culture and I was therefore culturally impervious to what was not obvious to me. I could not begin to understand the subtleties of her family's communication and its meaning for Sara, let alone try to give voice to it on her behalf, as I would try to do for someone from my own culture.

Nevertheless, my acceptance and culturally limited understanding of Sara still enabled me to support her in allowing her experiences more into her awareness and acknowledge their phenomenological meaning, even if she could not put them into words. This meant that Sara became much clearer about the meaning of her experiencing. At the end of this session, she recognised that she wanted some acknowledgment that her family still accepted her and that she was still part of them while, at the same time, being independent from them.

Voicing the culturally unacceptable

The next time I saw Sara, she was again very distressed. Her husband was now demanding custody of the children and was prepared to take them by force if necessary. This gave me an ethical dilemma, as I would be required to break her confidentiality if the children were at risk of harm. I asked myself whether I was looking at a case of potential abduction and whether I needed to act. Expressing her panic and distress until it had subsided, Sara then discussed the situation. She recognised that her family, although antagonistic towards her, were being both supportive and protective of her and the children and would not allow the children to be taken. Having raised the confidentiality issue, I was reassured by Sara that her children were being closely guarded and that, at the first sign of danger, she would call the police. I felt that breaking her confidentiality would destroy the trust she had in me and set back the improving situation with her family.

Subsequent events meant that the children remained safe. The family now believed some of Sara's story, and thus had taken the pressure off her to return to her husband. She now began to explore reclaiming her belongings and divorce. As she was married under Islamic law, but not English Civil Law, I knew little about what this entailed, either on a personal or legal level. This meant that I asked more questions than I would normally and felt intrusive and interrogatory. I found difficulty in understanding her frame of reference and struggled to understand the concept of being married in a religious and cultural sense but not a legal one. However, when I put my issues to one side, I could hear Sara's fear, turmoil and helplessness. I found that I could be more empathic with her when I was in touch with her feelings than when I was trying to understand the complications of her divorce.

CONCLUSION

Our different cultural backgrounds meant that I sometimes struggled to understand Sara's experiences and emotions. There are differences in cultures that go beyond words and which need to be taken into account when working with culturally different clients. While I lacked the personal experience of being part of Sara's culture and was restricted in terms of translating her experience into my cultural framework, I feel that using a person-centred approach enabled me to engage with her reality. It seems that the voice of person-centred counselling, particularly when incorporating recent developments that deal with a person in relationship with his/her society as well as an autonomous individual, can offer a medium that enables both therapist and client to cross the cultural divide. My analysis of Rogers' interaction with his black client as well as my own practice have shown me that unconditional positive regard and empathy are essential aspects of counselling culturally diverse clients. It is by identifying and engaging deeply with the client's reality that the therapist can fully and effectively support his/her efforts to construct a voice for him/herself.

REFERENCES

Clarke, C (2000a) Cultural Aspects of Person-Centred Counselling. Paper/workshop presented at 'A Question of Culture? Eighth Annual International Counselling Conference' at CESCO, School of Education, University of Durham.

Clarke, C (2000b) *I Sneeze Therefore I Am: The Culture of the Yorkshire Pudding: Examining cultural aspects of person-centred counselling.* Paper at CESCO, School of Education, University of Durham, webpage.

Hawtin, S and Moore, J (1998) 'Empowerment or Collusion? The Social Context of Person-Centred Therapy', in B Thorne and E Lambers (eds) *Person-Centred Therapy: A European Perspective.* London: Sage.

Holdstock, L (1996) 'Discrepancy between the Person-Centred Theories of Self and of Therapy', in R Hutterer, G Pawlowsky et al. (eds) *Client-Centred and Experiential Psychotherapy: A Paradigm in Motion.* Frankfurt am Main: Lang

Kierkegaard, S (1941) *Sickness unto Death.* Princeton: Princeton University Press.

Kirschenbaum, H and Henderson, VL (1990) *The Carl Rogers Reader.* London: Constable.

Rogers, CR (1951) *Client-Centred Therapy.* London: Constable.

Rogers, CR (1961) *On Becoming a Person.* London: Constable.

Van Kalmthout, M (1998a) 'Person-Centred Theory as a System of Meaning', in B Thorne and E Lambers (eds) *Person-Centred Therapy: A European Perspective.* London: Sage.

Van Kalmthout, M (1998b) 'Personality Change and the Concept of Self', in B Thorne and E Lambers (eds) *Person-Centred Therapy: A European Perspective.* London: Sage.

Chapter 11
CROSS-RACIAL/CULTURAL MATCHING: THREE APPROACHES TO WORKING TRANSCULTURALLY

SHUKLA DHINGRA AND RICHARD SAXTON

Our aim in this chapter is to consider the filmed sessions *The Right to be Desperate* and *On Anger and Hurt* in order to examine issues of race and culture in person-centred therapy, particularly the question of racial and cultural matching between client and therapist.[1] Most of what has been written on the issue of racial and cultural matching focuses either on the white counsellor/black client dyad (see, for example, Carter, 1995; Lago and Thompson, 1996), or the black counsellor/ white client dyad (see, for example, Alladin, 1993; Moodley and Dhingra, 1998). While work on the relationship between Carl Rogers and his black client seems to continue this trend, we nevertheless have attempted to avoid the straightforward and polarised focusing comparison between the black/white racial and cultural dyad. Our focus is on the relationship between Carl Rogers and his client as representing some of the complexities and contradictions

---

[1] We believe that race in simple biological terms is now outdated. Contemporary definitions include social, political and psychological variables. Pinderhughes (1989, cited in Carter 1995:15), has this to say: 'Over time race has acquired a social meaning in which these biological differences [skin colour, physical features, hair, etc.], via the mechanism of stereotyping, have become markers for status assignment within the social system. The status assignment based on skin color identity has evolved into complex social structures that promote a power differential between Whites and various people-of-color ' (cited in Carter, 1995: 14). Stemming out of this, racism is then: '… the construction of social relationships on the basis of an assumed inferiority of non-Anglo-Saxon ethnic minority groups and flowing from this, their exploitation and oppression' (Dominelli, 1988, cited in d'Ardenne and Mahtani, 1989: 5). Culture, in contrast, refers to: 'the shared history, practices, beliefs and values of a racial, regional or religious group of people' (d'Ardenne and Mahtani, 1989: 4). Race is assigned, culture is learned.

inherent in the white counsellor/black client dyad.

The second question approached in this chapter is the question of choice and being able to choose a counsellor as it is critical to the process of counselling, and the expectations of positive outcomes in therapy. In contemporary Western society getting to see a white counsellor is fairly straightforward, while accessing a black counsellor appears to be more difficult. For many black clients, the option of working with another black person is at present a theoretical one in the UK. In the current context black clients do not have a real choice. Their choice is restricted by the lack of black and ethnic minority counsellors, black specific counselling organizations, and white counsellors with a level of racial/cultural awareness which will enable them to work meaningfully with black clients. Certain settings, such as the voluntary sector services, have developed services for specific racial groups. In educational and medical settings, on the other hand, the assumption is generally made that black clients will work with the counsellor they are presented with (generally a white counsellor). In such settings racial matching is not an option and may even be discouraged. However, it is our contention that black clients should be able to work with a black counsellor (in the same way that women sometimes choose to work specifically with a female counsellor) as a way of taking into account social and cultural norms and counterbalancing the unequal distribution of power (see Moodley and Dhingra, 1998).

In the filmed sessions, the communication between Rogers and his client seems to indicate the possibility that the latter may have made a conscious choice in wanting to work 'trans-culturally' with a white therapist, although the extent to which the exchange between Rogers and his client is cross-cultural is open to interpretation since the two of them clearly share many values and beliefs. One piece of history they do not share, however, is their experience of racism since they have grown up on opposite sides of the racial divide. They may both have grown up in the American culture but have done so in different racial groups and have learned different cultural patterns within this culture (see Carter, 1995; Jones, 1985; Pope-Davis and Coleman, 1997). We shall focus primarily on the cross-racial nature of the work and on the cultural consequences of belonging to different racial groups.

CLIENT'S CHOICE OF WORKING TRANS-CULTURALLY

It appears that the client has made a conscious choice to work 'trans-racially'. His numerous references to race and trans-racial communication lead us to this assumption. This can be seen in the excerpt below in which the client says:

Client (C10): ... the activities that I was involved in terms of trans-racial communication, working with groups (T: Mmhm) and helping people

> *(T: Mmhm) and uhm I would hope very similar to what, what people like yourself do (T: Mmhm) uhm, you know, always being available for everybody ...*
> *(The Right to be Desperate)*

We believe this client not only wished to work trans-racially but wanted to do so because he wished to address issues of race with a white person. It seems that, all his life, he has been desperate to be accepted and valued by people outside his own racial group, as for example his white father-in-law. His identification with Rogers together with his repeated observations that he did not want only to be 'a credit to his own race' lead us to believe that not only was he looking to work trans-racially but also to get some acceptance/support from Rogers as a white person in the same way as he had from his white father-in law. This can be seen when he says:

> *Client (C12): ... we first married you know my father-in-law we just fought tooth and nail (T: Mmhm) but then after that we loved each other (T: Mmhm) for about six long good hard years (T: Mmhm) and basically he was my only connection when he died (T: Mmhm) I found that there was no support (T: Mmhm) there was absolutely no support.*
> *(The Right to be Desperate)*

The depth of this relationship is reflected in the client's sense of loss after the death of his father-in-law, as he felt he had become 'just another black person ... just another nigger'. These utterings seem to indicate that the client made a positive choice to work cross-racially. Given the client's desire to work cross-racially and his repeated references to the importance of race, one is tempted to wonder why Rogers failed to address this issue in therapy. Rogers makes no reference to the cross-racial nature of the dyad, does not pick up on the many references made by the client to his important relationship with his white father-in-law; neither does he pick up on the client's reference to his own cross-racial work being similar to that of Rogers.

It seems as if Rogers did not realise the importance to the client of working cross-racially. Although he and the client establish a working relationship within which they are able to explore a number of themes, such as hurt, anger, and death, the impact of race and racism on the client's life is not addressed despite the many references to it by the client. It is our contention that, had Rogers responded to the client's references to race and racism, a deeper exploration and understanding of his experience would have been achieved. Although this type of situation is not uncommon in the world of counselling, there have at the same time been attempts to integrate and understand issues pertaining to race and culture in the client's experience (see Kareem and Littlewood, 1992; Moodley, 1998; Sue and Sue, 1981; Westwood and Borgen, 1988). In this respect, the ways in which counsellors have viewed the idea of racial and cultural matching is quite revealing.

THREE APPROACHES TOWARDS RACIAL AND CULTURAL MATCHING OF CLIENT AND COUNSELLOR

There are different opinions about whether racial/cultural matching is necessary or desirable. These seem to fall into three predominant views that prevail in the therapeutic world which may be stated as follows:
- Race/cultural neutrality: *race and culture do not matter, anyone can work with anyone.*
- Racial/cultural compatibility: *race and culture shape our experience, cultural mathcing is to be preferred*
- Racial/cultural sensitivity: *race and culture shape our experience, beliefs and values.*

Race/cultural neutrality

This approach which focuses on 'persons', though in our opinion still quite common in the counselling world, was prevalent in the 1960s when the aim was assimilation. It is clearly indicative of the idea that blacks are to assimilate into the white culture and hence become invisible. In this approach, counselling is viewed as a process that can be applied to all irrespective of race, colour, religion, sex and other parameters of difference (Pedersen, 1985). This universalistic approach emphasises the 'commonality shared by humans' (Pedersen, 1985; Patterson, 1995). For example, Patterson argues that concepts such as 'self-actualisation' and 'fully functioning' are universal goals in psychotherapy. Furthermore, some advocates of this approach feel that differences of race and culture may present problems in the counselling relationship and encourage therapists to 'stress attributes that are shared by all people irrespective of race, ethnicity or culture—rather than stress the distinguishing characteristics of a specific racial group' (Thompson and Jenal, 1994: 484). This approach—often described as the 'race-avoidant' approach—is based on the idea that differences of race and culture can create difficulties which are best avoided by not focusing on race and culture (Thompson and Jenal, 1994). At the very beginning of therapy in *The Right to be Desperate* and *On Anger and Hurt,* the client's race is in the open arena as a crucial element which the client frequently mentions. His statements reflect his painful acknowledgement that he only became a credit to his own race and that, despite his outstanding achievement, he could not become credit to any other race (e.g., the white race). The fact that Rogers gives no acknowledgment to the client's race within the session (nor does he make any reference to his own race or approach to cross-racial working) is striking, given that the issue of race is raised by the client within minutes of the beginning of the first session.

> *Client (C5): I was a potential credit to my race ... I used to always wonder why I couldn't be a credit to somebody else's race ... I think I (was) really conditioned uhm to be something uhm, to be some kind of a symbol or whatever.*
> (The Right to be Desperate)

Rogers opts not to elaborate on this. What he does elaborate on is the client's reference to having had less than a year to live:

> *Client (C5): ... and uhm that was a trip (T: I bet, mmhm) that was, that was a trip and uh ...*
> *Therapist (T6): It was a trip into a fairly dark place I suppose.*

The client tries for a second time and says:

> *Client (C6): ... there's a lot of hurt ... there's an awful lot of hurt and I think I'm just beginning to realize that uhm because you know, in being a credit to your race in being outstanding student an outstanding (T:Mmhm) scholar an outstanding (T:Mmhm) football player whatever, uhm leaves you little room to, to be...*
> *Therapist (T7): ... You've been meeting other people's expectations of you and that it seems that what you should do now I guess you are really questioning that very much.*
> (The Right to be Desperate)

Rogers extracts the uses of the phrase 'meeting others' expectations' which is appropriate and meets with the client's approval, but for the second time he leaves race out. The client refers to race again in his 7th, 9th and 12th statements, but again Rogers does not elaborate on this. There follows a rather long period during which the client lets it drop. In his 21st, 22nd and 23rd statements, he again refers to race, but yet again Rogers fails to pick it up. Only after 35 minutes and nine references to race, colour, being married to a white person, and his identity being shaped by others (from his own race) does Rogers make reference to race:

> *Client (C41): ... and then other people were shaping me up you know.*
> *Therapist (T42): You are a credit to your race.*
> *Client (C42): Oh yeah ...*
> (The Right to be Desperate)

In the light of the above, our contention is that Rogers' behaviour within these sessions was racially neutral insofar as he (consciously or unconsciously) used race-avoidant interventions. While there may be limited research to prove how far race-avoidance can have a disruptive effect on the counselling relationship, the denial of the reality which is personal, social and political means the negation of significant aspects of the individual in therapy. Critics of race/cultural neutrality argue that not to acknowledge race and culture is 'naive and denies the real world in which people live' and that 'the assumption that counselling techniques can be applied universally and that common therapeutic goals exist for all clients is due to the counsellor's cultural encapsulation and denial of cultural differences' (Alladin, 1993:14). This assumption of universality has been challenged as 'a viable approach to counselling members of racial and ethnic minority groups' (Pope-Davis and Coleman, 1997:140). The other two perspectives on transracial/cultural matching address these criticisms in very different ways.

Racial/cultural compatibility

This approach to race and culture takes as the starting point the idea that matching the client and the counsellor enhances understanding, trust and empathy and as such is always to be preferred. It is the result of the black civil rights movements in the late 1960s and early 1970s which grew in response to continued racism. Blacks began to encourage each other to take pride in their own culture, colour and ethnicity. Black role models were actively promoted in educational and social settings, and cultural and racial matching in therapy began to be considered beneficial (see Carter, 1995; Moodley, 1998). This approach considers racial/cultural elements to be central to therapeutic intervention and argues that efforts should be made to match the racial/cultural background of the client with that of the counsellor in order to maximise outcomes in therapy. Singh and Tudor suggest that 'racial, cultural and ethnic (and other) barriers are minimised by the "matching" of therapist to client' (Singh and Tudor, 1997: 35). As Jones argues,

> models of therapeutic intervention as currently conceived and conducted are inappropriate for the black population. Many ethnic minority psychologists have maintained that because of important cultural differences between blacks and whites, traditional methods of psychotherapy are inadequate (Jones, 1985: 173).

Some of the arguments which have been made in favour of 'racial and cultural compatibility' or 'matching' include the idea that white counsellors are likely to be perceived by black people as inherently (and often unawarely) racist. This is likely to hinder the development of a therapeutic alliance with the white counsellor. Also, the fact that Western therapy is still predominantly a eurocentric, middle class phenomenom often means that '[t]herapists from middle-class backgrounds are not equipped to deal with people from different social classes or cultures' (Singh and Tudor, 1997: 35). Given this background, racial/cultural compatibility is often seen as the solution to some of the problems that arise as a result of the white counsellor/black client dyad as '[t]he integrity of the therapeutic alliance may be strengthened by matching clients to therapists with similar demographic backgrounds' (Beutler, 1998, cited in Singh and Tudor, 1997: 35). It is often argued that empathic understanding and self-disclosure are better achieved when racially and culturally similar dyads are working together (Alladin, 1993; Jones, 1985) and that failure to empathise tends to increase the likelihood of countertransference reactions which might result in the black client being viewed as 'unmotivated for treatment' (Jones, 1985:178). In addition, there is a high risk of early or 'premature' termination of counselling if the counsellor is 'unable to empathize with the oppression that many black clients feel in a dominant white society' (Alladin, 1993: 51). Generally, black clients are likely to disclose more to a black counsellor. Atkinson, Thompson and Grant (1993) after their reviews of research concluded that if race/ethnicity is relevant to the client's problem, then a racially/ethnically similar counsellor is perceived as more expert and trustworthy. However, critics of this perspective question the assumption that black people necessarily share the same values and warn that matching based purely on race or colour can imprison both the counsellor and client in their own cultural identity, and suggest that it may lead to segregation and a strict and inflexible approach (Kareem and Littlewood, 1992).

Racial/cultural sensitivity

This approach is a development from the previous approach as it focuses on persons in a racial and cultural context. In other words, if a counsellor develops a high level of cultural and racial awareness, she/he can develop the ability to work sensitively and appropriately with those of a different race or culture (Dupont-Joshua, 1997; Pedersen, 1995). This approach developed mainly in the late 1970s and 1980s as a result of the awakening of multiculturalism. It meant a greater acceptance of cross-cultural matching in therapy. Advocates of this approach argue that while racial/cultural diversity within a dyad may be problematic or divisive, it also has the potential to be enriching if worked with awareness (Pedersen, 1985; Pomales, Claiborn and Lafromboise, 1985). This viewpoint proposes the notion of the culturally sensitive and skilled counsellor who has developed a 'tripartite set of competencies': beliefs/attitudes (with an active awareness of personal assumptions regarding human nature and behaviour change); knowledge (to actively attempt to understand the world-view of the client); and skills (to actively develop and practise culturally sensitive and relevant interventions) (see Pope-Davis and Coleman, 1997). Pope-Davis and Coleman assert that lack of these competencies can lead to 'gaps in communication' which result in 'misunderstandings, distrust and lack of support' and that consequently minority clients will 'not benefit from counselling in the same way as clients who hold similar cultural values and worldviews as the counsellor' (*ibid.*: 140). Similarly, many writers argue that a client's needs can be best understood when a universalistic approach is combined with a level of understanding and skill which includes an understanding of the person's sociopolitical conditions (Thompson and Jenal, 1994; Lago and Thompson, 1996; Carter, 1995). Counsellors can then separate the issues related to race and culture and have the skill to address them as they become pertinent to the work. This approach requires a high level of racial and cultural awareness on the part of counsellors as well as their willingness to address issues of race and culture.

CONCLUSION

The communication between Carl Rogers and his client in the 'The Right to be Desperate' and 'On Anger and Hurt' films reveals some of the limitations of the approaches based on race/cultural neutrality. It also demonstrates the importance of factors pertaining to race and culture within the therapeutic relationship. Also, it raises the question of choice and whether clients are able to select a black or a white counsellor depending on their needs. Although racial matching seems to have many positive outcomes for the client, we believe that it should neither be imposed nor denied. Instead, its significance for the black client should be recognised and steps taken to facilitate real choice. In order to do this, some practical matters need to be considered. For example, counselling training institutions need to recruit more black trainees, make race and culture central to training in order to better equip white and black trainees in terms of skills and knowledge to respond to the needs of black clients, and finally develop more appropriate resources such as more films and videos of cross-racial/cultural dyads (including some with black counsellors) and of black/black dyads. Similarly, in order to achieve race/cultural compatibility and sensitivity, it seems necessary for counselling providers to: employ more black counsellors; offer more choice with regard to racial and cultural matching as well as gender matching; provide in-house training opportunities for counsellors to develop racial/cultural sensitivity and insight into the racial and cultural dynamics in a white-dominated society; and ensure that the environment of counselling services is racially and culturally diverse. These practical and logistical considerations go hand-in-hand with the efforts counsellors need to make in order to: acknowledge the cross-racial/cultural nature of the dyad when working with a culturally different client; create space for the client to talk about this if she/he so wishes; and be willing to examine her/his own feelings about her/his own race and culture.

REFERENCES

d'Ardenne, P and Mahtani, A (1989) *Transcultural Counselling in Action*. London: Sage.
Alladin, WJ (1993) 'Ethnic Matching in Counselling: How important is it to ethnically match clients and counsellors?', in W Dryden (ed) *Questions and Answers on Counselling in Action*. London: Sage.
Atkinson, DR, Thompson, CE and Grant, SK (1993) 'A three dimensional model for counseling racial/ethnic minorities. *Counseling Psychologist, 21*(2): 257–77.
Carter, RT (1995) *The Influence of Race and Racial Identity in Psychotherapy*. New York: Wiley.
Dupont-Joshua, A (1997) 'Race, Culture and the Therapeutic Relationship: Working with differences creatively.' *Counselling, 7*(3): 282–4.
Jones, EE (1985) 'Psychotherapy and Counseling with Black Clients', in P Pedersen (ed) *Handbook of Cross-Cultural Counseling and Theory*. New York: Praeger.
Kareem, J and Littlewood, R (1992) *Intercultural Therapy—Themes, Interpretations and Practices*. Oxford: Blackwell Scientific.
Lago, C and Thompson, J (1996) *Race, Culture and Counselling*. Buckingham: Open University Press.
Moodley, R (1998) '"I say what I like": Frank Talk(ing) in Counselling and Psychotherapy.' *British Journal of Guidance and Counselling, 26*: 495–508.
Moodley, R and Dhingra, S (1998) 'Cross-Cultural/Racial Matching in Counselling and Therapy: White Clients and Black Counsellors.' *Counselling, 9*(4): 295–9.
Patterson, CH (1995) 'A universal system of psychotherapy.' *Person-Centred Journal, 2*(1): 54–62.
Pedersen, PB (1995) 'Culture-Centred Ethical Guidelines for Counsellors', in G.J. Ponterotto, M.J. Casas, L.A. Suzuki and C.M. Alexander (eds) *Handbook of Multicultural Counselling*. London: Sage.
Pedersen, PB (1985) *Handbook of Cross-Cultural Counseling and Therapy*. New York: Praeger. Pomales, J, Claiborn, CD and Lafromboise, TD (1985) 'Effects of black students' racial identity on perceptions of white counselors varying in cultural sensitivity.' *Journal of Counseling Psychology, 33*: 58–62.
Pope-Davis, D and Coleman, HLK (1997) *Multicultural Counseling Competencies—Assessment, Education and Training and Supervision*. Newbury Park, CA: Sage.
Singh, J and Tudor, K (1997) 'Cultural Conditions of Therapy.' *Person-Centred Journal, 4*: 32–46.
Sue, DW and Sue, D (1981) *Counselling the Culturally Different: Theory and Practice*. New York: Wiley.
Thompson, CE and Jenal, ST (1994) 'Interracial and Intraracial Quasi-Counseling Interaction When Counsellors Avoid Discussing Race.' *Journal of Counseling Psychology, 41*: 484–91.
Westwood, MJ and Borgen, WA (1988) 'A Culturally Embedded Model for Effective Intercultural Communication.' *International Journal for the Advancement of Counselling, 11*: 115–25.

Chapter 12
GROWING RACE AWARENESS IN THE THERAPIST (REFLECTIONS ON CARL ROGERS' VIDEOTAPED SESSION WITH DADISI[1])

COLIN LAGO AND JEAN CLARK

In this chapter, we will attempt to illustrate what we consider to be a marked change in Rogers' therapeutic style (towards greater 'race acknowledgement') from the interviews recorded several years earlier. We believe the later recording of Rogers conducting therapy with the African-American client called Dadisi offers evidence of Rogers' ongoing development in awareness and sensitivity to majority/minority ethnic group issues since the 'On Anger and Hurt' sessions. Barrett-Lennard (1998) records Rogers' interest in and work with groups in tension from the mid-1960s onward and notes his proposal for a high-level interdisciplinary task force to be formed by Government that would become involved in, amongst other areas of tension, programmes and research concerned with race relations. These intense experiences, particularly in the late 1970s and early 1980s, we contend, must have had deep effects upon his appreciation and knowledge of their impact. His explicit reference to his racialised self in the interview with Dadisi, as we will demonstrate, reveals his awareness of the impact his whiteness potentially represented to the black client. In this example, we have an indication of Rogers uniting explicitly, not only the personal and the political aspects but also involving the structural and interconnected phenomena of life.

[1.] This film is now available in video as: *Person-Centred Approach: Carl Rogers Meets With a Black Client*, 1985, a newly re-edited version made in 1999, from the Center for the Studies of the Person.

THE 'DADISI' SESSION

In November 1984, Carl Rogers and colleagues attended a special college meeting to reflect, with students and staff there, upon the impact of the person-centred training courses that had been held in that particular neighbourhood college. Both students and staff of the courses, as well as staff members of the Center for Studies of the Person, were represented on a panel of speakers. Later in the meeting, Rogers conducted a demonstration counselling interview with a young black man from the college named Dadisi.

The whole proceedings of this meeting (i.e., the panel discussion and the interview) were recorded live, on a single camera, set up within the audience. Inevitably, there are many external noises and interruptions on this recording. The resulting video (featuring the following interview), therefore, is obviously not of studio quality, but it certainly does demonstrate Rogers' own enhanced appreciation, through his statements, of his own differential 'social situatedness' to that of the client, as compared to the 1977 recordings, *The Right to be Desperate* and *On Anger and Hurt*. In the intervening years between these two examples of filmed/videotaped interviews (1977 and 1984), Rogers and his colleagues had been exposed to a wide range of cultural, interracial and political influences (see Chapter 25, this volume). Our analysis of the interview with Dadisi clearly demonstrates Rogers' increasing capacity to recognise, acknowledge and address explicitly the societal conditions of discrimination and racism that affect minority group members.

Opening up to the client

Key extracts of Rogers' dialogue with Dadisi are detailed below providing evidence for the above assertion of Rogers' own development. The initial part of the interview (which lasts approximately half an hour in total) is taken up with the client's consideration of and reflections upon his personal history of development as a therapist and clinical supervisor, gained essentially through practical and clinical experience. He had, however, been very ambivalent about gaining academic qualifications and thus his involvement with formal learning had been sporadic over the years. So, for example, the client reports, some minutes into the interview:

> 1 D/C (Dadisi/client): ... *in a sense [I] have at times overcompensated for not having the educational background to back up ... and that's what's gotten me more into things I do out in the world which, I always feel are more important than the academic requirements.*
> 2 C/T (Carl/therapist): *I'm not quite clear about that but partly because of your anger and frustration you do more things out in the world uh ...*

>   *demonstrating your competence. Is that what you're saying?*
> 3 D/C: Right ... Part of it is demonstrating my competence and part of it is doing what I would do with a degree anyway ...
> 4 C/T: ... I get the feeling that you're saying to that ... you don't really expect anything out (of) the academic aspect except just to prove that you are who you are, that you are somebody, and that you've held good positions and you are competent.
> 5 D/C: (Several statements later) ... In fact my name is Dadisi and what it means is 'inquisitive and questioning'.
> 6 C/T: Mhm, hm. So your very name is a learning name.

The client's offering of the meaning contained within his name and Rogers' consolidating response (5–6) reflects a significant cultural heritage deriving from African (Burkina Faso) sources where the names given to children have great significance in terms of their task or role in this life (Some, 1989). The theme is expanded in the continuing conversation, the client feeling the frustration between his clinical and professional competence and others' views of his academic attainment, particularly when he considers those who are educationally qualified and yet not as effective in professional circumstances:

> 7 C/T: Mhm, mhm. There is a real, a real mismatch between the amount of education you've had and what you're doing. (D/C: Right.) And the education thing is way low and what you're doing is way high.
> 8 D/C: (nods) Mhm, mhm. (Pause 60 seconds) There is another piece, but I don't feel comfortable sharing with you.
> 9 C/T: I'd appreciate it if you would. If there is a little piece that you haven't brought up. (Pause 30 seconds) I guess it's a real puzzle to know whether you dare bring it up.
> 10 D/C: You're puzzled?
> 11 C/T: Mhm?
> 12 D/C: You say you were puzzled?
> 13 C/T: No. It sounds like you're puzzled as to whether or not to bring it up ... this other piece.
> 14 D/C: Yes, I am.
> 15 C/T: Mhm, mhm.
> 16 D/C: (Pause 10 seconds) Part of it someway has to do with, not who I am but, who you are.
> 17 C/T: Mhm, hm. Mhm, hm. Mhm, hm. Part of me ... the fact that I'm white or, that I'm well known or, what?

Rogers, here, offers his whiteness as one possible explanation for Dadisi's reluctance to continue at this stage, alongside the option of him being well known as well as acknowledging it could be something else. The following paragraphs focus upon the significance of Rogers' reference to his being white, but it is also important to note that this was offered within the context of a choice ('being white or well known') as well as an openness to something else ('what?'). This response characterises Rogers' wish and therapeutic intention to ensure that he both understands accurately and deeply the client's meanings in addition to assiduously avoiding both his own assumptions and interpretations.

Returning now to the issue of Rogers' whiteness, his capacity to state this, clearly and unequivocally, even if the client indicated that this was not the case, we contend, provides a clear opportunity for the client to appreciate that this subject is safe and acceptable to discuss with Rogers, as Rogers has already opened it up. One wonders if the client's earlier indecision to proceed on this track may have continued for a good while longer, or indeed not be further mentioned, without this offering from Rogers. Thompson and Jenal in their study of 'race-avoidant' therapists with black clients, noted significant impacts upon the therapeutic discourse in relation to whether and how clients raised issues of race (and how these were responded to), client's racial identity perspectives and 'what could be termed *kinship* factors, or the client's affiliation (or lack of affiliation) with the counselors based on race' (1994: 489). Thompson and Jenal noted that where black clients were not responded to in relation to specific references they had made to race-related issues, they ceased to raise these issues in their discourse. These researchers offer two possibilities of why this might have been so:

> Given the prevalence of this type of interaction among the interracial dyads, one might speculate that these clients sought acceptance from their white counselors by eliminating racial talk, perhaps sensing that the racial content was uncomfortable for these counselors or inappropriate to counseling. An alternate explanation is that clients with initial race-related concerns ... may have acquiesced to counselors' race-avoidant posture because they believed that their concerns could be understood from this posture and therefore, were comfortable with it (*ibid.*: 489).

In contrast to the term 'race avoidance', employed by Thompson and Jenal, Rogers, in this moment of therapeutic interaction, has provided 'race acknowledgement'; i.e., he has explicitly acknowledged the structurally different 'social positioning' of himself, as a white man, compared to the client, as a black man. In the following excerpt, we can see Rogers and the client delving deeper into the question of race:

18 D/C: *The fact that you're white.*

19 C/T: *The fact that I'm white. You don't feel comfortable bringing up something that really has a lot of meaning to you, because I'm a different*

color.

20 D/C: *Mhm, hm. (nods)*

21 C/T: *Will you take a chance?*

22 D/C: *I don't know yet. (The audience laughs.) No.*

23 C/C: *I guess I'd appreciate it if you'd try me out.*

24 D/C: *It's a little hard, a little difficult for me 'cause this is a live issue for me, something that I'm dealing with now. (C/T: Mhm, hm.) It has to do with you, the fact that you're white. It has to do with, plus, how I feel about school. (C/T: Mhm, hm.) And the fact I've always felt school, being a student um ... predominantly in America (C/T: Mhm, hm) ... and dealing with white educational systems (C/T: Mhm, hm) that never taught me anything about me. (C/T: Mhm, hm.) And for instance learning history and not learning anything about black contributions to American history, (C/T: Mhm, hm) world history in fact ...*

25 C/T: *So part of the resentment against school is that you're in a white system, they haven't taught you anything about yourself or, about your background or, your race, your history. Then that makes you mad.*

The rest of the interview proceeds towards a much more explicit exploration of the client's experience of racism and how it has operated through the various institutions of society including education. It is clear from the following excerpt that Rogers is willing to verbalise the themes of race and racism in his communication with the client:

26 D/C: *Yeah. It makes me mad but, it also motivates me to go and get it (C/T: Mhm, hm) myself and not (C/T: Uh, uh) expect white people ...*

27 C/T: *If you can't get it through the white system, you'll get it yourself.*

28 D/C: *Right. (C/T: Mhm, hm.) So some of my resistance with school has also been avoidance of acceptance, avoiding accepting ... all information that is transmitted in white institutions.*

29 C/T: *Mhm, hm. Mhm, hm. Yeah that makes it ... that helps to clarify it. So, underneath some dislike for school is the fact that you're saying, I don't like to take information or education from the white system. I resent that.*

30 D/C: *Mhm, hm. A totally white system with what felt like totally white interests at heart. (C/T: Mhm, hm.) I never felt like it had my interests at heart.*

31 C/T: *Mhm, hm, mhm, hm. They were just interested in the whites'. (Client nods yes) Mhm, hm. So that's much deeper than just a dislike of school isn't it? I mean it's a real, (Client nods yes) real strong feeling about, strong feeling against a system that doesn't have your interests*

at heart. (Client nods, yes.)

32 D/C: *Exactly. (Pause 30 seconds, nods yes) And I feel that with the experience I've had in the public school, kind of been of the belief that the higher in this white educational system you went, ah ... the more assimilated.*

33 C/T: *More?*

34 D/C: *The more assimilated ... (C/T: Mhm, hm, hm.) So part of my avoidance is to being assimilated.*

35 C/T: *The higher you go, the more likelihood of being assimilated. You don't want to be assimilated. (D/C: No.) You want to be a black person.*

36 D/C: *Right. (Pause 8 seconds.) And learn and teach about what are my interests now. (C/T: Mhm, hm.) And assist and help and heal my people (C/T: Mhm, hm.) And there's very few places where that's being taught. (C/T: Mhm, hm.) Or where that interest (C/T: Mhm, hm, hm) is a priority.*

37 C/T: *It narrows down a lot of the places where you might get the kind of education you would want. (D/C: Mhm,hm.) But you want to be of service to your people, and help them, heal them and you would like to get the information for that, not a white education. (D/C nods.)*

38 D/C: *(Pause for 15 seconds) Some of those pieces have always been there, some of those pieces of information have always been there but, I think it's probably taken me ... I turned 30 yesterday, (C/T nods) probably all this time to feel set in myself and set enough in my identity that I could take that on with probably a greater strength. (C/T: Mhm, hm) and to know that I won't necessarily ... lose me.*

39 C/T: *Uh, huh, I think I'm getting that. That you feel sufficient strength in your own identity (D/C: Mhm) that perhaps you could take what you want from a system you don't like. Um ... and not lose your identity, not be assimilated. Is that ... ?*

40 D/C: *And I realize I've been doing that all my life because white people are on top, (C/T: Mhm, hm.) you know? And white institutions and white information everywhere.*

41 C/T: *Now a white counselor, um.*

42 D/C: *Now a white counselor. You know (smiles, reaches forward and touches therapist's knee) I've always chosen a black counselor.*

(Several statements later)

43 C/T: *So understanding between black and white isn't impossible. You've experienced that.*

44 D/C: *Right. No, that was never really the primary issue. That is, understanding between races but um ... race is why I felt it to be a racist system. (C/T: Yeah) Um ... which included education.*

> 45 C/T: *Mhm, hm. Mhm, hm. So, with white individuals you've been able to understand and be understood but, a racist white system, that's a different matter.*
>
> *(And, nine interchanges later …)*
>
> 46 D/C: *And as someone who is aspiring to be a therapist, one of my conflicts has become well, how do I feel if I choose not to work with white people? (C/T: Mhm, hm.) And only third world people. (C/T: Mhm, hm.) They really are my primary interest. Um … but I've also come to the belief that white people need to be healed too.*

The above statements reflect aspects of the therapist's own 'race awareness' which seem to fit into some of the theories which have been developed about white racial consciousness.

Whiteness, power and un/awareness

The references to identity by the client, in this transcript, seem no accident, historically speaking, as much developmental theoretical work was being conducted at this time in the USA on what have become known as the Racial and Ethnic Identity Development Models (see Atkinson, 1989; Cross, 1991; Helms, 1984; Helms and Piper, 1994; Phinney, 1989). These are models that attempt to describe a developmental process that human beings may proceed through in their quest to achieve a healthy sense of racial and ethnic identity. Feeling good about who we are enables us to respect and value others. Consequently the counsellors' own sense of racial identity development becomes an important if not determining component in the multicultural counselling relationship (see Lago and Thompson, 1996; Thompson and Jenal, 1994; Tuckwell, 2002). Helms' (1984) white racial consciousness model suggests five stages of development: contact, disintegration, reintegration, pseudo-independence and autonomy.

1. The contact stage is characterised by an unawareness of self as a racial being, a tendency to ignore differences; an awareness that minorities exist yet searches for resolution through withdrawal.
2. Disintegration involves becoming aware of racism that leads to guilt, depression and negative feelings. There exists a sense of being caught between internal standards of human decency and external cultural expectations. Responses to this dilemma lead to over-identification with black people, the development of paternalistic attitudes towards them or a retreat into white culture.
3. Reintegration is typified by hostility towards minorities and positive bias in favour of own racial group.

4. Stage four, the pseudo-independent stage, is marked by an increasing interest in racial group similarities and differences accompanied by an intellectual acceptance of other groups. Limited cross-racial interactions or relationships with special black people are a feature also of this stage.
5. The stage of autonomy enables an acceptance of racial differences and similarities to be dealt with appreciation and respect. This is accompanied by a perception that does not equate differences with deficiencies and an active seeking of opportunities for cross-racial interactions.

Despite the above very succinct articulation of a process of attitudinal change in white identity development, it has to be noted that many whites are simply not aware of their 'positioning' within society in relation to matters of institutional power relative to members of minority groups. In the dominant power position, there is often little awareness of the problems and experiences of others who are situated differently in society. By contrast, the sheer impact of the dominant group's attitudes and behaviour upon the sense of self and identity of members of minority groups can be devastating and overpowering.

Whiteness, itself, has only become a serious arena for study in very recent years and it has proved an immensely complex, elusive and challenging domain to penetrate. Hitherto, it had only been understood in relation to minority group issues, to the 'racial other', to the impact of racism and poverty. Kincheloe et al. (1998: x) note that 'race, as a category, is usually applied to "non-white" peoples. White people are usually not seen and named. They are centered on the human norm; "others" are raced: "we" are just people.'

They proceed to quote the critic and cultural theorist Richard Dyer from his book, *White*:

> There is no more powerful position than that of being 'just' human. The claim to power is the claim to speak for the commonality of humanity. Raced people can't do that—they can only speak for their race. But, non-raced people can, for they do not represent the interests of a race (Dyer, 1997: 2).

A key point emerging from this perspective is that of the importance, indeed necessity, for white therapists to understand themselves as racial beings, that is, in relative (power) relationships to other racial beings, not solely as human beings. Texts such as Robert Terry's (1970) *For Whites Only*, Judy Katz's (1978) *White Awareness* and the book *White Reign* edited by Kincheloe at al. (1998) have developed the notion of 'race awareness' as an awareness that understands the myriad ways in which particular minority groups in society and individuals from those groups are discriminated against on the basis of their visibility of difference from the 'majority' population. For example:

> People of color ... usually experience racism differently ... they are constantly reminded by words, deeds, and unconscious gestures that they are outgroup members because they experience themselves collectively and historically as being treated differently based on their skin color (Scheurich, 1993, cited in Kincheloe et al., 1998: 81).

Authors, such as Van Dijk (1987, 1993), point to the unceasing capacity of racism to keep re-inventing and reasserting its existence through new mechanisms within interpersonal behaviour and institutional policies and practices. The term 'institutional racism' was apparently first coined in the USA in 1967 to represent the systematic and more covert forms of racism perpetuated by dominant groups, social systems and institutions (Coker, 2001). In the UK, institutional racism was raised as an issue in the McPherson Report following the Stephen Lawrence Inquiry and attributed not only to the police but to all the key institutions of British society. Only through an understanding of what has been termed 'structural inequalities' in society and the mechanisms that support them, including how each person within the majority group perpetuates discriminatory behaviour, however unconsciously, may insight be gained into the pervasiveness of racism and its damaging consequences upon black people (see Davis and Proctor, 1989; Fried, 2000; Lago and Smith, 2003; Ponterroto and Pedersen, 1993).

Rogers' race awareness with Dadisi

In reflecting upon the earlier selected extracts from Rogers' interview with Dadisi, we can see that there is a gradual development of the client's original statements from 'overcompensation for not having a conventional educational background and more involvement with things out in the world' (1) to expressing anxiety about his capacity to trust Rogers (7–16). This impasse becomes transformed, it seems, by Rogers' offering of his 'whiteness' as a possible reason for his perceived untrustworthiness (17). The client's ambivalence continues for a little while further (19–23) before embarking more directly (24) into his experiences of a white education system that has not offered any learning about black contributions to US history. Rogers' deeply empathic responses (25, 27, 29, 31, 33, 35, 37) demonstrate great understanding and appreciation of the client's experience of a racist educational system and the impact that such experiences have on personal and professional (identity) development. It is important to recognise that Rogers' way of working with Dadisi both facilitates the client's expression of how his experience has affected him historically and how he wishes to develop beyond that particular position to re-engage with the wider world. This subsequently leads to the expression of a new position, that 'white people need to be healed' too (46).

The interview with Dadisi, discussed above, is an indicator (a) of Rogers' ongoing development as a white therapist with black clients, (b) of an evolutionary developmental outcome of the particular events, experiences and workshops he and others had been engaged in during those intervening years, and (c) of the general changes in society occurring at that time demanding open and honest engagement with the historically embedded systems of oppression, discrimination and racism. Some scholars suggest that this societal openness to issues of racial inequality changed again in the post-1980s climate in the USA where a 'race-neutralizing' climate again began to prevail (Bell, 1992; Hacker, 1992; Thompson and Jenal, 1994). We contend that this therapeutic interaction filmed in 1984 demonstrates a significant shift by Rogers in his awareness and his verbal behaviour in relation to black/white issues compared to his response behaviour in the earlier videos recorded in 1977. A specific example of this development is Rogers' use of the term 'culture'. The term 'culture', besides being one of the two or three most complicated words in the English language (Williams, 1983), was then and to some extent still is a euphemism for other concepts such as race and ethnicity. 'Culture', in some way, has become a 'nicer' word to use, masking successfully the intricacies and ravages of power differentials and racism in society (see Lago, 1997). In the 'On Anger and Hurt' sessions, might Rogers' references to 'culture', rather than 'race', have reflected this earlier (and socially acceptable and conventional, though nevertheless euphemistic) usage? Might this aspect account, at least partially, for the astonishing difference between the 'On Anger and Hurt' sessions and the Dadisi sessions regarding the number of references to race by Rogers? Our analysis reveals only four references to 'culture' or 'cultured' being made by both the client and the therapist in the 'On Anger and Hurt' sessions.

CONCLUSION

We have argued in this chapter that Rogers' approach was explicitly 'race-acknowledging' with Dadisi, as opposed to the one demonstrated in the 'On Anger and Hurt' sessions. Rogers' 'uncharacteristic directiveness' noted by Barbara Brodley (1996) suggests that perhaps the 'On Anger and Hurt' sessions were not fully representative of Rogers' approach. Perhaps, in the end, what these videos do offer are a form of metaphor or case study for the sheer challenge and complexity of racism and its myriad impacts upon people's lives, a complexity that then, at worst, besets the interracial therapeutic relationship. These person-centred demonstration interviews featuring a cross-cultural counselling dyad are an original stimulus from which to consider, compare and reflect upon the particular challenges created in such situations, allowing also for the historical, intellectual and theoretical developments that have occurred since their recording. What we know from these tapes is just how much passion, debate, multiple viewpoints and disagreements these issues generate. Such tensions, we assert and hope, will prove in the future to be healthy for the therapeutic field in its search for enhanced sensitivity, efficacy and effectiveness in interracial counselling and psychotherapy.

ACKNOWLEDGEMENT

We are most grateful to Barbara Temener Brodley in Chicago, who brought this particular video to our attention. This tape has only recently been made available (through the Center for the Studies of the Person in La Jolla). Barbara notes that the tape is also located in the Carl Rogers Archive at the Library of Congress, Washington DC (in an email to the authors dated 4 February 2002).

REFERENCES

Atkinson, DR, Morten, G and Sue, DW (1989) *Counselling American Minorities: A Cross-Cultural Perspective* (3rd edn.). Dubuque, IA: W. C. Brown.

Barrett-Lennard, GT (1998) *Carl Rogers' Helping System: Journey and Substance.* London: Sage.

Bell, DA (1992) *Faces at the Bottom of the Well: The Permanence of Racism.* New York: Basic Books.

Brodley, BT (1996) 'Uncharacteristic Directiveness: Rogers and the "Anger and Hurt" Client', in BA Farber, DC Brink and PM Raskin (eds) *The Psychotherapy of Carl Rogers.* New York: Guilford Press. (Reproduced as Chapter 4a in this volume.)

Coker, N (ed) (2001) *Racism in Medicine: An Agenda for Change.* London: Kings Fund Publishing.

Cross, WE (1991) *Shades of Black: Diversity in African-American Identity.* Philadelphia: Temple University Press.

Davis, LE and Proctor, EK (1989) *Race, Gender and Class: Guidelines for Practice with Individuals, Families and Groups.* Englewood Cliffs, N.J: Prentice Hall.

Dyer, R (1997) *White.* New York: Routledge.

Fried, J (2000) 'Student Development Education as the Practice of Liberation: A Constructivist Approach', in K Eriksen and G McAuliffe (eds) *Creating Constructivist and Devlopmental Programmes.* USA: Association for Counselor Education and Supervision.

Hacker, A (1992*) Two Nations: Black and White, Separate, Hostile, Unequal.* New York: Ballantine Books.

Helms, JE (1984) 'Towards a theoretical model of the effects of race on counselling: a

black and white model.' *The Counseling Psychologist, 12*:153–65.
Helms, JE and Piper, RE (1994) 'Implications of racial identity theory for vocational psychology.' *Journal of Vocational Behavior, 44*: 124–38.
Katz, JH (1978) *White Awareness: A Handbook for Anti-Racism Training*. Norman, OK: University of Oklahoma Press.
Kincheloe, JL, Steinberg, SR, Rodriguez, NM and Chennault, RE (1998) *White Reign: Deploying Whiteness in America*. New York: St. Martin's Press.
Lago, CO and Thompson, J (1996) *Race, Culture and Counselling*. Buckingham: Open University Press.
Lago, CO and Smith, B. (eds) (2003) *Anti-Discriminatory Counselling Practice*. London: Sage.
Lago, CO (1997) 'Race, Culture and Language: A Redefinition of Terms.' *RACE Journal, 12*, Spring, British Association for Counselling.
Phinney, JS (1989) Stages of ethnic identity in minority group adolescence. *Journal of Early Adolescence 9*: 34–49.
Ponterotto, JG and Pedersen, PB (1993) *Preventing Prejudice: A Guide for Counselors and Educators*. Newbury Park, CA: Sage.
Scheurich, JJ (1993) 'Towards a White Discourse on White Racism.' *Educational Researcher, 22*(8): 5–10.
Some, MP (1989) *The Healing Wisdom of Africa: Finding Life Purpose Through Nature, Ritual and Community*. New York: Jeremy P. Thatcher/Putnam.
Terry, R (1970) *For Whites Only*. Grand Rapids, Michigan: WB Eerdmans Publishing Co.
Thompson, CE and Jenal, ST (1994) 'Interracial and Intraracial Quasi-Counseling Interactions When Counselors Avoid Discussing Race.' *Journal of Counseling Psychology, 41*(4): 484–491.
Tuckwell, G (2002) *Racial Identity, White Counsellors and Therapists*. Buckingham: Open University.
Van Dijk, TA (1987) *Communicating Racism: Ethnic Prejudice in Thought and Talk*. Newbury Park, CA: Sage.
Van Dijk, TA (1993) *Elite Discourse and Racism*. Newbury Park, CA: Sage.
Williams, R (1983) *Keywords: A Vocabulary of Culture and Society*. London: Fontana.

Chapter 13
USING VIDEOTAPES OF THE SESSIONS TO EXAMINE WAYS OF HELPING COUNSELLORS TO WORK WITH THE PERSON-CENTRED APPROACH IN A TRANSCULTURAL SETTING

MARY CHARLETON AND MELANIE LOCKETT

In this chapter we explore ways in which videotapes of the filmed sessions *The Right to be Desperate* and *On Anger and Hurt* could be used in a counselling training context. The chapter begins by outlining some of the general principles of Person-Centred Therapy and counselling. Some of these are demonstrated by Carl Rogers in the sessions. Observations and questions are offered as indicators of important transcultural issues. Keesing defines the term 'transcultural' to refer to the process of working across 'systems of shared ideas, systems of concepts and rules and meanings that underlie and are expressed in the ways that humans live' (Keesing, 1981: 68). While race is the focus of difference in this chapter, other differences, such as health, illness and age, could be considered as part of the 'transcultural' process. Also, our discussion examines both internal and external contexts. The internal context includes the beliefs and values of both the therapist and client, and the external context is defined, not only as the immediate environment in which the therapist and client meet, but also the wider society in which they both live. The sessions explore the loss of what Rogers calls the real self. They show a therapist working with a client as he recalls his childhood and remembers how and who he was at that time. The client realises that by rejecting standards and values imposed on him as a child, he can hope to return to what he regards as his real self and that he can accept and become that self. In this chapter, we explore the ways in which a client and therapist coming from different cultures work together to find the routes to this more authentic living. We see the Person-Centred Approach as being central in this and critically examine how the model works in a transcultural setting. We also highlight power, transference, countertransference, trustworthiness, self-disclosure, and perfection and finally examine the core conditions—genuineness, empathy and unconditional positive regard—as well as key counselling skills with the aim of offering 'learners' a further opportunity to reflect on their own practice.

The sessions are looked at in the light of the three core conditions and with the aim of considering whether or not they are present for the client. In addition, the chapter is aimed at helping 'learners' who are interested in using the videotapes to find out more about the Person-Centred Approach and how it works in a transcultural setting. 'Learners', who may be trainers or students, are invited to approach the tapes in a spirit of constructive criticism, deepening their understanding and finding questions to ask about the model's effectiveness with this particular client. Much of this chapter is about Rogers as a white therapist, but we hope that counselling trainees may be able to translate some of the issues raised to their counselling relationships where they too will encounter difference and a need to examine their internal systems. Finally, we take the view that 'transcultural' counselling is a positive development in person-centred counselling in the sense that the client and therapist are able to communicate in such a way that the relationship is appropriate and useful to the client.

BEING PERSON-CENTRED

Rogers focused on the relationship between therapist and client and considered that theory and technique are less important than the quality of the human interaction between two people. He believed that clients need an experience of love in therapy; given this, they will be able to work through periods of confusion and pain before arriving at a place where they are free to develop and learn. By 'love', Rogers meant the Greek word 'agape', the desire to fulfil the beloved. It demands nothing in return and wants only fulfilment of the loved one. It does not burden or obligate the loved one. Therapists strive to be available in this way to their clients, supporting them to be in touch with the whole of their experience and engage in what Rogers calls 'the organismic valuing process'. In other words, the client finds his or her values through acting in the world and reflecting on the consequences of those actions. The therapist is encouraging the expression of an inner, more genuinely experienced self and the finding of individual meaning.

Rogers encourages the client to respect that early organismic valuing. We see him working constantly on the assumption that his client's meanings and values are what counts, and the thrust of the work is to help the client find these again and discard his substitute self. There is a clear sense that the client is right there with him, jumping ahead even, being very clear and definite. Together they explore the consequences of being estranged from the childhood self. In the videotape the young man talks about how the unique meaning he found from his early experience of reading Jung and getting up at night to see the stars was repressed. Wordsworth puts it well in *Odes on Intimations of Immortality based on early childhood:*

> Shades of the prison house begin to close
>   Upon the growing Boy,
> But he beholds the light, and whence it flows,
>   He sees it in his joy   (Gill, 1984)

Instead his energy became focused on adjusting to his environment and competing constantly for excellence within it. The client has very clear memories of this self, and, with the whole of his adult being, wants to include that self now. He knows that 'it is Okay' not to want to be a credit to his race or the recipient of anti-discrimination policies which he feels objectify and dehumanise him. Through being accepted, the client learns experientially that it is all right to be himself. He is in a state of knowing and feeling which Kierkegaard calls 'true subjectivity'.

The role of the therapist is essential in conveying to a client that at last he or she is loved. Rogers asserts that if the therapist is quite open and transparent about his or her 'complex and changing and sometimes contradictory feelings in the relationship, all would go well. If, however, he (or she) was only part of his (or her) feelings and partly facade or defence, he (or she) was sure the relationship would not be good' (Rogers, 1961: 172). In the same passage he describes the client who gains benefit from therapy as having 'this desire to be all of (her)self in each moment—all the richness and complexity, with nothing hidden from (the) self—and nothing feared in (the) self ...' (*ibid.*). Finally, he concludes that the essential ingredients of a therapeutic environment must include: genuineness, empathy and unconditional positive regard. Therefore, we draw on the tapes to find evidence of Rogers' ability to demonstrate that he is using these three core conditions. In this transcultural context, we look for signs that the therapist is able to enter into and dwell within the experience of another person.

USING THE TAPES IN TRANSCULTURAL PERSON-CENTRED TRAINING

In this section, we invite learners to reflect on the questions that follow each of the descriptions and to critically analyse and assess their practice in the light of the transcultural issues highlighted. To further assist the learner in the development of transcultural practice, we explore some examples of communication that may have limited the therapy because Rogers did not appear to include full consideration of the transcultural issues. Finally, we briefly examine the core conditions and counselling skills in the light of transcultural counselling and offer the learner additional questions for discussion.

'The Right to be Desperate'

The client moves from presentation to exploration of his internal reactions and his own mortality. Rogers allows him to be 'desperate', an essential task of the therapist in helping the client uncover his world and peel back to the feelings underneath the words. The client is accepted and validated for who he is and what he feels. The core conditions seem to be in place so that the client is able to feel more powerful in being himself.

Similarly, the client decides where to go, and the therapist follows the feelings as they occur and tries to stay with the strongest. By accepting and validating what is in the client, the therapist helps him take the locus of evaluation back into himself and discard introjections from parents, teachers and others. The client moves nearer to his seven-year-old self who was in touch with the glory of the universe. He has been freed up to explore that loss of self and to recognise that illness put him in touch with what he values in his own being.

Questions to learners: 'The Right to be Desperate'
- How would you have established a relationship in the first moments with this client?
- What are your thoughts about dealing with the issue of difference in the early stages of this relationship? How have you done it? And why might it be important?
- Can you identify the qualities and skills Rogers uses to demonstrate that he has both understood the client and is able to communicate that understanding?
- How far do you agree that Rogers created a climate for experiencing buried feelings?
- During Part One of *The Right to be Desperate*, the client is, in different ways checking out Rogers' trustworthiness. Can you identify where this is happening?
- Much of what the client says about his race and the racism he has experienced is not directly responded to by Rogers. How would you respond to what the client has said?

'On Anger and Hurt'

Rogers continues to work with the client, establishing a quality of presence. Learners may wish to consider how far Rogers is willing to explore their differences and the impact of those differences in their relationship. Despite the fact that the client wants to talk about the impact of racism on his life, he fears not being heard. He implies that he feels the straitjacket of both racism and anti-racism; both positions deny him his individuality. Learners may wish to consider the possibility that Rogers, by colluding with the client at this point, misses an opportunity to deepen their relationship. By not discussing issues of race, this white therapist may have failed to maintain the core conditions. The client comes to believe that his experiences of racism may have caused his life-threatening illness and what he describes, as a deterioration of the mind. Rogers replies, 'What the culture did to you was to give you a cancer of the mind'. On this occasion Rogers' intervention seems to show that he has more fully understood the destructive powers of racism and the powerlessness of the client to express his rage. Learners may notice that Rogers encourages the client towards accepting all parts of himself, including those defences that are protecting him from himself. Toward the end of the tape, the client is beginning to express a more flexible and congruent self, which is more in touch with his feelings.

Social context is crucial in any therapeutic relationship, and it is important that the client is understood in the context of his experience as a black man living in a white majority culture. The client believes this experience has caused his cancer. Perhaps the client's fear of being congruent should not be addressed solely as his problem of perception or his particular response to racism, but also in the context of a society, which permits oppression. Although it seems that Rogers is, on the whole, successful in enabling the client to begin to feel his feelings and rely more on his internal locus of evaluation, there are many examples where he may have missed therapeutic opportunities because he largely ignored the transcultural nature of their relationship. For example, Rogers does not deal with his and the client's 'difference' around culture, race, health, illness or power (white healthy therapist/black ill client). He does not overtly support the client's black identity or take account of the context in which the client lives. He chooses not to develop the client's beliefs about culture, society and illness and does not fully explore the issues of trust within their relationship, or the potential father/son relationship between them. It seems that Rogers pays little heed to the client's black identity. There are some exceptions to this, but often they fall short of directly addressing the racism the client has experienced. For example, the client explains to Rogers how it seemed the whole community (white) was divorcing him. Although Rogers laughs briefly with the client he does go on to say, 'And I catch an amount of bitterness there, feeling that they really make judgments without knowing that they are judging'. Although this is an attempt at acknowledging the racism this client has faced, does it really reflect the full force of the client's experience?

Questions for learners: 'On Anger and Hurt'
- If you were working with this client, what issues would you need to be aware of, whether you are a black or white therapist, about your own prejudice/racism, or other differences you may have identified?
- How might you have to adjust your habitual way of working to empathise with this seriously ill black man?
- Does the white therapist/black client relationship actually reproduce the context in which the client has felt fearful of revealing his thoughts and feelings in the past?
- If the client had been encouraged to focus his anger against the racism he has experienced, would he have got in touch with his feelings of hurt and rage more easily? Would Rogers have increased his trustworthiness if he had chosen to self-disclose and discuss his own position regarding both his internal racism and the racism of the society in which both men lived?
- Is racism, as experienced by the client, a red herring to the work that was underway or an important omission by Rogers?
- How successfully has Rogers understood the world and experience of this black client, when as a white American he is part of the problem? What does the Person-Centred Approach offer about the context in which a client lives?
- Since these tapes were made, how has the Person-Centred Approach developed to include issues of transcultural counselling?

Transcultural considerations

In *'Transcultural Counselling in Action'*, d'Ardenne and Mahtani state that:
> Western counselling, nurtures self-centredness, self-exploration, self-disclosure and self-determination; this creates an intensity and exclusivity in the relationship, which may be alien for a client from another culture. The client needs to be seen as being an integral part of a community that consists of many significant people. The counsellor does not have a relationship with the client alone (d'Ardenne and Mahtani, 1989: 75).

How, we wonder, might Rogers' client see himself, as part of the Western culture or as both part and separate from it? As Owen (1996: 188) says, 'the importance of the communication code can only be understood when the context is known'. Owen refers to the 'internal' context: 'the psyche, beliefs, experiences, attitudes, culture and ideas of causation about misfortune and suffering' which applies to both client and therapist and the 'external' context, literally where the communication takes place. Rogers and the client meet in what looks like a studio. They are there to make a training tape. The environment offers the client no clues about therapy or Rogers as a therapist. Although, in the main, it seems as if the client copes well with the cameras, this must have had implications for the power dynamic in the therapeutic relationship. Learners may like to consider how they could ensure that the space they work in and the literature they may produce could help a client from a different culture to feel included in the therapeutic relationship.

d'Ardenne and Mahtani (1989) go on to describe what makes therapy more accessible for black clients. We have included here, for consideration, the issues of power, transference and countertransference, trustworthiness, self-disclosure and have added perfection as having had a particular impact on Rogers' client. Inevitably, power is a significant dynamic in the therapeutic relationship. In a transcultural relationship its significance is magnified. During the sessions, the client feels helpless, angry and hurt because of his experience of racism. He believes it has made him ill. Has he somatised his anger? If so, then he needs to find a way to express it, or he will literally die. He has many injunctions about expressing his rage and his hurt. Some of these injunctions are cultural; 'black men don't cry', and some are received racist messages, for example the idea that black angry men are militant and a threat in a majority white culture. These internal and external oppressions disempower this client. One way in which he tries to address this feeling in his relationship with Rogers is to liken himself to Rogers; they both care for people after all. The client says,

> Client (C10): ... but I think the activities that I was involved in terms of transracial communication working with groups (T: Mmhm) and helping people (T: Mmhm) and uhm I would hope very similar to what, what people like yourself do (T: Mmhm) uhm, you know, always being available for everybody (T: Mmhm) all the time (T: Mmhm, mmhm) and uh I that's, that's being a martyr or (T: Yeah, yeah) something you know.
> (The Right to be Desperate)

Is he suggesting that they are both wounded healers and therefore equals?

The second aspect that facilitates therapy for black clients—transference—is not emphasised in Person-Centred Therapy. However, transference attitudes do exist in the client and can be accepted and worked with in the light of the three core conditions. In general, the therapist will absorb the client's projections until the latter is ready to assimilate and integrate them, himself. It then becomes possible for clients to move towards incorporating more of themselves, including those aspects which frighten them. Therefore, therapists need to be aware of and accept black clients' angry feelings about white people as these may be transferred onto them. By working with the client's anger in a non-defensive manner, therapists will enable clients to move through their helplessness and empower themselves. Learners may like to identify interventions that successfully show Rogers' sanctioning of the client's anger and others where he appears more ambivalent.

It seems therefore that the onus is on white therapists to examine their own cultural and racial prejudices because, for many black clients, a white counsellor will be seen as belonging to a white racist society. In a sense, white counsellors are both part of the problem and part of the solution. Black clients have little or no choice about this paradox and have to work within it. In the tapes, we do not see Rogers sharing any of his internal process regarding his own racism, although he believed that clients should be empathically understood. In *A Way of Being* Rogers writes,

> When functioning best, the therapist is so much inside the private world of the other that he or she can clarify not only the meanings of which the client is aware but even those just below the level of awareness. This kind of sensitive active listening is exceedingly rare in our lives. We think we listen but very rarely do we listen with real understanding, true empathy. Yet listening of this very special kind is one of the most potent forces for change I know (Rogers, 1980: 116).

Learners may also like to consider what countertransference issues might arise, even though again these are not emphasised in person-centred counselling. When client and therapist are from different cultural backgrounds, countertransference may invade in a particularly insidious way. If a white counsellor is not in touch with her own prejudice and racism, there is a strong possibility that this unacknowledged prejudice is reflected back, unconsciously, to the client. As d'Ardenne and Mahtani point out,

> When this occurs the client may no longer experience unconditional positive regard, genuineness, and empathic understanding and is likely to withdraw. This is exacerbated if the counsellor sees the client's withdrawal purely as non-compliance or defensive. The beliefs of both about each other's culture are re-enforced (d'Ardenne and Mahani, 1989: 81).

In the end of the second part of *On Anger and Hurt*, one wonders whether Rogers is impatient to end as he seems deeply uncomfortable. When describing the client's material as 'fascinating', his response seems far from adequate, and he seems quite distant from his client. Rogers shows no sign of acknowledging the inevitable tendency of a white male to discriminate in all sorts of subtle ways against someone from a minority group.

Transculturally, self-disclosure by the counsellor can increase feelings of acceptance and levels of safety in the relationship. Nelson-Jones (1997: 173–5) summarises some advantages and disadvantages of self-disclosure. The advantages might be that the counsellor appears more human and more accessible to the client, and some of the disadvantages might be that the client feels overwhelmed and burdened by the counsellor. The work will be more effective if the white therapist shows in some way that he/she has examined his/her racism. A black client may measure whether or not the white counsellor is truly a 'companion', whether he/she senses that the white counsellor is prepared to fully enter the relationship, demonstrate empathy, show he/she is accepting of the client's culturally different experience, understand the client's needs, appreciate the client's background and cultural wisdom and show that he/she has some knowledge of what it means to be a black person in a majority white society. This may be done explicitly but, more often, will be through subtle communication.

In a transcultural relationship, therapists recognise their clients' daily battles with prejudice and may demonstrate their credibility by revealing similar personal experiences to their clients. This does not happen in these tapes and yet something may have been gained if Rogers had occasionally offered something of his own process and experience. He could have talked about how alienated he felt in some of the institutes of higher learning when his ideas were prejudged and misunderstood. Although a very different experience from racial prejudice, we know from his writings that he felt lonely, misunderstood and found it hard to break through institutional barriers to find a hearing for his beliefs and for himself.

Trustworthiness is linked to self-disclosure and is one effective means of achieving trust in the eyes of their clients (Sue and Sue, 1981). Mearns and Thorne (1998) describe trustworthiness as an ongoing process, which deepens as two parties increase their knowledge of each other. A therapist's trustworthiness enables clients to take risks and makes the relationship more profound. d'Ardenne and Mahtani (1989) remind us that clients from different cultures can find the world an untrustworthy place; therefore, their therapists are required to work hard to attain trustworthiness. An example of a missed opportunity for client and therapist to deepen the trust between them occurs when Rogers says, 'And so you are wondering "Yeah but can I trust him?"' and later 'Have I trusted him too much?' It is in character for this client to take responsibility and he replies, 'Well, I guess I'm just going to have to deal with that in terms of I'm just going have to, to trust myself to tell you'. Would the client have relaxed more if the issues of racial and cultural difference had been highlighted? An example of where the issue of trust is explicitly raised by the client is when he expresses the hurt he experienced after being rejected by his 'white' family. In the tapes, he speaks little of his birth family and this is not followed up or questioned in any way by Rogers:

Client (C81): ... they [the white family] wouldn't understand that, they

> *wouldn't understand how a black person could be hurt, you know, because if you don't accept a person as human, how can you, how can you think about you know like ... it's like thinking a dog could be hurt or whatever, you know people that don't have dogs and don't understand them you know?*
>
> (On Anger and Hurt)

Does Rogers really understand? His response seems to take the client away from his rising anger and hurt. Interestingly the client follows this by saying that he could not raise this with his 'family' because he wouldn't trust them to hear it and respond with care towards him. Is he also letting Rogers know that he does not trust him either? Rogers' next intervention seems to insist that the client should trust him:

> *Therapist (T83): So there are probably loads of people you wouldn't dare to open up to on that but I guess you're opening up to me to say 'Yes but I have been really wounded, badly, by a lot of people.'*
>
> *Client (C84): ... I maybe think you can understand that a little bit in terms of about hurt and that, you know, that... you know, that I, you know, that I'm a person ...*
>
> (On Anger and Hurt)

Perhaps he wants to trust Rogers and is asking for a sign that this could be possible. We have included perfection here as a transcultural issue particularly because the client on these tapes speaks movingly of his need to do everything two hundred percent perfect to be the 'littlest super star'. His path has had to be upward towards greater worldly achievement. His illness and his own insight into the imprisoning experience of being a black man in a predominantly white materialistic society gave him the opportunity to move off the conveyor belt and enabled him to experience life in its ebb and flow. He could abandon the struggle for perfection and the terror of failure, and his own life could be accepted 'as a process in which failure, rest, being, are just as important as success, activity, and doing' (Chaplin, 1988: 49). He started to honour other aspects of his being over his unrelenting pursuit of success and he followed values that were intrinsic to him.

There may be something to learn from F. Taylor-Muhammad's article, 'Follow Fashion Monkey Never Drink Good Soup: Black counsellors and the road to inclusion' (2001) about working with black clients as a white therapist. Although the article addresses the impact of eurocentric-style training of black and white therapists, it also offers some important insights into working with black clients' cultural wisdom. In her article, the author advocates some 'black' only training so that black counsellors can truly feel included and can explore the theorists of Africa and Asia. She highlights the success of including in the training 'African cosmologists and approaches to healing, the reality and relevance of ideas of race and internalised oppression as well as understanding the role of the "spirit" and "love" in counselling relationships'(Taylor-Muhammad, 2001: 10–12). None of this client's background, wisdom, beliefs or culture is explored. Is he only invited to express himself in 'white' ways? Indeed, he says that he has been brought up to fit in and negate part of his background and heritage.

A CLOSER EXAMINATION OF THE CORE CONDITIONS IN THE LIGHT OF TRANSCULTURAL PERSON-CENTRED COUNSELLING

The three conditions are briefly defined in this section. We identify an example of each of the core conditions to demonstrate times when an intervention by Rogers works well, and another example showing a time when Rogers may miss an opportunity to deepen the relationship by not using transcultural awareness.

Genuineness

This is sometimes referred to as congruence. The therapist has access to and uses his/her internal process, feelings, attitudes and moods. He/she strives not to be defensive and is transparent. This may be achieved silently with the therapist's inner qualities being revealed in his/her eyes, face and posture. The therapist may also tell the client how he/she is feeling in order to help him/her to be fully present with the client. The latter, when presented with the therapist's warmth and respect, feels trust and experiences willingness to self-reveal. In the tapes we see an example of congruence when the client is talking about how angry he feels. Rogers' intervention, which is slightly misunderstood by the client, is, 'I get what you're saying, and I also feel quite strongly that I want to say "It's okay with me if you're angry here"', in *On Anger and Hurt*. Conversely, in *The Right to be Desperate*, the issue of trust is being tested out by the client, and an opportunity to deepen their relationship may have been missed. As Rogers' voiceover explains, trust is often an issue for clients; is it safe for this black client to share a more vulnerable part of himself with his white therapist? When Rogers wonders if the client trusts him, the response is '… I'm going to have to trust myself to tell you … And even just sitting here talking with you, you know, whether you are Carl Rogers or Jesus Christ or whatever you know like'. Rogers' intervention seems to miss an opportunity for him to challenge the client on his view that Rogers is up there with Jesus Christ and reminds him of a former school teacher who held the client close to her bosom and told him that he was a credit to his race. The client says that, 'burned me up'. Rogers could have shared something of his own process at this point. What was it like for him to be put up there with Jesus Christ and likened to the teacher who helped to sabotage the process of the client becoming himself? The client had to live with the pressure of being a credit to his race, rather than be the individual he is. What did it mean to Rogers to be a white therapist, listening to the effect of white oppression on his client?

Empathy

An empathic therapist makes an effort to share the client's point of view, to experience the world as he/she does. He/she wants to be in contact with the emotional as well as cognitive experience of the client. The therapist then communicates that experience of the client to the client, giving the client back to himself. An example of empathetic understanding in the tapes is when Rogers, hearing the client say that he believes he went into remission when he decided to live, says, 'Mmhm ... that, perhaps, sounds as though you are saying several things here, that perhaps, uh, deciding you wanted to live, made a real difference, and also deciding that what you're experiencing is your needs and your wants and so on really had some validity'. In *The Right to be Desperate* the client is describing to Rogers the pressure of having to be 'two hundred percent better' than his white counterpart. Rogers replies to this painful admission of feelings of inadequacy, by saying, 'And, and in striving for that one reason you really weren't heard was that you didn't dare express the person you were, the sick person you were at that time'. Here Rogers seems to miss an important additional opportunity to empathise with the client who is reaching out to him. Although his response seems to have the effect of only confirming the client's inadequate sick and frightened self, it successfully leads to the client uncovering his desperate self. If Rogers had acknowledged the reality of being black in a white majority society and acknowledged the implications for their relationship, would he have increased the trust and deepened the work at this point?

Unconditional positive regard

Finally, it is the therapist, as a person, who is the healing agent, and it is the goal of the therapist to make it safe for the client to explore his deepest nature with praise and approval for who she/he is (unconditional positive regard). Thus the client will begin to own the whole of her/himself and not disown parts she/he has judged as being full of negativity. In the tapes, the client is once again recalling his seven-year-old looking out at the stars. Rogers' next intervention offers the client total acceptance. He says, 'At seven you were really part of the universe and you knew it'. In *The Right to be Desperate* Part Two, Rogers accepts the client's experience as a seven-year-old and therefore what has been lost to the client as an adult.

At the end of the second session of *The Right to be Desperate*, the client is angry and says, 'I would like to go back and kick some butts I think'. There is a three-second pause in the conversation and then the client introjects his anger, 'Well enough of the militancy'(pause three seconds). Rogers swiftly brings the session to a close, 'Okay, however, shall we call it quits for today?' Rogers missed an opportunity to support the client at this important moment for being angry or to demonstrate his acceptance of the client's anger. One is left speculating about what was happening for Rogers at this point and about his feelings about angry black men. Can he accept the client's experience of racism and work with the tension of being, as a white therapist, part of the problem, as well as part of the solution for this black client? It is interesting that at the beginning of the next session the client returns to the issue of anger and Rogers says, 'I've thought a lot about what you had to say about that then,' but does not self-disclose. The closest he gets at this point, some minutes into the session, is to offer a non-defensive reflection of the client's meaning, 'what the culture did to you was to give you a cancer of the mind'.

COUNSELLING SKILLS

At the heart of person-centred counselling is the therapist, aware, respectful, genuine, interested and accepting. A number of essential qualities and counselling skills, both verbal and non-verbal, enable the relationship to be therapeutic. In the tapes, these skills are seen in action and some examples are given here.

- Non-verbal communication, particularly eye contact and whole body contact.
- Reflective skills ('Yeah the way you describe sounds like a lot of err real hatred for yourself, for your body doing such things to you').
- The use of 'I' to directly reflect the client's voice ('I've been wounded').
- Thinking and feeling interventions ('And just for a moment there I thought you really were experiencing that too, really feeling that stick shoved up your arse').
- Occasional interpretations (You could practically disappear if you let me know how hurt and beaten and awful and …').
- Acceptance ('What the culture did to you is give you cancer of the mind').
- The use of the client's images ('It seems to me more like a spiral').
- Paraphrase ('If I have caught your meaning you have never felt so much being beaten as you do right now').
- Projection. For example, the client describes a 'wino' he has seen and uses

this example to describe his own feelings of desperation. Rogers reflects back the projection to convey to the client his empathic understanding of the client's feelings of desperation ('It seems to me that you, err, you feel, know what it is like to be in desperation and you know what it could drive you to and so maybe that's what has happened to some of them. Something like that').
- The use of the notion of being a companion to the client. Rogers' voiceover in the tapes describes his relationship with this client as a companionship ('I like the way I am being a companion to him trying to discover just how the prospect of death seems to him').

Learners may like to critically comment on the examples above and find other interventions that serve to demonstrate some of the skills of person-centred counselling. Furthermore, they may use the questions below to help to focus discussion and thinking about what changes, challenges and new ways of working are needed to develop their practice.

Questions for learners
1. Can you distinguish between an empathic response and a full use of empathy by Rogers?
2. Pick out at least one response where the client's awareness of his feelings is increased?
3. Give an example of a depth reflection.
4. Find three metaphors and discuss their effect.
5. Can you identify any occasions when Rogers' empathic sensitivity appears blunted?
6. What effect does Rogers' unconditional positive regard have on the client?
7. Do we see any attempts by Rogers to try to get to the personal meanings of the client?
8. Imagine Rogers taking this client to supervision. How might the session go?
9. Do you think Rogers imposes his own values?
10. Do you think Rogers is self-accepting?
11. Does Rogers appear to trust the client?
12. What do you think of the client's readiness for counselling?
13. Would you say Rogers freed the client's ability to self-heal?
14. What issues would you be taking to supervision?

Finally learners are invited to go back over their responses to the questions above and see how a transcultural approach would alter, amend or add to their answers.

CONCLUSION

We have seen Rogers' work with a client who can look back and remember himself as a child possessed of his own organismic valuing process. The client's experiences as an upwardly mobile black man took him so far away from this process and alienated him from his inner or real self. How successful Rogers was in helping the client become his whole self in a white society can only be estimated or guessed at by two white authors. The client was grateful to his illness for taking him back to himself, and Rogers by honouring this process supported him further by recognising difficult feelings and at times encouraging the expression of those. We set out to demonstrate ways in which the videotapes can be used to become familiar with the effectiveness of Rogers' approach while raising the question of what else is needed. We ask whether or not Rogers is aware of the effect of cultural difference on a therapeutic relationship and suggest that the learner might reflect on what they might do instead or as well. One view is that a more direct method could be used to attempt to address as well as redress racial prejudice. Can ways be found to help white therapist and black client deal with their experience of living in a predominantly white racist society and reach a more complete and more empathic level of understanding?

REFERENCES

d'Ardenne, P and Mahtani, A (1989) *Transcultural Counselling in Action*. London: Sage.
Chaplin, J (1988) *Feminist Counselling in Action*. London: Sage.
Gill, S (ed) (1984) 'Ode to the Intimations of Immortality', in *William Wordsworth 'The Major Works'* pp. 297–302. Oxford: World Classics.
Keesing, RM (1981) *Cultural Anthropology: A Contemporary Perspective*. New York: Holt, Rinehart & Winston.
Nelson-Jones, R (1997) *Practical Counselling and Helping Skills: Text and Exercises for the Lifeskills Counselling Model* (4th edn.). London: Cassell.
Mearns, D and Thorne, B (1998) *Person-Centred Counselling in Action*. London: Sage.
Owen, IR (1996) 'The Person-Centred Approach in a Cultural Context', in S Palmer, S Dainow and P Milner (eds) *The BAC Counselling Reader*. London: Sage.
Rogers, CR (1961) *On Becoming a Person*. Boston: Houghton Mifflin.
Rogers, CR (1980) *A Way of Being*. Boston: Houghton Mifflin.
Sue, DW and Sue, D (1981) *Counseling the Culturally Different: Theory and Practice*. New York: Wiley.
Taylor-Muhammad, F (2001) 'Follow Fashion Monkey Never Drink Good Soup: Black counsellors and the road to inclusion.' *Counselling*, 12(6): 10–12.

Chapter 14
THE 'ON ANGER AND HURT' SESSIONS: A NARRATIVE SOCIAL CONSTRUCTIONIST PERSPECTIVE

JOHN McLEOD

The films *The Right to be Desperate* and *On Anger and Hurt* were made in 1977, a time of a great deal of racial tension in the USA, where the films were shot. Both the client and Rogers lived in California, which was a centre for not only racial conflict, but also intergenerational and political conflict that had arisen from resistance to the Vietnam War. During the film, we learn that the client is a person who has had direct personal experience of racism and oppression. The therapist, Carl Rogers, represented, at that time, for many people, an image of an intelligent and good white man. There are some clues in these sessions that the client perhaps viewed him in this light, at least to some extent. Carl Rogers was probably old enough to be his grandfather. The client presents himself as an intelligent, educated and ambitious person. There is no information conveyed in what will be referred to here as the 'On Anger and Hurt' sessions about the immediate context in which these therapy sessions took place. It is impossible to tell whether the two protagonists were in a studio, accompanied only by a film crew, or if there was also an audience present. As the sessions unfold, we observe Carl Rogers actively engaging with the inner feeling state of the client.

As a viewer of the film, there were many occasions when I was unsure about the meaning or significance of what I was seeing and hearing. I am Scottish, and although I have spent my life in regular contact with American culture through watching television programmes and movies, there were many moments when both Carl Rogers and the client appear to use forms of language for which I possess no more than an approximate understanding. For instance, there are several times when Rogers summarises key themes in what the client has said, and the client responds by pausing, and then stating 'for sure' in a deliberate and considered kind of way. What could this signify? I found myself returning to this phrase again and again. I imagined that, possibly, this could be a somewhat deferential means of signalling a qualified agreement: 'what you have said is correct, or interesting, but it does not really get to the heart of what the real issue is for me'.

Although the client certainly talked in these sessions about what appeared to be some of the central concerns in his life, my sense was that he had not shifted, to any significant extent, in relation to these issues by the end. I was uncomfortable at several points during the films, from a sense that there was more going on behind the scenes, things unsaid by both participants. The conversation did not appear to flow smoothly. My discomfort, as an audience to, or consumer of, this performance, was heightened by the extent to which the voice of Carl Rogers was privileged. The client is not given a name; he is 'the client'. Carl Rogers, on the other hand, has a big name. Also, edited into the films are a series of voiceovers, where Rogers comments on his understanding of what has been happening in the preceding interactions. Most of the voiceovers seem, to me, to express a detached position in relation to the client. For example:

> Voiceover 1. *Clearly he has rehearsed this first portion and yet the material is of interest. Whether it is superficial or deep I want to understand the exact meaning his experience has for him. Whether it's true or false, real or imaginary, this kind of presenting material is very common in first sessions and is to be expected and respected.*
>
> Voiceover 2. *I like the way I'm being a companion to him trying to discover just how the prospect of death seems to him. I find that important because a client needs most to be understood in the darkest portions of his experience.*
>
> (*The Right to be Desperate*)

In these statements Rogers adopts a privileged stance. How does he know that the client's opening statement has been rehearsed? How does he know that this person (rather than clients in general) 'needs most to be understood in the darkest portions of his experience'?

A recurrent theme in my personal or subjective response to these films was that of *not knowing*. I have worked often enough with recordings of therapy sessions to know that what is captured on tape does not necessarily capture the felt quality of the encounter between the therapist and client. I have found that there are several ways in which a therapy session captured on tape may be open to misinterpretation. Sometimes, it is difficult to understand the meaning of what has been recorded in the absence of knowledge about what has led up to the session. For example, the contract or agreement between participants can influence their approach. In the 'On Anger and Hurt' sessions, how much control, or confidence did the client have in what would happen to the tape?

Did this make him cautious about disclosing personal details? Recordings may fail to represent fully shared feelings: there can be a subtle emotional contact between client and therapist that just does not come through on a recording. Also, there can be important covert processes or 'things unsaid' that result in puzzling 'gaps' in the recorded discourse. If therapist and client are interviewed following the session, they may be able to provide explanations, in terms of their internal dialogue, of what appear to be incomprehensible topic shifts or silences occurring in the external dialogue. Knowledge of context, feeling states and covert processes supply a perspective from which the words and actions captured on film can be interpreted with confidence. The film record of the 'On Anger and Hurt' sessions represents a version of what happened—a version that in many respects is incomplete.

It is with these reservations, and from this position of uncertainty, that I would like to offer a narrative social constructionist reading of the 'On Anger and Hurt' sessions. My aim in offering this reading is to contribute to the on-going dialogue around the nature and operation of person-centred counselling and psychotherapy.

A NARRATIVE SOCIAL CONSTRUCTIONIST APPROACH: KEY IDEAS

Social constructionism is a philosophical framework that became increasingly influential in the social sciences during the latter half of the twentieth century. Currently, the most prominent social constructionist writer is the American psychologist and philosopher Kenneth Gergen (1994, 1999). Perhaps the most distinctive characteristic of a social constructionist approach is its tendency to question the capacity of individual persons for autonomous action. Instead, human identity and action are viewed as historically and culturally constructed: we are shaped and defined by the social world into which we are born. From this perspective, the role of language is of crucial importance. Social realities are constructed and maintained through the collective use of language. The words we use have effects: they bring experience into being, draw attention to certain features of that experience and hide other aspects. Language also serves as a vehicle for the formation of relations of power and control in relationships between people. A social constructionist analysis of therapy, therefore, pays special attention to the way that language is used in the therapy relationship—how some words come to be used, while other words and voices are silenced.

The concept of narrative represents a useful addition to social constructionist theory, in relation to making sense of therapy. Narrative can be viewed as a particular use of language. Narratives and stories are linguistic structures that communicate human interaction over time, in a manner that places action within a moral context. The idea of narrative also possesses a large degree of flexibility and adaptability (McLeod, 1997; Meier, 2002). For example, on a 'macro' scale, it is possible to think about life-narratives (the story of a person's life) or 'dominant narratives' (the typical story of 'being a man' or 'being black' that exists within a culture). At a 'micro' level, it is possible to locate specific stories that convey how a person thinks, acts, feels and relates in particular situations.

Much of my own writing and thinking has been concerned with exploring the implications for therapy of a narrative social constructionist perspective (McLeod, 1999a, b; McLeod and Balamoutsou, 2000; McLeod and Lynch, 2000). This endeavour has involved developing a set of techniques for displaying and analysing narrative processes in therapy cases, using transcript material (McLeod and Balamoutsou, 2001). Some of these techniques have informed the analysis of the 'On Anger and Hurt' case which follows.

The invitation to enter the world of the client

One of the main tasks for clients at the beginning of therapy is to allow the therapist to enter their personal world, in order to enable collaborative exploration of any areas of tension or difficulty that might exist (McLeod and Balamoutsou, 2000; Willi, 1999). Clearly, the 'world' of a person covers a potentially vast amount of information and autobiographical memories that could be relevant to the work of therapy. This mass of information is conveyed as a narrative—the client's 'story'. It is possible to identify three different modes of storytelling, each of which has its own significance in terms of the therapeutic relationship (McLeod, 1997). *Habitual narratives* are broad-brush accounts of 'what used to happen' and are employed to provide a general account of themes within a life. An example of a habitual narrative in the 'On Anger and Hurt' case occurred when the client described his response to learning that he was ill:

> Client (C11): ... *I worked so hard and so long uh that uh ... it was, it was just really, really difficult for me to get used to you know being sick, not working, uhm, and not being in control.*
> (The Right to be Desperate)

This statement introduces the general theme of 'not being in control'. Another type of narrative is the *chronicle*—a list of key events that are organised in terms of temporal sequences. For example, early in the first session the client described a series of events and times:

> Client (C8): ... *I went back this year in March ... and I had four weeks or less to live at that time, I was told on March 15th ... I got worse and I got worse and ... I proceeded to develop a plan to move my family*

out here ... and we moved out in approximately November.
(The Right to be Desperate)

By locating these events in time, the client here makes it possible for the therapist to begin to organise the information that has been received into some kind of order.

The production of habitual narrative and chronicles are essential aspects of the task of allowing the therapist to learn about the world of the client. However, these forms of storytelling contain relatively little concrete detail about actual events and experiences. As a result, the therapist is provided with a somewhat distanced and generalised account of the client's experience. It is only when the client tells *vivid personal stories* that the therapist can begin to understand the client as an active agent, a person who creates his or her own personal world. Personal stories have a beginning, middle and an end, are set in a specific time and place, and refer to concrete events. Such stories are rich sources of information on the ways in which a person relates to others, and on his or her intentions and desires, ways of feeling, and moral values (McLeod, 1997). A personal story can be viewed as an invitation to the therapist to move closer to the experienced reality of the client's world. It is possible to view therapy as a process of retrieving and making sense of the implicit meanings that are conveyed through the telling of vivid personal stories that operate almost as defining moments in the biography of the teller.

Typically, clients recount between five and eight such stories in each therapy session. The 'On Anger and Hurt' sessions are characterised by a relative absence of such narratives, and the brevity of the personal stories that are produced. It may be that the conditions under which the sessions were conducted may have made the client cautious about moving beyond a generalised account of the issues in his life. Nevertheless, the two vivid personal stories that he tells in the first session offer remarkable testimony to his way of being in the world:

Closing the outside world out

I was sitting in the room
And waiting beforehand
And I was thinking about

I was about seven or eight years old
And I remember reading a book
I believe I can't recall the name of this book
By Jung, I think it was
And I recall

When I was reading that at that time
I used to go down the basement of my home
And turn off all the lights
And in a way that was kind of closing the outside world out
And concentrating on what I wanted to do
And what I wanted to be

And at seven years old
I was I was into that
And today I am in the same position

Really you know trying to find out
What I want to do
What I want to be

And I've learned a lot of things
I've learned a lot of things
Since I found out that I had leukemia
Which is about a year ago this June
I learned an awful lot of things
(The Right to be Desperate)

In this story, told right at the beginning of the first session, the teller introduces a powerful and poignant image of himself as a seven-year-old boy. Rogers returns to this image several times in the therapy, in an attempt to explore its meaning for the client as a representation of parts of himself that may have become lost or hidden as a consequence of the pressures of adult life. The boy is alone and has deliberately put himself in a position of being alone, even though he is in the family home. Again, the theme of aloneness recurs across the two sessions as a thread through the client's life. There is even a sense, particularly in the second session, that he is alone, and can only be alone, with his strong emotions of hurt and anger, even though he is in the presence of a therapist who is willing to be his companion. The teller also repeatedly describes himself as a person of knowledge who reads and studies, and who is 'trying to find out' and has 'learned a lot of things'.

A second story is told later in the first session:

I couldn't see

I recall
When I went back

And I and I
It was the first time my parents had learnt that I had leukemia
 What do you say to your mother?
 What do you say here to your father?
I remember I got a phone call
I was staying at my wife's house
We were going
 Keep in mind now we were going through a divorce
 The whole bit
And we're
I am celebrating my children's birthday
At the same time
My mother calls 'We are coming over'
Nobody at the house
All of a sudden I lose my vision goes
 That's one of the symptoms of leukemia
And and and it scared the hell out of me
Like I really wanted to run
But I couldn't run
I couldn't see
(The Right to be Desperate)

This story introduces a 'peopled' world, and affirms the central relationships in the client's life: his wife, children and parents. However, even though these people are mentioned, the teller is once again portrayed as alone: 'nobody at the house'. It is not 'we' who are celebrating the children's birthday, it is 'I'.

There are important differences between the first and second stories that encapsulate the transformation of the client's life that had taken place in recent months. He is described again as being in a family home, but this time it is not 'my home' but has become 'my wife's house'. He is no longer a person who learns, knows and finds out: he has become unable to see. He is not in a position of intentionally turning off the lights—the lights are, in effect, turned off by forces beyond his control. He is scared.

Through the second half of the first therapy session, and the whole of the second session, there are no further examples of well-formed vivid personal stories. There are many examples of fragments of narrative that might, in different circumstances, have been worked up into personal stories. For example, the death of the client's father-in-law comes across as a highly significant event for the client, but it is recounted in general terms, as a chronicle. The effect of this absence of personal stories, particularly in the second session, is to construct a discourse that is oddly detached from the actual world of the client. The session focuses on the expression of an emotion—anger—that is apparently felt in the moment by the client and by the therapist. From a narrative perspective, however, emotion is never an entity in itself but is part of a story, and is causally linked to intentions, relationships and situations. The lack of 'emplotment' (Parry, 1998; Sarbin, 1989) of the client's feelings of hurt and anger may be a factor in the failure of the client to resolve these emotions, either by expressing them or finding what they might mean or signify to him.

THE RACISM NARRATIVE: 'IT HAS SOMETHING TO DO WITH THE RACE THING'

From a narrative social constructionist perspective, the horizons of the client's world are usually communicated through habitual narratives and chronicles that provide a generalised account of key themes and issues, which then crystallise into vivid personal stories that invite the therapist closer to the purposeful, interpersonal texture of that world (McLeod, 1997). From the earliest moments of the first session, the client in the 'Anger and Hurt' sessions produces a generalised *racism narrative* to which he returns again and again. However, at no point in the case does this narrative theme become the topic of a specific, vivid personal story.

The racism narrative is introduced in the form of a phrase that is voiced in such a way that its bitter irony is obvious to any listener:

> *I remember in second grade I, uhm, was a I was ... a potential credit to my race. (T: Mmhm) that was one of the (T: Mmhm) I used to always wonder why I couldn't be a credit to somebody else's race also but ... I think I really conditioned to be something ... to be some kind of a symbol or whatever ... and ... and not really being a person you know. (C5)*

The theme of racism is expressed many other times throughout the sessions. Examples of these statements include:

> *... in a majority society I had to I had to be a hundred per, two hundred percent better that my white counterpart (T: Mmhm) or my brown counterpart ... (C16)*
> (The Right to be Desperate)

> *... I had a young wife who had two children and those children were of mixed, uh, mixed heritage (T: Mmhm) living in a, in a (pause) isolated community what would happen to those children ... (C33)*
> (The Right to be Desperate)

> ... I've always felt like this ... you only have about two options, you know, when you deal with race ... you either have to be ... you're either a racist or you're an antiracist.(C7)
>
> *(On Anger and Hurt)*

> ... that part of me that's, that's my culture or is a part of the total ... is saying that it's not all that good to be angry, you know, because militancy is frowned upon or whatever, you know ... when blacks become angry they're, they're not angry ... they're militant ... (C15)
>
> *(On Anger and Hurt)*

> I'm afraid to ... show anybody that I'm hurt, you know ... (T: Mmm,mmm) Scared to death ... terrified ... (C48) ... it has something to do with being a man and it has something to do with ... with the race thing, you know.(C49)
>
> *(On Anger and Hurt)*

> A man doesn't admit he's hurt ... a black man especially doesn't admit that he's been hurt by anything. (T60)
>
> *(On Anger and Hurt)*

> ... so little chance for that group of people understanding me ... it would just, it would be like me trying to, uh, to understand or to, to tell Dick Nixon or something about my feelings ... (C19)
>
> *(On Anger and Hurt)*

> ... they wouldn't understand how a black person could be hurt, you know, because if you don't accept a person as human, how can you, how can you think about, you know, like ... it's like thinking a dog couldn't be hurt ... you know ... people that don't have dogs and don't understand them ... (C81)
>
> *(On Anger and Hurt)*

Although they permeate the sessions, these references to the experience of resisting racism do not become a specific focus within the conversation between the therapist and client, either in the form of a personal story or in the form of a topic for reflection. Why is this? It appears as though Rogers uses two linguistic strategies that operate to deflect the client from developing his racism narrative. These strategies can be defined as *process direction* and *restatement*.

Process direction refers to a response by a therapist which leads the client in the direction of a specific way of talking about emotional or cognitive data

(Rennie, 1998). For example, a request to 'say more' about an issue invites a client to present more data, while 'can you give me an example?' may elicit a story or concrete event. In some approaches to therapy, process direction may involve complex activity, such as two-chair interventions in Gestalt Therapy. In the 'On Anger and Hurt' sessions, Rogers consistently prompts the client in the direction of naming and expressing feelings. For instance, near the start of the second session, the following interchange takes place:

> Client (C7): ... It's ... it's almost like in this country ... and, and I've always felt like this ... you only have about two options, you know, when you deal with race ... you either have to be ... you're either a racist or you're an antiracist. (T: Mmm.) And that doesn't really seem to be the kind of thing that I'm, you know ... I don't really care to be an antiracist, if you know what I mean (T: Mmm) anymore. Uh, and I don't wanna be a reflection of any other ... of any other larger society at all. (T: Mmm.) I really don't want to ...
> Therapist (T 7): You'd like to get in touch with what's going on in you.
> (On Anger and Hurt)

Here, the client can be seen to focus on what is, for him, a significant personal dilemma ('in this country ... you're either a racist or you're an antiracist'). The therapist response directs attention to one aspect of this dilemma ('what's going on in *you*'). The preceding exchanges between client and therapist support the relevance of this statement, as an invitation to continue on the track of exploring 'the anger'. However, it is also important to recognise, also, that the therapist's words fail to acknowledge both the existence, and the nature, of the dilemma being confronted by the client.

Another linguistic strategy used by the therapist is *restatement*. There are several places in the transcript of the case where the client uses the terms 'race', 'racism' and 'black', and the therapist restates his understanding using words that refer to more generalised experiences of hurt, or the imposition of cultural standards, rather than naming the specific experience of racism. Examples of these interactions include:

> Client (C6): ... being a credit to your race in being outstanding student an outstanding (T: Mmhm) scholar an outstanding (T: Mmhm) football player whatever er leaves you little room to to be ...
> Therapist (T7): You've been meeting other people's expectations of you ...
> (The Right to be Desperate)
> Client (C12): ... I gave a lot to that family you know for five I don't know seven years I guess and uhm when I went back there were just some things that happened ... all of a sudden, you know I became uh you know I, I became just another black person I became just another

> *nigger.*
> *Therapist (T13):* ... *perhaps I catch a little bit of resentment* ...
> *(The Right to be Desperate)*
>
> *Client (C81):* ... *they wouldn't understand how a black person could be hurt, you know, because if you don't accept a person as human, how can you, how can you think about, you know, like ... it's like thinking a dog could be hurt or whate-ver, you know, people that don't have dogs and don't understand them, you know?*
> *Therapist (T81): But you get some satisfaction out of saying, 'You people don't realize how much you hurt me' ... out of letting, letting yourself know, letting others know that, 'God, I've been hurt!'*
> *(On Anger and Hurt)*

These therapist statements may be viewed as representing a consistent use of a language that stripped the client's talk of almost all references to the social reality of racism, and downplayed the intensity of this aspect of his life. Instead of staying with the theme of racism, the therapist offered back an account that was framed in terms of individual feelings and reactions. The point here is not that the client did not recognise these individual feelings as part of his world—he certainly appeared to value this opportunity to move closer to what appeared to be pent-up feelings of anger, hurt and pain. But, at the same time, he kept returning to a 'race narrative', as if attempting to incorporate this theme into the therapeutic conversation.

DECONTEXTUALISING THE PERSON: THE PROBLEM OF CULTURAL EMPATHY

Throughout the case, the therapist guides the conversation away from the actual social world of the client, and toward a discourse grounded in expression of, and reflection on, what was being felt by the client in the moment. This is a therapeutic approach that lies at the heart of the client-centred, experiential and person-centred tradition in therapy. The 'On Anger and Hurt' sessions provide an opportunity to examine the impact, in one case, of this kind of decontextualised reflection of meaning. In this case, the client generates powerful images of a social world permeated by racism. If the words of the client are read on their own, it seems clear that the experience of 'being a credit to my race', 'a black person not being human', being cut off from his own children by barriers of race, always struggling to prove himself, and other facets of racism, represent the dominant narrative (White and Epson, 1990) within which he was at that time living his life. If, by contrast, the words of the therapist are read in isolation, they outline a therapeutic metanarrative that can be summarised as 'feeling those feelings inside and really feeling them fully ...' Anyone watching the tapes of these sessions can observe the connection between therapist and client: there is contact and dialogue. But there is also a lack of contact, a sense of 'talking past' each other.

The decontextualised reflection of meaning that is apparent in the 'On Anger and Hurt' case can be understood, at least in part, through the consideration of recent theory and research in the area of cross-cultural or multicultural counselling and psychotherapy. Thompson and Jenal (1994) carried out a quasi-experimental study in which black clients (students in a university in the USA) were exposed to a single counselling session with counsellors who were instructed to avoid following up any references that their clients might make to racial issues. They found that some clients conceded to their counsellors, by eliminating all mention of race. Other clients disengaged from their counsellors, and appeared to lose interest in the process. A third category of client ' ... persisted in attempting to be heard ... in their efforts to maintain a race-centered stance in the face of the race-avoidant [counsellors], these clients appeared frustrated and exasperated' (*ibid.*: 489). The researchers reported a 'tugging-match quality' evident in the sessions of these 'persistent' clients (*ibid.*). In another study which explored client and therapist experiences of race-avoidant discourse, Tuckwell (2001) concluded that the disruptive therapy process associated with this kind of therapist response could be attributed to the unconscious 'threat of the other'. An important implication of these studies, taken together, is to raise serious doubts about the validity of a 'universalistic' approach to therapy, in which cultural differences can be ignored by virtue of the therapist's capacity to access universal human experiences such as self-acceptance, acceptance, loss and despair. The message from Thompson and Jenal (1994) and Tuckwell (2001) is that cultural differences must be collaboratively addressed before therapeutic work can be done.

It appears to have been generally accepted within multicultural counselling that the achievement of empathic engagement is more difficult in situations where client and counsellor belong to different cultural groups (Scott and Borodovsky, 1990; Ridley and Lingle, 1996). It seems that there are several factors that make it hard for a counsellor or psychotherapist to enter the 'frame of reference' or emotional world of a client from another cultural background. The 'feeling language' used by each participant may be different; the same words may have different meanings, or there may not even be words that correspond to certain culturally-specific states of feeling. The understanding of which social and interpersonal situations elicit particular emotional responses or behaviours is likely to be imprecise. There may also be different conversational and interactional 'rules', for example, concerning how acceptable it is to disclose intimate information, or around the 'expert' status of the therapist. These contrasting rules or behavioural norms may inhibit open communication. To counteract these barriers, Dyche and Zayas (1995) propose that it is important for counsellors to be actively curious around dimensions of cultural difference, and be willing to take time in therapy to discuss such matters. Moodley (1998) has characterised this kind of approach as being one of encouraging 'frank talking' around cultural and racial issues in the therapy room.

These ideas open up the possibility of an alternative interpretation of the 'On Anger and Hurt' tapes. To what extent can the unusual amount of control and directiveness that Rogers appeared to exhibit in these sessions (Brodley, 1996) be seen as a reflection of his own way of coping with the threat presented by this cultural 'other'? To what extent could the anger and hurt expressed by the client be understood as a response to an experience of being blocked in his desire to use the session to allow others—a global audience—to be witness to the effects of racism in his life? Could the client pattern of behaviour that Rogers described in his summing-up as being that of an 'armour-plated man' be understood as similar to the constricted and resistant posture of some of the clients exposed to race-avoidant counsellors in the Thompson and Jenal (1994) study? In the absence of information which is not available—for example, retrospective interviews with the therapist and client—it is impossible to gauge the plausibility of this alternative reading of the 'On Anger and Hurt' case.

CONCLUSION

My hope and expectation is that readers of this chapter will be able to reflect on the value of a narrative social constructionist reading of the 'On Anger and Hurt' sessions in enriching their appreciation of the possible meaning and significance of the interplay between Carl Rogers and his client. This reading of the sessions represents a return to a genuinely hermeneutic form of inquiry (McLeod, 2001). In recent years, a hermeneutic approach has been understood as a form of qualitative analysis that involves the use of interpretation. I believe that the true meaning, and value, of hermeneutics is much wider than this. Classical hermeneutic studies always involved a number of scholars offering competing interpretations of a religious or literary text that was already known to readers (e.g., the Bible). This situation empowers the reader or consumer of the analysis, who already possesses her/his own interpretation of the text, and is in a strong position to judge whether any new analysis that they read enhances that pre-existing understanding.

The aim of this social constructionist interpretation is to place the interaction in its social context, and to draw attention to the ways in which the use of language within this therapy session positions each of the participants in relation to the social, cultural and historical traditions which 'speak through' them. From this perspective, the 'On Anger and Hurt' sessions can be viewed as a microcosm of race relations in the USA in the mid-1970s. A white man who has accumulated status and privilege is in the position of seeking to assist a younger black man who reports a troubled life. As a liberal, the white man does his best to be helpful. The black man appears to be willing to believe that help can be gained from this source, but in places is also wary, as if testing out the other. Time and again they seek to identify a shared American cultural experience, defined by notions of success, effort, family life and honesty and the sharing of jokes and profanities. Behind these efforts, though, can be glimpsed quite different cultural narratives. The black man lives in a world in which racism and discrimination are central, and where someone like him may struggle to find a home. The white man lives in a world in which he enjoys a high degree of control and respect, reflected in a narrative of authenticity. And, in the end, the white man is the ultimate beneficiary of the interaction. He, and his colleagues, gain further status and income from publishing it.

To suggest that the 'On Anger and Hurt' tapes can be seen as a microcosm of race relations is not intended as a criticism of Carl Rogers. At the time when the sessions were recorded, the body of theory, research and experience in cross-cultural or multicultural counselling and psychotherapy, to which we now enjoy access, did not exist. The 'On Anger and Hurt' case can be regarded as a documentation of an example of client-centred counselling from a particular stage in its historical development. The case exhibits the application of a universalistic approach to therapy, in which empathic engagement is almost entirely directed toward the inner feeling state of the client rather than toward his sense of his social and cultural identity. It would be interesting to determine the degree to which contemporary counsellors and psychotherapists, faced with the same client, would be observed to adopt a more culturally-sensitive approach.

REFERENCES

Brodley, BT (1996) 'Uncharacteristic Directiveness: Rogers and the "Anger and Hurt" Client', in BA Farber, DC Brink and PM Raskin (eds) *The Psychotherapy of Carl Rogers*. New York: Guilford Press. (Reproduced as Chapter 4 in this volume.)

Dyche, L and Zayas, LH (1995) 'The value of curiosity and naivete for the cross-cultural psychotherapist.' *Family Process, 34*: 389–99.

Gergen, KJ (1994) *Toward Transformation in Social Knowledge* (2nd edn.). London: Sage.

Gergen, KJ (1999) *An Invitation to Social Construction*. Thousand Oaks, CA: Sage.

McLeod, J (1997) *Narrative and Psychotherapy*. London: Sage.
McLeod, J (1999a) 'Counselling as a social process.' *Counselling, 10*: 217–26.
McLeod, J (1999b) 'A narrative social constructionist approach to therapeutic empathy.' *Counselling Psychology Quarterly, 12*: 377–94.
McLeod, J (2001) *Qualitative Research in Counselling and Psychotherapy*. London: Sage.
McLeod, J and Balamoutsou, S (2000) 'Narrative process in the assimilation of a problematic experience: qualitative analysis of a single case.' *Zeitshcrift fur qualitative Bildungs—Beratungs—und Sozialforshung, 2*: 283–302.
McLeod, J and Balamoutsou, S (2001) 'A method for qualitative narrative analysis of psychotherapy transcripts', in J. Frommer and DL Rennie (eds) *Qualitative Psychotherapy Research: Methods and Methodology*. Berlin: Pabst.
McLeod, J and Lynch, G (2000) 'This is our life: strong evaluation in psychotherapy narrative.' *European Journal of Psychotherapy, Counselling and Health, 3*: 389–406.
Meier, A (2002) Narrative in psychotherapy theory, practice, and research: A critical review. *Counseling and Psychotherapy Research 2*: 239–52.
Moodley, R (1998) '"I say what I like": frank talk(ing) in counselling and psychotherapy.' *British Journal of Guidance and Counselling, 26*: 495–508.
Parry, TA (1998) 'Reasons of the heart: the narrative construction of emotions.' *Journal of Systemic Therapies, 17*: 65-79.
Rennie, DL (1998) *Person-centred Counselling: an Experiential Approach*. London: Sage.
Ridley, CR and Lingle, DW (1996) 'Cultural empathy in multicultural counseling; a multidimensional process model', in PB Pedersen, JG Draguns, WJ Lonner and JE Trimble (eds) *Counseling across Cultures* (4th edn.). Thousand Oaks, CA: Sage.
Sarbin, TR (1989) 'Emotions as narrative emplotments', in MJ Packer and RB Addison (eds) *Entering the Circle: Hermeneutic Investigation in Psychology*. Albany: State University of New York.
Scott, NE and Borodovsky, LG (1990) 'Effective use of cultural role taking.' *Professional Psychology: Research and Practice, 21*: 167–70.
Thompson, CE and Jenal, S (1994) 'Interracial and intraracial quasi-counseling interactions: When counselors avoid discussing race.' *Journal of Counseling Psychology, 41*(4): 484–91.
Tuckwell, G (2001) '"The threat of the Other": Racial and cultural dynamics in the counselling process.' *Counselling and Psychotherapy Research, 1*: 154–62.
White, M and Epston, D (1990) *Narrative Means to Therapeutic Ends*. New York: Norton.
Willi, J (1999) *Ecological Psychotherapy: Developing by Shaping the Personal Niche*. Seattle, WA: Hogrefe and Huber.

Chapter 15
POINTS OF DEPARTURE: A HUMANISTIC-SPIRITUAL VIEW

WILLIAM WEST

I write this chapter as a counsellor, counselling supervisor, ex counsellor trainer, researcher and research supervisor. I am white and male and my work as a counsellor is sited within an integrative, humanistic (West, 2000b) body-orientated (West 1994a, b) and spiritual frame (West, 2000a). Rogers was a hero of mine during my Masters in Counselling Studies in the early 1990s. Much of what he said rang true for me and seemed to resonate with much of my experience gleaned from a decade of practice as a therapist during the 1980s. There was striking honesty about Rogers and an iconoclastic quality that I admired. An example of this is the way in which he valued his own experience above everything else including his own thinking or any outside authority. I was excited by his idea of 'presence' which also for me seemed to wreck the neat research ability of his core conditions and of his insistence on their being necessary and sufficient for client therapeutic progress. I felt that his concept of presence and its full implications including its innate spirituality was never followed up by him before he died or by the person-centred world since then, except for some notable exceptions (Geller, 2001; Geller and Greenberg, 2002; Thorne, 1991, 2002). Thus, while valuing Rogers' approach, I could not 'convert' and give up insights and practices that were not person-centred. I write here from the viewpoint of deeply valuing Rogers but also being able to question his approach from within a more broader spiritually informed humanistic perspective to therapy.

ISSUES RELATING TO THE FILMED THERAPY SESSIONS

As a former trainer on an integrative British Association for Counselling and Psychotherapy accredited course it was of great value to be able to show trainee counsellors some quality examples of counselling in practice. There has been a relative lack of good films and videos available in recent years especially made in Britain—the confidentiality issue seems to be a key one here. In the absence of much recent British video material, it is even harder to resist the urge to show videos of the founding fathers (and mothers, but usually fathers) of some of the key therapeutic approaches. In recent years, I have become increasingly troubled by the showing of such films and videos as Rogers and others working with the clients Gloria or Cathy, or Rogers working with the man in *The Right to be Desperate* and *On Anger and Hurt*. I have therefore explored my concerns in conversations with colleagues and in emails—especially with members of a person-centred email list—and recently in print (West, 2002a). One of my concerns is that, in repeatedly viewing these videos, I feel as if the clients involved are not making progress. It is as if they remain forever stuck and I hear nothing of their future lives, except for Gloria who asks Rogers and his wife to be her spiritual parents (Rogers, 1984).

Another concern is that of consent. We know for instance that Gloria, the client who worked with Rogers, Perls and Ellis, was a client of Shostrum who introduced and set up the filming. We do not know what kind of consent was sought for Gloria's participation. How much of it was about pleasing her therapist, or getting sessions from famous and effective therapists? Or did it feed into an unhealthy narcissistic side of her? Similarly, is the client in the *The Right to be Desperate* and *On Anger and Hurt* films motivated partially by a need to make a public confession of how he sought money off his friends by deceit because he was unable to tell them he was dying? We don't know. What are the healthy reasons for giving consent to be so filmed? Are there any? How informed can consent be in a power relationship such as any therapist-client relationship however client-centred it may be? How informed can consent be between a white female client and a white male therapist, or, with the case of *The Right to be Desperate* and *On Anger and Hurt*, between a black client and a white therapist? How come these filmed and videotaped clients are usually young, female or black and the therapists older, white and male?

If people are facing serious difficulties in their lives, are they able to freely consent to counselling, let alone taping? If you are desperate enough you will agree to almost anything. For example, Gloria saw all three therapists as 'doctors', again pointing to the power differential. Also, the fact that she had these three sessions in one day has to be queried on health, therapeutic and ethical grounds. Did she know that counselling trainees and others in their thousands would continue to view her tape for years after it was made and years after her death?

Did she consent to that? What of the client of *The Right to be Desperate* and *On Anger and Hurt*? What happened to him? What did he consent to? How does he feel about us viewing him in Britain today? Who got/gets the royalties? A person-centred view that is sometimes expressed is that Gloria and the other clients were capable of an emancipatory decision to give consent to being filmed. However, if clients could take emancipatory decisions they probably would not need to have therapy. It is hard not to get caught up at some level or other in pleasing one's therapist. As Rennie (1994) has shown, client deference is a key feature of being a client.

MY VIEW OF THE CLIENT'S POSSIBLE THERAPEUTIC WORK

In the films *The Right to be Desperate* and *On Anger and Hurt* in which Rogers is counselling a young man who is black, the client is never given a name, unlike Gloria, Kathy and the others. This resulted in him being referred to on one occasion by a counselling tutor on our diploma course as the 'black man with leukaemia', which was rightfully challenged by one of the course members who insisted he be granted a name: she suggested Karl. This name will be used in the rest of this chapter.

Reviewing these films today, it is important to acknowledge the culture or rather cultures in which we live. Britain is still struggling to accept itself as a multicultural society. The word 'postmodern' is in vogue, partially as a way of recognising that we do not have cultural unity anymore (if we ever did), and as a way of recognising that our society consists of a range of cultures and sub-cultures with all kinds of crossovers occurring (e.g., in food, music, complementary medicine, marriage and other aspects of our lives). This is a different world to that of 1977 Britain and even more to that of the USA in 1977 when the *The Right to be Desperate* and *On Anger and Hurt* films were made.

Rather than go through the text of the films and indicate in great detail what other interventions someone from my therapeutic persuasion would make, I shall instead give some indication of my understanding of the client's possible therapeutic work and point out some key moments when my approach would significantly be different to Rogers'. I have to say, however, that it is Rogers, not I, who is the one in the film, who is in the therapy room with this client. It is therefore relatively easy for me to make my remarks, viewing the film and the transcript from the safety of my armchair. However, the value of this process is in our thinking and feeling through the therapeutic possibilities available, so that, when we are in that unique encounter with our own clients, we have the best possible opportunity to be of use.

At the end of the first therapy session, *The Right to be Desperate*, I feel there are two therapeutic tasks that ask to be addressed and which I would have wished to have discussed with the client, albeit in very provisional terms. These two tasks could be part of the process of setting a possible agenda and seeing if the client agreed to it, while being very open to further reflection by myself and more importantly by the client. They could possibly have been explored in the second session but might well have taken longer. One task is to further explore the hurt and anger feelings. Although Karl does so in the second session, the process feels frustrating and unfinished. The second task would be to explore the seven year old child state in order to give it voice, perhaps in a Gestalt fashion, but certainly to invite the child to be present and to link the adult Karl with his inner child. It might be possible and useful to explore Karl's need to retreat from the world, asking how much has he given himself that opportunity, and asking how much was his illness asking him to do this, what would be a more healthy way of doing this.

FURTHER POINTS OF DEPARTURE

At a crucial point in the second film, *On Anger and Hurt*, Karl speaks of 'vomiting up green slime.' (C117, *On Anger and Hurt*). This is a key moment for me and as someone with a background in bodywork approaches to humanistic therapy (West, 1994a, b), Karl's comment could be taken further. A possible intervention would be to invite the client to make the noise he would associate with vomiting up this green slime. The client could chose not to, or feel, and be, unable to. However, there is a distinct possibility the client could respond with a sound that was expressive of the feelings indicated by this powerful metaphor. I can imagine a mix of feelings being released if the client was able to so do. This mix would need appropriate processing and making sense of by the client. This process is a common experience in some forms of humanistic therapy (West, 1994a) and is valued by the clients involved (West, 1994b). In the case of Karl, this could well be the moment at which he ceases to walk around the pit of his feelings to actually feel them more deeply and come to some new and deeper realisation of himself and his life. If he was able to do this he would no longer be the 'armour-plated man' that Rogers calls him in his commentary after the session. We do not know what would actually happen, but I believe that there was a possible and highly significant turning point available at that moment.

Indeed, if the client was unable to follow this therapeutic direction, there are other possible ways of exploring this powerful 'green slime' metaphor. The client could be invited to associate with this phrase 'green slime'. What does 'green slime' mean to him? Who or what produces such slime? What would he wish to do with this 'green slime'? There are many possible ways forward if we stay with this image and work with the client with it. For instance, at another point in the session, the client talks about 'somebody [who] took a big goddamned tree and just rammed it up ...'. (C125, *On Anger and Hurt*) Again this is a key moment and a gift to a humanistic body-orientated therapist. The approach might be something like, 'Can I ask you to stop there? Can you feel that tree inside you? What is it like? What do you want to do with it? What does it feel like when you breathe more deeply?' Or, using a more imaginative, possibly transpersonal approach (Rowan, 1993), 'Can you imagine that tree inside?, What does it look like? What is it doing to you? What would you like to do to it? What help would you call upon in your imagination to help you deal with it?'

These suggestions would, I believe, occur quite naturally to a humanistic-orientated therapist. We could then see Brodley's discussion of Rogers' departure from a person-centred approach in a new light (see Brodley, 1996, also Chapter 4 in this volume). Rogers is acting in many ways like a humanistic therapist in the parts of *On Anger and Hurt* which Brodley criticises him for. My position is that Rogers did not go far enough into a more general humanistic way of working with Karl. Karl could well have benefited from the kind of interventions suggested above. If he did not, then it is likely that nothing will have been lost given the effective therapeutic relationship already established. As Brodley has demonstrated, Rogers is able to resume his person-centred working with Karl, despite his forays into more directive work. Also, information will have been gathered about what does not work at that point with Karl, a process which feeds into further therapeutic choices and developments.

Viewing the second film, *On Anger and Hurt*, I become increasingly frustrated. I think this is, at least in part, my response to the feelings that Karl is wrestling with but not able to let go of. I surmise that this frustration might have well been experienced by Rogers and possibly led him to be more directive. This could, in person-centred terms, have formed the basis of a congruent statement sharing this feeling of frustration or a humanistic comment of a kind I use fairly frequently: 'Listening to you I get a real sense of frustration and I feel it' (name body part in which I feel it, or describe it metaphorically). The hope is that the client will pick up this comment/bodily sensation/metaphor and own and develop it himself.

SPIRITUALITY

Rogers can be viewed as a key humanistic figure bridging into the spiritual and transpersonal, in contrast to other humanistic figures like May who argued that there was no room in the American Psychological Association for transpersonal psychology (Menahem, 1996). He seemingly was increasingly open to spirituality in his life and work as he got older. For example, his concept of 'presence' with its talk of his and his client's inner spirits being in contact (Rogers, 1980) has a clear spiritual ring to it. In Karl's therapy with Rogers, there are odd moments that have a clear spiritual feel. At one point when Karl is saying that he wished he had told his father-in-law that he loved him before he died, Rogers suggests, '… telling me in place of telling him and maybe even speak to him, I don't know.' (T74, *On Anger and Hurt*). The implication being that perhaps Karl's father-in-law would somehow be able to hear what was said.

Menahem (1996) suggests that Karl talking about his desire to help winos was a reflection of a developing compassionate nature which can be viewed as a spiritual development. Many people facing the possibility of dying from cancer and other such illnesses go through a spiritual shift. From a truly person-centred approach it would perhaps not be easily possible to ask Karl questions about his spirituality. From a spiritual way of working therapeutically, this would be a natural part of the process right from the start. Richards and Bergin (1997) advocate asking clients about religion and spirituality as part of a formal assessment process which will thereby indicate to them that it is very appropriate to explore such matters during the counselling process. Even without a formal assessment process, the raising of spiritual questions can serve the same purpose. I would have been interested in hearing how Karl felt about his therapeutic work with Rogers and whether he would feel it had something of a spiritual quality to it or not. There is certainly the potential for the encounter with Rogers to have had something of a healing nature to it.

Case study: Matthew

Although my therapeutic orientation is humanistic-integrative (West, 2000b), in the last six years I have sought clients who see spirituality as part of the solution to their problems (West, 2002b). I felt it necessary to stipulate this as I wished to work in a more explicitly spiritual, though not necessarily religious, way. This gives me and my client's greater freedom in how we could work together therapeutically. Consequently I have attracted a number of clients to whom their spirituality is important. Curiously, they are not usually Christian; many have been New Age, and some have been Buddhists.

The following case study (further discussed in West, 2004) is included with the explicit permission of my ex-client who has asked for some aspects of his story not to be included here. We have agreed to refer to him as Matthew (his name and some personal details having been changed). In his early thirties, Matthew is of mixed race origins but was raised within a white working-class family. Although brought up within a fairly devout Christian (Church of England) family Matthew had become a Sufi in his adult life and had regular contact with his Sufi teacher or master. His spiritual life was of great importance to him, and he would quote from Sufi poets like Rumi during his therapy sessions. He was working as a psychiatric nurse at the time of his therapy with me. Matthew's immediate presenting issue was that of a tension with members of his team at work. He also reported that he was 'out of touch with his feelings' and had some sense of 'not taking his place in the world'. He said that he did not feel grown up, and was not 'coming into his power'. He also expressed regret that he was not married or in a committed long-term sexual relationship.

Rather than cover Matthew's therapy in some detail, which to do it justice would take a whole book, I have decided to select some parts of the case narrative that especially reflect the spiritual interventions used. However, it must be recognised that much of the work could be seen and understood in fairly conventional therapeutic terms. Also, for Matthew and me, this was a therapeutic encounter that was infused with spirituality and reflected the spiritual paths and spiritual journey we both saw ourselves as being on. From this perspective the whole of life is both sacred and spiritual. There were several key moments some months into his therapy. In one session I was moved to share with him that his spirituality had a feeling or flavour of the Middle East or Istanbul, a sense of a place where East meets West. This reflected my feeling, which I had not expressed to him, that his spirituality was in some way different to Christianity. He was pleased by what I said and shared the fact that he was a Sufi.

Matthew and I were able to share the frequent silences which appeared to have a huge therapeutic value for him during his sessions with me. We seemed to share the spiritual nature of our encounter rather than try to make a shared theological sense of it, a focus on experiencing rather than on theorising or theologising.

However, these silences were not always unproblematic. One session, a few months into his therapy, he said that he was afraid of the 'spiritual intimacy' that was occurring between us. I was very struck by this phrase. Exploring what this meant, he referred to the silences that arose in our sessions that had a healing affect on him, the synchronous way in which words and images that overlapped came to both of us, and the feelings of interconnectedness that especially arose in the silences. It seemed important to me to check out with him what role he was experiencing me in, as I was wary of becoming his spiritual teacher and what that could mean. He replied that I was his counsellor, that he had a spiritual teacher, but that because his spirituality was important to him, he wanted to be able to explore it in his therapy with me. I was relieved to hear this.

A few sessions later, during one of our silences, I had an experience of dropping into a very deep place that I can, and do, reach on occasions in meditation or spiritual contemplation. I felt that I was on the edge of going so deep that I would lose all ordinary consciousness. I knew that it was not appropriate for me to go any deeper in the middle of a counselling session but I was reluctant to bring myself out of being on the edge of this very deep and very spiritual space. I was thus able to relate to him from that deep space. It seemed very important. I assumed that my going there had a meaning and was not just an accident. It felt important to stay there in that deep space and not to break contact or consciousness. I did find a way of speaking to him from that deep space without losing it. I felt that I was on an edge in that I could go either deeper into the space or come back to a more ordinary way of relating. It was almost as if I was on the edge of falling or dropping down inside myself. In that moment, I did not quite know what this meant. It was, I think, part of that spiritual intimacy that he had referred to earlier, part of which was not always knowing exactly what was going on but trusting in the spiritual process that was unfolding. Some of it, I think, was saying to him that this is okay, that it was okay for him to be in a similar deep and spiritual space. At some level, being in silence with him from a deep space, not having to come out of it, and staying with that space and with him at the same time felt like a kind of mentoring. There was something different about being there with him in that session and an extraordinary feeling of 'holding' that deep space, not having to come out of it, and not going so deep that I lost that connection. It felt risky but very important.

Some of Matthew's therapy could be seen in non-spiritual terms about a developmental need on his part to heal the trauma of his adoption soon after birth and to deal with his difficulties at work and his need to find a sexual partner. However, this misses the truth that Matthew saw himself as being on a spiritual path, that he chose to have therapy with me because of my spiritual approach to therapy, and that there was for both of us some explicitly spiritual experiences and spiritual content in the therapeutic encounter. There is a growing body of literature and research that covers spiritual moments in psychotherapy (e.g., Mearns and Thorne, 1988; Richards and Bergin, 1997; Rogers, 1980; Rowan, 1993; Thorne, 1991, 2002; West, 2000a). Rogers, in particular, spoke of his experience of what he called 'presence':

> I find that when I am closer to my inner, intuitive self, when I am somehow in touch with the unknown in me, when perhaps I am in a slightly altered state of consciousness in the relationship, then whatever I do seems to be full of healing. Then simply my presence is releasing and helpful ... I may behave in strange and impulsive ways in the relationship, ways which I cannot justify rationally, which have nothing to do with my thought processes ... At these moments it seems that my inner spirit has reached out and touched the spirit of the other ... Profound growth and healing energies are present (Rogers, 1980: 129).

Was this experience described by Rogers possibly a version of the 'spiritual intimacy' that Matthew feared? Does it not also encompass the deep spiritual and meditative space that I found myself in with Matthew in the session described above? I think both interpretations are true.

I learnt much about working with my clients' spirituality through working with Matthew. I also learnt a lot about my own spirituality. It was a challenging and rewarding experience to share his spiritual unfolding. It was, and is, a rare privilege to share that aspect of my nature so frequently in the human encounter that is the therapeutic relationship. I am left wondering why Rogers did not draw on, or perhaps could not draw on presence with Karl? I am aware that with differing clients, differing parts of my therapeutic self are engaged. Perhaps Karl did not call forth or 'allow' Rogers to engage 'presence'.

CONCLUSION

My own students always rate highly the live counselling demonstrations we as tutors offer on our counselling courses. From a training point of view perhaps we need to reconsider the balance we strike between such live demonstrations (and these could be videotaped for short-term feedback purposes) and what use we make of videos available either from Britain, the USA or elsewhere. Perhaps it has become too easy to put on a video of a Rogers' film like *On Anger and Hurt*, trusting that the students will get the opportunity to see some good therapy in practice but being less aware of the implications of these actions. I am not advocating a ban on such videos but more the kind of careful consideration that usually does go into the design of a counsellor training programme.

Finally, in the light of my feelings about viewing and re-viewing the videotapes of these films of Rogers working with Karl, Gloria, Kathy and others which I have discussed in this chapter, I now feel that I can understand the fairly common aboriginal fear that photographing someone somehow captures a piece of their soul. Maybe it is time for Gloria, Kathy and Karl to be released from these soul-trapping video recordings perhaps by a ceremonial burning of the videotapes?

ACKNOWLEDGEMENTS

Many people have contributed to my understanding of the issues around the use of the films *The Right to Be Desperate* and *On Anger and Hurt*. These include: Roy Moodley, Barbara Temaner Brodley, Pete Sanders, Henry Hollanders, Mary Berry, Celia Hindmarch, and Bob Colderley.

REFERENCES

Brodley, BT (1996) 'Uncharacteristic Directiveness: Rogers and the "Anger and Hurt" Client', in BA Farber, DC Brink and PM Raskin (eds) *The Psychotherapy of Carl Rogers*. New York: Guilford Press. (Reproduced as Chapter 4 in this volume.)

Geller, SM (2001) Therapists' Presence: The Development of a Model and a Measure. PhD thesis. York University, Toronto.

Geller, SM and Greenberg, LS (2002) 'Therapeutic Presence: Therapists' experience of presence in the psychotherapy encounter.' *Person-Centered and Experiential Psychotherapies, 1*(1 and 2): 71–86.

Mearns, D and Thorne, B (1988) *Person-Centred Counselling in Action*. London: Sage.

Menahem, SE (1996) 'The case of 'anger and hurt', Rogers and the development of a spiritual psychotherapy', in BA Farber, DC Brink and PM Raskin (eds) *The Psychotherapy of Carl Rogers: Cases and Commentary*. London: Guildford Press, pp. 322–33.

Rennie, DL (1994) 'Qualitative analysis of the client's experience of psychotherapy: The unfolding of reflexivity', in SG Toukmanian and DL Rennie (eds) *Psychotherapy Process Research: Paradigmatic and Narrative Approaches*. London: Sage, pp. 11–33.

Richards, PS and Bergin, AE (1997) *A Spiritual Strategy for Counselling and Psychotherapy*. Washington: American Psychological Association.

Rogers, CR (1980) *A Way of Being*. Boston: Houghton Mifflin.

Rogers, CR (1984) 'Gloria—a historical note', in RF Levant and JM Shlien (eds) *Client-Centred Therapy and the Person-Centered Approach: New directions in theory, research, and practice*. London: Praeger, pp. 423–5.

Rowan, J (1993) *The Transpersonal: Psychotherapy and Counselling*. London: Routledge.

Thorne, B (1991) *Person-Centred Counselling: Therapeutic and Spiritual Dimensions*. London: Whurr.

Thorne, B (2002) *The Mystical Power of Person-Centred Therapy: Hope Beyond Despair*. London: Whurr.

West, WS (1994a) 'Post-Reichian Therapy', in D Jones (ed) *Innovative Therapy: A Handbook*. Buckingham: Open University Press, pp. 131–45.

West, WS (1994b) 'Clients' experience of bodywork psychotherapy.' *Counselling Psychology Quarterly, 7*(3): 287–303.

West, WS (2000a) *Psychotherapy and Spirituality: Crossing the Line Between Therapy and Religion*. London: Sage.

West, WS (2000b) 'Eclecticism and integration in humanistic therapy', in S Palmer and R Woolfe (eds) *Integrative and Eclectic Counselling and Psychotherapy*. London: Sage, pp. 218–32.

West, WS (2002a) 'Some ethical dilemmas in counselling and counselling research.' *British Journal of Guidance and Counselling, 30*(30): 261–8.

West, WS (2002b) 'Being present to our clients' spirituality.' *Journal of Critical Psychology, Counselling and Psychotherapy, 2*(2): 86–93.

West, WS (2004) *Spiritual Issues in Therapy: Relating Experience to Practice*. Basingstoke: Palgrave.

Chapter 16
HORIZONS OF ALIENATION: CULTURE AND HERMENEUTICS

SUSAN JAMES AND GARY FOSTER

When I (Susan James) was at the University of Chicago, I showed students videos of various types of therapies; part of this exercise was to note the cultural and moral assumptions within them. It was an exciting place to show a video of Carl Rogers conducting therapy as Rogers had been teaching in that same department 40 years earlier. I got the sense of the type of students that Rogers would have had in his classes: students with extensive knowledge of other disciplines such as philosophy, anthropology, literature and theology. This experience helped me to understand the reason why Rogers was so well versed theoretically across many disciplines. For example, Rogers (1955) sought to understand the human psyche not only by reading the work of psychologists but also philosophers, such as Kierkegaard and Buber. Additionally, Rogers' early training in theology also undoubtedly shaped his work.

My (Gary Foster) interest in Rogers' work emerged indirectly through my reading of Kierkegaard. Rogers speaks of how he came to encounter Kierkegaard through the recommendation of several theology students at the University of Chicago. The phenomenological picture of selfhood that Kierkegaard presented—that selfhood should not be simply understood in an externalized, behavioristic manner, but as a dynamic progression which could be understood only indirectly through personal articulation—would have a profound influence on Rogers' own worldview. Rogers appropriates Kierkegaard's notion of a 'becoming self' which develops in the realm of freedom, our creative or spiritual capacity dimensions which have been at the heart of many 'phenomenological' approaches to selfhood, particularly the client-centered approach; a view which we also share. We believe that Rogers demonstrates this clearly with his client in the 'The Right to be Desperate' and 'On Anger and Hurt' sessions. This approach, we feel, displays certain characteristics of what could be called the hermeneutic situation.

We believe that hermeneutics, the science of interpretation, provides a somewhat natural theoretical framework for doing cultural psychotherapy. Cultural psychotherapy explores the role that tradition and culture play in shaping the meanings, beliefs and assumptions that constitute a client's intentional world. The therapist's task is to try to understand that world which includes the dialectical relation between the individual client and his/her culture. Likewise, hermeneutic methodology is based on the assumption that a dialectic exists between the part and the whole in any act of interpretation. Whether it be a text or a client's problem, which needs to be understood in a cultural context, the two-way relation between the client (part) and their culture (the whole) needs to be examined. We argue that a cultural psychotherapy framework is helpful for examining intercultural therapeutic encounters. We will examine key dimensions of this multidisciplinary approach and its relevance for our discussion. We will give examples from the client's utterances in *The Right to be Desperate* and *On Anger and Hurt*. Our intention here is to demonstrate the need for an interpretative methodology for approaching cultural/cross-cultural psychotherapy and to show why we think that the hermeneutical method suits this task well.

ROGERS AND THE CLIENT IN SESSION

In the sessions with the African-American client, we see Rogers employ the elements of a successful interview that he had outlined in previous work (Rogers, 1989). For instance, he was successful at creating a climate of acceptance and gaining a deep understanding of the client's feelings. As he describes in his writings, Rogers reflects the client's feelings to test his own understandings of the situation (*ibid.*). He also uses this strategy because he is working under the assumption that the client's feelings and meanings seem sharper through the eyes of another (*ibid.*).

> *Client (C39): I am certainly not trying to indite all doctors and the medical profession (T: sure) but what happened to me. I hope in some way that, uhm, other people who have life-threatening illnesses can deal with because (T: Mmhm) you know, I think it, that I have, I do have that control since I was seven to some extent when I went down that basement turned that light off and like, and I shut the outside world off or whatever, somehow I lost that. Because somehow in the process of becoming educated, and socialized (T: Mmhm, mmhm) and*

> whatever, I let other people control what I wanted, what I wanted to do. And I really, I did and that was, Jesus, that was ... Yeah, well, what can you say?
>
> Therapist (T40): That has a lot of meaning to me and I want to make sure that I'm getting it straight. Down in that basement as a seven-year-old, with the lights out, you are really finding yourself and I gather trusting yourself (C: Mmhm) and then life has said to you 'no no don't do that we have the standards for you live up to our expectations. You got to be the image, you got to be just right and everything' and now you are gradually recapturing what you found as a seven-year-old.
>
> Client (C40): I, I, I believe that to be true ...
> (The Right to be Desperate)

It was also clear that Rogers was following a number of assumptions that he had previously outlined in his work (*ibid.*) such as the notion that the primary difficulty for people is that they are not in touch with themselves and that clients have within themselves resources for self-understanding and for altering their self-concept (*ibid.*). Rogers also assumes that these resources are tapped when there is a facilitative climate (unconditional positive regard, empathy, and genuineness), which he demonstrated with this client (*ibid.*).

From our perspective, which will be discussed more fully later, the cultural therapist relates to the client in a way that is similar to Rogers in many respects. Thus, we see our cultural framework as an extension of Rogers' work. Cultural therapy, like Rogers' framework, is grounded in multiple disciplines. Our framework is holistic and suggests that the individual is affected, not only by psychological processes, but also by familial, societal, religious and moral domains. These various levels or contexts are interrelated. The framework challenges traditional psychotherapy models (based solely on psychological theories) by integrating psychology, philosophy and anthropology (James and Prilleltensky, 2002). We use a dialogical framework that is process-oriented rather than one that focuses on the final result. Thus, cultural psychotherapy is more a basic philosophy rather than a technique or method. There are also some places where we modify Rogers' approach. Although we agree with Rogers that clinicians must try to get rid of the prejudices that they bring to the session, we are less hopeful that this can actually be fully accomplished. Thus, we see the importance of having clinicians recognize that they are bringing their own biases to the sessions. It is important also to constantly monitor how this process happens and how it affects the sessions.

In addition, we disagree with Rogers' theory of universal pathology (i.e., all problems are caused by being out of touch with one's feelings) for two reasons.

First, we must ask whether the therapist is really allowing the client to guide the session if he/she has already decided *a priori* that the client's problem is caused by the client being out of touch with his or her feelings? In practice, it is the intention that the client guide the session, but an underlying belief of universal pathology constrains the shape that the session actually takes. Secondly, how can there be a universal pathology when clients are so different? The cultural psychotherapist tries not to impose a predetermined pathology on the client but rather helps the client identify the problem. The universal pathology, of not being in touch with one's feelings, is high on Maslow's hierarchy of needs (Maslow, 1970). The needs of ethnic minority clients, however, are often much more basic and are often related to economic constraints. Thus, the realities of their situation mean that a successful counseling session might involve ensuring that they are adequately connected to social service resources. Finally, for some clients, the notion of listening to, or being in touch with oneself is foreign (Rogers, 1989). This is a Western framework that would not fit for all clients. Many clients, especially of more collectivist societies, would find it selfish to spend so much therapy time focusing on themselves.

Using hermeneutics to situate clients in their socio-historical context

The encounter between Rogers and the client reflects what might be called a hermeneutic situation. Even though the client is encouraged to direct the concerns of the therapeutic encounter, it is evident from Rogers' interaction with the African-American client in the filmed sessions that Rogers' own input is highly significant. This situation may be understood as an attempt on the part of the therapist to enter into the 'horizon' of the client, that is, the client's 'range of vision that includes everything that can be seen from a particular vantage point' (Gadamer, 1999: 302).

The concept of a horizon
The notion of a horizon is not that of a static framework but rather one that marks the ever-changing context of understanding through which a person experiences the world (Gadamer, 1999). Our horizon may be described as 'narrow' or 'broad' depending on the effort we make to see beyond that which is most familiar to us (*ibid*.). The notion of horizon is to be understood in a double sense. It describes my 'perspective', that is my sphere or field of subjective understanding, but it also characterizes the sense in which my subjective field is 'open' to change both through my experience of the physical world and my interaction with other people. Horizons take into account both social and historical dimensions of our self and our experience (*ibid*.).

The importance of the notion of horizons for the clinical encounter should be obvious. To understand a client is not to merely understand him or her according to broad classifications based on race, gender or other factors, but to develop a composite out of the various elements of the client's horizon gathered from the encounter itself as one hears the client's own self-interpretations. Horizons themselves can be multi-layered as is demonstrated by the sessions. The client in this case understands his situation in the context of being male, black, American, having leukemia, having had a failed 'mixed marriage' and as being the victim of racism. Rogers allows the client to explore these various aspects of his horizon, but he is by no means a neutral observer in the encounter. The feedback that Rogers gives to the client while he is trying to clarify the meaning of his situation plays more than the role of clarification. Rogers adds to the client's own self-understanding through the dialogical situation. Rogers' words help the client to articulate who 'he' is.

What must be understood here is that the notion of horizon does not represent a distinct and isolated sphere in which we operate. Rogers' ability to develop an understanding of the client rests on the fact that they share a historical horizon to a large degree (American, educated, male). This 'shared' horizon allows the encounter to begin so that Rogers can explore the more distinct aspects of the client's horizon, moving from what is common in the two horizons to what distinguishes the client (*ibid.*). Hence, the encounter between Rogers and the client takes on a dialectical structure which exemplifies what we have earlier called the 'hermeneutic situation'. Understanding both one's own view of the world as well as that of the client in terms of 'horizons' means that one recognizes that their consciousness is 'historically effected' (*ibid.*). This implies that therapists 'necessarily' bring their own 'prejudgments' or 'prejudices' into the shared horizon with the client, contrary to Rogers' claim. These prejudices need not remain 'blind'. Indeed, part of the task of therapy, or more generally human communication, is to become aware of one's own prejudices and to limit their negative effect.

Alienation and Hegel's master/slave story

During the sessions, we see that the client feels a strong sense of alienation for which he identifies various sources. He feels alienated as a black man in America. He recalls a childhood incident where one of his schoolteachers, in recognition of his intelligence, called him 'a credit to his race'. It is clear from his repeated recollection of this event that it had a profound effect on him. He feels alienated from his ex-wife's family whom he believes to have shunned him for racial reasons. He experienced alienation due to his leukemia and possibly due to his financial problems. He regrets feeling that he had to lie in order to borrow money from friends while being sick. He feels a strong sense of loss over the death of his former father-in-law. After a rocky start in their relationship, they had finally developed a friendship that obviously meant a great deal to the client. What is interesting to note is the client's constant focus on the anger and frustration associated with the rejection he felt from his ex-wife's family and the silence surrounding his own biological family.

Aspects of the client's alienation seem to bear an ambiguous relation to issues of race. For instance, his hurt, which resulted from the lost relationship with his wife's family, would probably have existed if his marriage had not been 'interracial', at least to a great degree. His understanding of the break-up of his marriage on racial grounds adds another dimension to the hurt. This introduces issues of historical consideration. The historical aspect is illustrated by G.W.F. Hegel's 'master/slave' dialectic as he presents it in his *Phenomenology of Spirit* (1977). Hegel characterizes the emergence of human freedom in terms of a struggle between two primitive consciousnesses. In this struggle, each stakes his/her life in an effort to break free from the necessity of nature and to become an 'essential being' (that is, a being who creates or determines his/her own 'essence' or 'purpose' rather than being an 'inessential' or passive part of nature). The loser of this struggle agrees to be the slave of the winner (the master) rather than submit to death. In this way the master gains the recognition he/she desires. The slave, on the other hand, lacks such recognition and only understands his/her own being through the eyes of the master. The master determines the slave's existence. This history of slavery and inequality becomes internalized in the historical consciousness of the oppressor and oppressed (*ibid.*). The 'oppressed', over time, come to understand themselves through the eyes of their oppressor (who largely determines language and other cultural structures); indeed, they may even come to despise themselves. This notion is of relevance to other types of situations such as ones resulting from gender inequalities which Feminist writers have commented on. For example, Simone de Beauvoir carries Hegel's master/slave dialectic over to the historical relation between the sexes in *The Second Sex* (1989). The 'second sex', like the slave in Hegel's story, is the inessential, the being who finds her essence in the other 'essential' being. In the case of Rogers and his client, the history of racial inequality that informs the 'master-slave' relationship forms the background of the interaction between the therapist and his client and, therefore, cannot be ignored.

Horizons of alienation

The internalization of this inequality is reflected in the horizon of the client; indeed, it plays a major role in shaping it. The formative childhood incident of being told he was 'a credit to his race' added to his sense of alienation. His marriage problems and rejection by his 'in-laws' created a new or further sense of alienation.

Client (C12) : Lost my father-in-law (T: Mmhm) which was uhm a terrible

> loss to me (T: Mmhm) and was a loss that I never could talk to my wife or anybody else about (T: Mmhm) and uhm I gave a lot to that family, you know, for five, I don't know, seven years I guess, and uhm when I went back there were just some things that happened that uh, uh showed me there wasn't, there wasn't very much of a connection, there wasn't very much of a connection between uh, between all of that love and whatever that I put in and then all of a sudden you know I became uh you know, I, I became just another black person I became just another nigger you know and I think it's important to understand that my my wife is Ge-, you know is, is white (T: I see) German-Irish (T: Hmm, I see) and I think that is part of the whole thing (T: Mmhm) that uhm when we first married you know my father-in-law we just fought tooth and nail (T: Mmhm, mmhm) but then after that we loved each other (T: Mmhm) for about six long good hard years (T: Mmhm) and basically he was my only connection when he died (T: Mmhm) I found that uh there was no support (T: Mmhm) there was absolutely no support.
>
> *(The Right to be Desperate)*

What this particular client's experience illustrates is a double alienation through two layers of his horizon: his personal experiences of illness, separation and his more general sense of social alienation (interracial marriage; comments by his grade school teacher; perhaps Carl Rogers as a 'white therapist'). This double sense of alienation illustrates a fundamental aspect of the hermeneutic dimension of cultural therapy whose aim is to understand the part (one's life and the particular episodes of one's life) in light of the whole (one's social-historical context) and the whole in light of the part (Gadamer, 1999). As self-interpreting beings who carry our history through language and memory, we not only internalize our direct experiences, but, to a large degree, the history of our cultural groups. This affects our consciousness through myth, religion, historical accounts, and the historical character of words themselves. Our direct personal experiences (the 'part') are always experienced by us through this larger historical web (the 'whole'). If we are Black, Jewish, German or other, our self-understanding is formed in the context of specific historical meanings. The theme of alienation is implied by Rogers in the videotapes in several places where he discusses the client's 'felt' need to live up to the expectations of others. Rogers discusses this elsewhere in the context of freeing one's self from external 'oughts' and expectations (Rogers, 1961). These 'oughts', when imposed on us from the outside rather than coming from our own internalized morality, appear to us in an alienated form as Hegel delineated (Gadamer, 1981).

We see justification for understanding Rogers' approach in hermeneutical terms when we look at his writings. Although he does not call his work hermeneutical, the description that he gives of a 'third approach' in his article 'Client-Centered Theory' demonstrates the notion of a 'shared' or 'fused' horizon (Rogers, 1956). When discussing his encounter with a client named Paul, Rogers (*ibid.*) indicates the limitations of behavioral approaches that seek to identify a causal sequence of events responsible for certain behaviors. Such an approach seems doomed to 'an infinite regress of fact-seeking' he tells us (*ibid.*: 115). Rogers presents us with an alternative way of understanding the client:

> We can form a relationship with Paul in which we can fairly readily come to know his phenomenological field, his field of perceived meanings as these occur in consciousness. We can learn how he sees himself, his behavior, his father, his mother, his teachers, his friends. We can learn how he perceives the attitudes of each of these toward him. We can learn the meaning that each of these perceptions has for him. We can even predict that if the relationship has certain qualities, the area of his awareness will broaden and come to include experiences which have occurred in his organism, but of which he has not previously been aware. Consequently we can broaden his perceptual field and come to know these additional meanings (*ibid.*:116).

How is it possible to come to understand the 'phenomenological field' of another person that is, by definition, subjective? How can we know 'his field of perceived meanings, as these occur in consciousness'? This, we would argue, is accomplished by a fusion or sharing of horizons. Communication of such subjective meaning is possible on the basis of our horizons being open enough, and shared enough for us to enter the field of meaning of another person. Gadamer calls this 'transposing ourselves into a situation' (Gadamer, 1999).

CLINICAL TOOLS

One of the goals of cultural psychotherapy is that there is a 'reconciliation' of the client's fractured or alienated sense of self. In Hegel's dialectic, reconciliation was the projected goal or answer to humankind's fundamental alienation. Narrative becomes a valuable tool at this point for both client and therapist in reconciling the various aspects of the client's life (Ricoeur, 1992). For example, narrative therapy has been a culturally appropriate tool for the Portuguese immigrants with whom we work (James, 2002). We found in our research with the Portuguese community that most of the participants spontaneously tell stories about their situation and what is important for them. The community that we studied found it difficult to use therapeutic language, whereas a narrative description of the situation was both natural and familiar. For the Portuguese immigrants, the narratives help them to reconcile their fractured horizons by finding a way to integrate life in Portugal with life in America. Similarly, in the sessions, we see Rogers allowing the client to tell his story, to provide a narrative that makes sense of his suffering and gives structure to his life, his self. The feedback that Rogers gives to the client helps him work out the details of his narrative as he seeks for a coherence that will reconcile the suffering in his life. His pain over the loss of his father-in-law is expressed in terms of his regret for not having told him he loved him.

> *Client(C75): ... We were getting so close, but that I really never told him that, 'Hey Dad, you know, hey Dad, I love you, I really love you'. And we told each other, I guess, in some ways or whatever, but it's not the same as saying it, you know, as saying, 'Dad, I really love you. I really care.'*

(On Anger and Hurt)

This obviously creates in him a sense of incompleteness that has been amplified by the further alienation he experiences in relation to his wife's family. By encouraging the client to articulate his/her self in terms of a story or narrative, the therapist gives the client a form for understanding and attempting to reconcile his or her suffering. Seeing one's suffering and alienation in the form of an individual story that is part of a bigger story (of America, Christianity, oppression) helps the client to understand who he/she is. Such historical self-understanding may provide the comfort of reconciling one's self with one's cultural group. From such a narrative framework the client develops a reflexive experience or understanding of his or her own self. The dialogue that begins with the therapist continues as an ongoing internalized dialogue, empowering the client with a new sense of being the author (or at least co-author) of his/her own story. The client begins to understand the circumstances (social, religious, educational) as well as the relationships that have helped constitute the client's sense of self. By identifying the important factors that have contributed to the shaping of his/her identity, the client is in a position to work through the obstacles that this identity entails (Ricoeur, 1992). The client is ready to set his/her story (or self) aright.

Cultural psychotherapy also tackles the client's alienation in pragmatic ways. Given that interracial mistrust is a theme for Rogers' client, we would not do client case notes that appear to be secretive (i.e., in the client's file) but rather adopt White and Epston's (1990) suggestion of mailing the client the case notes in the form of a letter. In this way, the client is not going to be worried about how his white therapist is evaluating him and he will be able to think about responses to the letter throughout the week. Further to this, besides working on an individual level with this client, we can also work on other levels to help his alienation. At the family level, finding ways for him to connect with his children would be important for the client. Also, providing an opportunity in therapy to talk about his family of origin (whom he rarely mentions) could be beneficial for tackling his alienation. From the moral domain, we are interested to learn what kind of obligation the client feels towards his children. Doherty (1995) provides an effective framework for helping clients work through moral dilemmas in therapy including those that arise in the context of co-parenting. It would be helpful to learn how the client envisions co-parenting from such distance.

In addition, cultural psychotherapy seeks to explore the client's spiritual reality. In the American health care system, 'illness' is separated into explicit domains. When the client experiences 'illness' of the mind (e.g., depression), a therapist is consulted. For the client with bodily 'illness' (physical ailment), a physician is recommended. Further, 'illness' of faith is mediated through a religious healer. However, for some clients, it is not functional to fragment these experiences. Thus, mental health providers need to be cognizant of the client's experiential dialogue (including a holistic approach) and incorporate healing methods that align with the client's interpretation of her/his 'illness'. In our research with Portuguese immigrants (James and Clarke, 2001), we found that they often demonstrated a worldview in which the mind, body and spirit are connected. For instance, we found that community members would seek healing for a culture-specific phenomenon known as 'the agonies' from physicians, traditional healers and priests. It was not a problem to seek healing from more than one healer at a time and, in fact, many of them believed that more was better.

In the case of Rogers' client, it seems that his experience of cancer has caused him to turn away from his faith. James and Clarke (2001) have found that some religious patients have a crisis of faith upon learning about their own cancer diagnosis (see also Pargament et al., 1995). We would explore that further with this client especially since he still makes Christian references. For instance he said, 'I was thinking I really conditioned myself to, to, to, really uh get ready and find the nearest cross and crawl up on that.' Does he feel a sense of loss either spiritually or socially because of leaving his faith? Does he feel guilt about this? What form does that take? Further, the client endorses a holistic perspective when the therapist states:

> *Therapist (T119): You wonder about that ... whether if you, if you let out all the ... all the hell that you've experienced inside, it might uh, it might bring back your illness ...*
> Client (C120): And that doesn't sound logical, does it?
> (On Anger and Hurt)

We would reassure the client that this kind of thinking is common in cancer patients (Clarke, 1985). The client's illness narrative allows him to once again take control of his life and try to prevent any illness from (re-) emerging. For the client whose life had been dictated for so long by others (physicians, technicians, nurses, creditors), creating this framework is probably an empowering experience. This notion of the culturally empowering therapeutic process could also be seen with Teresa who was in therapy with Susan James. A discussion of the case vignette is offered below.

Case study: Teresa

Teresa is a 58-year-old woman from the Azores. Like many Azorean widows she dressed in black, even though her husband had been dead for several years. She had been referred by a social worker who worked at the local Portuguese community centre. She came to see me because she had many pains that she experienced during any kind of activity. During the intake interview it became clear that she frequently visited her physician because of her many ailments such as diabetes and rheumatoid arthritis. When I asked about her medications, she pulled four pill bottles out of her purse to show me. Although she was taking a number of medications, her pain had not disappeared; she still had pains in her legs, pains when she stood and other pains when she lay down. In fact, for most of the first three sessions she nearly only spoke of her pain even if I tried to discuss other topics.

During the fourth session I asked her 'are there times when you are not in pain?' and 'what helps with that?' The next week she came back and she was much worse than during the previous three weeks. My attempt to try to help her to focus on the times that she was not in pain had backfired. As I forced her to find days she was feeling better she was sure to tell me about days that she was feeling worse. Fortunately, I was aware that this had happened so I decided that I would not force her to talk about the times that she felt better but rather have her direct the course of therapy and really try to understand her situation. As I gave up trying to find ways to get rid of the pain, her conversation moved in the direction of other areas of life such as her daughter's poor treatment of her.

What I learned through this experience (and was later confirmed through my research) was that with this client, and many Portuguese immigrant women, taking the time to listen to all their physical symptoms is important for several reasons. First, for this community, sharing aches and pains is a natural way to connect with another human being. Thus, with my client it was a way to open up a compassionate bond and build rapport. Secondly, listening to physical complaints is a test that needs to be passed until more personal issues are broached.

Thirdly, I discovered that my client thought that therapy would terminate, and our relationship would end, if her pains subsided. Lastly, from my client's perspective, a good person suffers. Suffering is part of the human condition that brings you closer to God and others. Asking her about when she was not suffering was not a helpful question. Now when I conduct therapy, I try to understand as soon as possible the client's 'horizon' including his or her notion of a good person, a good family and a good society. I also try to understand the biases that I bring to the session. With my first client it was clear that I found it difficult to listen to her suffering and that I held the bias (implicit in many psychotherapy theories) that suffering needs to be removed immediately without even trying to understand its web of significance.

CONCLUSION

Like Rogers' framework, cultural psychotherapy has been influenced by multiple disciplines resulting in a complex understanding of the client. It demonstrates its value with ethnic minority clients by situating the client within the context of his/her multi-layered social reality. This approach allows the therapist to try to understand clients through exploring the various dimensions of their 'horizon' by way of client-therapist dialogue. Meanwhile the client gains a better understanding of his or her own self by coming to understand this 'horizon' and by articulating a story or narrative which gives coherence to this self.

REFERENCES

Clarke, J (1985) *It's Cancer: The Personal Experiences of Women who have received a cancer diagnosis.* Toronto: IPI Publishing.
de Beauvoir, S (1989) *The Second Sex.* New York, NY: Vintage Books.
Doherty, W (1995) *Soul Searching: Why Psychotherapy Must Promote Moral Responsibility.* New York, NY: Basic Books.
Gadamer, H-G (1981) *Reason in the Age of Science.* Cambridge, MA: The MIT Press.
Gadamer, H-G (1999) *Truth and Method* (2nd edn) trans. J Weinsheimer and DG Marshall. New York: Continuum.
Hegel, GWF (1977) *Phenomenology of Spirit,* trans. AV Miller. Oxford: Clarendon Press.
James, S (2002) 'Agonias: The social and sacred sufferings of Azorean immigrants.' *Culture, Medicine and Psychiatry, 26*(1): 87–110.
James, S and Clarke, J (2001) 'Surplus suffering: The case of Portuguese immigrant women.' *Feminist Review, 68*: 167–70.
James, S and Prilleltensky, I (2002) 'Cultural diversity and mental health: Towards integrative practice.' *Clinical Psychology Review, 22*(8): 1133–54.
Maslow, AH (1970) *Motivation and Personality* (2nd edn.). New York, NY: Harper &

Row.

Pargament, KI, Sullivan, MS, Balzer, WK, Van Haitsma, KS, et al. (1995) 'The many meanings of religiousness: A policy-capturing approach.' *Journal of Personality,* 63(4): 953–83.

Ricoeur, P (1992) *Oneself as Another*. Chicago, IL: University of Chicago Press.

Rogers, CR (1955) 'Persons or science? A philosophical question.' *American Psychologist,* 10: 267–78.

Rogers, CR (1956) 'Client-centered theory.' *Journal of Counselling Psychology,* 3(2): 115–20.

Rogers, CR (1961) *On Becoming a Person*. London: Constable.

Rogers, CR (1989) *The Carl Rogers Reader*. H Kirschenbaum and VL Henderson (eds). Boston: MA: Houghton Mifflin.

White, M and Epston, D (1990) *Narrative Means to Therapeutic Ends*. New York, NY: W.W. Norton.

Chapter 17
THERAPIST'S FACES CLIENT'S MASKS: RACIAL ENACTMENTS THROUGH PAIN, ANGER AND HURT

ANISSA TALAHITE AND ROY MOODLEY

Given the society's history of complex racial relations, therapists must be prepared to accept the rage that clients of different racial backgrounds may hold toward therapists as symbols of the country's racial dynamics
(Helms and Cook, 1999: 149)

It seems that the pain, anger and hurt created by the racial tensions in society that clients and therapists (black and white) experience, can often be unconsciously acted-out as part of their intersubjective relating. In this respect, the 'On Anger and Hurt' sessions offer an interesting, and at times complex process characterized by the presence/absence of race. Although very much 'silent' in the verbal communication between Rogers and the client, race is at the same time an unavoidable meaning which impinges on the client's and Rogers' clinical reflections. Race acts as both the signifier and the signified of the physical and the psychological self, and in turn inhabits the psychic space of client and therapist. The silence of race or 'the absent presence of race' (Walcott, 2003) then creates a 'voice' which articulates a fixed, essentialist and physical explanation of the subject. This limits the interpretation and understanding of the self to the confines of the epidermal layer; skin deep, as it were, of any cultural, social and historical manifestations of the self. In this way, the silence of race constructs and reinforces a place of memory where historical pain, anger and hurt can be re-experienced. Race in the therapy room is then an omniscient presence dislocating and alienating the client, to the point where the pain, anger and hurt lie in wait, as it were, for the therapist.

In this chapter, we examine the ways in which race perhaps unconsciously takes on this pervasive role in the client's discourse. Using some of Frantz Fanon's ideas about 'alienation of the self' theorized in *Black Skin White Masks*, we explore the client's interactions with Rogers, particularly focusing on the question of 'trust' and 'mistrust' which becomes part of the socio-historical and cultural memory (Fanon, 1967). In the 'The Right to be Desperate' and 'On Anger and Hurt' sessions, we are offered an opportunity, through a particular direction and technique in the filming, to be part of the visual gaze: of black and white, of anger and hurt, of coloured metonym and metaphor, of life and death, and of therapist's faces and client's masks. It is these masks that the therapist must face and at the same time unmask the hidden sometime invisible distressed part of the self. The uncovering of the suffering—pain, anger and hurt—is what constitutes the 'work' and the 'working through' in therapy which is precisely what Rogers tries so hard to do. The client resists. Rogers insists and continues to insist in a directive fashion (see Brodley, 1996). The client continues to resist Rogers' efforts. If we consider that these masks of pain, anger and hurt are 'defensive masks' necessary to maintain a semblance of ego boundary in an otherwise devastated and fragmented individual, it then stands to reason why Rogers was, as Brodley (1996) suggests, uncharacteristically directive. The release of these points of racial tension perhaps may be possible if client and therapist are willing to step outside the clinical room, at least metaphorically, to confront, according to Helms and Cook (1999), the 'symbols of the country's racial dynamics'.

Two decades before the meeting between Rogers and his anonymous black client, Fanon engaged in the dialogue of faces and masks in *Black Skin White Masks*. Many of Fanon's ideas about questions regarding imposed identity and the existence of the black person in a world dominated by systemic racism—and the ensuing pain, anger and hurt—came from personal experience, very much like the narrative of Rogers' client.[1] Fanon writes, 'I believe that only a psychoanalytical interpretation of the black problem can lay bare the anomalies of affect that are responsible for the structure of the complex'. This complex, he argues, results from 'two facts': '… White men consider themselves superior to black men … Black men want to prove to white men, at all costs, the richness of their thought, the equal value of their intellect' (Fanon, 1967: 10). In our viewing, it is the second fact that seems most evident, especially as the client appears to intellectualise his feelings to a point of being unable to express them in therapy. This defence mechanism appears to be often seen in middle-class black clients irrespective of race or ethnic differences. For example, Moodley (1999) through the analysis of a same race/culture client shows how this kind of defence system can be problematic.

[1.] In *Frantz Fanon and the Psychology of Oppression*, Hussein Abdilahi Bulhan (1985: 138) suggests that in *Black Skin White Masks,* Fanon 'emphasised the experiential features and hidden psycho-affective injuries of blacks and the various defense maneuvers they adopted'.

A comprehensive analysis of such defence mechanisms are examined by Liggan and Kay (1999). They argue that the three primary internal models that drive psychological defences in relation to African-American clients and white therapists—the internal parental models, the internal model of the whites, and the internal models of blacks—impair the ability to resolve interracial conflict and limits adaptation. In terms of the internal model of whites, they argue that the 'image is distorted by the power and privilege ascribed to representations of a superior class ... and an underlying image of self as inferior, primitive and "non-white"' (*ibid.*: 199), and that 'the narrative of race offers an explanation of how these attitudes affect the African-American psychological being' (p. 200).

Fanon's definition of alienation seems of particular relevance to the analysis of the ways in which Rogers' client articulates his distress and his relationship with the therapist. One of Fanon's main ideas was that the Manichean divide created by racism is responsible for creating an existential alienation for those who are regarded as racial 'others'. Abdul Jan Mohamed describes this phenomenon as the 'economic, social, political, racial and moral elaboration and distortion of a fundamental ontological opposition between self and other' (Jan Mohamed, 1983: 264). Homi Bhabha gives it a more pathological definition calling it, after Fanon's phrase, 'a constellation of delirium' (Bhabha, 1987: 119). It seems that some of the characteristics resulting from what Fanon describes as the psychological violence of racism are being re-enacted by Rogers and the client in the 'The Right to be Desperate' and 'On Anger and Hurt' sessions. Although the therapist and the client are able to communicate with each other, they also express some of the tensions of racially segregated society—e.g., as it will be demonstrated, aggression, guilt and mistrust can be observed as part of their communication. We will suggest that a possible way of averting these negative projections is to understand the client's distress as the product of social, cultural and historically constructed parameters that need to be taken into account in the therapeutic process.

MASKS AND ALIENATION: 'I FORGOT THAT I WAS BLACK'

One recurrent theme in the client's narrative is that of denial, particularly in relation to his comments about the difficulty of being black in a white-dominated society. The denial of blackness has historical associations in relation to the construction of the racialised 'other' as theorized by Fanon in *Black Skin White Masks*, a text which anticipates some of the major debates on race and identity in contemporary Western society. His observations as a psychiatrist treating patients dealing with the trauma of racism and colonisation in *Wretched of the Earth* have added to the knowledge about the psychological violence of racism (Fanon, 1965). Fanon was writing at a time when de-colonisation was starting to shake Europe's former colonial empire and around the period when the voice of resistance against racism and segregation in the United States was making itself heard through powerful figures, such as Martin Luther King and Malcolm X. One of Fanon's main observations is that the black client's distress is primarily the result of an ontological need to find a meaningful self, his/her sense of self having been displaced and negated or distorted in the process of assimilating the dominant culture.

Fanon also writes about the projections that have historically been associated with blackness as 'otherness' and as 'negativity' in the European psyche (Fanon, 1967). In the first session, the client describes the intense feeling of alienation he experienced as a boy when his school teacher commented on his being 'a credit to [his] race'. This phrase is used later by both Rogers and the client when trying to describe the difficulty of having to live up to others' expectations. These expectations are often articulated by the client in terms of race. In fact, the issue of the 'racialised' self permeates the client's discourse. For example, in the first session, the client explains that he 'forgot' that he was black at the time he was living with his ex-wife in a white community:

> *Client (C27):* ... *I forgot for, for may be a couple of years you know and I am going to oversimplify this next thing (T: Hmm) but, but I forgot that I was black (T: Hmm mm) in that family (T:Hm mm) in that community (T: Hm mm) or whatever you see. (T:Hm mm) Then I quickly learned that uhh—*
> *Therapist (T28): You were reminded all over again.*
> *Client (C28): Oh for sure and I think that also caused a lot of bitterness or whatever (T: Hm mm) and that kind of stuff I want to get out of me.*

Fanon describes the condition of the racialised 'other' as a permanent state of psychological tension resulting from the impossibility of belonging to neither the 'white world' nor the 'black world'. For Fanon, to search for recognition from the 'white world' means to realise that it is impossible to enter that world, for its very existence is based on the exclusion of black people (Fanon, 1967). Similarly, Rogers' client seems to have become alienated from his self, having acquired as it were a 'white mask', a psychological disguise which allowed him to survive in an all-white community. This creates a feeling of hurt and 'bitterness' towards those who originally denied his difference but later rejected him because of his race. This of course raises two important questions: first, can the black client successfully engage in therapy with Rogers, a white middleclass man who could represent for the client this oppressed history? and second, is Rogers' presence itself a catalyst for the pain, anger and hurt to surface? According to Liggan and Kay (1999), race transferences that represent powerful early feelings towards white people are projected onto the therapist through feelings of mistrust, anger, acknowledgement of ambivalence and acceptance of disparate parts of the self.

Fanon argues that race is above all a meaning constructed by white society, stating that '… it is not I who make a meaning for myself, but it is the meaning that was already there pre-existing, waiting for me' (Fanon, 1967: 134). Rogers' client seems to gradually recognize his alienation in relation to his blackness, a process that Rogers senses but does not articulate in terms of race. For the client, his experience of being in the presence of Rogers may allow for him to experience the whiteness of the therapist as a representation of a idealized, lost, never-achieved object (Holmes, 1992). From a slightly different geopolitical situation but a similar socio-historical perspective, Biko (1978) asserts that black people have internalized a negative self-image and consequently identify with white society, supporting the view that the ego in these contexts is constructed through the distorted mirroring from whites. For the therapist grappling with these issues, Lacan's (1977) mirror stage and alienation theory appears to be one way of understanding this process. Lacan suggests that the development of the subject's ego takes place through a process of identification of the image outside itself which is fragmented, distorted and displaced. Since the ego itself is in the place of the imaginary, false images of identity will be internalized in which case the therapist would need to 'rediscover in the ego the function of the real' (*ibid.*: 90). Furthermore, Lacan maintains that 'you cannot possibly achieve this if you cling to the idea that the ego of the subject is identical with the presence that is speaking to you' (*ibid.*: 90). In clinical terms, a therapist would need to locate, for the client, his or her position of the 'I' (first person pronoun) in his verbal interactions. The intention here is to alienate the 'I' of the client from his or her ego which is in the imaginary, a place of distortion, fragmentation and mutation. This seems to have been the position of Rogers with his black client. For example, in the voiceover to *The Right to be Desperate*, Rogers comments on the client's progressively becoming more self-accepting, describing his growing awareness as 'a real step into … [t]he acceptance of himself as a desperate person'. The client experiences a sense of loss when recalling the 'wholeness' which he felt as a seven-year-old boy. This feeling could also be seen as resulting from the process of assimilating into the white world and shaping an ego which remains in the imaginary. In his voiceover, Rogers comments on how the client's sense of being 'part of the universe' which he felt as a child was disrupted by society, thus showing some awareness of the socio-historical forces which caused the distress experienced by the client.

RACE AS AN INEVITABLE MEANING

Internalised processes involving self-objectification and self-depreciation are part of the contradiction experienced by the client. His relationship with his wife in particular seems to be closely connected to his sense of alienation within white-dominated society. The fact that his children are, as it were, 'absent' from his personal narrative accentuates this sense, as fatherhood as a means of asserting one's reality seems to have been denied to the client. It is interesting to note that this process of denial that the client experiences seems, in many ways, to be accentuated through the way in which the therapeutic process is conducted. The fact that Rogers appears to avoid the focus on race or ethnicity seems to accentuate the experience of alienation.

To us as viewers (and to the generations of therapists who have been using the videotapes over the years), the absence of a name for the client and the silence surrounding his blackness reinforce the idea of denial. The client's constant references and allusions to race and racial issues, for example ('a credit to my race' and many similar comments), appear to have been avoided by Rogers, who uses the concept of 'culture' rather than race or 'racism' as the basis for an exploration of the client's narrative. One interpretation, albeit psychoanalytic, is that Rogers' apparent disavowal of race with this particular client could be a clinical strategy to engage unconscious material in the transference relationship. Another interpretation is that Rogers may have used the core conditions (viz., empathy, unconditional positive regard, and congruence) in a conscious and deliberate attempt to enable the client to realize his 'true' self through the removal of the 'false' masks imposed by society. As Rogers' comments in the voiceover (V18), 'I'm trying, as in all my therapy, to help him get back to the kind of realness he had as a child.' A third interpretation, and one that is very difficult to assess, is that Rogers may have unconsciously denied the client's racial identity.

These interpretations must be seen in the context of the social, cultural and historical forces that shape relationships between blacks and whites. In other words, the therapist's silence about race echoes in many respects the silence of white society over the client's identity. It is often through this kind of silence that race becomes absolute and essential. Rogers' silence on race and its corollary, the client's overt articulation of it, could eventually result in one or the other making race absolute and essential. This is what may be happening in these sessions, a process seemingly Rogers wants to avoid. In other words, if one considers race an inevitable meaning between Rogers and the client that none can escape, the client's insistence on race and Rogers' silences become loaded with powerful significances. What is the meaning of the client's desire for asserting his 'otherness' to Rogers? Is he seeking recognition of his 'black self' by a white therapist and therefore some kind of reassurance that he exists? The fact that he is seeking this recognition from a white male figure (who he even associates with Jesus Christ in the course of the therapy!) is not without significance. Does the client need to be acknowledged as 'black' by Rogers for 'blackness' to exist for him as a meaning? If this is the case, his constant references to race are part of a deep sense of alienation, rather than an act of self-assertion. As Fanon explains,

> Ontology—once it is finally admitted as leaving existence by the wayside—does not permit us to understand the being of the black man. For not only must the black man be black; he must be black in relation to the white man (Fanon, 1967: 110).

It is also interesting to note that, while the client seems to be willing to address issues of racism, his overall communication shows that he is also resisting the interaction with Rogers. Many of his responses could be seen as avoidance and defence mechanisms. Although Rogers identifies moments when the client is able to 'experience his buried feelings rather than describe them or be told about them' (V17), these are very rare. For most of the time, the client is able to explain his distress to the therapist without experiencing the affects. One interpretation is that the client is building intellectual defences that seem to alienate him even further. The client seems aware of this process in himself when he says at the beginning of the 'On Anger and Hurt' session:

> Client (C3): ... being angry now, is a part of the process and I've got to do that, but I'd like to ... I guess my uh ... I guess mind uh academically or something, you know, and something other than emotion or whatever you like, would like to tell me that, uh, I'd like to uh ... to not be angry and to skip over that part.

The intellectualized version of his 'self' acts as a fortress where he cannot be reached. Rogers appears to be aware of this defence mechanism as a constant shield against various therapeutic attempts encouraging the client to be more affective and open about his feelings. This leads him to describe the client as 'an armour-plated man' in his final comment about the session.

DISAVOWAL OF THE 'OTHER'

The resistance on the part of the client and the reluctance to acknowledge race on the part of Rogers represent a double process that has been observed between white therapists and black clients. Holmes (1992) suggests that there is significant resistance in patients and countertransferences in therapists associated with race. A denial of race, ethnicity and culture of the 'other' in psychotherapy, either consciously or unconsciously, can lead to negative transference and countertransference reactions. The therapeutic relation is then based on mistrust, negative tension, resistance, repression and pseudo-identification on the part of the therapist. Clearly, this position limits the treatment and may incapacitate the therapist from interpreting intrapsychic material. Holmes indicates that there are several factors that limit therapeutic intervention when therapists do not fully interpret intrapsychic conflicts in relation to clients' racial explanations. She suggests, 'these issues include white therapist guilt, black therapist over-identification with the downtrodden (a particular form of countertransference problem) and warded-off aggression in patients and therapists' (*ibid.*: 1). Similarly, another view is that when black clients explore racial and cultural identity in psychotherapy, the denial of race or the disavowal of the racial 'other' creates a particular anxiety that exposes the tensions between the patient and the therapist. As Bhabha says,

> The disavowal of the Other always exacerbates the edge of identification, reveals that dangerous place where identity and aggressivity are twinned ... At the edge, in-between the black body and the white body, there is tension of meaning and being, so some would say demand and desire, which is the psychic counterpart to that muscular tension that inhabits the native body ... It is from such tension—both psychic and political—that a strategy of subversion emerges (Bhabha, 1994: 62).

The racial, cultural and ethnic denial of the 'other' creates negative conflicts, confusions and tensions and may be experienced as aggression by either patient or therapist or both. This is particularly poignant in a black and white dyad, such as the therapeutic encounter of Carl Rogers with the black client. For example, taking a close look at the dialogue between Rogers and the client, one is struck with the violence of some of the images as in the following excerpt of *On Anger and Hurt*:

> Client (C125): ... *just like somebody took a big goddamned tree and just rammed it up ... ooh, so, you know? (Sighs). Hard to describe, you know, you know?*
> Therapist (T125): *Took a big stick and rammed it up your ass, / is that what you're saying?*
> Client (C126): *(Laughs) I, I didn't say that.*
> Therapist (T126): *Is that what you meant?*
> Client (C127): *That's what I meant.*
> Therapist (T127): *Okay. That's what I want to know, whether I was catching your meaning correctly.*

Although the client accepts that this is 'what he meant', the image is still being completed by the therapist for the client in a directive manner (Brodley, 1996: 318). Is Rogers reflecting his own tensions regarding race through this image? It is interesting that he returns to the image of the tree in his final comment on the session:

> Rogers (Final comment): ... *Along the way we see how powerful metaphor is in the deeper ranges of psychotherapy. Metaphor is so much more expressive than an intellectual description ... The lump in his throat ... The*

ability to speak from 'up here' and not from 'down there'... The goddamn tree stuck up his ass ... The green slime that must be vomited ... They all speak vividly of his feelings, without naming those feelings.

One wonders whether such examples are reflective of the complex projections of anger and aggression engendered by the denial of race in the therapy.

This denial of race can become dominant in the therapeutic dialogue at the expense of intrapsychic material that could be facilitated creatively to engender trust, openness and cross-racial therapeutic possibilities. It seems that an avoidance of race, culture and ethnicity as clinical variables can have considerable consequences for the client who is already in a very vulnerable state about his/her self-concept, self-esteem and self-perception. One consequence is the projection of aggression and anger. If these are not dealt with openly as part of the therapeutic process, they are at risk of being projected onto the client. Another example is Rogers' articulation of the client's anger in the following excerpt:

Therapist (T22): I get what you are saying and I also feel quite strongly that I want to say, 'it's okay with me if you're angry here'...
Client (T23): (Pause) ... But I don't ...it's hard to know how to be angry, you know ... hard to ...
Therapist (T23): Sure, sure, I'm not saying you have to be. (C: Sure.) I'm saying it's okay with me.
Client (C24): Mmm.
Therapist (T24): If you feel like being angry, you can be angry.
Client (C25): You really believe that?
Therapist (T25): Damn right.
(On Anger and Hurt)

In this dialogue, the therapist appears to be very directive about the patient's expression of anger. This aspect of Rogers' method in *On Anger and Hurt* is surprising, particularly as it is atypical of the Person-Centred Approach.[2] Is the therapist speaking for the patient, or could he have been expressing his own anger? Tillett suggests that therapists do 'become aware of recurrent

---

[2] In her chapter titled: 'Uncharacteristic Directiveness', Barbara Temaner Brodley (1996 and Chapter 4a this volume) offers an interesting critique on the second of the two video presentations: *On Anger and Hurt*. In it she explores the inconsistency in the therapy with Rogers. For example, Rogers appeared to be 'uncharacteristically directive' in a process which is named after him purporting to be non-directive. She says, 'Rogers was trying to influence the client toward specific objectives to immediately and intensely experience anger, sadness, and hurt feelings' (p. 139,1996, and page 44 this volume). This response raises critical questions in relation to issues of race and the Person-Centred Approach, or perhaps, of Rogers and this particular black client.

countertransference anger, though obviously the sources of this need exploration in supervision to distinguish between projective identification and stimulation of the therapist's own unresolved psychopathology' (Tillett, 1998: 289). In the context of projection of negativity onto the 'other' (Fanon, 1967), the 'unresolved psychopathology' are all the more 'unresolved' as they have to do with the historical processes which are beyond the control of the therapist and the client.

The issue of exploring anger and aggression is a complex one for psychotherapists. This gets further complicated if the anger and aggression are released and expressed as a result of the disavowal of race, culture and ethnicity. However, addressing aggression is critical because,

> Many patients, especially those whose psychopathology is the result of inappropriate aggression or abuse will respond positively to an approach which is not only containing but also confronting. Avoidance of therapeutic aggression may lead to failure of therapeutic engagement or, worse, to the accidental covert or unconscious use of aggression by the therapist which will certainly replicate earlier damage (Tillett, 1998: 288).

The exploration of the anger and aggression would need to be contextualised and situated within the client's psychological, as well as social worldview models. It seems therefore important to recognise the psychological alienation experienced by Rogers' client in relation to his place in a white-dominated world. The history of racial domination needs to be taken into account when looking at the relationship between Rogers and his black client, particularly in the context of trust and mistrust within the therapeutic relationship.

(MIS)TRUST: 'I HAVE THAT HISTORY ... '

In addition to aggression and guilt, the disavowal of race also promotes mistrust between the patient and the therapist.[3] The issue of trust and mistrust are seldom

---

[3] Scholars and researchers have devoted much attention to clarifying the definition and meaning of trust in different contexts and the conditions or determinants which engender trust (Jones and George, 1998). For Rosseau et al. trust can be generally defined as 'a psychological state comprising the intention to accept vulnerability based upon positive expectations of the intentions or behaviours of another' (Rosseau et al., 1998: 395). Although scholars are in agreement about a general definition of trust, there appears to be a widespread disagreement about a suitable definition for specific situations (Bigley and Pearce, 1998). For example, trust is viewed by sociologists as a willingness to be vulnerable (Mayer et al., 1995), and by psychologists as individual attribute and behaviour (Sitkin and Roth, 1993). While Gambetta (1998) suggests that trust enables cooperative behaviour, Sztompka (1999) offers a detailed and systematic study of trust from a sociological perspective by examining the emergence and decay of trust cultures.

explored in detail in psychotherapy but always get a mention in the literature on therapy with the culturally diverse. d'Ardenne and Mahtani (1989) suggest that in monocultural therapy, there is often an assumption by both parties that the therapist is trustworthy whilst in a transcultural context, where the relationship can be more complicated, it can become an issue. The development of trust is an ongoing process which deepens as the two parties increase their knowledge of each other (Mearns and Thorne, 1988). Gaining knowledge about each other is often a complex and confusing process and can sometimes be problematic depending on the personalities of the two people involved and the therapeutic approach. Other factors, such as the particular therapist's style and the depth and willingness of the patient to risk-take and self-disclose, also play an important role. According to d'Ardenne and Mahtani, the therapist's self-disclosure is an important means of achieving trustworthiness when employed 'truthfully, appropriately and economically' (d'Ardenne and Mahtani, 1989: 84; see also Sue, 1981). On the other hand, many psychoanalytic and psychodynamic approaches actively discourage therapist self-disclosure. However, minority patients may more readily be trusting of therapy and the therapist, irrespective of the therapist-patient match or the methodological approaches, if psychotherapists acknowledge race, culture and ethnicity.

Vontress (1971) suggests that when a black client mistrusts his/her white therapist because of their different worldviews, the therapeutic process is in danger of failing. A number of studies, mainly North American, have examined the trust and mistrust in therapy, particularly the white therapist–black patient interactions (see, for example, Nickerson et al., 1994; Watkins and Terrell, 1988; Watkins et al., 1989). Nickerson, Helms and Terrell found 'higher levels of mistrust of whites were associated with more negative general attitudes about seeking psychological help from a clinic staffed primarily by whites' (Nickerson et al., 1994: 383). This view is also articulated by Sue and Sue who assert, 'The services offered are frequently antagonistic or inappropriate to the life experiences of the culturally different client' (Sue and Sue, 1990: 7). Kareem (1992) reminds us that a mistrust of psychotherapy and its practitioners prevails amongst many black and other minority groups in Britain. To remove mistrust from the therapeutic process is not an easy task, given that its socio-historical sources go beyond the personal therapist-client relationship. However, it seems that to understand and acknowledge the issues of trust and mistrust within the process of therapy could be a first step towards alleviating some of its negative effects.

Sue and Sue (1990) contend that the responsibility for proving to the client that the therapist is trustworthy lies with the therapist. Furthermore, they argue that it is the therapist who is likely to experience severe tests of his or her trustworthiness before serious therapy can proceed. Therefore, it behoves white (and black) psychotherapists to adopt appropriate clinical strategies that will engender trust, and contain and hold mistrust when it is experienced. Indeed, the understanding and interpretation of mistrust may be the significant moment and movement of change for the patient in psychotherapy. A failure to trust the therapist or the therapy may allow clients to slip into idiomatic expressions or other culture-specific colloquialisms that the therapist is not aware of; patients may also appear to be shy and withdrawn, and offer a position of being 'cool', until they 'sus' out the hidden agenda of the therapist (Moodley, 1998). In this situation patients and psychotherapists develop a relational trust that evolves over time through the repeated transference and countertransference interactions and transactions. The reliability and dependability of previous exchanges will determine the level of risk-taking, the degree of interdependence and the quality of emotions that the two individuals experience. Since trust in therapy is not static, these states of trustworthiness may change from time to time depending on the patient's and the therapist's emotional and cognitive states. For example, in the videotaped sessions, the issue of trust becomes critical for the client who seems to feel the need to address the issue with Rogers in the first session:

> *Therapist (T52): Maybe part of that reason is you feel, 'My God I have told him a lot. I've trusted him. Have I trusted him too much?'*
>
> *Client (C52a): For sure. Well I guess I'm just going to have to deal with that in terms of I'm just going to have to trust myself to tell you. (T: Mmhm, mmhm) You know. But I, but I do have that. You know. I have that history ...*
>
> *(The Right to be Desperate)*

The statement by the patient: 'but I do have that ... I have that history...', seems to suggest that he may be referring to both a personal but also a group history—a race, culture and ethnic history. Could the issue of trust be about the difficulty of trusting white people because of the power structure and historical legacies? It is interesting, and surely significant, that Rogers interprets the issue of trust in relation to himself when he says, 'and so you are wondering, "yeah but can I trust him?"' It seems that the therapist is aware of the moment of mistrust, perhaps in relation to the history of slavery and the civil rights.

d'Ardenne and Mahtani (1989) suggest that clients from different cultures who have suffered prejudice and lack of economic opportunities find the world to be an untrustworthy place. These experiences can manifest themselves either consciously or unconsciously in psychotherapy to the extent that therapeutic efficacy is challenged. Many black therapists have indicated anecdotally that they have held back feelings, information and critical thoughts with white therapists as well as with white supervisors. Fong and Lease argue that black therapists who are 'culturally mistrusting' in supervision with white counsellors 'may have lower expectations of gaining from the white supervisor and less inclination to reveal affective concerns in the supervision sessions' (Fong and Lease, 1997: 394). In the case of Rogers and his client, the question of trust is clearly a critical one and could perhaps account for the defences that the client is building around him. Rogers reflects on the way in which clients often have doubts about trusting the therapist when he says in his voiceover (V21): 'Is it safe to trust me with this more vulnerable part of himself? Clients often have such doubts and I respond in a way which helps him to realize that I recognize and accept that question.' Surely, Rogers' technique of relating the client's mistrust to his relationship with the therapist is appropriate and effective given that it enables the client to reflect on this important issue. However, whether the process of therapy would have been enhanced if the therapist had phrased the question in racial terms ('can I trust him as a white therapist?') is difficult to ascertain.

CONCLUSION

In this chapter we have focused on the socio-cultural and historical realities of race, racism and the question of identity as a way of understanding how these issues are negotiated and integrated in therapy. Our conclusion is that notions such as gender, disability, sexual orientations and class cannot be ignored, as they determine to a great degree the quality of the relationship between the therapist and the client, and the consequences for therapeutic process and outcomes. As demonstrated in the 'The Right to be Desperate' and 'On Anger and Hurt' sessions, one of the main obstacle for the therapeutic process results from the projections of aggression, the mistrust and the historical tensions that undermine the relationship between the white therapist and his black client. At some level, Rogers seems to have understood this process as he raised both the issues of anger and trust during the therapy sessions, even if these were not contextualized in relation to the question of race. Perhaps what is needed is not only a recognition of the client as a 'racial being' by the therapist but also an acknowledgement by the therapist of his/her own tensions regarding race. With a history of mistrust that exists between black and white people, particularly in the context of the United States and from a more global perspective if one looks at slavery and colonisation, it seems that the complexities that inform constructions of race and identity must be understood as inherent in and inseparable from the relationship between the white therapist and the black client.

This is what Fanon advocates when he states that 'the effective disalienation of the black man entails an immediate recognition of social and economic realities' (Fanon, 1967: 11). Therefore, for the therapeutic process to be effective, it is crucial to acknowledge the economic, social and historical place that black clients occupy in a world which has confined their being as racial 'others'. The example of Rogers' therapy with his black client in the 'The Right to be Desperate' and 'On Anger and Hurt' sessions illustrates some of the ways in which race permeates the therapeutic relationship, often to hinder it. For these negative effects to be avoided, it seems essential to go back to race to attempt to understand the roots of the problem. This is what Rogers' client does when exploring his sense of being alienated in the white world, his feelings of fragmentation and the 'wholeness' that he has lost through the process of acquiring 'white masks'. Whether this process would have been enhanced if Rogers had articulated an understanding of race more explicitly in his communication with the client is difficult to tell. Perhaps race does not need to be acknowledged by Rogers for it to exist as a meaning for the client. Although not articulated by the therapist, race is made present by the client throughout the therapy sessions. By constantly bringing it back to the centre and articulating it as part of his personal narrative, the client is clearly attempting to construct a meaning for himself as opposed to some pre-existing meaning constructed for him by others.

REFERENCES

Bhabha, H (1987) 'What Does the Black Man Want?', *New Formations*, No.1 (Spring).

Bhabha, H (1994) *The Location of Culture*. London: Routledge.

Bigley, GA and Pearce, JL (1998) 'Training for Shared Meaning in Organization Science: Problems of Trust and Distrust.' *Academy of Management Review, 23*: 405–21.

Biko, S (1978) *I Write What I Like*. Aelred Stubbs (ed). London: Heinemann Educational Books.

Brodley, BT (1996) 'Uncharacteristic Directiveness', in BA Farber, DC Brink and P M Raskin (eds) *The Psychotherapy of Carl Rogers*. London: Guilford Press, pp. 310–21. Reproduced as Chapter 4a this volume.

Bulhan, HA (1985) *Frantz Fanon and the Psychology of Oppression*. New York: Plenum Press.

d'Ardenne, P and Mahtani, A (1989) *Transcultural Counselling in Action*. London: Sage.

Fanon, F (1952/1967) *Black Skin White Masks*, CL Markmann (trans.). New York: Grove Press.

Fanon, F (1965/1973) *The Wretched of the Earth*, C. Farrington (trans.). Harmondsworth: Penguin Books.

Fong, ML and Lease, SH (1997) 'Cross-Cultural Supervision: Issues for the White Supervisor', in DB Pope-Davis and HLK Coleman (eds) *Multicultural Counseling Competencies*. Thousand Oaks, Cal.: Sage, pp. 387–405.

Gambetta, D (1998) *Trust: Making and Breaking Cooperative Relations*. New York: Basil Blackwell.

Helms, JE and Cook, DA (1999) *Using Race and Culture in Counseling and Psychotherapy: Theory and Process*. Boston: Allyn and Bacon.

Holmes, DE (1992) 'Race and Transference in Psychoanalysis and Psychotherapy.' *International Journal of Psycho-Analysis, 73*: 1–11.

Jones, GR and George, JM (1998) 'The Experience and Evolution of Trust: Implications for Cooperation and Teamwork.' *Academy Management Review, 23*: 531–46.

Kareem, J (1992) 'The Nafsiyat Intercultural Therapy Centre: Ideas and Experience in Intercultural Therapy', in J Kareem and R Littlewood (eds) *Intercultural Therapy: Themes, Interpretations and Practice*. Oxford: Blackwell, pp. 14–37.

Lacan, J [1966] (1977) *Ecrits: A Selection*, trans. Alan Sheridan. London: Routledge.

Liggan, DY and Kay, J (1999) 'Race in the Room: Issues in the dynamic Psychotherapy of African-Americans.' *Transcultural Psychiatry, 36*(2): 195–210.

Mayer, RC, Davis, JH and Schoorman, D (1995) 'An Integrative Model of Organization Trust.' *Academy of Management Review, 20*: 709–34.

Mearns, D and Thorne, B (1988) *Person-Centred Counselling in Action*. London: Sage.

Mohamed, Abdul R Jan (1983) *Manichean Aesthetics: The Politics of Literature in Colonial Africa*. Amherst, Mass.: University of Massachussetts Press.

Moodley, R (1998) '"I Say What I Like": Frank Talk(ing) in Counselling and Psychotherapy.' *British Journal of Guidance and Counselling, 26*: 495–508.

Moodley, R (1999) 'Challenges and Transformation: Counselling in a Multi-Cultural Context.' *International Journal for the Advancement of Counselling, 21*: 139–52.

Nickerson, KJ, Helms, JE and Terrell, F (1994) 'Cultural Mistrust, Opinions about Mental Illness, and Black Students' Attitudes towards Seeking Psychological Help from White Counselors.' *Journal of Counseling Psychology, 41*: 378–85.

Rosseau, DM, Sitkin, SB, Burt, RS and Camerer, C (1998) 'Not So Different After All: A Cross-Discipline View of Trust.' *Academy of Management Review, 23*: 393–404.

Sitkin, SB and Roth, NL (1993) 'Explaining the Limited Effectiveness of Legalistic 'Remedies' for Trust/Distrust.' *Organization Science, 4*: 367–92.

Sue, DW (1981) 'Evaluating Process Variables in Cross-Cultural Counseling Psychotherapy', in AJ Marsella and PB Pedersen (eds) *Cross-Cultural Counseling and Psychotherapy*. Honolulu, Hawaii: East West Centre, pp. 102–25.

Sue, DW and Sue, D (1990) *Counseling the Culturally Different: Theory and Practice*. New York: John Wiley & Sons.

Sztompka, P (1999) *Trust: A Sociological Theory*. Cambridge: Cambridge University Press.

Tillett, R (1998) 'Therapeutic Aggression.' *British Journal of Psychotherapy, 14*: 284–93.

Vontress, CE (1971) 'Racial Differences: Impediments to Rapport.' *Journal of Counseling Psychology, 18*: 7–13.

Walcott, R (2003) *Black Like Who?* (2nd edn.). Toronto: Insomniac Press.

Watkins, CE and Terrell, F (1988) 'Mistrust Level and its Effects on Counseling Expectations in Black Client–White Counselor Relationship: An Analogue Study.' *Journal of Counseling Psychology, 35*: 194–7.

Watkins, CE, Terrell, F, Miller, F and Terrell, S (1989) 'Cultural Mistrust and its Effects on Exceptional Variables in Black Client–White Counselor Relationships.' *Journal of Counseling Psychology, 36*: 447–50.

Chapter 18
Twenty-First Century Reflections on 'The Right to be Desperate' and 'On Anger and Hurt'

COURTLAND C. LEE

It is interesting to watch *The Right to be Desperate* and *On Anger and Hurt* at the beginning of the twenty-first century almost 30 years after they were conducted. So much has transpired in terms of both the history of American society and the evolution of the counseling profession. Racial issues and relationships are at a different place today from where they were when Rogers and this Black client recorded these sessions. Likewise, issues of race and culture have become much more centralized and accepted in the profession of counseling than they were in the 1970s.

It is within this context that I, a Black man myself, who happens to be a professional counselor reflects on *The Right to be Desperate* and *On Anger and Hurt*. It is interesting to watch Carl Rogers, who in my opinion is the father of counseling in the modern era, work with a client who is so different from him in many ways. The first thing that strikes me in this video session is that the issue of race lies between Rogers and the client like a huge dead elephant. It is there but neither wants to address the issue that there is a dead elephant in the room. While the client makes noble efforts at addressing his own issues and challenges of being Black, he stops short of saying 'Hey look this is a Black thing, Dr Rogers, let's deal with it.'

Rogers, because of the tenets and parameters of his theoretical approach, will not address the issue of race directly. Hence, it is the dead elephant between himself and the client. Rogers, in his voiceover, states that he wants the client to experience his hurt, desperation and anger. It appears as though the client does experience these emotions. However, what the client does not seem to be experiencing is his Blackness in a profoundly meaningful fashion. Rogers seems to be reluctant to allow (or perhaps fearful of allowing) the client to experience his Blackness. In listening to the client's story unfold, it is obvious that his Blackness and his experience of it is at the root of his issue. He talks of his struggles to be a 'credit to his race', how race affected his marriage and family life, and how it is an ongoing struggle to be Black in White America. However, Rogers makes few attempts to actually reflect the affect associated with these issues. Such reflection could perhaps have promoted a deeper exploration of racial feelings on the part of the client. Rogers comments on his giving the client permission to experience many things; however, I feel he fails to give the client permission to experience his Blackness. Unique windows of opportunity to explore the affect around racial issues were not seized upon.

While I am no doubt guilty of presentism here, it is important to consider what is going on in this session in an early twenty-first century context. This consideration comes with the benefit of almost 30 years of thought with respect to cross-cultural counseling that was not evident when Rogers sat down with this client. We now have a body of scholarly cross-cultural counseling work with respect to racial identity development and culturally responsive counseling with Black clients that was nonexistent or in its infancy in the 1970s. Using this modern perspective, let us consider this client. He is a young Black man in remission from leukemia. He talks of layers of affect starting with a top layer of anger followed by hurt, and then a layer where he describes feeling beaten because of his physical and emotional pain.

What is evident from a racial/cultural perspective is that this is a Black man who has reached a high stage of racial identity development and has acculturated to the dominant White society with which he must interact. While he has acculturated he still experiences the trials, tribulations and pain of racism in a deeply personal way. On top of this, he is also dealing with societal messages about what it means to be a man with respect to exhibiting strong emotion. He is afraid to show his hurt and anger because it will betray his image as a 'credit to his race' and will bring the leukemia back.

While Rogers is able to give him permission to experience many aspects of his affective domain, he does not allow him to experience his Blackness in a meaningful way. This is because Rogers' passive approach refuses to go to that level (at least with this client). From my perspective, a far more effective approach would be one that actively allows the client to engage in an expressiveness that would promote the positive experiencing of his Black identity. My approach would provide for the use of Black expressiveness in the therapeutic interaction. Through the use of Black art forms, such as music, literature, poetry, or graphic expression for example, I would provide mechanisms for the client to fully explore his Blackness and what it means to him with respect to his issues and challenges. Another method would be to invite the client to listen to Black music, be it blues, jazz, or even rap, and explore the messages and meaning in that music for his own life and challenges; or the client could also do some bibliotherapy by reading some prominent Black male authors or poets who write about the Black experience and by reflecting on that writing in an exploration of his own life and circumstances.

In short, I want to find ways to both help the client truly experience his Blackness and get the hurt and anger out in growthful ways. Sitting there with Rogers, I see him as a time bomb on the verge of explosion. Rogers' approach is not lighting the fuse. I want that fuse lit and a positive explosion to take place. I want the client to be able to cry, get angry, and process his hurt as a Black man. I want him to be able to experience the power of hurt, anger and Blackness in an active rather than passive way.

From my worldview, the client is an angry and hurting young 'brother' who needs to get it all out and deal with it. I do not have faith in Rogers' approach accomplishing that. This session gives credence to the notion in multicultural counseling that the Person-Centered Approach may be too passive for many clients of color in dealing with painful and racially-tinged issues. This view is underscored by the fact that Rogers does not really deal with the issue of race in a meaningful way.

In fairness to Carl Rogers, it is important to acknowledge that he is a product of his time and cultural realities. His approach has much merit, and he certainly made significant headway with this client. However, through twenty-first century Black male eyes, this client could be better served by a more active and creative approach on the part of the helper.

Chapter 19
A Credit to One's Self, One's Race and One's Community

WILLIAM A. HALL

As I viewed the videotapes of the filmed interviews in which Rogers is counselling the African-American client, I was struck by the number of similarities of experiences that I had with his client. For example, just as he is, I am a Black professional who was married to a White woman; we had two children just like the client. My wife's father and I were good friends as were the client and his father-in-law. My marriage came unraveled after the death of my father-in-law as did his. I have also suffered the fright of having had cancer that is now in remission. However, a key difference between the client and myself was that my teachers did not talk about being 'a credit to your race'. I wonder about the race of the teacher who held the boy's head (the client) 'between her big bosoms' as she praised him in this manner. My Black teachers, in the racially segregated public school system, instilled pride and self-confidence and dignity in us. Somehow, as a little boy, I knew that there was a collective responsibility for Blacks to not only excel for individual gratification, but for the race as a whole. I suppose that this translates into one being a credit to one's self, one's race and one's community. I am reminded of Rosa Parks who was 'a credit to her race' because she refused to give up her seat on the bus as Black folks normally have done for White folks. They did not think she was 'a credit to her race' because her actions resulted in the Montgomery Bus Boycott. So, too, was the story of Martin Luther King. He was not only a credit to his race, but also to the nation.

Perhaps the client's reference to being 'a credit to his race' needs to be understood as a complex process which generates ambivalent feelings in the client about his identity. Although Rogers' approach appeared to be effective as an initial means of getting the client to explore below the comfortable surface, my experience is that African-American clients generally enjoy more successful outcomes with counselling models that include goal-oriented processes following self-exploration. This process meant that the therapist would need to move the client from an almost exclusive reflective approach to a more proactive one that took account of the socio-economic and cultural aspects of their lives. Also, responses by the counsellor that acknowledge an unspoken sense of a collective past and a collective present have been known to enhance the direction and speed of developing a trusting rapport between client and therapist. In other words, the therapist would need to consider using ideas from African philosophies, such as the Nguzo Saba (see Hall and Moodley, 2001, for discussion). An approach which incorporates the client's world-view will support the development of a trusting relationship.

TRUSTING RELATIONSHIPS

One discerns a hint that Rogers' client began the journey of losing trust at an early age when his closest adults disappointingly failed to protect him. It seems that such failures were to continue right up to the moment of the filmed session. It is therefore not surprising that the client expressed doubts about placing confidence in Rogers late in the interview. It is noticeable that Rogers' client had serious reservations about trust, in spite of his having already revealed some things about his life that might have caused a lesser skilled counsellor to mistakenly think that he/she had a license to proceed full speed ahead.

The responses by Rogers to challenges of trustworthiness seem to have gradually reassured the client that it was safe to inch forward in self-exploration mode. However, I suggest that acknowledgement of the place of racism in the equation would have been helpful in building the necessary component of trust. Rogers effectively reassured his African-American client by not expressing surprise at challenges at various points throughout the counselling session that were aimed at testing the trustworthiness of the counsellor. In my experience, although the dynamics are different in every case, as a counsellor in multicultural situations, openness and honesty are very important elements in trust-building. Such openness and honesty will avoid the pitfall of defensiveness, a development that will most certainly hinder the building of a trusting relationship.

One possibility is that the client is able to build trust in the therapist and in the therapeutic process as a result of Rogers' approach and the fact that he views the client as a distinct individual with unique perceptions and emotions. This means that Rogers does not stereotype the client into a group identity, a common problem in cross-cultural counselling situations. To avoid the mistaken tendency to group all members of an ethnic minority group into a single stereotypical viewpoint, it may be helpful to apply an identity development model as a means of acquiring insight into the client's inner world, such as developed by Cross (1971) and Helms (1984).

It was noticeable that, as the client became more comfortable and trusting with Rogers, he was prepared to share more of his hurtful past, much of which had probably been suppressed since the early childhood escapes to the dark basement in his home. This is suggested by his statement, 'I let myself be hurt by giving and sharing so much ... just beaten; I could tell you about some things that would just blow you away.' It becomes clear that the client perceived that he had been hurt, abused and betrayed at different stages of his life; perhaps by close adults, then by his teachers, and finally by his wife's family that he had attached himself to in his apparent seeking for solace. All of this, in addition to a complex mixture of racial abuse and a life-threatening disease as he faced the world alone, placed him in a desperate situation in which it is not surprising that he experienced emotions of hurt and anger.

Rather than becoming intimidated by expressions of anger, Rogers seems to be aware of the socio-cultural and historical dimensions of the client's distress, anger and hurt. He recognizes that the release of tension by the expression of these historically suppressed emotions is a necessary part of the 'cure'. It is well known that suppressed anger can cause both physical and emotional illness. The fact that Rogers' client suffered a vision problem when his wife called, as well as when parents visited, reveals evidence that such suppression has a negative effect on one's physical and mental health. It seems that Rogers was aware of this process and tried to engage the client to express this suppressed anger that was causing his cancer. The client was finally able to tell Rogers that he wanted 'to call somebody a few names'; that he needed to 'get it out to my teachers and the family I had'. He didn't feel that he could adequately describe the depth of the hurt that he endured. He sometimes felt that if he 'could get it out' his illness might go away.

CONCLUSION

Finally, while viewing the videotape of the session between Rogers and the African-American client, I was reminded of counselling interactions that reach back 20 or more years when I was intimately involved in the BAC (British Association for Counselling) as one of the chairs of the RACE (Race Awareness in Counselling Education) group. As chair of RACE, I was co-opted onto the BAC Executive Committee where decisions were made to encourage the various divisions to adopt race-awareness methods. In the RACE group it appeared to us that our outreach efforts were failing to meet desired goals because some of the ethnic minority counsellors that were working on the 'front line', so to speak, did not trust the predominately White BAC. This led to the formation of the Association of Black Counsellors (ABC). Remembering this and looking at the videos got me thinking about the possibility of trust in a situation which is embedded in historical mistrust and inequalities. Thinking about Rogers' client in this way makes me understand the difficulty that both Rogers and the client were experiencing during the therapy sessions. The fact that they were able to proceed and come to some resolution offers hope for not only Black and White counselling dyads but organizations and institutions of counselling and psychotherapy.

REFERENCES

Hall, WA and Moodley, R (2001) 'Using an African orld view in therapy with black clients.' *Counselling and Psychotherapy Journal, 12*(3): 10–13.

Cross, WE Jr (1971) 'The Negro to Black conversion experience: Towards a psychology of Black liberation.' *Black World, 20*(9): 13–27.

Helms, J (1984) 'Towards a theoretical explanation of the effects of race on counseling: A Black and White model.' *The Counseling Psychologist, 12*: 153–65.

Chapter 20
THE 'ARMOUR-PLATED MAN' IN CROSS-RACIAL COUNSELLING

JOSNA PANKHANIA

The 'On Anger and Hurt' sessions were not only challenging in terms of race and culture in therapy but clearly offered an opportunity to see Rogers attempt a challenge to his own theory of non-directive Client-Centred Therapy. At various times in my viewing of a videotape of the films, I found Rogers' presence, his commitment to the client and his compassion deeply moving. And yet, I was troubled watching the process unfold. At first, I was not sure what was troubling me and so I watched the video over and over again, carefully thinking about Rogers' responses and the client's narrative. I did not have the privilege of meeting Carl Rogers, but his work played an important role in my training as a counsellor. I was inspired by the fact that the person-centred, humanist therapy emerged as a challenge to the hegemony of psychoanalysis characterised by the conflict-laden and pathological view of the therapist as the expert and even omnipotent. And yet, the more I worked as a counsellor with people from marginalised groups, such as women survivors of rape and incest and black women who had been at the receiving end of institutional racism, the more I struggled with the Person-Centred Approach. Does the Person-Centred Approach offer an avenue for the counsellor to explore the possibility of the impact of the present day and historical manifestations of the power of racism? And if the person-centred counsellor was to offer some exploration of race in cross-racial counselling settings, to what extent would the Person-Centred Approach be compromised by such a directive intervention?

I wondered if my struggle with the Person-Centred Approach was also to do with my struggle with the discourse of counselling itself, and the groups and organisations that claim their right to exist on the healing agenda. I remember feeling uncomfortable at often being the only black counsellor in the late seventies at the various British Association for Counselling (BAC) conferences, and I wondered what kind of counselling a predominantly white group of counsellors might be providing for black people if at all. At the BAC's Counselling in Education (CIE) division's annual conference in 1983, I said to the group that had gathered that 'as an Asian counsellor I felt as though I did not belong there' amongst a sea of white faces. I wondered if 'the time to go our separate ways had come' (BAC, 1983: 2–5). Fortunately, we did not move away but formed a working party which met in Leicester on 8 May 1983 for the first time (*ibid.*: 5) and called itself the RACE group—Race Awareness in Counselling Education. Over time, this working group of five white counsellors and myself attracted more black counsellors and eventually became a subdivision of the BAC. But the process of 'separating' from white colleagues was critical; not exclusionary of our white colleagues; but a brief respite from these joint adventures to ones which looked at our history and psychology; ones in which we could share our stories. Almost a year later, on the 19th May 1984, initiated by Dr William A. Hall (Bill) who himself is African-American, like Rogers' client, four black counsellors of the RACE group (Shukla Dhingra, Bill Hall, Roy Moodley and myself) met in Derbyshire, at the home of Roy Moodley; this was the beginnings of the Association of Black Counsellors (ABC) (see Moodley and Dhingra, 1998: 295). It was RACE and ABC that paved the way for a national focus on the issue of appropriate counselling services for black people and the question of racism in counselling education and practice.

TROUBLING INTERVENTIONS

It was with all of this history that I came to view a videotape of the *On Anger and Hurt* film. I was troubled by the extent to which Rogers appeared to me to be directive and pursuing specific objectives on behalf of the client. I was surprised to see Rogers offering interpretations such as, 'I feel also you're afraid of crying for yourself.' and asking leading questions such as, 'If you did cry, what would some of the themes of that crying be?' I felt somewhat uncomfortable to see Rogers encouraging the client to feel angry and to cry in the session and to see Rogers encouraging the client to express emotions of intense hurt and anguish. My understanding of the Person-Centred Approach is that the counsellor offers the client the space to express emotions that the client wishes to express. Other than through interpretations and encouragements, Rogers appeared to me to be directive in other ways and this was through the introduction of profanity, such as 'You'd like to just tell off the bastard' and 'Took a great big stick and rammed it up your ass—is that what you're saying?' What were such interventions about? Was Rogers trying to press the client to express further intense feelings? Why? Or was this something about Rogers' own inner world? Whatever the reason, I found the use of such profanity by Rogers somewhat shocking and wondered if he might have used the same approach if the client had been a white, middle-class male (see also Brodley, 1996; also Chapter 4a, this volume).

I was surprised to see that Rogers did in fact have a clear idea of where he was trying to get to with the client. To me, it looked like a conscious and calculated path along which Rogers was directing the client. The following comments by Rogers are examples of this mindful process. 'I can let him feel desperate. Friends and family cannot allow this. It is important that someone can really permit it. I also go back to his earlier feeling of hurt. I want to get a more complete feeling for his inner world but he as you will see doesn't pick up on this particular portion.' How are Rogers' plans here non-directive? Brodley (1996) argues that Rogers was 'uncharacteristically directive' with this client. I wonder if race had anything to do with this uncharacteristic dimension. To what extent can a white therapist offer a black client empathy? The historical relationship that white people have had with black people has included the assertion of power, slavery and colonisation. This historical relationship continues to impact on the way black and white people relate to each other. The ongoing structures of neo-colonialism and cultural imperialism keep the oppressive nature of this historical relationship alive. This historical and present-day unequal relationship between black and white people can manifest itself either consciously or unconsciously in counselling and psychotherapy to the extent that the therapeutic efficacy is challenged. A clinically skilled therapist will acknowledge the historical and present-day experiences of power appropriately in context so that the impact of the power can be explored without any defences being raised by the client or the therapist experiencing guilt (Moodley, 2001).

THE ARMOUR PLATE AROUND COUNSELLING

Rogers states in his voiceover: 'This is the very heart of therapy. When I can provide a climate in which the client can experience his buried feelings rather than describe them or be told about them, it has a much more powerful and enduring effect' (V17, The Right to be Desperate). I am wondering if the kind of directive approach that Rogers used with his black client helped the client to release buried feelings, which Rogers states was the intended goal, or did the approach actually prevent the feelings from finding expression? Towards the end of the sessions, the client was overwhelmed as tears came to his eyes and he asked if the interview can be stopped. As the session closed, Rogers leaned towards the client and gently touched his knee as an expression of concern. As

Brodley (1996: 139) says, '... Immediately after this emotional sequence of events, in his post-session comments (not in the client's presence), Rogers began his remarks by describing the client as an "armor-plated man"'. I was surprised by this description of the client as an 'armour-plated man' having witnessed a man who had expressed a range of emotions to Rogers during the session. I could not understand what appeared to me to be a contradictory comment by Rogers about the client—how could Rogers call this client an 'armour-plated man' after such an emotional counselling session?

Metaphorically, I am wondering if it was Rogers' approach that was the armour-plate around the client's therapeutic journey. Where did the armour-plate lie when Rogers says: 'I always try to sense the feelings just below his words and welcome that. I try to catch the resentment and the hurt which he hasn't yet voiced very clearly.' Does the armour-plate lie in Rogers' directive approach here or within the client? Who was the 'armour-plated man'? Was it the black client or was it Rogers? Or are the organisations, institutions and Western European therapeutic approaches the 'amour-plated man' that surface in the therapeutic journeys of black people?

I am left with many other questions.

REFERENCES

Brodley, BT (1996) 'Uncharacteristic Directiveness: Rogers and the "Anger and Hurt" Client', in BA Farber, DC Brink and PM Raskin (eds) *The Psychotherapy of Carl Rogers: Cases and Commentry.* New York: Guilford Press.

British Association for Counselling, *Newsletter* No. 22, August 1983.

Moodley, R (2001) Trust and Mistrust in Counselling and Therapy. Unpublished paper.

Moodley, R and Dhingra, S (1998) 'Cross-Cultural/Racial Matching in Counselling and Therapy: White Clients and Black Counsellors.' *Counselling,* 9(4): 295–9.

Chapter 21
The Man He Has Become

STEPHEN M. WHITEHEAD

One aspect of the 'The Right to be Desperate' and 'On Anger and Hurt' films is the interconnectedness of the discourses of race and masculinity which underlie the communication between Carl Rogers and his client. The client's narrative of self and his description of the felt experience of cancer suggest a strong link between his internalised anger at the pressure to conform to prescribed social norms and the subsequent 'decaying' of his body. Carl Rogers recognises this tension and sensitively supports his client's apparent desire to express such anger and to feel release from these social constraints. However, within this process, it seems that two key areas which contribute to shaping the client's sense of a self are left unexplored, at least explicitly. One is racism, and the other is the masculine body.

THE UNSPOKEN RACISM

The word 'racism' is never spoken throughout the two sessions, yet it is very clear from early on that it is racism which the client is recognising and grappling with in his 'post-cancer' life. He feels that the purity, innocence, and conviction of his seven-year-old self have been corrupted by the racist attitudes of the system (represented by his school teacher who told him that he was 'a potential credit to his race'), and by those to whom he unreservedly 'gave love' (his white wife and her family) but who failed to return such love at the very time when he most needed it—when he experienced acute desperation at his leukaemia and impending death. As the client says, '… I gave a lot [of love] to that family [but in the end to them]... I [was] just another black person ... just another nigger.'

Moreover, this emergent, and for the client, troubling resentment, appears encapsulated in his acknowledgement that he was somehow pressured to 'live up to those standards ... that told me what I must do'. These discourses were presented to him from an early age as the means by which he would become accepted and acceptable in a white society. However, as discourses, their identity signifying properties remain powerful (Butler, 1993). Their subsequent effect on the client was to initiate and substantiate a process through which he would become a new self, an individual who, in his words, 'let other people control what I wanted to be'.

Although there is deep bitterness in the client's narrative (both in and in-between the actual spoken words) at the racism he experienced, it is not expressed in such stark and direct terms. Instead, the client and Carl Rogers talk around that which apparently cannot be spoken. Indeed, the client still appears to experience a certain guilt at talking 'radically' as a black man. He cannot quite overcome the conditioning which works at positioning him in a respectful and subordinate relationship to white authority. Later in the interview, the term 'civilised' is used by the client to justify his reluctance to directly confront the social and cultural racism which he feels so effectively took his seven-year-old self from him. He now seeks that boy back. In finding that younger self, so the client feels he can, somehow, detach himself from the political reality of his adult ethnic identity.

The client's reluctance to explicitly confront the racism which rendered his younger self from him, may well be partly due to the fact that he is talking and revealing himself to a white man, someone who he remains a little ambiguous about with regard to what degree he, the client, can trust him. As he so revealingly says towards the end of the two sessions, 'Can I trust you?' The words white and black remain silent, unspoken, but all the more potent for their apparent invisibility. It is in these sensitive and telling interactions between two individuals caught, through no fault of their own, in political categories that we confront the stark reality of the black/white dichotomy and the discreet relations of power and privilege which accompany it (Hall, 1997).

The client's anger, as it surfaces during the two sessions, is a manifestation of his sense of betrayal by white society and white individuals, but also a recognition that he himself seemed to collude in this process. Thus, he is angry at his own act of betrayal, at his adult self. His seven-year-old self was not simply taken from him: he gave him up in return for 'acceptance' and others' recognition of himself as a man. His subsequent move to California, together with his divorce, signify both a physical and explicitly emotional detachment from a self who he now feels did not resist enough.

THE REPRESSED AND REPRESSIVE MASCULINITY

While 'racism' surfaces throughout the sessions as a key theme and influencing discourse, the paradoxes surrounding the (black) masculine body remain totally unexplored and undeveloped. In post-structuralist terms the 'sexed/gendered body materialises through the dynamics and processes of discourse' (Whitehead, 2002: 193), and in so doing it conceals the means of its own invention. Thus, it is important to recognise that gendered and racial bodies are not a natural expression, but acutely linked to the power effects that form their constitution (Butler, 1993). In the case of the client, we can clearly see these power effects in operation and the subsequent difficulty he has had in coming to reposition his body outside of them—to retake control of his body. As he says, 'I didn't like myself (T: Mhhm) you know, maybe I didn't like myself at all because I couldn't control it [the cancer].' This comment seems to act as a metaphor for the client's depowered self. Cancer, therefore, comes to represent other controlling process which restricts the self.

The power effects, as discourse, materialising the client's body can be understood to be firstly the masculine/feminine polarity (Connell, 1995), and secondly, the white gaze upon the black body (Whitehead, 2002). Thus, it can be argued that the client's point of departure from his 'purer' seven-year-old self was precisely around that time in his life when his body was changing, maturing, beginning the process of graduation into manhood. As he moves into high school, so the client adopts a more explicitly adult masculine bodily representation of self. Part of this is a natural maturing physical process and part is a 'desire to be a man' (*ibid*). But an additional expression of this new bodily presence is, significantly, exercised through his football activities, which themselves take place within a racially signified domain. It is no coincidence that the client's masculine body presence begins to reshape itself in the signifying 'image' presented to him as appropriate for a young black male. The client's sporting activities are clearly driven by this desire to 'give 200%', in order to live up to that early marking as a 'potential credit to his race'. In giving to this degree, the client is giving his body to a white society in return for being accepted and deemed acceptable. However, his masculine sense of self is reinforced and validated by this very process, since the constructions of blackness and masculinity overlap. Consequently, there is little or no ambivalence for the client in the relationship between his masculine body and his masculine body activities, even though neither dimensions of self have been constructed in any wholly agentic fashion by him.

TRANSFORMING THE BODY

Through the process of talking and reflecting, the client is now able to recognise that if he had not 'competed in sport (and schooling)' he 'would not have had anything'. In short, he would not have been elevated as a (black) man in a white, male-dominated society. His masculinity would have been undermined, whereas through sport it was reinforced (Majors, 2001). The subsequent cancer has, for the client, fundamentally rendered his masculine body insecure. It has corrupted that which for so long he felt some control over and which gave him some control, but which he now recognises to have been in part constructed for him. His sovereignty over his body is now increasingly rendered illusory and at least contingent upon the journey of his illness. This aspect of his new self is one he continues to grapple with, not least because it undermines his masculine presence and thus renders his black male body identification less potent. Not only did the cancer trigger a process of 'decaying' his body, a body still in every other respect very much in its prime, it also highlighted the long-standing tension between his desire to control the gaze of others upon him, and his desire to return to that younger self. But the younger self has gone. It disappeared as his body changed. He is now a man with a man's body. The external gaze upon the client is not the same external gaze which would settle on the young child. His desire to return to that young child, and that young child's view of the world, cannot be fulfilled, although the hope that he may well do so does offer him some inner comfort and a focus point for his emergent black identity.

The client is now in the process of re-forming his body and self, a process triggered by the desperate crisis he experienced through having his body fail him. Although his bodily identification remains central to this process, there are two key interconnected dimensions—blackness and masculinity. The client's acceptance that his black identity is not one to retreat from but to embrace and develop seems to have begun or to have been clarified through the session with Carl Rogers. However, the client's desire to retreat to the boy he was suggests that he has yet to fully come to terms with his weakened adult male body. As his body remains in question, so too does his sense of masculine potency. In his desire for the child he was, he is, in effect, no longer desiring to be the man he has become.

REFERENCES

Butler, J (1993) *Bodies That Matter: The discursive limits of 'sex'*. New York: Routledge.
Connell, RW (1995) *Masculinities*. Cambridge: Polity.
Hall, S (ed) (1997) *Representation: Cultural Representations and Signifying Practices*.

London: Sage.
Majors, R (2001) 'Cool Pose: Black Masculinity and Sports', in SM Whitehead and FJ Barrett (eds) *The Masculinities Reader*. Cambridge: Polity.
Whitehead, S (2002) *Men and Masculinities: key themes and new directions.* Cambridge: Polity.

Chapter 22
"Tripping" in 'The Right to be Desperate' and 'On Anger and Hurt'

GELLA RICHARDS

'Tripping' is a word that was originally coined by African-Americans as a way to capture both experiences and interactions of Black people in a White-dominated world (Wolfram and Thomas, 2002). It is typically seen as coming under the category of Ebonics since it mixes African language patterns with English words. This term seems relevant in the 'The Right to be Desperate' and 'On Anger and Hurt' sessions since the client who is an African-American uses it at different semantic levels to describe a variety of experiences. For instance, at the beginning of therapy, the client uses it to talk about experiences that represent for him a 'bad' trip: 'being a credit to [his] race', his cancer and his anxiety of death and dying. In order to understand the variety of meanings that the client attributes to 'tripping', the counsellor would have to appreciate the richness of this word and its use in many different contexts in African-American linguistic variations. The resourcefulness of the word 'tripping' aptly reflects the variety and the richness of the client's life.

In order to be able to empathise with this client and to enable him to resolve his issues, the therapist would need to be sensitised to the use of the word 'tripping' as a multilayered metaphor. By achieving this understanding, the therapist will be able to grasp the different levels at which the client is expressing his feelings and therefore respond appropriately with different types of intensity of empathy. In therapy, it seems that Rogers attempts to get an understanding of 'tripping', although at times it appears to be unidimensional in the way it is understood. But at other times, it is clear that Rogers senses in the client his 'tripping', when he says that he wants to understand 'the exact meaning that the [his] material has for him [the client]'. The depth of the reverberations of the client's experiences on how he perceives his identity will need to be understood for therapeutic movement to take place. In this respect, the linguistic dimension of the client's experiences—as expressed, for instance, in the notion of 'tripping'—needs to be fully appreciated and integrated in the therapeutic dialogue.

Throughout the therapy sessions the client is reflecting on the 'bad tripping' that he has experienced. Since it seems that he has not been allowed to reveal his anger and hurt to those around him, I feel that he may also benefit from exploring what it was about those 'tripping' experiences that prevented him from doing so. No doubt the client will need to express his hurt and anger in the therapeutic encounter and may possibly want to convey his feelings of hurt and anger in relation to significant others. By helping the client explore these options, we are likely to see that the reasons behind his suppressed anger lead us to the underlying theme of 'tripping' that explains and connects many issues in his life. To be able to appreciate the true extent of the client's fight as a Black man struggling to achieve his own racial identity and to work with his feelings and his emotional needs, an extra layer of empathy and a deeper level of understanding and compassion would be required from the therapist. As a Black female psychologist who has adapted the Rogerian approach to work with some Black clients and also cross-racially, I would make particular use of the self in therapy, which is a trademark of person-centred counselling. There are many ways in which the client could relate to me, and this would provide him with the opportunity to explore the various feelings he has about various significant others in his life. My gender is likely to have an influence on the therapeutic relationship. Not only am I a woman, but I am also a Black woman. Though not an occurrence in every encounter that Black men have with Black women, it is not unusual for there to be an uneasy dynamic when a Black man reveals to a Black woman that he has a White wife. The client may have 'scrutinised' me for evidence of disapproval. At one level, as a Black person, the client may feel that I can really appreciate the pain of racism and the anger one feels since other people decide that because you are Black you are to be controlled by other (White) people and that you are to be accepted or rejected purely on the basis of your race. On the other hand, he may be wary of revealing that he was married to the 'other' (a woman from the White race), since he may (erroneously) suspect that I may perceive him to have 'sold out' or betrayed his 'race'. Indeed, he may be particularly alert to this notion now that he has realised that the 'other' that he seemed to want to become part of is rejecting him.

As a therapist, I would attempt to make particular use of congruence in my response when the client states that being with his wife's family he actually 'forgot that he was Black'. My own awareness of my race would lead me to be curious as to what this meant for the client when it dawned on him, that although he had forgotten his ethnicity, his in-laws had actually seen him as 'just another nigger'. When he revealed this, the depth of his pain was very apparent; yet it was left unexplored. In cross-cultural work, this is a potentially very difficult area for the counsellor to broach, particularly when the latter is from the 'race' that has rejected the client, and even more so if that 'race' is the one that historically has dominated that of the client and made slaves of his ancestors. I wonder if this could be the reason for Rogers not overtly mentioning race, and the 'anger and hurt' that the client felt after the event. However, as a Black person, I feel that it is essential to provide the client with an opportunity to get to grips with his bewilderment.

Finally, to be fully empathic and congruent with the client, it is important to understand and acknowledge the issue of 'love' which the client has contextualised as part of his experience of 'tripping'. The client found it very difficult to understand how all the love he had bestowed on his in-laws mystifyingly disintegrated once his father-in-law died. It was as if the love that he had invested suddenly meant nothing to them. The feelings of rejection were made even more painful since there was no valid reason for them. While the client should be allowed to express his anger, the unjustness and spitefulness of his in-laws' ignorance and bigotry, empathy by the counsellor at this time is crucial. Without over-identifying with the client, I feel that, as a Black therapist, I would need to make an empathic response. Depending on the client's reaction, I may even have gone further and mentioned the racism that Black people experience. My value as a Black female counsellor to him would be to witness his narrative, not as a bystander but as a person of colour who could 'trip' with him on different levels.

REFERENCES

Wolfram, W and Thomas, E (2002) *The Development of African American English*. Oxford: Blackwell.

Chapter 23
MULTIPLE INTERPRETATIONS: STORIES, LIES AND VIDEOTAPES

WILL STILLWELL

When Roy Moodley invited me to write about the 'The Right to be Desperate' and 'On Anger and Hurt' films, I believed it would provide me with an opportunity to reflect on some of the controversies that have shadowed the recording of this particular client with Carl Rogers. The controversies take the form of rumblings and rumors (that the client was hiding from the police, never had leukemia, and so on) that somehow call into question the validity of the filmed interviews. The shadow-stories and what I have accomplished by reflecting upon them have been a learning experience for me.

Carl and I were associates at the Center for Studies of the Person in the late 1970s when these films were previewed. At that time, and since then when I watch them, I have the impression that while Carl defined this as an occasion primarily for the client to further understand himself, the client was actively defining the situation otherwise. I saw the client in a posture of relaxation, active in thinking his way from one to another topic of supposed emotional desperation. My guess then was that the client had put himself into a verbal contest, playing 'pretend patient' making up a sad, difficult story or two as he went along, improvising in a game to outwit—out-talk—someone he perceived as having an opposing purpose. Two men, two intentions, each leading in different directions. At that first viewing, I felt the contest and recall I felt embarrassed that ('my man') Carl, seemingly unwitting, fell into a straight-man role against which the client displayed his cool.

I was not alone in my discomfort with these films. Nel Kandel, also from the Center for Studies of the Person, found these demonstration interviews unsatisfying. She was the founding Director of the Carl Rogers Memorial Library, and spent many hours working with Carl's career-long print and visual presentation efforts. She considered *On Anger and Hurt* and *The Right to be Desperate* atypical. Nel attributed this quality to the client having been 'picked up off the street' by our Center coordinator, Dr Earl Burrows—sometimes an improvisational trickster himself. Earl Burrows was a radical person-centered educator and consultant, known (even infamous) for the interpersonal and professional risks he was willing to take. I surmise that, as was typical for Carl in his later-life demonstration interviews, Carl did not pre-screen the client he was to meet. However that may be, this man who volunteered to be a client for demonstration interviews was not recruited from Carl's usual pools of such volunteers in 'educational', 'personal growth' or 'mental health' environments.

Several years later I informally chatted with the client when he revisited the Center. He told me that in the meantime he had been a gas station attendant in Salt Lake City, Utah. He reported that Carl had come in for gasoline and not recognized him, which, he said, was disappointing. I had my doubts. Carl driving around in Salt Lake City seemed highly unlikely to me. These untidy bits of information swirl like dust-devils outside what we witness in the demonstration interviews. Yet I find disquiet sometimes deserves to be addressed. Around any significant event there are multiple interpretations—stories, lies and videotapes. Each throws in the 'true' dirt. As Center member Dr Robert Lee reminds me, a person-centered therapist functions to help a client see and hear the depths of his own world. Their time together is for the client to use as he is able. He will shift to 'make up something else' when he is ready to work on different feelings and meanings. The therapist is doing his or her best work, Bob Lee maintains, when his or her own investments in a 'self' are minimal. Nothing to defend. No contest offered or entered to demonstrate 'help,' 'truth,' 'compassion,' or 'skillfulness' (or 'cool').

My own congruence differs from Carl's. Had I been interviewing this client, I now assert I would have spoken to him about my doubts and confusions as I tried to follow his sense of his world. I would have followed my native tendencies that I have seasoned and implicitly trust. I would have mixed myself into the client's game in order to embody it and struggle myself free of it. But one of Carl's extraordinary and essential gifts comes clear to me as I contrast my fantasy counseling to his attitude toward his interaction with the client. As a therapist, Carl did not play his reciprocal part in our culture's customary (for men) 'power' exchanges gauging personal worth; he would not engage concerning his own self-confirmation. Indeed, in therapy Carl was almost never in an attitude of 'over-against' the other person.[1] His kind of affirmation was the same attitude

---

[1]. 'Over-against' is the translators' most consistent rendition of Martin Buber's ontological essence of face-to-face relationship. Much has been written about Buber's influence on

he offered as a gift to facilitating peace later in his life. My irony is that I never did what I now assert: never did mix it up, never did take occasion to speak to Carl or the client about my doubts, challenges, and confusions concerning these interviews.

Carl Rogers often characterized his therapeutic efforts as attempts to understand what the client wanted him to know. He wished to convey the extent of his understandings to the client. Most importantly, he was keen to hear from the client about the client's perception of being accepted and accurately understood. In this demonstration, Carl kept *his* accepting, understanding contact with *this* particular person in the way he was best able. Carl persistently maintained his therapeutic integrity through the client's shifts in story and feelings. As the client expressed perhaps newly formed feelings and meanings Carl was perceptive and supporting.

I, and maybe most of us seldom are *really* consciously available for existential person-in-world understanding and acceptance. Surely I do give attentive effort to constructing myself as a point of reference, a center of gravity to defend against a universe in change. Perhaps even in my conscientious sincerity and hope I am more like this man meeting Carl than I would care to know. What does it take to open opportunity for him, and for me?

In reconsidering my opinions about these interviews of Carl's, I remember that an Argentine colleague, Andres Sanchez Boda, used the 'On Anger and Hurt' session in a 1992 workshop to reflect on psychotherapy. He had seen videotapes of both films of Carl with this client and seems to have none of the suspicions I have held about the work. He takes the sessions as straight psychotherapeutic interviews. I admire Sanchez Boda's contextualization of Carl Rogers' work in broader currents of European and American thought. Like me, Sanchez Boda uses the videos for his own inspiration and as a basis to further advance his own passionate understanding. Maybe I can let his inspirations help me understand how a person comes to accepting.[2]

Sanchez Boda sets the scene with summary remarks about the client (who he names 'Hurt'):

Rogers, and much about the essential differences between the two men. As close as they might have been in honoring the possibilities of what both—Rogers appropriating Buber—were to call 'I-Thou' relating, I believe their native and seasoned attitudes differed right here in their respective approaches to encountering an other.

[2.] Sanchez Boda's paper was republished in 1995 as a part of a more comprehensive discussion of his own multidimensional holistic psychotherapeutic methods. It appeared as a chapter in *Estar Presente: desde Carl Rogers al Enfoque Holístico Centrado en la Persona*, Holos Editorial, Buenos Aires. I have translated from Spanish those brief excerpts of the writing (pp. 208, 210–11) which directly comment on Carl Rogers in his work with the client in *On Anger and Hurt*.

> We encounter a person who perceives himself wounded and damaged by a hostile world … He considers that his black skin in a racist society is a mark of his *self*. He finds himself paralyzed and in great difficulty connecting with his own feelings. He is preoccupied more with the 'cancer' of his mind than that of his body (perhaps one generated the other).

Sanchez Boda continues:

> The introjection of cultural patterns has distanced [Hurt] from himself. His militancy in the battle for rights for black people permits him to express his internal fight 'out there', but has not made easy his own integration. He fears to express what he feels, his illness is in remission, but he fears contact with the unfolding in which he finds himself and with the paradox that it is fully probable that his own fear has caused his leukemia. [Hurt] is truly preoccupied by the possibility of dying, but he wants to engage in not being more disconnected, which would imply something like being dead in life (to live is to feel and account for it) (1995: 208).

Carl Rogers' therapeutic approach has been an inspiration for Sanchez Boda during much of his career. In the videotape he sees that '[w]ith Rogers [Hurt] manages to get close to his true feelings, he is able to express them within this bond and permits himself a certain degree of loss of control' (*ibid.*: 210). He also states that,

> [i]t seems excellent to us how Rogers facilitates this interview … [T]he method of Carl Rogers to accomplish psychotherapy is a verbal form where he is perceived as a therapist WHO IS PRESENT. He locates himself in a phenomenological posture, creates a climate of unconditional acceptance, and reveals his authentic and spontaneous self. From empathic comprehension he makes 'reflective' responses, wherein he intends to facilitate that Hurt perceive himself more adequately, initiating thus the road to his transformation (*ibid*: 208).

Sanchez Boda sees 'reflection' as central to the process which Carl Rogers engages in:

> 'Reflection' is the response conceived by Carl Rogers which we can define as a phenomenological reduction that emerges from empathic understanding, stripped of theoretical-structural prejudgments. It is a response that intends to take the essence of the discourse (words, gestures, spirit) and express it as a synthesis. If the client is able to see himself reflectively and recognize himself in the response, he begins the road to re-perception, remaking his 'manner of seeing himself', and thus is able to get closer to the distortions and negations that have generated his ill-being (*ibid.*: 208).

'Reflection', 're-perception', and 're-visioning' are key therapeutic activities for Sanchez Boda. He utilizes various modalities of reflection in his own work with clients:

> We believe that for Hurt it will be very useful, in the following sessions, to include other resources which make possible the reconnection and coming together of himself … [W]e think that the utilization of the method of Focusing will enable Hurt to make a respectful and gradual approach to his felt sense. It also might be useful to suggest later that Hurt be included in a therapeutic group, where from psychodrama and Gestalt he would be able to confront his fearful episodes, play them from other places, attain acceptance and better his self-esteem. It is probable if he opens his perceptions to other constructs that he himself creates, from a created reconstruction he would be able to unfold his emotions and have more spontaneous conduct (*ibid.*: 210).

Finally, Sanchez Boda argues that,

> Hurt fervently desires to feel himself free, this has been his battle for years, but he is surrounded in the trap of a system created by others and which he 'bought into', he is not able to give himself this permission. Our work is that he revisions and recreates through various perspectives, from there we know that persons, when they are able, look for the best for themselves and others … Without 'courage to exist' life is merely survival, and probably cancer (*ibid.*: 211).

Carl Rogers and a man whose real name we are not given to know were filmed in their duet. We view their encounter here as Person-Centered Therapy. We attend these men improvising together, each in relation to his interior melodies and to the melodies he heard from the other. Was their song a beginning of successful therapeutic work as Sanchez Boda seems to accept, or were Carl's efforts misled? If a person tells lies, part of what he communicates is true. If only to make it pass as real, my lies (inadvertently, perhaps) invest some of my true hopes and fears into my fantasy. *If* (even beyond my hearing) *I can hear how all my telling*—feelings, wishes and disappointments, associations, prejudices, and alternative fantasies, thoughts, diseases, assumptions and values—*is received as melodies of prized being*, I may hear other than I have thus far heard from my story, I may give myself to open opportunity.

These demonstration interviews are a fine example of Carl Rogers relating in his therapeutic best to the vitalities he perceived in the other person. His reflective comments following the interviews show that, as well as accepting and attempting to understand the client, he was developing some psychological ideas about him. That Carl and the client were (or were not) in the room under widely different assumptions, that the client was (or was not) genuine, that Carl was (or was not) 'fooled', seem to me now less important issues than my raw witnessing of Carl's untiring persistence trying to understand another human being in the intention of that person better accepting and understanding himself.

REFERENCE

Sanchez Boda, A (1995) *Estar Presente: desde Carl Rogers al Enfoque Holistico Centrado en la Persona,* Holos Editorial, Buenos Aires, pp. 208, 210–11.

Chapter 24
INTERVIEW WITH CARL ROGERS ON THE USE OF THE SELF IN THERAPY[1]

MICHELE BALDWIN

In 1986 I had the privilege and pleasure of interviewing Carl Rogers about the way he uses himself in therapy. My original request was for him to write an article on the topic and he informed me that he was too busy at the time to accept another assignment. When I expressed my disappointment, and in view of his interest in the topic, he graciously invited me to his home and what follows is my write-up of the conversation we had in his living room.

Over time, I think that I have become more aware of the fact that in therapy I do use my *self*.[2] I recognize that when I am intensely focused on a client, just my presence seems to be healing, and I think this is probably true of any good therapist. I recall once I was working with a schizophrenic man in Wisconsin whom I had dealt with over a period of a year or two and there were many long pauses. The crucial turning point was when he had given up, did not care whether he lived or died, and was going to run away from the institution. And I said, 'I realize that you don't care about yourself, but I want you to know that I care about you, and I care what happens to you.' He broke into sobs for 10 or 15 minutes. That was the turning point of the therapy. I had responded to his feelings and accepted them, but it was when I came to him as a person and

---

[1.] This chapter was originally published in Baldwin, M. and Satir, V. (eds) (1987) *The Use of Self in Therapy*, pp. 45–52. New York: The Haworth Press Reproduced with permission.
[2.] Whenever the term *self* is first employed in a chapter as part of the concept of the use of self in therapy, it is italicized to call attention to its special use.

expressed my feelings for him that it really got to him. That interested me, because I am inclined to think that in my writing perhaps I have stressed too much the three basic conditions (congruence, unconditional positive regard, and empathic understanding). Perhaps it is something around the edges of those conditions that is really the most important element of therapy—when my self is very clearly, obviously present.

When I am working, I know that a lot of active energy flows from me to the client, and I am now aware that it probably was present to some degree from the first. I remember a client whose case I have written up, who said toward the end of therapy: 'I don't know a thing about you, and yet, I have never known anyone so well.' I think that is an important element, that even though a client did not know my age or my family or other details of my life, I became well known to her as a person.

In using myself, I include my intuition and the essence of myself, whatever that is. It is something very subtle, because myself as a person has a lot of specific characteristics that do not enter in as much as just the essential elements of myself. I also include my caring, and my ability to really listen acceptantly. I used to think that was easy. It has taken me a long time to realize that for me, for most people, this is extremely hard. To listen acceptantly, no matter what is being voiced, is a rare thing and is something I try to do.

When I am with a client, I like to be aware of my feelings, and if feelings run contrary to the conditions of therapy and occur persistently, then I am sure I want to express them. But there are also other feelings. For instance, sometimes, with a woman client, I feel: 'This woman is sexually attractive, I feel attracted to her.' I would not express that unless it comes up as an issue in therapy. But, if I felt annoyed by the fact that she was always complaining, let us say, and I kept feeling annoyed, then I would express it.

The important thing is to be aware of this feeling, and then you can decide whether it needs to be expressed or is appropriate to express. Sometimes, it is amusing. I know in one demonstration interview, I suddenly was aware of something about the recording. I believe they had not turned on the recorder or something like that. It was just a flash and then I was back with the client. In discussing it afterward, I said, 'There was one moment when I really was not with you.' And he replied, 'Yes, I knew that.' It is very evident when there is a break in a relationship like that. I did not express that concern because it seemed irrelevant and yet, it was relevant. It would have been better had I said, 'For a moment there, I was thinking about the machine, and now I am back with you.'

I think that the therapist has a right to his or her own life. One of the worst things is for a therapist to permit the client to take over, or to be a governing influence in the therapist's life. It happened to me once, and was nearly disastrous.

It was with a schizophrenic client of whom I got tired, I guess. I had done some good work with her—and sometimes not—and she sort of clung to me, which I resented, but did not express. Gradually she came to know me well enough to know just how to press my buttons, and she kept me very upset. In fact, I began to feel that she knew me better than I knew myself, and that obviously is nontherapeutic and disastrous to the therapist. It helped me to realize that one of the first requirements for being a therapist is that there be a live therapist. I think it is important to realize that one has a need and a right to preserve and protect oneself. A therapist has a right to give, but not to get worn out trying to be giving. I think different therapists have different kinds of boundaries: some can give a great deal and really not harm themselves, and others find it difficult to do that.

A number of years ago, I would have said that the therapist should not be a model to the client, that the client should develop his or her own models, and I still feel that to some degree. But, in one respect, the therapist is a model. By listening acceptantly to every aspect of the client's experience, the therapist is modeling the notion of listening to oneself. And, by being accepting and nonjudgmental of the feelings within the client, the therapist is modeling a nonjudgmental self-acceptance in the client. By being real and congruent and genuine, the therapist is modeling that kind of behavior for the client. In these ways, the therapist does serve as a useful model.

The way I am perceived by the client also makes a difference, but not in the therapeutic process. If I am seen as a father figure, for example, then that makes a difference in the therapy; it makes a difference in the client's feelings. But, since the whole purpose of therapy, as I see it, is to hear and accept and recognize the feelings that the client is having, it does not make much fundamental difference whether the client sees me as a young person or a lover, or as a father figure, as long as the client is able to express some of those feelings. The process is the same regardless of which feelings are being experienced.

This is why I differ so fundamentally with the psychoanalysts on this business of transference. I think it is quite natural that a client might feel positive feelings toward the therapist. There is no reason to make a big deal out of it. It can be handled in the same way as the fact that the client might be afraid of the therapist, or of his or her father. Any feelings are grist for the mill as far as therapy is concerned, providing the client can express them and providing the therapist is able to listen acceptantly. I think the whole concept of transference got started because the therapist got scared when the client began to feel strong positive or negative feelings toward the therapist.

The whole process of therapy is a process of self-exploration, of getting acquainted with one's own feelings and coming to accept them as a part of the self. So, whether the feelings are in regard to the parents, or in regard to the therapist, or in regard to some situation, it really makes no difference. The client is getting better acquainted with and becoming more accepting of his or her self and that can be true with regard to the transference feelings. When the client realizes: 'Yes, I do love him very much', or whatever, and accepts those as a real part of self, the process of therapy advances.

I think that therapy is most effective when the therapist's goals are limited to the process of therapy and not the outcome. I think that if the therapist feels, 'I want to be as present to this person as possible. I want to really listen to what is going on. I want to be real in this relationship,' then these are suitable goals for the therapist. If the therapist is feeling, 'I want this person to get over this neurotic behavior, I want this person to change in such and such a way,' I think that stands in the way of good therapy. The goal has to be within myself, with the way I am. Once therapy is under way, another goal of the therapist is to question: 'Am I really with this person in this moment? Not where they were a little while ago, or where are they going to be, but am I really with this client in this moment?' This is the most important thing.

Another important element is the maturity of the therapist. I recall that in Chicago, a graduate student did some research that seemed to indicate that the more psychologically mature the therapist, the more effective the therapy was likely to be. It was not a definitive research, but I suspect that there is a lot of truth in it. Not only experience in living, but what one has done with that experience in living makes a difference in therapy. It ties in with another feeling I have—that perhaps I am good at helping people to recognize their own capacities, because I have come to value and represent the notion of self-empowerment. However, somebody else may be good at helping them in another way, because they have achieved maturity in another realm. What I am saying is that different therapists have different characteristics of their mature personality and probably these different elements help clients move in those directions.

The mature person is always open to all of the evidence coming in, and that means open to continuing change. Often people ask me, 'How have you changed over the years?' And I can see from the way they phrase their question that they are asking, 'What have I rejected, what have I thrown away?' Well, I haven't rejected much of anything, but I have been astonished at the fact that those ideas which started in individual therapy could have such very wide implications and applications.

My career as a therapist has gone through a number of phases. One of the earliest and most important was when I gave up on a mother and her son. My staff was handling the boy and I was dealing with the mother, trying to get across to her the fact that her problem was her rejection of the boy. We went through a number of interviews and I had learned to be quite attentive and gentle. I had been trying to get this point of view across but I was not succeeding, so I said, 'I think we both have tried, but this is not working, so we might as well call it quits. Do you agree?' She indicated that she thought so, too. She said 'goodbye' and walked to the door. Then she turned and said, 'Do you ever take adults for counseling here?' I said 'yes,' and with that she came back and began to pour out her story of problems with her husband, which was so different from the nice case history I had been taking that I could hardly recognize it. I did not know quite what to do with it, and I look back at this as being the first real therapy case that I ever handled. She kept in touch with me for a long time. The problems with the boy cleared up. I felt it was successful therapy, but did not quite know how it came about.

Later, another change occurred. I had been impressed by Rankian thinking. We had him in for a two-day workshop and I liked it. So I decided to hire a social worker who was a product of the Philadelphia School of Social Work, Elizabeth Davis. It was from her that I first got the idea of responding to feelings, of respecting feelings whether she used that terminology or not I am not sure. I don't think she learned very much from me, but I learned a lot from her.

Then, another stepping-stone. I had long been interested in recording interviews, but it was very difficult to do in those days. The equipment required that somebody be in another room, recording three minutes on the face of a record and then brushing off the shavings of glass, since we could not get metal during the war. Then, they had to turn the record over and continue. Anyway, it was really difficult. But when we began to analyze these interviews and we gradually got better equipment—it was astounding what we learned from these microscopic examinations of the interviews. One could clearly see where an interview had been going along smoothly—the process flowing—and then one response on the part of the counselor just switched things off for a while, or perhaps for the whole interview. We also began to see that some of the people in my practicum came to be called 'blitz' therapists, because they would seem to have a couple of very good interviews with their clients, and then the client never came back. It was not until we examined the recordings that we realized that the therapist had been too good, had gone too far, revealed too much of the client's inner self to them and scared the hell out of them. Another important development in my career was the writing of a very rigorous theory of the client-centered approach. I was very excited that what had gradually been developing quite experientially could be put into tight cognitive terms which could be tested. This gave me a great deal of confidence, and a great deal of satisfaction. Another change in my career occurred when I moved out to California. Having had the opportunity to realize the power of relatively brief intensive group experiences, I directed my energy to the development of intensive encounter groups. I also developed the applications of my theories to education, and then to large groups.

Finally, early in life I acquired a strong belief in a democratic point of view, and that belief has impacted my therapy. I became convinced that the final authority lies with the individual and that there is no real external authority that can be depended upon. It comes down to one's internal choice, made with all the evidence that one can get and the best possible way that one can cope.

I have always been able to rely on the fact that if I can get through the shell, if I can get through to the person there will be a positive and constructive inner core. That is why I hold a different point of view from Rollo May. He seems to feel that there is a lot of essential evil in the individual, but I have never been able to pin him down as to whether it is genetic or not. I feel that if people were evil, I would be shocked or horrified at what I found if I was able to get through to the core of that person. I have never had that experience—just the opposite. If I can get through to a person, even those whose behavior has a lot of destructive elements, I believe he or she would want to do the right thing. So I do not believe that people are genetically evil. Something must have happened after birth to warp them. It has often been said that I could not work with psychopaths, because they have no social conscience. Well, my feeling is: yes, it would be difficult and I don't think they would come easily into one-to-one psychotherapy. But if they could be part of a group for a long period of time, then I think they could probably be gotten to.

Recently my views have broadened into a new area about which I would like to comment. A friend, who is a minister, always kids me about the fact that I am one of the most spiritual people he knows, but I won't admit it. Another time, a group of young priests were trying to pin me to the wall, saying that I must be religious. I finally said to them and it is something I still stand by, 'I am too religious to be religious,' and that has quite a lot of meaning for me. I have my own definition of spirituality. I would put it that the best of therapy sometimes leads to a dimension that is spiritual, rather than saying that the spiritual is having an impact on therapy. But it depends on your definition of spiritual. There are certainly times in therapy and in the experience I have had with groups where I feel that there is something going on that is larger than what is evident. I have described this in various ways. Sometimes I feel much as the physicists, who do not really split atoms; they simply align themselves up in accordance with the natural way in which the atoms split themselves. In the same way, I feel that sometimes in interpersonal relationships power and energy get released which transcend what we thought was involved.

As I recently said, I find that when I am the closest to my inner, intuitive self—when perhaps I am somehow in touch with the unknown in me—when perhaps I am in a slightly altered state of consciousness in the relationship, then whatever I do seems to be full of healing. Then simply my presence is releasing and helpful. At those moments, it seems that my inner spirit has reached out and touched the inner spirit of the other. Our relationship transcends itself, and has become part of something larger. Profound growth and healing and energy are present.

To be a fully authentic therapist, I think that you have to feel entirely secure as a person. This allows you to let go of yourself, knowing confidently that you can come back. Especially when you work with a group, you have to surrender yourself to a process of which you are a part and admit you can't have a complete understanding. And then when you get to dealing with a group of 500 or 600, you surrender any hope of understanding what is going on, and yet, by surrendering yourself to the process, certain things happen.

The therapist needs to recognize very clearly the fact that he or she is an imperfect person with flaws which make him vulnerable. I think it is only as the therapist views himself as imperfect and flawed that he can see himself as helping another person. Some people who call themselves therapists are not healers, because they are too busy defending themselves.

The self I use in therapy does not include all my personal characteristics. Many people are not aware that I am a tease and that I can be very tenacious and tough, almost obstinate. I have often said that those who think I am always gentle should get into a fight with me, because they would find out quite differently. I guess that all of us have many different facets, which come into play in different situations. I am just as real when I am understanding and accepting as when I am being tough. To me being congruent means that I am aware of and willing to represent the feelings I have at the moment. It is being real and authentic in the moment.

I am frequently asked what kind of training is necessary to become a person-centered therapist. I know some very good person-centered therapists who have had no training at all! I think that one could go to small remote villages and find out who people turn to for help—what are the characteristics of these people they turn to? I think to be a good person-centered therapist, one needs to experience a person-centered approach either in an intensive group for some period of time, or in individual therapy, or whatever. I don't, however, believe in requiring such an experience. I feel that the opportunity should be available, but not required.

Then, in addition to that, I think that breadth of learning is perhaps the most important. I'd rather have someone who read widely and deeply in literature or in physics, than to have someone who has always majored in psychology in order to become a therapist. I think that breadth of learning along with breadth of life experience are essential to becoming a good therapist. Another thing: the importance of recording interviews cannot be overestimated. Videotaping is even better, although I have not had much experience with that. But to have the opportunity to listen to what went on, be it right after the interview or one year later, to try to understand the process of what went on, should be a tremendous learning experience. I think that one should let the beginning therapist do whatever he wants in therapy, provided that he records the sessions and listens to them afterward, so that he can see the effects on the process. I think that the careful review of recorded interviews is essential.

I think that my present viewpoints are difficult to admit in academic circles. In the past, I could be understood at a purely cognitive level. However, as I became clearer as to what I was doing, academicians had to allow room for experiential learning, which is quite threatening, because then the instructor might have to become a learner, which is not popular in such circles. I think it is much easier to accept me as someone who had some ideas in the 1940s that can be described, than try to understand what has been happening since. I know very few people in major universities who have any real or deep understanding of my work. In some of the external degree institutions, yes, and outside of institutions there are a number of such people. It is interesting that the degree of understanding does not depend on the degree of contact with me. When people are philosophically ready for that part of me, they can pick it up entirely from reading. If they are not philosophically ready, they can do an awful lot of reading and still not get the point. Basically, it is a way of being, and universities are not interested in ways of being. They are more interested in ideas and ways of thinking.

People have asked me what effect I think my work has had on other professions. I think that my most important impact has been on education. I don't feel that I have had much influence on medicine or psychiatry or even on psychology. I have had much more influence in counseling, but not on the mainstream of psychology. I think I have had some impact on nursing. Nurses don't need to defend themselves against change and new ideas. I am also intrigued with the thought that the idea of leaving a human being free to follow his own choices is gradually extending into business.

Finally, I have been interested to see an evolution in the practice of medicine, where the idea of empowering the patient has brought medicine 'back' to the idea that patients can heal themselves. I am also pleased to see the development of personal responsibility in health. One of the most important things is that we have opened up psychotherapy and substituted the growth model for the medical model.

Chapter 25
CARL ROGERS ON MULTICULTURAL COUNSELLING: EXCERPTS FROM LETTERS FROM CARL ROGERS TO JEAN CLARK, 1979–1983

COLIN LAGO

Jean Clark was a one of the founding members of RACE (Race Awareness in Counselling Education), a subcommittee of the BACP (British Association of Counselling and Psychotherapy). She worked with Carl Rogers as a staff member and as a participant on several intercultural communication workshops and wrote to him, from time to time, as a way of keeping him appraised of the activities of RACE. His replies were always enthusiastic and supportive as some of the following extracts demonstrate. These extracts are taken from five of Carl Rogers' letters to Jean Clark from 18 September 1979 to 12 July 1983. All the letters were signed 'most cordially' before his signature and the role of 'Resident Fellow, Center for the Studies of the Person' written after. Only extracts from the correspondence relevant to the material of this book have been included below, the personal and other references having been appropriately edited.

LETTER NO. 1 (18 SEPTEMBER 1979)

This letter is only half a page in length and, in part, was a response to Jean Clark enquiring about the possibility of working with and or involving Carl Rogers in a large group workshop on the theme of intercultural relations.

Dear Jean Clark,

It is always so good and refreshing to hear from you …

I, too, have been through some very difficult workshops this summer. I don't quite understand why they have been more struggling than in the past … your ambitions for an intercultural workshop*… excite me. I would like to work with you on a staff ...

*During the late 1960s, Carl Rogers and colleagues had begun to focus their work much more on groups (than on therapeutic work with individuals) and by the early 1970s, Wood records the first long (17 days' duration) large group workshop being organised in the United States (Wood, 1999: 142). In 1977, staff of the Center for the Studies of the Person (including Carl Rogers) convened a large group workshop for 300 participants in Brazil (*ibid.*: 152). The Facilitator Development Institute in the UK had commenced running annual summer workshops in 1975 (modelled on Rogers' theoretical ideas) and Rogers himself attended the El Escoriel workshop in 1978, where Jean Clark had met him. Intercultural dimensions and possibilities within these group workshops were already an acknowledged dimension of this work and Jean Clark could see the potential for its application, certainly in the British context as well as more widely.

By this time, Carl Rogers had already published writings on the resolution of intercultural tensions (Rogers, 1977; see also Kirschenbaum and Henderson, 1989). These, however, were not new concerns for Carl Rogers. Barrett-Lennard, in his excellent and wide-ranging book covering the development of Rogers' work and its spread of application, notes that by the mid-1960s Carl Rogers was involved in simulation experiments at the Western Behavioral Sciences Institute to explore international tensions and, subsequently, made proposals for further research into 'tension processes and conflict resolution', involving, among others, programmes concerned with race relations (Barrett-Lennard, 1998: 220).

LETTER NO. 2 (8 SEPTEMBER 1981)

This second letter in the series contains the most relevant material to this book and is, therefore, reproduced in its entirety. Rogers was writing in response to Jean Clark and the RACE committee who had written to him about their emerging work (and dreams).

Dear Jean Clark,

This is a letter to all of you who signed the letter to me.

I am genuinely enthusiastic about your plans to establish a viable program of workshops which would tackle the difficult problems of multiracial and intercultural tensions.

I have had enough experience in such work to know that it takes dedication, a deeply empathic, nonjudgmental stance, and a willingness to innovate and adapt. With such qualities it is possible, as I know from my own work, to achieve mutual understanding between hostile racial groups, feuding intercultural groups, angry members of the 'haves' and 'have-nots'.

Often it is necessary for the facilitative staff to listen to, absorb, and understand, hostile, contemptuous attitudes towards the staff itself. This is not always easy.

It is most certainly important to have members of the different races or cultural groups represented on the staff.

I applaud your plan to train just such people as facilitators so that the work you do can be a center from which many workshops and other programs will spread. I wish I could help in establishing the person-centered training institute of which you dream.

You may be sure that if I am in England (or Europe) at a time when it would be possible for me to be involved in your program, I would like to take part.

Your plan and program has my heartiest approval and support. It is a vitally needed venture, and I wish you all success as you undertake it.

LETTER NO. 3 (8 MARCH 1982)

This letter was only one paragraph in length and thanked Jean Clark for having sent 'a long and fascinating letter. I am glad you are keeping me up to date …' The letter finished with: 'I am delighted that I will be seeing you in Mexico'. Mexico was the location for the first International Forum of the Person-Centered Approach, held in the summer of 1982. Jean Clark presented a paper at this Forum on the use of the Person-Centred Approach in a multiracial society (Clark, 1982).

LETTER NO. 4 (2 MAY 1983)

In this letter, Carl Rogers comments on his visit to South Africa. Accompanied by Ruth Sanford, he had been invited to South Africa by Len Holdstock, a professor at the University of Witwatersrand in 1982. There, they facilitated a small group experience involving black and white, male and female, participants. This group had formed in answer to an invitation for volunteers to a large assembled audience of 600 and was conducted, on stage, in front of that audience. Apparently, the proceedings proved extremely powerful in enhanced communication between the various participants (Sanford 1,999).

Dear Jean Clark,

I have just gotten round to reading your most interesting letter in the network newsletter put together by Ann Weisner ... I wish we could talk together because I seem to be more and more involved in intercultural and interracial situations. Ruth and I had a marvelously enriching and challenging time in South Africa where we held, for example, a black/white encounter group onstage in front of 600 people. The people in the group were very open and deep and strong feelings emerged; also the possibility of real dialogue between the races.

Now, in a few days, Natalie and I take off for Japan where Naoko has invited us to conduct a workshop there. Again, the intercultural and interracial aspects are uppermost in my mind ...

Good luck to you in your work. I hope you will share with me anything that you write about developing communication and dialogue between people of different cultures, values and customs.

With cordial good wishes ...

LETTER NO. 5 (12 JULY 1983)

This six-paragraph letter comprises Carl Rogers' clarification of an impending visit he was to make to London during that summer and, at which, amongst other things, he was engaged to be in dialogue with the psychiatrist R. D. Laing. Carl Rogers also apologises for not being able to be available for a workshop on 'class issues' that had been proposed earlier by a British colleague. His time in London, he explains, is already filled with obligations.

> In regard to the book that you are doing,* I have made it a hard and fast rule (of necessity) that I do not write forewords to books that I have not had a large part in preparing. I would, however, be willing to write a blurb for your volume when it is finished...

* Jean Clark had written to Carl Rogers on behalf of the RACE committee asking if he would kindly consider writing a foreword to an edited collection of chapters on the topic of 'multicultural counselling' that the committee wished to publish. Eventually, and despite many of the chapters having already been written, it was not possible to obtain a publishing contract for this venture.

CONCLUSION

The above extracts from Carl Rogers' letters to Jean Clark provide evidence of an important and sustained commitment that Carl Rogers demonstrated over several years to the importance of intergroup (cultural, ethnic, racial, national) communications and relations. The reference to the extracts from Barrett-Lennard further indicate that this commitment had been part of a much longer-held view by Carl Rogers, a view that was concerned to explore, research and establish hypotheses and methods that would underpin the enhancement of communication between people. The subsequent application of his ideas, in therapy, in small and large groups, in educational environments and in international situations reveals his deep concern for understanding and promoting peaceful relations between people.

REFERENCES

Barrett-Lennard, G (1998) *Carl Rogers' Helping System: Journey and Substance*. London: Sage.

Clark, J (1982) 'Change is Boundaries Dissolved': Person Centred Approaches in a Multi-Racial Society', in A Segrera (ed) *Proceedings of the First International Forum on the Person-Centered Approach*. Mexico: Universidad Iberoamericana.

Kirschenbaum, H and Henderson, VL (eds) (1989) *The Carl Rogers Reader*. Boston: Houghton Mifflin.

Rogers, CR (1977) *Carl Rogers on Personal Power: Inner Strength and its Revolutionary Practice*. New York: Delacorte Press.

Sanford, R (1999) 'A Brief History of My Experience of the Development of Group Work in the Person-Centered Approach', in C Lago and M MacMillan (eds) *Experiences in Relatedness: Group Work and the Person-Centred Approach*. Ross-on-Wye: PCCS Books.

Wood, JK (1999) 'Towards an understanding of large group dialogue and its implications', in C Lago and M MacMillan (eds) *Experiences in Relatedness: Group Work and the Person Centred Approach*. Ross-on-Wye: PCCS Books.

Contributors

Michelle Baldwin

I am a marriage and family therapist with an MSSW from the Simmons College School of Social Work (1966), and a PhD from the Union Graduate School (1976). As an AAMFT approved supervisor, I teach and supervise at the Chicago Center for Family Health and the Family Institute at Northwestern University. I trained with, taught with and co-authored two books with Virginia Satir, *Satir Step by Step* in 1984 and *The Use of Self in Therapy*, in 1987. (Second edition, 1999). For over ten years, together with my husband DeWitt C Baldwin MD, I have taught PAIRS (Practical Application of Intimate Relationship Skill) in the US and overseas and know how to create a safe environment for experiential work. In 2002, I became a Certified Sageing™ Leader of the Spiritual Eldering® Institute, and I am conducting workshops focusing on successful aging for people who are retired or thinking of retirement. I knew and met Carl Rogers on a number of occasions in the 1970s in La Jolla, California, where he, my husband, and I were conducting workshops for the Human Dimensions for Medical Education Program, which was one of the programs at the Center for the Studies of the Person. Although, I was familiar with Carl's work, I very much appreciated seeing him in action, and also had the opportunity to know him over time in informal settings. In 1986, when Virginia Satir asked me to co-author an edited book on the *Use of Self in Therapy*, I thought that Carl should be the lead contributor. The problem was that when I approached Carl, he stated that he was working on too many other projects and that he could not accept the invitation. I then suggested the format of an interview, which would be audio taped, and he graciously welcomed me in his home.

Selwyn Black

I am a lecturer in counselling and Course Director of the Post Graduate Diploma/MSc in Counselling and Therapeutic Communication in the School of Communication at the University of Ulster. I have been involved in developing a unique course—the Post Graduate Certificate in the Management and Care of Psychological Trauma. My PhD research presented both a longitudinal study with a team of trauma counsellors from Northern Ireland in which I explored the long-term impact of vicarious traumatisation on counselling identity, and a comparative study with a surgical team from Travnik County Hospital, Central Bosnia. The research identifies and tracks the biographical, societal and cultural influences that directly shape the assimilation and integration of traumatic experience. My research interests include understanding the psychological impact of caring in trauma counsellors and other professionals; exploring the distinction between traumatic experience that emanates from the sexual abusive arena and traumatic experience that emanates from the combat/terrorist/disaster arena; and understanding the shape of the 'trauma story'. I have published several articles on the issues of trauma and counselling identity. My interest in trauma, particularly the experiences of professionals working with traumatised clients, arises out of my experiences as a military chaplain in several international contexts. I have addressed many international audiences on self-care issues for professional helpers working with the traumatised. My escape from academic life is a shared passion for 'jazz' with Catrin Rhys.

Debora C Brink

I taught Developmental Psychology in the School of Education at the City College of New York, New York for more than 20 years before retiring in 1986. I now live in New Orleans, Lousiana.

Barbara Brodley

I was born in 1932 on the south side of Chicago and lived there in a lower-class all White neighborhood during the Great Depression. My father was a first generation Italian-American, and my mother came from English and Scottish people who arrived in the US in the 1600s. The 'Black Belt' was only two streets away from our apartment building, but the line was rigidly drawn, so I had no personal contact with Blacks as a child. In fact, I rarely saw Black persons in stores or on the street until college, when I had friends of color; racial segregation in Chicago had been so profound and ubiquitous. My parents were dedicated supporters of Roosevelt with strongly felt democratic and egalitarian values. I was not exposed to racial, ethnic, social class or religious prejudice within the family, and from childhood I experienced any such attitudes as repugnant. In high school I began to identify my socialist leanings with Marxism. Then, through a series of fortunate circumstances, I was helped to attend the University of Chicago where I was given a broad education and exposed to Enlightenment philosophies of freedom and the equality of persons. In 1953, I began to study Rogers' theories and in 1955 started to practice client-centered therapy. I did not meet Rogers personally until 1960 although I was committed to his philosophy of persons and therapeutic approach—as I have continued to be. I received my doctorate in Clinical Psychology from the Committee on Human Development at the University of Chicago, and I was a staff member for seven years at the University of Chicago Counseling Center founded by Rogers. I had five years of psychotherapy experience working in a large state 'mental hospital'; then in an inpatient drug treatment program, in a general hospital with the physically ill, in a student health service and in a geriatric home as well as having a private practice for the past 35 years. My clients have included Black, Asian, Arab and Latino, as well as White individuals and couples. I have been teaching and supervising client-centered therapy for many years in Chicago and abroad. Since 1980, I have taught client-centered therapy at Argosy University Illinois School of Professional Psychology in Chicago.

Khatidja Chantler

I currently work as a counsellor and supervisor in private practice, and have worked as a tutor on social work and counselling courses. I am also an independent researcher, and honorary research fellow at the Manchester Metropolitan University, UK, and undertake consultancy and evaluation work. I have worked in health and social care settings, in both the statutory and voluntary sectors, for over 20 years.

My personal experiences of racism, sexism and classism in the UK context have helped to shape my fundamental belief in the need for fairness, justice and egalitarianism. Fairness and justice are claimed as desirable by practically everybody as well as by society at large. Within this context, the problem has been how to make visible the invisible, i.e. injustice and oppression where dominant and/or majority groups do not see it, or believe it exists. I came to see that how I, or others, are treated is not to do as much with inherent qualities that we possess, but with wider structural issues and power relations. Structural issues (such as racism, sexism and class) and personal issues are frequently presented as two separate dimensions. For me, it has been helpful to see these two dimensions as intertwined. Hence our internal world is both part of, and constituted by, the external, and this formation of our internal world influences how we interact, and are in the external. It is these issues that have been a key influence in my working (and personal) life. My interest in the 'internal' led me train as a person-centred counsellor. In many ways I found this a frustrating process, as I felt that structural issues were not seen as integral to the ways in which we relate and conduct our relationships. It is from this sense of frustration that I have written my chapter in an attempt to grapple with, and hopefully elucidate, some key issues for person centred therapy as I see it.

I am committed to working towards more inclusive and innovative approaches to health and social care, particularly around 'race', culture, gender and class. I have published in a range of UK, European and international journals and co-authored two books: *Attempted Suicide and Self-harm (South Asian Women)* (2001) and *Domestic Violence and Minoritisation: Supporting women to independence* (2002) both published by the Women's Studies Research Centre, Manchester Metropolitan University.

Mary Charleton

I work as an independent trainer, supervisor and consultant. Since the 1970s I have been strongly influenced in my living and working by ideas in Humanistic Psychology and have welcomed the emphasis on human potential rather than problems or deficit. The ideas and practice of Carl Rogers and Fritz Perls encouraged me to honour my own experience and from that standpoint work with and encourage others.

In the 1980s I started teaching on the South West London College counselling course. This was a training run by Brigid Proctor and other well respected staff. The programme was student directed and self and peer assessed. As well as being influenced by John Heron, the course took on board Rogers' ideas about the method of learning being compatible with what is being taught and Harvey Jackins' views about the capacity to learn being impeded by previous hurtful learning experiences. Working on this course enabled me to live the Person-Centred Approach to people and learning. It opened up the possibility of having power with others and was as much of a challenge to the staff as the students. In particular, managing the interface with a traditionally administered educational organisation was a stressful task. Rogers acknowledges this in some of his writing, and I empathised with him when I witnessed the persecutory rage that this and other counselling courses at times attracted.

I became senior tutor (course leader) and after the demise of the Inner London Education Authority negotiated the transfer of the course to another organisation. Here we were presented more forcibly with the task of reconciling our ideas with statutory requirements regarding equal opportunities. Direct action to protect minorities was required of us and to white staff who were well imbued with a particular tradition this seemed to jar with self-directed practice. This was an inner city. Tensions were high, emotions raw, and difficult lessons were learned. Many of us became more interventionist in our way of working, and it is from this altered standpoint that some of the criticisms of the film arise.

Bias and prejudice are obstacles to an individual's growth and development. In education and in therapy, prejudice and white European bias within counselling theory should be acknowledged. If the people experiencing injustice are left on their own to work against it they will have little time and energy left to meet their own goals in therapy and education. A way of combating prejudice is to notice it, comment on it and work actively against it by, for example, devising training exercises which help white people become aware of the significance of being white in a multi-racial society.

In my book *Self-directed Learning in Counselling Training* published by Cassell in 1996, I describe this kind of work in considerable detail. I have also published a number of relevant articles on counselling and counselling training and have edited several editions of the *European Journal of Humanistic Psychology (Self and Society)*. These editions were about self-directed learning, counselling and choice, and sexual politics.

Now that I work privately in a more rural setting I continue to confront the inevitable bias of a white middle-class heterosexual majority and help people become aware of prejudice within themselves. Tagore speaks of helping people knock at the doors of their own minds. I hope I do this a bit.

Jean Clark

When I was 12 years old the second world war broke out and I was sent to live with a family in Cambridge, my first experience of culture shock. Three months later I returned to London, and then my father's work in a government department was evacuated to North Wales. I now found myself living in a town where there was prejudice against 'these English evacuees' where people spoke Welsh, as well as English with a different accent, and where I went to my fourth school in sixteen months! My friends were mainly the 'other English kids' who had also been evacuated to Wales. These experiences led me to writing a paper many years later, 'Change is Boundaries Dissolved' (1988) which explored 'the place between in the process of change'.

After the war ended, I moved to London, and worked as a secretary at the National Council of Social Service. Here many of the pioneers of social welfare were working-people who had established the Citizens' Advice Bureaux, the Community Association movement, the Old People's Welfare Council, the National Association of Voluntary Youth Organisations, the Village Hall movement and the Women's Clubs movement (set up for the wives of coal miners, who became unemployed in the economic depression of the 1930s). I met and worked alongside these exceptional people who had created important social movements—and discovered that it was possible to 'make things happen', to work for change in society.

In 1949, aged 23, I studied for a social work qualification at the University of Oxford, then married two years later. My husband began working in an adult residential college for men who had left school early and were working in industry, and now wanted to further their education. Looking back, I recognise that the one-year course at Fircroft was a person-centred learning community, where students took responsibility for their own growth in a respectful and caring environment where they had freedom to learn. I became the mother of two children and my only social concern during this time was an involvement with a hostel being set up for refugees from Eastern Europe.

In 1963, the family moved and settled in Leicester, and I felt ready to begin part-time work. For two years I job-shared a lectureship at the National College for the Training of Youth Leaders (where I remember meeting Colin Lago). Then in 1968, I read in a higher education journal, an article on 'Student Counselling' and *knew* that this was what I wanted to do next, even though I was not clear what the role might involve. There were very few student counsellors in Universities or Polytechnics in the UK at that time. I gained a further qualification in psychology in 1969, but for a year no student counselling post occurred in Leicester.

But again I seemed to be in the right place at the right time, when I was offered a one-year part-time post as research assistant at the Centre for Mass Communication Research at Leicester University for a project funded by UNESCO. It was to prove a profoundly life changing experience and of direct relevance to the subject matter of this book. My task was to undertake a major content analysis of the British national daily press, identifying and analysing all items of news which related to race for the years 1960–68. The results were published in *Race as News* UNESCO (1972). That year's work was to have a profound influence on my awareness of the racism which was endemic in Britain during the 1960s.

In 1971, I was appointed as the first student counsellor at Leicester Polytechnic, an institution which had a large intake of students from overseas and increasingly was receiving young people who were the first generation of children of immigrant parents who were living and working in Leicester. Over the next decade the counselling service developed as did my awareness of the complexity of working with students who were now living in two cultures. After Colin joined me as second student counsellor, our concern for issues about cross-cultural counselling developed. We met with a group of Asian mothers so that we might learn about their cultural assumptions and expectations for their daughters and sons who were coming into higher education. Then in 1978, I was invited to attend the first person-centred workshop on cross-cultural communication facilitated by Carl Rogers and an international staff in Europe, and for me this 12-day experience of living and working with people from 26 countries was very powerful; subsequently, I was invited to be a facilitator for similar workshops in Germany, Italy and Hungary. I corresponded with Carl Rogers over this period; he was supportive and very interested in the work which was going on in the UK, where racism was now being addressed.

Though I left the Polytechnic and moved to Norwich in 1985, where I work in independent practice, my concern for issues to do with counselling, race and culture has continued. At age 75, I edited my first book, *Freelance Counselling and Psychotherapy—Competition and Collaboration* (2002) which deals with a wide range of practical and internal challenges for trainees and qualified practitioners in independent practice.

CHRISTINE CLARKE
My spirit descended to earth on the first day of the first month of 1955. Struggling to survive physically, emotionally and intellectually in a white poverty-stricken town, near Middlesbrough, England, left its mark. At 18, a boyfriend and Alnwick College of Education warmed and nourished my starved soul. The College's student-centred

philosophy, based on the belief that everyone learns at their own pace, and given the right conditions, can find their own way, growing and developing in a positive direction, ignited my fire of passionate belief. Teaching practice with severely physically and intellectually challenged children led to my later involvement with Mencap.

Marriage, bits of jobs, and 2 children later, I was ready to once more face the employment market. However, the devastating tide of unemployment that swept through the 1980s left thousands washed up on the desolate beach of the dole office. Lack of confidence, low self-esteem, depression and isolation took their toll of all communities and cultures. Recognising these barriers to employment, an enlightened back-to-work scheme in a local Further Education College, ran therapy groups as an integral part of the programme. As a participant I shared my experiences and listened to others as they shared theirs. I learnt from Arabs, Muslims, Hindus, to name but a few, what it was that made them who they were and gave them the potential for what they could become.

I was soon employed to 'teach' on these schemes, and I listened to hundreds of people's life experiences, valuing their lives and achievements and gaining a rich knowledge of different cultures, races, and religions. Counselling Mencap carers and their dependants, I built on Alnwick's philosophy and trained in both Person-Centred and Gestalt Approaches and changed my career.

Gaining my British Association for Counselling and Psychotherapy Accreditation in 1991, I set up a small private practice. At the same time, working as a student counsellor for the University of Teesside, I set up the counselling service at the new joint College with the University of Durham at Stockton. My previous multi-cultural experience gave a solid background for me to work with students from a variety of cultures, furthering my knowledge and understanding. In parallel, I gained my MA in Counselling, and, having taught on counselling courses for the local Further Education College, I became a part-time counselling tutor with the University of Durham.

At the time of writing, I have taken time out from teaching, but work for Tees and North East Yorkshire NHS Trust, as one of their counselling managers, as well as continuing with my private practice. Working in GP's surgeries, serving poor inner-city multicultural populations, I encourage referrals from all cultures and on occasions have worked through interpreters.

I aim for equality in a counselling relationship where each person's contribution is of equal value. Clients contribute their life experience and I, my counselling expertise. I warmly accept and cherish difference, and acknowledge that my empathy is culturally defined. I endeavour to provide a climate for clients to discover for themselves what it means to live life to the full, in the context of themselves, their families and their cultures.

Shukla Dhingra

I recently took a job at Trent University as a counsellor, having been at Loughborough University for the last five years. I am also a trainer and supervisor and have a lifelong passion for issues of equality, widening access for black minority groups and women's issues especially Asian women. I enjoy offering workshops on the influence of race and culture on counselling and supervision.

My journey about cross-cultural/multicultural issues started long before I became a counsellor back in the 1970s when I was a teacher. I realised that when norms and values are taken mainly from the white majority group and are applied to every situation, people from minority groups are left feeling alienated and disadvantaged.

Ten years ago when I came into counselling, I thought all counselling work, regardless of orientation, paid special attention to the cultural, social and racial differences of clients, but I found this practice was not widespread. I wanted to meet other black counsellors to share my views. In one of the British Association for Counselling conferences in 1984, I had the opportunity to meet three other black counsellors— Josna Pankhania, William (Bill) Hall and Roy Moodley (who have all written in this book). We all experienced isolation in our individual situations and wondered whether there were other black people who might be feeling the same. So this gave birth to ABC (Association of Black Counsellors) and our active involvement with the RACE division of BAC.

I am pleased that now on my journey I have met many professionals, both black and white, who are exploring similar issues and have had opportunities to offer workshops on the influence of race and culture on the counselling relationship. I believe that all counselling should be cross-cultural and that all counsellors need to reflect this in their practice regardless of orientation.

GRAHAM FALKEN

I was born in Cape Town, South Africa, in 1952, racially labelled at birth as a 'coloured'— ironically the same year in which Britain welcomed its new monarch— ushering in the second Elizabethan age. Nine years later, I was on the SS Windsor Castle heading for Southampton, England and a new life in the 'mother country'. We were fleeing the horrors of Apartheid South Africa—pariah state (and former British colony)—a country which had just sunk to new lows with the Sharpeville massacre in 1960. Within a few short months, I was made aware that racism and racial discrimination were not confined to the southern tip of Africa. Strange as it may sound, it was in London that I first experienced the personal pain of hate speech and social exclusion. As a child in Cape Town, extreme segregation had 'protected' me from this by denying me any direct contact with white children. I recount some of these early experiences by way of explanation for my lifelong interest in issues of race and inequality.

I came to counselling almost by accident in 1990—ironically again the year of Nelson Mandela's release from Robben Island—because the job I had been doing at City College Manchester disappeared in a restructuring process. But perhaps it was no accident I chose to retrain for work in the college's Counselling Department. The Chinese say that out of crisis come both danger and opportunity, and the path I had been forced to take was to open up a wealth of opportunity at both the personal and political levels. I had been active in radical left politics since my teens and viewed racism as primarily a function of class oppression. But maybe as a direct result of the challenge of feminist perspectives in the 1970s and 1980s I had been forced to re-evaluate the personal as political too. My training has almost all been within the framework of person-centred therapy, and it seemed a natural home for an old 'leftie' with lingering Marxist tendencies because it seemed to allow for diversity of identity. But nothing was simple. Contradictions continued to abound. The women's movement had still to deal with the invisibility of black women within its own ranks. I vividly recall a presentation by Susie Orbach in the early 1990s to a conference hall full of counsellors and therapists, the majority women, where I was shocked, perhaps a little naïvely, to find only a handful of black faces. Something of this same sense of shock was present when I first saw Rogers in 'On Anger and Hurt'. How could the father of person-centred therapy miss something so blindingly obvious? Perhaps he was just a person after all!

I spent another six years at City College, dividing my time between the College Counselling Service for staff and students and facilitating the training of new counsellors. During this time, along with my good friend and colleague Yvonne Harris, I ran the first (I think) 'black' only introductory courses in counselling skills with the specific aim of bringing more black people into the profession. There was a fair amount of criticism from those who felt threatened or excluded, but for most of our students it was to prove the safest space they had ever experienced in their lives. For us as black trainers, it was both challenging and exhilarating. We also ran a number of workshops for counsellors who wanted to work in culturally and racially sensitive ways. Towards the end of my time at the College I was responsible for running the theory module of the Diploma programme. Despite some resistance from a few of the trainee counselors, 25% of the course lectures and 33% of the assessed coursework were devoted to issues of inequality in psychological theory and in the therapeutic relationship.

During my own training, I was privileged to be a fellow student of Anne Kearney (*Counselling, Class and Politics*, 1996, PCCS Books). In the course of much heated debate and discussion, she helped me re-integrate my political core into the new person I was becoming. It was a classic case of not throwing the baby out with the proverbial bathwater! My final two years in Manchester saw me move more into supervision. I was fascinated by the dynamics of the supervisory triangle. In 1998, I returned to Cape Town. Hardly anyone had heard of Carl Rogers, but there were a lot of black people experiencing 'anger and hurt'. The counselling profession, as it exists in the US and the UK, is not replicated here. The clinical psychologists and psychiatrists still seem to hold absolute sway. But things are changing, albeit slowly. In the meantime I now manage a small NGO working in arts and media—older and growing!

GARY FOSTER

I was born in 1964 in the village of Blacks Harbour, New Brunswick, Canada. Blacks Harbour was mainly a company town, which based its livelihood on the sardine industry. My parents both worked for Connors Brothers, the company that was founded by two Irish immigrants, Patrick and Lewis Connors, and which more or less established the village.

I experienced very little cultural diversity in my early years. The population of our village was almost exclusively comprised of English and French labourers. The French population moved to Blacks Harbour from the northern part of the province in order to find employment.

Following high school, I attended a small, Protestant, religious college with the intention of becoming an ordained minister in the Wesleyan Methodist Church. Following graduation I worked as an assistant pastor (in charge of youth programs) in Halifax, Nova Scotia and then in Tampa, Florida. During this time, I realized that the

Christian ministry was not where I really wanted to be. My growing interest in philosophy, combined with an intense questioning of my faith, drew me away from the church and back into the university classroom.

My time in Tampa exposed me to more cultural diversity than I had previously experienced, even though there was a fair amount of segregation between the black and white populations. Much of my contact with culturally diverse groups during this time was with the American Hispanic community. When I moved back to Halifax to pursue my education in philosophy, I experienced more contact with the black community (Halifax has one of the longest established black communities in Canada).

After studying philosophy at St Mary's University in Halifax, I moved to Waterloo, Ontario to pursue graduate studies. I finished both my MA and PhD at the University of Waterloo and have since been teaching at Wilfrid Laurier University (also in Waterloo). It was at Wilfrid Laurier that I first met Susan James, who, at the time was teaching in the Department of Psychology there. After numerous discussions of our work, we decided to try writing some articles that combined my interest in hermeneutics, existentialism, and ethics with her work in cultural psychology. This decision has resulted in a very fruitful, cooperative effort, which has been most beneficial to my own work.

The current work on Rogers helped me to realize the extent to which his work, especially his view of the self, was greatly influenced by one of my favourite philosophers, the Dane, Søren A. Kierkegaard. Kierkegaard's notion of the 'becoming' self which experiences freedom fundamentally as *angst* or 'anxiety', and which realizes authenticity by overcoming a condition of 'despair' or 'guilt' influenced Rogers as well as the entire 20th century movement called Existentialism.

My own interest in the self, both from an existentialist and hermeneutic perspective, has given me a greater appreciation and perspective for the work of Rogers and the work of contemporary psychology. My work with Dr James has helped me come to understand my own work in a more concrete way.

MICHAEL GOLDMAN
My interest in cross-cultural therapy has evolved from a curiosity about human diversity and its relationship to the community; specifically, the way in which society accepts and rejects differences. This has led to my development both personally and professionally. While working as a therapist in children's mental health within both outpatient and inpatient settings, I was fortunate to have the opportunity to collaborate with a diverse group of people who often faced multiple stressors in their lives. There were times when families faced hardships that related to immigration, which often caused complications in parent-child relationship as a result of differential cultural adjustments. This had an influence on my own desire to learn more about the impact of immigration on individuals and families and the way in which it could be accommodated and addressed effectively in the therapeutic process.

Furthermore, I was able to relate to the complexities of these experiences through my family history, which involved a cultural integration into Canada and has continued to be an ongoing process on multiple levels. This has also initiated my desire to learn experientially and has resulted in an exploration of narratives across the globe. I have lived in Japan for two years and was challenged to adapt culturally and linguistically, which raised my interest and awareness of the process of cultural adjustment. I have continued to appreciate a range of perspectives through extensive travels to Southern Africa, the Middle East, South-East Asia, and Eastern Europe as well as North and South America. These journeys have also increased my insight and interest in understanding the multiplicity of issues that are embedded in the cross-cultural therapy dynamic.

Clinically, I have diverse interests ranging from psychodynamic to client-centered approaches to therapy. I am currently in the midst of completing a doctoral degree in Counselling Psychology at the University of Toronto and have continued to explore research on the way in which cultural variables influence the process of psychotherapy.

WILLIAM ALEXANDER (BILL) HALL

I am an experienced school psychologist, family therapist, and human systems consultant. I worked extensively with clients from multicultural settings with backgrounds in North and South America, Asia, Africa and Australasia.

I retired from the American Department of Defense Dependents School system where I, consecutively, filled positions of teacher, counselling psychologist, principal and, finally, Evaluation Coordinator for schools in the North Atlantic Region. I also lectured in the Language Institute of the University of Heidelberg, Germany. I am currently director of an international counselling and consulting service that is based in London, England.

My primary and secondary education was experienced at a time when segregation of the races was enforced by statutory requirements in Tennessee, USA. However, the experience of being in an all black school and being taught by black teachers instilled in me a positive self-concept and a strong sense of pride and confidence. I hold degrees from the University of Maryland, Boston University and Vanderbilt University. Additionally, I completed an externship at Saint Elizabeth Mental Health Hospital, Washington, DC and a post-doctoral year in Cognitive Behavior Therapy at the Philadelphia College of Osteopathic Medicine. Among others, I hold professional memberships in the American Psychological Association, American Mental Health Counselors Association, American Association of Marriage and Family Therapist, the British Association for Counselling and Psychotherapy, and the multicultural divisions of these organizations. I chaired BACP's RACE group which eventually became a sub-division. Also, together with Josna Pankhania, Shukla Dhingra and Roy Moodley, I was instrumental in founding the Association of Black Counsellors in Britain.

Since retirement from the Defense Dependent Schools System, my professional pursuits have taken me into the realm of intercultural cooperation and understanding. My clinical practice follows an eclectic model of client-centred counselling and cognitive behavior therapy, which has produced positive results with psychological disorders such as depression, anxiety, panic and grief. In addition to individual, family and group therapy, I also offer organizational consultancy—a range of workshops in the workplace and life skills.

SUSAN JAMES

I was raised in a small town, outside of Toronto, Canada. Although Milton is primarily white, I was aware of the richness that other cultures bring because I am from a mixed family where my cousins and uncle are from Nigeria. I also learned about diverse cultures in Milton as I had many interactions with the deaf community. These experiences, as well as time spent living in Brazil, Nepal and Algeria, led me to appreciate other cultures.

My studies too reflected my interest in other cultures. After completing a clinical psychology doctorate at the University of Ottawa, Canada, on the adjustment of sojourners living in Nepal, I did a post-doctoral fellowship in medical anthropology at Harvard University. Still wanting to learn more about the intersection of culture and psychotherapy, I did a post-doctoral fellowship at the University of Chicago's Committee on Human Development. My time at Chicago gave me a better appreciation for Rogers who had been there 40 years before. As an institution that promotes interdisciplinarity, the faculty are well versed in multiple disciplines and issues from diverse theoretical perspectives.

I have adopted an interdisciplinary framework for my work that integrates psychology, anthropology and philosophy (James and Prilleltensky, 2002). This framework shapes my teaching at the University of British Columbia, Canada, and my psychotherapy with culturally diverse clients. It also influences the research that I do with Portuguese immigrants and leads me to take a holistic perspective that integrates the individual, familial, social and religio-moral domains.

COLIN LAGO

I retired from the position of Director of the University of Sheffield Counselling Service (UK) during the summer of 2003 after 16 years of service. Previously, I had worked for ten years as a counsellor in higher education at Leicester Polytechnic, (now De Montfort University).

Leaving school at sixteen, somewhat under qualified, (a sure sign of a misspent youth!), I ended up taking a full engineering apprenticeship before discovering full-time youth work in my early twenties. Following an excellent but short training in Leicester I obtained a youth work post in the London Borough of Havering where I stayed for five years. Working with young people proved an absolute joy, although it was not without its moments of strain, exhaustion and elation. A two-year stint in Jamaica then followed where I had been appointed (in addition to some classroom teaching) to develop an outdoor activities programme. Most afternoons were thus spent with groups in canoes, sailing boats, caves, walking and climbing in the hills and occasional evenings spent struggling to learn astro-navigation and painting.

My interest in counselling, which had been stimulated by the many experiences I had in youth work, was further developed in Jamaica through my association with the school counsellor whom I began to assist. Fortunately, my applications to the UK to train in counselling were successful, and I completed the Diploma course at Keele University in 1977. I was immensely lucky and privileged to be appointed to the student counsellor's post at De Montfort University, where the head of service, Jean Clark, proved to be an excellent mentor and role model. During those early years, Jean and I became very involved in multiracial issues in counselling and developed, with others, different training programmes and videos, providing contributions to national conferences and becoming founder members of what was then the RACE sub-committee of the British Association for Counselling.

My interest and passion in this field of concern first originated, I believe, in my early childhood experiences of multiple school moves and the ensuing difficulties these caused me. Consequently, the theme of 'insiders/outsiders', and its concomitant issues related to power, discrimination and equality of opportunity have continued within me to this day, and I have been most fortunate to have various writings published in this and other spheres of interest.

COURTLAND C. LEE

I was born in Philadelphia, PA in 1949. I am the oldest of four children. My father worked for the US Post Office and my mother was a homemaker. From my father I got the value of hard work, and from my mother I received an aesthetic appreciation as well as a social consciousness. I am a product of the Philadelphia public school system, in which I received a first-rate education. My most important developmental experiences took place during my high school years. I attended an all-male, all-academic, highly competitive high school. While in high school, I developed two important skills that have been and continue to be crucial to my life and career—the ability to write and to think critically.

I attended college as an undergraduate student during the late 1960s and early 1970s. This was a period of great social and political change in the United States. The Civil Rights Movement and the war in Vietnam permeated my college experience. Both of these events and the powerful issues surrounding them helped to develop my views on access, equity and social action which form my core values with respect to my work in multicultural counselling.

In 1972, I enrolled in graduate school to pursue my Masters degree in counselling. It was during this time that I met my mentor, Dr Alfred Pasteur. Pasteur was one of the founding fathers of the discipline we know today as multicultural counselling. He was a prolific writer and a noted international lecturer. Dr Pasteur took me under his wing, and it was from him that I began to develop a passion for issues related to ethnic minority mental health, particularly the mental health of African Americans. He would constantly challenge me with new ideas and concepts. It was Pasteur who encouraged me to pursue my doctorate in counselling. Upon completion of my doctorate in 1979, I accepted a faculty position in the Counselling Psychology Program at the University of North Carolina at Chapel Hill. I then began my career as a counselor educator and scholar. I proceeded to develop a line of research and began to achieve a national reputation for my work on African American mental health issues.

In 1987, I accepted a position as director of the Counselor Education Program at the University of Virginia. I consider the University of Virginia years to be the most prolific period of my career. During this period I published two of my most important and influential scholarly works. The first of these was my edited book, *Multicultural Issues in Counseling: New Approaches to Diversity*. This book, now going into its third edition, has become one of the American Counseling Association's best-selling works. The second work is *Counseling the Native Son: Empowerment Strategies for Young Black Males*. The three editions of this book have been best sellers not only among counselors, but a broad range of educators and other mental health professionals as well.

In 1997, I was elected President of the American Counseling Association, the first Black man to achieve this position. This gave me the 'bully pulpit' for a year to advance the things that I believed to be important in counseling and represented what

I stood for as a professional.

In 2001, I accepted a position as Professor and Director of the Counselor Education Program at the University of Maryland. My major contributions to the profession will continue to be through my writing and presentations on multicultural issues in counseling as well as mentoring students and young professionals.

Germain Lietaer

After receiving my PhD in experimental social psychology in 1966 at the Catholic University of Leuven (Belgium), I participated in a two-year training program in Client-Centered Therapy at the same university. During the academic year 1969–70 I studied as a post-doctoral fellow with Carl Rogers at the Center for Studies of the Person in La Jolla. Since then—being a professor at Leuven University—teaching client-centered/experiential psychotherapy, and doing process research have been my main professional activities. During these thirty-five years I have enjoyed being on the staff of a three year half-time post-master's training program in client-centered/experiential psychotherapy.

My theoretical and empirical research and the resulting publications have gone in several directions (for a survey, see: <http://perswww.kuleuven.ac.be/~u0004824/>): the editing of books on client-centered/experiential psychotherapy, construction and adaptation of research scales and questionnaires, process studies on helping and hindering factors, comparison of therapeutic orientations and theory building around issues of psychotherapy integration, history and overviews of client-centered/experiential psychotherapy, in-depth studies of microprocesses, group psychotherapy process studies, theoretical-clinical elaboration of client-centered/experiential concepts, and analyses of session transcripts of Carl Rogers. Characteristic of my work—and of the Leuven team in general—is an attempt at integrating new evolutions and related approaches into a broadly conceived paradigm of 'client-centered/experiential/humanistic' psychotherapy: working towards a peaceful co-existence and cross-fertilization of classical client-centered therapy, focusing-oriented and process-experiential therapy, interpersonal and existential psychotherapy. In this vein I organized the first International Conference on Client-centered and Experiential Psychotherapy in 1988 in Leuven, and together with other colleagues I have been active in the founding process of the World Association of Person-centered and Experiential Psychotherapy and Counseling of which I have been Chair during the years 2000–2003. My integrative stance is clearly visible in the Leuven conference book *Client-centered and experiential psychotherapy in the nineties* (Lietaer, Rombauts and Van Balen, 1990, Leuven University Press) and in the *Handbook of experiential psychotherapy* (Greenberg, Watson and Lietaer, 1998, Guilford Press).

As to the topic of this book, I must confess that ethnicity issues have never been in the foreground in my work. For example, in analyzing Rogers' interview 'On anger and hurt' it never came into my mind to give special attention to the difference in ethnicity between client and therapist. Partially, this relates to the fact that I have never worked in a multicultural setting. More importantly, however, I think it relates to my conviction that client-centered therapy is very suitable for working with diversity — be it ethnic or of whatever kind — because of its strong emphasis on 'following the client within his or her own frame of reference'. However, I gradually became more conscious of possible intercultural pitfalls in our therapy approach. A few experiences were impactful in this regard. During the eighties I went several times to Saint Louis

University in Baguio in the Philippines to teach a course on client-centered/experiential psychotherapy. Being in a totally different culture and listening to my students, I came to realize the individualistic nature of Rogers' image of the human being, his concept of the fully functioning person and his view on 'the person of tomorrow': a strong emphasis on autonomy at the expense of interconnectedness. Furthermore, in my group work with these students, I learned that giving critical feedback and openly expressing negative feelings towards others ran deeply counter their group norms. Another more recent experience brought to me that in our clinics and mental health centers, we do not easily reach clients from a totally different culture. A national survey research asked Belgian psychotherapists to describe one therapy case in detail: of the 900 respondents only one therapist described a therapy with a culturally diverse client! These and other experiences have made me more attentive to intercultural issues in our profession. Never too old to learn (I am sixty-five), or as Rogers said: 'older and growing'.

MELANIE LOCKETT

I run an independent counselling, supervision and training practice in London and work in the NHS, and the not-for-profit sector. I have a particular interest in supporting people affected by cancer, and I am an Associate Trainer with 'Cascade', a Diploma Course in supervision training. I am a 50-year-old white woman.

Some years ago I was listening to the radio and I heard something that stopped me in my tracks and has influenced my beliefs about the power of the therapeutic relationship. A guest on the programme was explaining that the Hebrew at the beginning of Old Testament had been wrongly translated. The correct translation is, he said, 'In the beginning is the conversation' (not the 'word'). To me this conveyed a sense of equality, the sharing of reflections, the possibility of learning, being engaged, being connected to another, of discovery and of not knowing. This is the essence, I believe, of a counselling, supervising or training relationship. A further influence on my work came from Carroll's *The Supervisory Life* (1998), a talk on spirituality in supervision. Here, Caroll says that spirituality is like counselling and supervision. It is about seeing, maintaining and holding connections. I have found in my practice that if I centre myself sufficiently, I meet those I work with differently. It is at these times that I am at my most receptive both hearing the client and understanding the context in which they live, most clearly.

I encourage clients, trainees and supervisees to search, to think through and find their own pathways or not. I am excited by the notion of 'focused contemplation' where we think deeply, attend to actions, emotions and thoughts, examine, inquire, be open and use theory and experience. When I am truly in retreat with my client, trainee or supervisee, I am intuitive, an equal, creative, clear, truly present and pleased to be so. This is the 'being' state I strive to achieve and at these times I hope that all the insights, experiences and learning I have had, and all that I can be, are present. My early training at South West London College established by Bridget Proctor was strongly influenced by the work of John Heron. It was here that I met Mary Charleton, the co-author of our chapter, who was a tutor on the course.

Since my original training, I have been particularly interested in the theories of Rogers, Perls, Berne and Jung. At the same time I was aware that euro-centric models can be transculturally limited, I therefore sought out other arenas that would stimulate my thinking and awareness about diversity. As I work within a multi-cultural society, many people have influenced me, but feminist psychotherapy offered me a political framework that has helped me work transculturally. This model asserts that certain groups can be described as 'risk groups' in a majority white, male, heterosexual society; for example, individuals may be at risk of more stress, poverty, alienation, oppression and powerlessness simply because they are different from the majority. Society may even organise itself so that it excludes some groups of people. This can result in some clients feeling less trusting, less understood and less accepted by me, than their majority counterparts. Sometimes I have needed to overtly address these issues of difference in order to establish a more collaborative, ethical and contained environment for some clients.

JOHN MCLEOD

I was born and grew up, as did my parents, in Dundee, an industrial city on the east coast of Scotland. However, until I was six years old my family mainly lived in India. The prosperity of Dundee had largely developed on the back of the jute trade. My father, like many other promising working-class young men in Dundee, had found work as a clerk for a jute trader in Calcutta, and had done well. The earliest years of my life are a hazy set of images of colonial privilege—servants, monogrammed shirts, being treated as someone special. Our return to Dundee, and my entry into a state school, was a shock. I didn't speak the language. In fact, I spoke Hindi better than I spoke Dundee dialect. I believe that this experience lies behind my interest in the perspective of the outsider, the one who looks in on the apparent warmth and comfort of those who are 'at home'. This sense of being both inside and outside the dominant culture was reinforced by the journey through university. The first in my extended family to enter higher education, I seemed to acquire a way of thinking and talking about things that was different, that marked me apart. And yet, at the same time, I knew I was not a member of the middle-class Edinburgh professional elite that—quietly—ruled Scotland.

These aspects of my biography have contributed to the development of a perspective, as a counsellor, researcher and theorist, that emphasises the social and cultural dimensions of personal identity, and therapy. Although I trained as a person-centred counsellor, and learned a great deal from this process, I no longer find that a therapy of the individual self is sufficient. Instead, my attention is drawn to the way that counsellors and clients use language to co-construct realities, and to the resonance of history and culture within that language. I view counselling and psychotherapy as arenas in which those who are excluded, silenced and 'outside' (for whatever reason) can tell their story and choose to engage actively with cultural and political life. In this context, the idea of 'culture' can encompass many different aspects of social life—the cultures of men and women, the culture of 'disability', the culture of social class, and much more. It seems to me that, fundamentally, we live in a society in which counselling is necessary, and popular, because it is a society that is fragmented: each of us takes parts of our identity from a huge range of sources, and we need help to be able to hold these bits together in some kind of minimally coherent fashion.

My own practice in recent years has been largely centred around being a trainer and educator, and researcher. I particularly enjoy making opportunities for members of training groups to share their cultural experiences and identities, and so develop a broader appreciation of the possibilities of being in relationship.

These are some of the interests and values that I bring to my interpretation of the Carl Rogers film of the 'On Hurt and Anger' case, and which have shaped my analysis of this material.

SHARON MIER
I worked between 1996–2000 in the UK with a focus on the impact of race and culture in the delivery of mental health services to Black and Asian communities. I am currently working as a clinical psychologist, providing mental health outreach services for Cornell University in Ithaca, New York. In this position, I work with a large number of East Asian and Asian American students. Personally, I have been profoundly affected by my experience as a White mother raising an African-American /Vietnamese daughter in the United States. I also have a Black Brazilian daughter-in-law, and two Black Brazilian grandsons.

ROY MOODLEY
I spent just as many years in England (where I met both Colin Lago and Anissa Talahite—the co-editors of this book) as I did in South Africa where I was born and raised to believe that 'the struggle is my life'. Over the years, in exile in London, Derby and Leeds, I learnt that the struggle was not just about race and the colour of one's skin—as apartheid had constructed for me—but that women, gay men and lesbians, the deaf and other disabled people, and working class communities were also at the forefront of the 'struggle'. This awareness greatly helped me survive those 'dark shadowy moments' when existential questions and ontological musings tended to create neurotic turbulences and psychotic conflicts in me—I survived by attempting to painting pictures, writing poetry and a play or two, the best of which never got on stage at the Royal Court, perhaps may not have even if I acquiesced to the revisions suggested. It was also during this time that as a member of the RACE sub-committee of the British Association for Counselling, colleagues asked me to join them in attending the Person-Centred Convention in Dublin, Ireland in 1984 where Carl Rogers was present. I refused to attend since Rogers had broken the cultural and academic boycott set by the African National Congress (ANC) and Anti-Apartheid movement by going to South Africa to conduct workshops.

Today South Africa is governed by the ANC and is free (relatively speaking) and I live and work in Toronto as a university teacher and researcher. After all these years I am once again invited to meet Carl Rogers (and his black client). This time I accepted, unreservedly. Unraveling the meanings of my involvement will be an interesting journey into my psychological self, perhaps revealing hidden cultural metaphors which my Jungian analyst so often tried to bring to consciousness all those many years ago in the middle of England somewhere in the rolling hills of the Pennines. Editing this text has been a similar journey with its multiple 'struggles', but also just as many moments of creativity.

JOSNA PANKHANIA
I was born in East Africa of Indian parents, and at the age of twelve I went to England with my family. The opportunity to grow up in post-colonial East Africa and Britain

offered me a rich international heritage and perspectives. In Africa, at school, we talked in English as our mother tongue was not encouraged. In England, at school, I learned in so many ways how and why Britain is Great. Throughout my schooling, I learned so little about my own culture, history and philosophy. I learned so little about the contribution of my people to the advancement of this world. After leaving school, I became involved in anti-racist and feminist politics. Writing *Liberating the National History Curriculum* (1994, Falmer Press) was an expression of my break away from the racist education that I had received both in East Africa and in England.

My training in counselling predominantly offered me a person-centred framework, but the work in the inner city of Manchester in England as a school counsellor soon paved the way towards a more politicised form of counselling. I expressed some of this journey in 'Black Feminist Counselling' (M.Jacobs, 1996, *In search of a Therapist*, Open University Press). Within the British Association for Counselling and Psychotherapy, I was involved in the setting up of the RACE (Race Awareness in Counselling Education) Committee. I was also one of the founder members of the Association for Black Counsellors in the UK. My work as a counsellor in Manchester led me to realise that there was no culturally appropriate institutional support for Asian girls who had left home. Thus, with a group of Asian women, I was involved in the setting up and the running of SUBAH, a sheltered home for young Asian women victims of violence, abuse and neglect.

Since 1996, I have been living with my husband and two children in the Blue Mountains of New South Wales, Australia where I have continued my work as a counsellor. I am interested in the inclusion of eastern healing systems in mainstream health provision in westernised countries and in Australia, I have argued for the inclusion of Traditional Chinese Medical knowledge in the provision of mental health services: *Alternative Health Care: Learning from Traditional Chinese Medicine in Untangling the Threads: Perspectives on Mental Health in Chinese Communities* edited by Wai-On Phoon and Ian Macindoe published by Transcultural Mental Health Centre, Sydney, 2003.

At present, I am engaged in doctoral research examining the impact of yoga at a personal level in a post-colonial, post-modern world with entrenched systems of racism and xenophobia. Yoga is a significant part of the multi-cultural and diverse world in which we live, and I hope that my research will contribute towards a greater understanding and a celebration of the spiritual dimension of yoga.

CATRIN S. RHYS

I am the Undergraduate Coordinator of Academic Affairs in the School of Communication at the University of Ulster. After an undergraduate degree in linguistics (York University), and a year's British Council scholarship in China (Liaoning University), I completed a PhD at the Centre for Cognitive Science (University of Edinburgh), including an Advanced British Scholarship in China (Fudan University) and a Linguistics Institute scholarship for the Summer Institute in Chinese Linguistics. I taught in Spain, England and Northern Ireland and have been working at the University of Ulster for eight years. I am a member of the International Clinical Phonetics and Linguistics Association and a member of the International Pragmatics Association. My major research interests lie in the linguistics of clinical interaction in a variety of therapeutic contexts. Other research interests include the linguistics of interaction, the influence of politeness on interactive practices in problem interactions; and linguistic structure as a local resource in interaction. I have published in core theoretical syntax, with a specific focus on the syntax semantics interface. My recent publications are in the conversation analysis arena, particularly focusing upon clinical contexts. My escape from academic life is a passion for jazz.

Gella Richards

I was born in London, UK, to a mother from the Caribbean and a father from South America, though historically both of my parents are of Afro-Caribbean descent. Both my parents are religious, being heavily involved in the Church; and my paternal grandfather was a minister. For me, it is important that I mention my birthplace because I think it indicates my parents' aspiration for me, and for all their children. They both wanted us to enjoy the dream of living in a so-called meritocracy, even though they themselves had not personally seen any evidence of this. When they came to Britain, they both experienced racism and exclusion (e.g., signs in windows of houses that rented rooms stated that although there were vacant rooms 'no dogs, no Gypsies and no Blacks'). This was despite the fact that my parents (like many other Black people at that time) were simply responding to the invitation from the 'Mother' of their Commonwealth: the British Queen.

Having heard their narratives of discrimination, I was always surprised at the optimism they had for us to 'succeed' in British society. I think their strong religious faith helped maintain their belief that good will prevail for their children even in a society that seemed to neither want to understand them, nor appreciate the richness they could bring to their environment. To some degree, I have also inherited this optimism. My parents thought that is was extremely important that we achieved some type of success in Britain, so they invested very heavily financially in us. We all had private education. I, for example, went to a public all girls school in Knightsbridge, London (where I was the only Black pupil for many years), and then a boarding school in Berkshire. Realising that this could potentially result in me becoming overly acculturated into the dominant culture, my parents made every effort to ensure that I did not forget or neglect my culture of origin. We had a close relationship with extended family members including my parents' brothers and sisters who had also immigrated to Britain. We had links with both the Caribbean and South America and also our Dutch relatives. I got a sense from all of this socialisation that my parents had felt that they had been discriminated against because, not only was the colour of their skin different from those of the host culture, but also their schemas and worldviews seemed contrary to those of the White people in Britain. Somehow, I thought that they wanted their children to sufficiently integrate into the dominant culture to be able to understand people of that culture and communicate with them in their 'language'. Yet, on the other hand, it was also clear that they did not want us to forget our 'roots' and they wanted us to be proud of our heritage. This I feel they have achieved.

It is this straddling of two cultures that has enabled me to work with both Black and White clients and colleagues. I feel that by having an experience of both cultures, in my role as a Chartered Counselling Psychologist and Senior Lecturer in Counselling Psychology, I am able to 'switch' between cultures when required. In addition, and more importantly for me, my 'bi-culturalism' helps me to sometimes 'translate', as best as I can, the experience that Black clients have living in a White society. I also think that I have a wider and more varied worldview as I have taken the good components from both cultures, yet acknowledged the distasteful processes in both cultures. I am happy that I do not have dichotomy thinking, observing experiences as belonging to one or the other category. My practitioner's doctorate helped me to explore this further and I found out a lot about myself as I investigated Black people's attitudes towards counselling and their therapeutic outcomes. Interestingly, I also noticed the encouragement and support that I received from many White colleagues who showed genuine interest in my research. Again, these experiences highlighted to me the need to share knowledge with colleagues from the dominant culture about working with ethnic minority clients, and to recognise the richness and opportunities that can be gained from such discourses and exchanges.

Conceiving my chapter presented somewhat of a challenge since, having taught on a humanistic programme for four years, I had always presented Rogers' work as client-centred (rather than culture-centred) and the most attentive to the use of the self and the therapeutic relationship. However, now I had been invited to deconstruct his work and indeed the schemas that I had cultivated in my students about his therapy. I have enjoyed writing this chapter because it made me re-visit my views and my own training on Rogers. It also enabled me to feel that I was 'worthy' enough to indicate how I would depart from one of the great 'masters' interventions and use my own style. This meant that I would be exposed. My fear was that readers (including students) and colleagues alike would be critical and may even question how I, a young Black woman, could do better than the distinguished Rogers in counselling a client using *his* model. However, the beauty of the client-centred approach is that it specifically calls for the therapist to be congruent and genuine and to use herself. Besides, I feel that I am not saying that I would do better, but that I would provide an alternative way in working with this client, even though I would be using a client-centred model. I hoped to show how the client-centred framework could be modified when both the client and the therapist are from ethnic minority communities, yet from different genders.

Having now become very involved in using CBT with many of my clients, I feel that having different approaches to working with the same client is very useful and resourceful. Indeed, I think that I have my parents to thank for this, and would like to dedicate my chapter to them. 'Thank you', mum and dad for giving me the best 'trip' and developmental experience which, I think, has transformed me into an adult who can see possibilities and appreciate differences in most people and many things.

Debra Rosenzweig

I am a clinical psychologist practicing individual and group psychotherapy and psychological testing in Greenwich Village, Manhattan. I believe in specializing my approach toward the treatment depending on the unique symptoms, history, and needs of each individual with whom I work. In addition to psychotherapy, I teach psychology courses at New York University, and supervise doctoral students in psychotherapy at Columbia University.

Shauna Savage

I was an undergraduate on the BSc (Hons) Language and Linguistics course at the

University of Ulster. I discovered a fascination for counselling after a second year option. When the time came to select a topic for my undergraduate dissertation, I asked Catrin Rhys (co-author of chapter we wrote) about applying linguistics to counselling. Catrin already had an interest in the interactive practices involved in counselling and suggested to me that I transcribe Rogers and reflect on the relationship between Rogers' talk and the principles of Person-Centred Counselling. Hours of transcription later, I felt that Rogers only ever said 'uh huh', and so we arrived at the focus of this work which was to raise the question of whether 'uh huh' is always a way of 'doing' empathic listening.

RICHARD SAXTON

I have long been interested in the impact of race and culture on personal, interpersonal and social relationships and attended my first workshop around those themes about twenty-five years ago. For the first 19 years, despite hard work and good intentions on my part, I seemed to be stuck at Helm's stage two (opposed to racism, idealistic and guilt-ridden.)

When I began working at Loughborough University in 1998, I was fortunate in having a colleague (Shukla Dhingra) who was also interested in issues of race and culture, who had done a great deal of work around them and who brought her own personal perspective. It was for me a source of joy and satisfaction to be able to work alongside someone with whom I could discuss these issues as a part of day-to-day life, whether in terms of interpersonal relationships, clinical work, supervision, or the workings of the staff team. I learned and developed a great deal as a consequence and would now describe myself as generally fluctuating between stages 2–5 depending who I am with, where I am, and what is going on (internally or externally). Writing this chapter has been an integral part of that process.

GERALDINE SHIPTON

I am a senior lecturer in the School of Health and Related Research at the University of Sheffield, and a psychoanalytic psychotherapist in private practice. I have worked in several different professions in the past, including language teaching, occupational therapy and student counselling, as well as in psychotherapy and university teaching, management and research. I helped set up the first community mental health team in Sheffield. I have written several books including *Working with Eating Disorders: A Psychoanalytic Approach* (2004); *Long-term Counselling* (1998), co-authored with Eileen Smith; and edited *The Supervision of Psychotherapy and Counselling: Making a Place for Thinking* (1997). I am interested in how a sense of self and identity develops or is produced in response to both inner phantasies and external realities, and the way that culture and technology function in this. I personally find psychoanalysis has the most explanatory potential for understanding these matters and for understanding how issues related to difference can be captured by unconscious and destructive processes. I do not believe, however, that any one form of psychotherapy has all the answers or is the right approach for everyone. Indeed, I am all too aware of the human resistance to change, however one might want to bring it about. Yet, people are always surprising me in their capacity to find creative solutions to difficult problems.

Will Stillwell

My personal and professional life are conjoined in my journey participating in, and understanding, intimacy. In togetherness, who am I? Who are you? How do I now experience my alone individuality and corporate belonging?

Yesterday I was present as a man was fired from his job. I accompanied him later as he started his long process of finding himself and his spirit again. Consulting with people in their day-to-day workplace organizations, dialoguing with my students, clients, and colleagues, over and over, I'm enveloped by our immense freedom. What are the freedoms you want? How do you live them? How is my freedom virtue? How am I responsibly facing Fate who always changes her game?

I am a person concerned with optimal qualities of life and work in today's organizations. I aim to liberate creative excellence. I apply my skills and heart with individuals and small work groups. In our interactive environment we will find new ways to deal with conflict, morale, leadership, quality of work and accountability. I have maintained a consulting practice for a quarter century. I have worked with civil service personnel, volunteers, boards of directors of non-profit organizations, laborers, skilled manufacturers, agency personnel, educational professionals, research design and engineering people. I have worked in settings as diverse as an office, a wilderness, a shop floor, a conference center, a park bench. But the settings and the categories of people are less important to me than our focus on the relationships between people trying to work together, and our finding individuals' clarity in what they want to accomplish in their work lives.

I have associated myself with humanistic psychology for more than thirty years at The Center for Studies of the Person in La Jolla, California. This has been for me a community of people with whom I could really be my own inarticulate self. With these colleagues I touched again my non-self-consciousness. Some folks call that spontaneity, and I do too some of the time, but lately I've been calling it innocence.

I have served on the faculty of several universities and as staff member of numerous workshop programs, most particularly with the La Jolla Program. I am author of the narrative script for the videotape *Unconditional Positive Dialogue* and co-author of the book, *Conflict is Inevitable—War is Optional*.

People want to understand themselves, I believe, and people sometimes want others to understand them too. It's not rare for me, and maybe you too, to avoid our own paths to our own truths even as we try to communicate these truths. But sometimes we are given to re-experience ourselves and others as we truly are, and as we truly want to be. I resonate with the Jewish hope of justice, and the Christian hope for love, the Buddhist hope for liberation, and the Hindu hope for multiplicity, the Islamic hope for community, and the Animist hope for spirit in all beings. Sometimes I curse, sometimes I despair, but most often I praise what we've made of what we've been given.

Anissa Talahite

Rogers with his black client presents a cross-cultural dynamic which reflects in many ways my own life. I was born of mixed French-Algerian parentage and came to understand from an early age the impact that historical and racial conflicts can have on interpersonal relationships. Cultural hybridity can be a source of richness and multiplicity but can, at other times, also bring pain, hurt and anger if the society we live in is not prepared for it. As I grew up, I tried to disentangle the various threads that contributed to my identity. Academic study has been one of the ways I tried to understand these issues. What was in childhood felt, experienced, but never fully understood, became the subject of a PhD on race and gender in the novels by South African women writers, at the University of Leeds. Choosing a field of study outside my own cultural experience gave me the necessary distance in order to deal with my own issues of identity. As in the Rogers' interview with his black client, I found in the narratives of South African women an echo of my own cultural conflict. Teaching and researching literature at Manchester Metropolitan University and now at the University of Toronto has been another learning experience which has brought me close to my own 'diverse and multiple self'.

Another way in which I have learnt about myself is through my children. Through 'the joys (and the pains) of motherhood', I have learned how to survive as a mother of four young children and an academic in a society where the two are not always compatible. The second challenge has been raising black children in a society still dominated by constructs of race. The daily challenges I have experienced as a mother have taught me as much as—if not more than—my intellectual journeys.

Finally, editing this book has been one of the few moments where I felt a sense of unity and wholeness in the face of the many fragmentations that make up our daily experiences. Bringing together the very diverse 'voices' and interpretations of Rogers and his client in this volume made me realize the very different ways in which to understand the multi-cultural dialogue.

Clemmont E. Vontress

In 1952, I graduated from Kentucky State University (BA, French and English). Subsequently, I enrolled at the State University of Iowa. In 1953, I went to Europe. In France, I saw Josephine Baker, black American immigrant and entertainer, perform at a Parisian show hall. She asked her audience to 'forgive me for being black.' They responded, 'It's better that way!' With young people, I sat in cafés where Jean-Paul Sartre and his companion, Simone de Beauvoir, talked about human existence. In Germany, I encountered Sidney Bechet, a black American musician, who also left the United States for Europe, where he 'could be a human being!'

Back home in 1955, I enrolled in graduate school at Indiana University, where I received the MS and PhD degrees in counseling. Usually, I was the only black student in my classes. The professors lectured about culture and how some people were deprived of it. Feeling personally assaulted by their views, I swore to pursue the matter when I graduated. Thus, I have devoted my entire professional career to studying culture and its impact on counseling.

After receiving my PhD in 1965, I defined culture as a human necessity. Nobody is deprived of it. People are 'culturally deprived' only when others try to deny them their humanity, as all humans are alike. During my career, I found Existentialism the most effective counseling approach to use with all clients. My 25 years of research in Africa reveals how closely related traditional healing methods are to existential counseling. My research on counseling African immigrants in France shows that traditional and modern healing methods can be used conjointly. Finally, I deplore the use of medicine to help people adjust to culturally induced problems such as racism and oppression.

William West

I am senior lecturer in Counselling Studies at the University of Manchester where I am overall Director of Courses and Director of the Professional Doctorate in Counselling. I currently have 11 PhD-by-thesis students and make a significant contribution to our Masters in Counselling Studies programme. I am a Fellow, an accredited practitioner, and Special Adviser on Research to BACP. I also serve on the Board of Counselling Psychotherapy Research journal. I have written many papers, book chapters, and two books on various topics including: spirituality and therapy, supervision, qualitative research, and humanistic therapy. My first book *Psychotherapy and Spirituality: Crossing the Line between Therapy and Religion* was published by Sage (2000) and my second book *Spiritual Issues in Therapy: Relating Experience to Practice* is currently at press with Palgrave Macmillan.

Spiritually I have been a member of the Religious Society of Friends (Quakers) since I found myself at a Quaker Meeting at the start of the first Gulf War in 1991. The Quaker emphasis on our experience of spirituality and the valuing of this above any religious dogma or creed sits well with me and is congruent with my humanistic approach to therapy. There is a profoundly egalitarian basis to Quakerism in Britain who have no priests and the voice of anyone—child or newcomer—is listened to as potentially the voice of God or Spirit.

I wrestle with the implications of multiculturalism and culture in general in my work with a diverse range of students especially among my group of PhD students, where there is something of a shared focus on spirituality, culture and qualitative research methods and also a valuing of traditional healing practices. It is especially within this group of students that I find such issues are deeply engaged in since a number of this group are directly addressing cultural issues in their studies. I have been deeply and profoundly changed by contact with people from different cultures. I think it has been through the generosity of a few key people such as Kam Dhillon, Roy Moodley, Wayne Richards, Rebecca Sima, Linda Ankrah and Pittu Laungani that I have made what limited progress I have.

I am attracted to postmodern thinking with its valuing of local sub-cultures, although perhaps not its 'anything goes' excesses, and to social constructionism with a deep respect for the other person's take on reality which probably puts me in the phenomenological camp. My own spiritual experiences have led me to value the sense of interconnectness that I can experience alone (with creation) or in the company of others. Martin Buber would call this I-Thou relating which I feel is at the heart of my approach to multiculturalism, to therapy, and to life in general. The I-Thou relationship is said by Buber to be not possible in the classroom or therapy room where there is inevitably a power imbalance. Nevertheless my approach whilst acknowledging the power, gender, class and cultural issues is to look for the potential of authentic meeting. I make no claims on my abilities to achieve this but my life has been changed by such contact with the people mentioned above and others.

Stephen Whitehead

I was born and raised in the North West of England, in a genteel seaside resort called Southport. It was, mostly still is, an enclave of the white middle, and aspiring middle, classes. My family were, in Marxist language, *petit bourgeois,* local shopkeepers with a strong 'common-sense' view of the world, a determined Protestant work ethic, and confident of their place in the scheme of things. Although I enjoyed learning, I left school at 15 with no qualifications and immediately went to work in my family's retail business. I didn't physically leave Southport until I was 25, and it was a further 15 years on from that before I really started to experience some psychological space between myself and the values and expectations of my past. This distancing of my self from a rapidly receding life was triggered by several critical incidents, catalysts for what were to turn out to be a series of major life changes occurring from aged 40 onwards. Firstly, I got the opportunity to teach in a college of further education in the inner city of Leeds. This work brought me face-to-face with some of the realities of black and white working class teenagers, forms of social and racial subjectivity pretty much absent from my earlier life. Secondly, I undertook a part-time MA in sociology. This study introduced me to critical thinking and feminist theories in particular, thereby giving me a basis from which start to explore gender, both intellectually and reflexively. The combination of my new professional experiences and the MA study lit a fire in me that still burns. In 1993 I started a PhD exploring the masculine subjectivities of men managers in further education. As a man manager in further education at the time, there was clearly an element of self-exploration going on here. One PhD and several books later, the process continues largely unabated.

I am now established as an academic in a UK university. I am still white, I am still male, and I am probably now more middle class than my parents. Perhaps not much has changed after all. And this is the difficulty we all have—to be someone different, to utterly and totally leave our histories behind. For no matter how much we'd like to think so, shifting our discursive positioning cannot be achieved by simple intent. Mostly, change is done for us and to us. Environment and relationships are forces that should not be underestimated. We are not knowing, rational subjects, grounded individuals in control and capable of standing outside our subjectivity. To imagine otherwise is an illusion, an ontological trap baited with more than a touch of arrogance. My subjectivity has certainly broadened over the past decades, and I don't see the world in quite the way I used to, but some things I cannot change. This slowly dawning realisation has brought me to see the value of feminist post-structuralism as a theoretical tool by which to critically explore masculine and racial subjectivities and identities. It is the tool I draw on in my interpretation and analysis of *On Anger and Hurt*.

MARGE WITTY
I come to this discussion as a bisexual woman with a history of involvement in the Women's and Gay Liberation movements and the New Left. In addition to my work as a client-centered therapist, I have been involved in providing supportive services to women and returning adult students at Northeastern Illinois University, to first-generation Latino students at Mundelein College in Chicago, and currently, at St. Leonard's Alternative High School for persons coming out of prison, the majority of whom are African American men. I also teach a course entitled 'Social Psychology and Difference' at the graduate level with racially and culturally diverse students.

INDEX

'a credit to my [your/his] race' 6, 8, 89, 94, 123, 131, 170, 204, 218, 229, 231, 244
actualizing tendency 24, 37–8
African-American culture ii
aggression 215, 220, 221, 225
Ahmad, WIU 106, 113
alienation x, xiii, 204–8, 214–18, 222, 225, 280
    of the self 214
Alladin, WJ 139, 144, 145, 147
aloneness 180
anger 8, 10, 25, 40–1, 66, 96, 110, 125, 133, 136, 166–7, 170, 180, 214, 216, 221, 240
anti-discriminatory practice 116
anti-racism 104, 164, 184 (see also 'racism')
Arciniega, GM 20, 32
arranged marriage 135
Association of Black Counsellors (ABC) 234, 236
Atkinson, DR 19, 32, 106, 113, 145, 147, 154, 158
autonomy of the person 87
Balamoutsou, S 178, 189
Baldwin, M xiv, 37, 38, 45
Barfield, G vii, xv
Barrett-Lennard, GT 158, 262, 265
Batsleer, J 120, 129
British Crime Survey (BCS) 120, 129,
Bell, DA 17, 32, 113, 157, 158
Bergin, AE 195, 197, 199
Bernstein, BL 17, 35, 115
Bhabha, H 109, 113, 215, 220, 226
Bhugra, D 21, 32
Bhui, K 21, 32
Bigley, GA 222, 226
Biko, S 109, 113, 217, 226
Bimrose, J 79, 83
Black, S xi
bodily identification 242
Bondi, L 128
Borgen, WA 141, 147
Borodovsky, LG 186, 189
boundaries 255

Bowen, M Villas-Boas ix, xv
Bozarth, JD 48, 81, 82, 83
Brink, DC ix, x, xvi, 36, 84
Brodley, BT ix, xv, 18, 22, 32, 39, 45, 46, 47, 52, 67, 70, 83, 85, 89, 95, 104, 157, 158, 187, 188, 194, 199, 214, 220, 221, 226, 237, 238
Brody, AF 39, 46, 69, 70
Buber, M 200, 248
Burke, AW 109, 113
Burman, E 128
Burrows, E 248
Butler, J 240, 242
Cain, DJ vi, xvi, 18, 21, 23, 32
Carkhuff, RR 17, 32, 114
Carl Rogers Archive at the Library of Congress 158
Carter, RT 21, 105, 106, 107, 114, 139, 140, 144, 146, 147
category system for therapist responses 37, 52, 57, 59
Center for Studies of the Person 148, 149, 158, 247, 248
challenge 57, 62, 133
Chantler, K xi, 117, 129
Chaplin, J 169, 174
Charleton, M xii
Civil Rights Movement i, iii, v, 106
Clark, J xii, xiv, 261, 263, 265
Clarke, C x, xi, 130, 131, 138
Clarke, J 209, 210, 211
client
    direct references to 'race' 121
    self-understanding 204
    racial identity 86, 151
    self-differentiation 87
Coker, N 156, 158
Coleman, HLK 19, 34, 140, 144, 145, 147
colonial-paternalistic relations 119
Combs, AW 24, 31, 32
conditions of worth 122, 123, 131
    racialised and gendered 122–4
confidentiality 137, 191
confrontation 57, 59, 62, 64–5, 68

congruence 38, 130, 133, 246, 254
Connell, RW 241, 242
continuers 73, 78
conversation analysis 71, 73, 75, 82
Cook, DA 20, 33, 214, 226
core conditions 24, 87, 130, 161–3, 166, 170
counsellor
    own sense of racial identity 154
    personal development 128
    training 146, 160
countertransference 107, 145, 160, 166–7, 219, 222
Cox, JL 19, 32
Cross, WE Jr 19, 106, 107, 114, 154, 158, 233, 234
cross-cultural
    counselling/therapy 17, 126, 127
    encounter groups vii
    matching 145
    therapy 17
cross-racial counselling/working 140, 143, 235
cross-racial/cultural matching 139
cry(ing) 12, 41, 63, 166, 236
cultural
    competency templates 19
    difference 86, 119, 130, 138
        and the core conditions 130
    empathy 185
    identity 132, 145 (see also 'racial/cultural identity')
    limitations 136
    psychotherapy 201–2, 208
    stereotypes 121
    -sensitive approach 188
culture 27, 47, 85, 131, 157
'Dadisi' (client) 22, 25, 88
D'Andrea, M 19, 20, 33
d'Ardenne, P 19, 21, 33, 125, 128, 139, 147, 165, 166, 167, 168, 174, 223, 224, 226
Davis, E 257
Davis, LE 156, 158
de Beauvoir, S 205, 211
death and dying 11, 22, 69
Devereux, G 19, 33
Dhingra, S xii, 139, 140, 147, 236, 238
diagnosis 132, 209
directivity 36, 38, 43, 44, 47, 54, 96, 98
discrimination 104, 119, 149, 157
Dixon, DN 17, 33, 114
Duncan, BL 79, 82, 83

Dupont-Joshua, A 107, 114, 145, 147
Dyche, L 187, 188
Dyer, R 155, 158
ebonics 244
Egan, G 72, 82, 83
Elliott, R 53, 70
empathy 38–9, 44, 47, 58, 71, 82, 89, 103, 130, 135, 145, 156, 161, 168, 171, 173, 202, 237, 244, 246, 254
    following responses 36, 44
encounter groups 257
Epston, D 185, 189, 208, 212
ethnic minority counsellors 21, 140
ethnomethodology 71, 82
eurocentricism 21, 83
existentialism 19, 20
expert 116, 132, 187
Falken, G x, xi, xvi, 34
Fanon, F xiii, 109, 114, 214, 215, 216, 217, 219, 222, 225, 226
Farber, BA ix, xvi, 36, 72, 84
feedback 56, 62
Feltham, C 21, 33
financial burden 122
five-stage theory for black identity development 106
Fong, ML 17, 33, 114, 224, 225, 226
Foucault, M 108, 114
Freud, S 33
Fried, J 156, 158
Friedlander, ML 53, 70
Gadamer, H-G 203, 206, 207, 211
Gambetta, D 222, 226
Garrett, H 130
Gates, HL Jr 106, 114
Geller, SM 190, 199
gender 122–7, 245
Gendlin, ET vi, xvi, 63, 70, 82, 84
genuineness 161, 170, 202
George, JM 222, 227
Gergen, KJ 177, 188
Gestalt Therapy 184, 193
Gill, S 162, 174
glass ceilings 120
'Gloria' (client) 191, 192, 198
Goffman, E 102, 103, 104
Goldman, M x
Goodwin, C 76, 77, 84
Grant, SK 145, 147
Greenberg, LS 53, 66, 70, 190, 199
Grillo, RD 106, 114
guilt xiii, 15, 107, 154, 209, 220, 237

Gundrum, M 53, 69, 70
Hacker, A 17, 33, 114, 157, 158
Hall, S 240, 242
Hall, WA xiii, 33, 232, 234, 236
Hawkins, S 128
Hawtin, S 136, 138
Hegel, GWF 204, 205, 211
Helms, JE 19, 20, 32, 33, 34, 106, 114, 154, 158, 159, 214, 226, 227, 233, 234
Henderson, VL 18, 33, 118, 119, 120, 129, 130, 131, 135, 138, 262, 265
Heppner, PP 17, 33, 114
Heritage, J 71, 84
hermeneutics 187, 200–1, 203
Hill, CA 53, 70
Hill, CE 53, 70
Holdstock, L 20, 21, 33, 104, 130, 131, 138
Holmes, DE 107, 114, 217, 219, 227
homophobia 103, 118, 120, 125
horizons 203, 205, 207, 211
 of alienation 205
intepretation 56, 62, 172
intercultural therapeutic encounters 201
Ivey, AE 18, 19, 20, 33
Ivey, MB 18, 19, 20, 33
James, S xiii, 207, 209, 211
Jefferson, G 72, 84
Jenal, ST 115, 142, 146, 147, 151, 157, 159, 186, 187, 189
Jones, EE 105, 114, 140, 144, 145, 147
Jones, GR 222, 227
Jung, CG 27, 162
Kandel, N 247
Kareem, J 19, 21, 33, 141, 145, 147, 223, 227
Katz, JH 155, 159
Kay, J 215, 216, 227
Kearney, A 116, 118, 128, 129
Keesing, RM 160, 174
Kennedy, J 21, 33
Kierkegaard, S 130, 138, 200
Kincheloe, JL 155, 159
King, Martin Luther 106, 216, 231
Kirschenbaum, H 18, 33, 118, 119, 120, 129, 130, 131, 134, 138, 262, 265
Kleg, M 104
Lacan, J 217, 227
Lafromboise, TD 34, 115, 145
Lago, C xii, xiv, 24, 33, 116, 115, 118, 129, 139, 146, 147, 154, 156, 157, 159
Laing, R 264
language 131, 135, 175, 177, 244

Laungani, P 19, 21, 33
Lease, SH 17, 33, 114, 224, 225, 226
Lee, C xiii
Leijssen, M 53, 70
leukaemia 2, 3, 9, 12, 22, 69, 124, 127, 132, 192, 229, 239
Lietaer, G vi, xi, xvi, 52, 53, 69, 70, 72, 82, 84
Liggan, DY 215, 216, 227
Lingle, DW 186, 189
Lipsedge, M 21, 33
Littlewood, R 19, 21, 33, 141, 145, 147
Lockett, M xii
locus of evaluation 8, 31, 117–8, 123–4, 128, 163–4
Lynch, G 178, 189
MacMillan, M 24, 33
Mahrer, AR 53, 70
Mahtani, A 19, 21, 33, 125, 128, 139, 147, 165, 166, 167, 168, 174, 223, 224, 226
Majors, R 242, 243
Malcolm X 106, 216
Margison, FR 53, 70
marriage viii, x, 2, 5, 18, 135, 204–5, 229, 231
masculinity 25, 116, 125, 126, 239, 242
masks 213, 216, 218
Maslow, AH 211
May, R 194, 258
Mayer, RC 222, 227
McIntosh, HS 129
McLeod, J xii, 19, 34, 117, 129, 178, 179, 182, 187, 189
McPherson Report 156
Mearns, D vi, xvi, 78, 84, 168, 174, 197, 199, 223, 227
Meier, A 178, 189
Menahem, SE x, xvi, 194, 195, 199
Merry, T 23, 26, 34, 47
Mier, S xi
militancy 10, 96, 110, 125, 172
Millington, M 109, 115
minimal responses 53, 75, 81, 82
'mm hmm' 72–6, 78, 80
Mohamed, Abdul R Jan 215, 227
Monte, CF vii, xvi
Moodley, R x, xi, xiii, xvi, 17, 18, 19, 21, 34, 109, 115, 139, 140, 141, 144, 147, 187, 189, 214, 224, 227, 232, 234, 236, 237, 238
Moore, J 136, 138
Morten, G 19, 32, 113, 158

Moynihan, DW 79, 82, 83
'Ms G' (client) 23, 26
multicultural
    counselling 19, 21, 29, 31, 47, 230
    politics 50
narrative(s) 55, 175–89
Nathan, T 19, 34
Natiello, P 77, 84
Nelson-Jones, R 168, 174
Newlon, BJ 20, 32
Nickerson, KJ 34, 223, 227
non-directivity 81, 37, 85, 86
non-verbal communication 25, 105, 113, 172
O'Hara, M 20, 31, 34, 79, 84
oppression 119, 139, 145, 175
organismic valuing process 161, 174
Osborne, J 18, 34
Owen, IR 165, 174
Pankhania, J xiii, 19, 34
Pargament, KI 209, 212
Parham, TA 19, 32, 114
Parker, I 109, 115
Parks, Rosa 231
Parry, TA 182, 189
patriarchal 21
Patterson, CH vi, xvi, 18, 20, 34, 48, 142, 147
Pearce, JL 222, 226
Pedersen, PB 19, 34, 142, 145, 147, 156, 159
Perls, F 191
phenomenology 200, 205
Phinney, JS 154, 159
Pierce, R 17, 32, 114
Piper, RE 154, 159
pluralistic society 103
Polanyi, M 66, 70
political conflict 175
Pomales, J 17, 34, 115, 145
Ponterotto, JG 19, 34, 35, 106, 115, 156, 159
Pope-Davis, DB 19, 34, 140, 144, 145, 147
poverty 120, 155
power 116, 128, 130, 140, 154, 155, 157, 160, 166, 237
    differentials 157
    -lessness of the client 164
prejudice 128, 165, 174
presence 64, 164, 190, 197, 254
privilege 118, 123, 125, 128, 176
process direction 183–4
Proctor, EK 156, 158
profanity 43–4, 125, 236–7
Psathas, G 71, 84

psychological contact 135
race 48, 85, 116, 125–7, 131, 139
    -acknowledgement 151, 157
    -avoidant 142, 144, 151, 186
    -awareness 156, 148
    disavowal of 22
    -neutral 17, 142, 146, 157
    white consciousness model 154–5
Race as News 270
Race Awareness in Counselling Education 233, 236, 261, 262, 264
racial and cultural matching 139, 142
racial and ethnic
    identity development models 154
    difference 102
    identity (development) 19, 86, 105–8, 110, 113, 151, 154, 229
    prejudice 167
    self-understanding 105
    tension 175
racial/cultural
    compatibility 144
    sensitivity 142, 145
    identity 105, 108, 113
    self-understanding 105
racialised and gendered
    being of clients 127
    conditions of worth 122–4
    self 126, 127
racism 48, 93–5, 100, 104, 110, 112, 118, 119–20, 122, 124, 127, 139, 141, 144, 149, 152, 154–7, 163–7, 174–5, 182, 184–5, 215, 218, 235, 239–41
Raskin, PM ix, xvi, 25, 35, 36, 37, 38, 84
Raskin, NJ 38, 46
reflection 28, 55
rejection 246
Rennie, DL 184, 189, 192, 199
response categories (of therapist) 37, 52, 57, 59
Rhys, CS xi, 77, 84
Rice, LN 53, 70
Richards, PS xvi, 195, 197, 199
Ricoeur, P 207, 208, 212
Ridley, CR 186, 189
Rogers, CR vi, vii, ix, xv, xvi, 18, 23, 24, 28, 35, 37, 39, 47, 48, 52, 67, 70, 72, 82, 84, 116, 119, 120, 129, 130, 134, 138, 162, 174, 195, 197, 199, 200, 202, 203, 207, 212, 262, 265
Rombauts, J vi, xvi
Rosseau, DM 222, 227

Roth, NL 222, 227
Rowan, J 194, 197, 199
Saba, Nguzo 232
Sabnani, HB 19, 35, 106, 107, 115
Sacks, H 72, 84
Sanchez Boda, A 250, 251, 252
Sanford, R vii, xvi, 24, 35, 251, 252, 265
Sarbin, TR 182, 189
Sashidharan, SP 105, 115
Savage, S xi
Saxton, R xii
Schegloff, EA 71, 72, 73, 74, 84
Scott, NE 186, 189
Second World War 104
self
   -acceptance 255
   -actualizing process 87
   -determination 66
   -disclosure iv, 57, 145, 161, 168, 172, 223
   -exploration 255
   use of 253–60
'seven-year-old'[self of the client] 6, 7, 27, 42, 63, 163, 180, 217, 240
sexism 51, 103, 118–20, 125
shame 107, 135, 136
Shipton, G x, xi, xvi, 34
Shostrum, E 191
silence(s) 53, 117, 196
   and power 117
Simek-Morgan, L 19, 20, 33
Singh, J 144, 145, 147
Sitkin, SB 222, 227
social constructionism xii, 175, 177, 187
Sollod, RN vii, xvi
Solomos, J 107, 115
Some, MP 150, 159
spirituality 190, 194–8
Squire, C 119, 129
Stephen Lawrence Inquiry 156
stereotypes 21, 104, 119, 121, 125
Stiles, WB 53, 70
Stillwell, W xiv
Sue, D 19, 35, 105, 106, 107, 112, 115, 141, 147, 168, 174, 223, 227
Sue, DW 19, 35, 105, 106, 107, 113, 115, 141, 147, 158, 168, 174, 223, 227
'Sylvia' (client) 79
Sztompka, P 222, 227
Talahite, A xiii
Tan, R 107, 115
Taylor-Muhammad, F 169, 170, 174
Terrell, F 34, 223, 227

Terry, R 155, 159
therapist
   frame of reference 36
   responses 22
   unresolved psychopathology of 222
Thomas, E 244, 246
Thompson, CE 115, 142, 145, 147, 151, 154, 157, 159, 186, 187, 198
Thompson, J 33, 115, 117, 118, 129, 139, 146, 147, 154, 159
Thorne, B vi, xvi, 78, 84, 116, 129, 168, 174, 190, 197, 199, 223, 227
Tillett, R 222, 227
training of therapists xii, 101
transference 25, 107, 160, 166
transitional relevance place (TRP) 72–3, 76, 81
'tripping' 244–6
trust 7, 160, 163, 166, 168, 215, 216, 219, 222, 224, 225, 232, 240
Tuckwell, G 154, 159, 186, 189
Tudor, K 144, 145, 147
turn construction units (TCU) 72–3, 77, 79
unconditional positive regard 38, 130, 133, 161, 171, 173, 202, 254
unconscious 27, 28, 186, 214, 218, 222
universal human qualities 79
universal pathology 202, 203
Van Dijk, TA 156, 159
Van Kalmthout, M 132, 138
Vanaerschot, G 53, 70
voiceover 27–9, 176, 217, 237
Vontress, CE 19, 35, 111, 115, 223, 227
Wade, P 17, 35, 115
Walcott, R 213, 227
Waterhouse, RL 118, 120, 129
Watkins, CE 223, 227
West, WS xiii, xv, 190, 193, 197, 199
Westwood, MJ 141, 147
White, M 185, 189, 208, 212
white racial consciousness model 154–5
Whitehead, S 243
Whiteley, JM viii, xvi, 8, 16, 36, 46
Wilkins, P vi, xvi, 21, 35, 79, 82, 84
Willi, J 178, 189
Williams, R 157, 159
Williamson, EG iv
Witty, M xi
Wolfram, W 244, 246
Wood, JK 262, 265
Wrench, J 107, 115
Zayas, LH 187, 188